THE MOSES AMES HOUSE, LOT 4 OF THE SEVEN LOTS
From a pencil drawing by Samuel A. Bradley

See page 278

Fryeburg Maine

An Historical Sketch

John Stuart Barrows

HERITAGE BOOKS
2015

HERITAGE BOOKS
AN IMPRINT OF HERITAGE BOOKS, INC.

Books, CDs, and more—Worldwide

For our listing of thousands of titles see our website
at
www.HeritageBooks.com

A Facsimile Reprint
Published 2015 by
HERITAGE BOOKS, INC.
Publishing Division
5810 Ruatan Street
Berwyn Heights, Md. 20740

Originally published
Pequawket Press
Fryeburg
1938

— Publisher's Notice —
In reprints such as this, it is often not possible to remove blemishes from the original. We feel the contents of this book warrant its reissue despite these blemishes and hope you will agree and read it with pleasure.

International Standard Book Numbers
Paperbound: 978-0-7884-1509-8
Clothbound: 978-0-7884-6271-9

TO THE INHABITANTS OF THE TOWN OF FRYEBURG,

TO THE DESCENDANTS OF THOSE HEROIC MEN AND WOMEN

WHO SETTLED IN OLD PEQUAWKET; AND

TO ALL, WHO HAVE AT ANY TIME RESIDED HERE,

THIS SKETCH IS RESPECTFULLY INSCRIBED

WITH THE HOPE THAT IT WILL STRENGTHEN THEIR LOVE

FOR THE BEAUTIFUL TOWN

IN THE GREEN VALLEY OF THE SACO RIVER.

In threefold sort hath Heaven its bounty poured
   On thee, Dame Fryeburg, sitting 'mid thy hills;
   For thou hast beauty such as stirs and thrills
The heart of Nature's lover; thou hast hoard
Of frugal competence and plenty stored
   Within thy barns and fields; and, still the best,
   As e'er by mothers' souls must be confessed,
Brave sons, fair daughters, round thy ample board.
   But some have left thy hearthstone, far to roam;
      And some lie in thy churchyards near at hand,
      Here where thou smiledst on their infancy;
   And some there be who left thy rural home,
      And fell in battle for their native land—
      Their graves known unto God, but not to thee!
One glory else thou hast. Here Webster came
   Among thy shady lanes, and here he taught;
   To thee first service of his manhood brought,
Ere wider fields his giant strength did claim.
His noble life adds lustre to thy name.

                                           —John S. Colby.

CONTENTS

Introduction		vii
I.	The Indians	1
II.	The Battle at the Pond	13
III.	Colonel Frye's Grant	28
IV.	Joseph Frye	34
V.	The First Settlers	49
VI.	Early Life and Customs	60
VII.	First Proprietors	70
VIII.	The Church	80
IX.	Parson Fessenden	94
X.	The New Town	101
XI.	The Common Schools	118
XII.	Fryeburg Academy	123
XIII.	Saco River	133
XIV.	Mountains, Ponds, Brooks	144
XV.	Fryeburg in the Wars	153
XVI.	Business and Industry	170
XVII.	Town Developments	188
XVIII.	Important Events and Organizations	199
XIX.	People in Professional Life	216
XX.	Notable Townsfolk	227
XXI.	Casualties	249
XXII.	Miscellany	254
XXIII.	Little Stories	267
Sources of Information		280
Index		283
Names		293

ILLUSTRATIONS

The Moses Ames House . . . . Frontispiece

The Old Weston House
The Chase House . . . . Facing page 49

Temperance House and Bradley & Warren Store
Jockey Cap . . . . Facing page 177

The Oxford House
The Dana House . . . . Facing page 217

INTRODUCTION

The demand for a History of Fryeburg has been insistent through many years. The compiler of this sketch has endeavored to collect material from reliable sources, and to record the facts in exact language. Minor incidents are mentioned as being illustrative of the conditions of life and the manners and customs of the people. Names have been given when it would make the incident more interesting, also to preserve the traditions and facts rapidly being lost with the changing generations. The progress of the Town has been shown, with especial detail regarding the improvements that have helped to make it a place suitable for safe and successful life and happy homes. Less attention has been given to the events of later years, as they are small in comparison with the efforts made by the earlier residents to develop the township. Therefore this story of the beginnings of the settlement of the Pequawket Valley; of the "Seven Lots"; of the changes made in the physical area; of Lovewell's Fight with the Pequawket Indians; of the growth of the township until it reached its present degree of importance, may be of interest and give information. The treatment is topical rather than chronological.

Fryeburg was the first town settled in the White Mountain region of either New Hampshire or Maine. That makes it also the first town in Oxford County, being settled before the County was erected in 1805.

A very important factor in developing Fryeburg was the remote location of the town. Separated from other towns by long distances, the first settlers were thrown on their own resources, and almost everything they had, they produced from the land and the forests. The families of the first settlers were from the best of the frontier towns of New England, and they came with a determination to make a living and rear strong, healthy families. The first experiences were hard, but they trained the next generation to meet hardships, and as they were trained, so they lived.

As "God sifted the wheat of a kingdom to find the seed for the planting" of the Plymouth Pilgrims, the first settlers were of a second sifting. They were God-fearing, law-abiding, self-respecting people. They believed in education, as was evidenced by the number of college-bred men who came to Pequawket in the early years. They were respecters of religion, as shown by the unanimity with which they sustained through many years a community church. It is doubtful if a better group of people ever undertook to found a town in the wilderness anywhere in this country than made their homes in this valley of the Saco River.

The various war periods that this country has experienced, the changes that the introduction of a railroad brings, the debilitating effect of abandoned farms, have made less change than might be expected, and the sprinkling of other nationalities in the faces, speech, and mode of life of the present inhabitants has not been noticeable, so that there may be found the same types that existed two centuries ago. Meanwhile the same energy that brought the first settlers here has sent their descendants along the extent of the Atlantic coast and across the continent to the Golden Gate.

This high standard of citizenship of Fryeburg has been stimulated by the presence of Fryeburg Academy. The influence of this institution has given to the town a marked position among the towns of Western Maine. As early in the history of the town as the beginning of the XIX Century, the character of Fryeburg society was such, that Daniel Webster, when Preceptor of the Academy, remarked on the select standard maintained; he also was impressed by the number of good libraries that he found. Webster's experience has been repeated by many persons sojourning in the town. They have found educated, congenial people whom they enjoyed meeting, and in whose acquaintance they took delight. The standard of excellence and the variety of subjects treated in the Academy stimulated students to acquire further education in other and higher institutions of learning. The number of college-bred men and women in the town has steadily increased from the early beginnings and a better standard of life has resulted.

It is hoped that this necessarily abbreviated sketch may help the citizens and those who are to follow them to place a higher value on the town and its possibilities, and that they may continue to maintain the reputation for integrity and high citizenship that the Town of Fryeburg has always borne.

Fryeburg, March, 1938.   J. S. B.

I

THE INDIANS

> Alas for them!—their day is o'er,
> Their fires are out from hill and shore;
> No more for them the wild deer bounds;
> The plough is on their hunting-grounds;
> The pale man's axe rings through their woods,
> The pale man's sail skims o'er their floods.
> —*Charles Sprague.*

Of the prehistoric and aboriginal inhabitants of the Saco River valley there is but little or no detailed information on record. Whatever the origin of the people called Indians, who have been inhabitants of North America since the continent became the home of human beings, it is with those who occupied the New England area that we are most concerned. These people in following the shore of the Atlantic came to the territory now the State of Maine and settled around the bays of the rivers, which furnished them food. The great kitchen middens of the Penobscot and Kennebec rivers' bays give evidence of great age, and of a time when the inhabitants made much use of shell-fish for food. As the climate became more salutary they pushed up the rivers, following the movement of wild animals, from which they obtained skins. These Maine Indians became the recognized ancestors of later tribes and clans.

The name Abenaqui, or as Fr. Sebastian Rasle wrote it, Abnaki, was applied solely to the Indian people occupying the eastern part of Canada, Nova Scotia and the Province of Maine. These Abnaki people were recognized by the other Indian tribes as the oldest people of their race. They were at the head of those who after the Ice age turned to the most eastern sea-coast. In the dialects used by the Indians of the North Atlantic coast was the word "Wapabachi," which became Abnaki and meant Men of the East or Eastlanders. The word was variously rendered by the different dialects, Wapanachki, Wabanakis, Abenaques, and Abnaki. The recognized correct spelling, as nearly as the word can be reduced to English, would be "Wanbanaghi," which literally translated meant: People of the Aurora Borealis, or Of the place where the sky commences to appear white at the day-break. Thus was the poetic nature of the aborigine shown in a characteristic word.

It must be remembered that the Indian language was a series of guttural sounds, with no orthography. The French voyagers, hearing a word uttered by several individuals, tried to reconcile the various expressions and to reproduce the sound. The French language being more liquid, it was difficult to get the exact expression of the Indians. When they tried to render the sounds of the Indian tongue into a written language they had to use a phonetic spelling.

Again, when the English explorers visited America, and often made use of French charts and maps, they encountered a similar difficulty. They tried to render into English the French spelling and translation of the Indian word. Therefore it is difficult to try to reconcile different Indian words in English orthography to mean a single form of expression. Our modern rendering of the Indian words is three steps away from the original. Father Rasle, a Jesuit missioner, did as careful work as any of the lexicographers, and even he can not be relied upon as an unquestioned authority, since his research was confined principally to a single locality and nation in Maine.

It is safe, however, to accept the Abnakis as the first Indian family that occupied the area between the Piscataqua River and the eastern coast of America, and to accept their name as the race-name of all the State of Maine Indians.

The Abnaki nation, of which the Pequawkets were a tribe, was peculiar for its intelligence and refinement, beyond the other nations. It had a language which was extensive in its vocabulary. The people lived in villages and were not wanderers. They had a rude sort of government, in which merit received recognition. They had legends and a religion, in which the Great Spirit was the leading divinity, and a Hereafter of rewards and punishments was accepted. The family relations were strong and sincere, and the traits of friendship and hospitality were highly developed.

Occupying stable homes, skill in domestic arts was acquired, and the men became skillful hunters and men of strong character, with great physical endurance.

When they came under the influence and control of the French, a people of such characteristics required but little urging to develop into fierce fighters against those to whom their new allies and rulers were opposed, and the Pequawket tribe was noted throughout the settlements on the border for their activity on the war-path.

The Abnakis had five great villages. Two, in Canada, St. Joseph, or Sillery, and St. Francis de Sales. In Maine, one on each of the three rivers—Saco, Androscoggin and Kennebec. Their principal village was at what is now Norridgewock, the Indian name for which was "Narrantsonack". We are concerned with the territory along the Saco, which derived its name from that of a sagamore, and was called "Almuchicoitt", the Land of the Little Dog.

The Saco river was a natural route between the ocean and the Canadian country, and permitted the Indians to move widely. After the French with their Jesuit missionaries came, the town of St. Francis was established, and the route through the White Mountain Notch became better known.

Dr. N. T. True, in his time the most eminent archaeologist and student of historical matters in Oxford County, gives the word "Crockemago" as being the oldest name of the country around Fryeburg (Pequawket), on record. It seemed to resolve itself into two words: auroc—hoeing, and Kemago—an enclosed place, i.e., the enclosed place where they planted (corn). The Pequawkets cultivated fields in Fryeburg, and there is still a field that the early Indians in the township told of as being a corn field, saying that no one ever knew trees to grow where the Indians had a corn field. The inference of Dr. True seems logical, and as nearly correct as any attempt to translate the various dialects. His study of the word Pequawket, in its various spellings, satisfied him as to the translation, "Pequa-auk-et" "at the cleared place", which would seem to harmonize with the word Crockemago, "The hoeing place."

Father Rasle presented the definition as: "Sandy Land", claiming that as being an Indian definition. It would be fitting, if accepted, as the land in the vicinity of the Indian village, where now the village of Fryeburg is located, is a sandy plain filling the greater part of the southern end of the township.

Just as the great difficulty in translating Indian dialects is to reconcile the differences in spelling the same word, the task of establishing authoritative spelling is difficult. This is illustrated by the various ways of spelling PEQUAWKET, which is generally accepted as the proper spelling.

Pequawkitt,	Writer on Portland Advertiser, 1835.
Pequackett,	Penhallow.
Pequawket,	Belknap.
Pequawkett,	Farmer & Moore.
Pequakett,	Samuel G. Drake.
Pequauquake,	Potter.
Pigwacket,	Rev. Thomas Symmes. Walter Bryant, 1741.
Pegwacket,	Indian Treaty, 1717.
Piggwacket,	Rev. Paul Coffin, 1768.
Paqukig,	Capt. John Giles.
Pecwalket,	
Pegouakky,	Vaudreuil.
Pegwackuk,	1676.
Pigwackett,	Jacob Wendell, 1745.
Peguawett,	
Pigwocket,	Boston Gazette.
Pigwackitt,	
Pequ'at,	Old Poem.
Pigwakkett,	Samuel Willard.
Pequakeket,	
Pigwackitt,	
Pequaket,	
Pauquaukit,	
Pegouakki,	Ferland's History of Canada.
Pequa'tt,	Old Poem.
Pickwacket,	Granite State News.
Picwacket,	John Moulton, in Granite State News.
Pequauket,	Dr. J. V. C. Smith.
Peguaket,	
Pequagget,	Edward Elwell.

Dr. True's study of the word Saco, is as follows: "properly Sauk-tuck. Sauk, an outlet or discharging-place. Tuck, a stream moved by tides or wind, and you have Sauk-tuck-et, at the tidal stream discharging-place."

Mr. C. E. Potter, of Manchester, N. H., also a student of Indian words gives the definition of Saco, in this way: Saco, Sawacatauke. Sawa (burnt) Coo, (pine) Auke, (place) Sawa-coo-t-auke, The Burnt Pine Place.

Mr. William Willis, translates the word Saco, as "Mouth of a River", which is in line with Dr. True's ideas.

When the aboriginal inhabitants of the Saco valley made their settlements no one knows, but the instinctive reason of the red man led him to see that a locality where the river wound in quiet solitudes for many miles was the place where the fish and animals that he required for food and clothing abounded. Search the entire course of this river, from its beginning in the notch of "The Mountains with Snowy Foreheads" to where it falls over the cliffs to join the waters of the ocean, there was no other locality with such a combination of desirable conditions.

The great bend of the Saco was good reason for the Pequawkets selecting this as their home, for it was possible after following the thirty-two miles of winding river, hunting and fishing, to turn their canoes into the pond, early known as "Saco Pond", and after passing over two and a half miles of sparkling water, to draw their canoes on the beach about two miles from their starting point at their village, a distance over which it was easily possible to carry their light craft.

It is practically impossible to locate with exactness the site of the Indian village, but in all probability, from statements of historians and from signs found in the ground, it was at the site of Fryeburg Village, along the high bank above the intervale, from the point where the river comes close under the height known as Pine Hill, and along the high ground for quite a distance. Darby Field, who came up the Saco in 1642 and stopped to get Indian guides, reported 200 inhabitants. The old settlers told of an "Indian clearing" below where is now the Weston homestead. An Indian mound was opened near the Evans place at the northern end of the Village and some bones were found. Not far away from this locality was what was known as "The Indian Hole", a hollow in the ground, but it was filled later to allow the road to be built. When the barn of Robert Bradley was being built, in digging the cellar an Indian skeleton was found. The enlargement of the Oxford House produced portions of a skeleton and some other relics. The stones of their fire-rings have been found around Lovewell's Pond. In 1821 Rev. Amos J. Cook wrote that "pipes, gouges, hatchets and bones of the human frame and sepulchral ornaments are frequently found." Several hatchets of iron were found at one time, and recently some arrow heads were unearthed on the plains in the vicinity of Fryeburg Academy. Otherwise traces of the past residents are very few.

In Williamson's History of Maine, a manuscript letter from Fryeburg is quoted as follows: "Hereabouts (near the site of the Indian village) are several mounds of earth left by the natives, of singular aspect. Whether they were ancient burying grounds, fortifications, or encampments cannot now be ascertained. The circumference of one of these banks is 60 feet, and in its centre is another, in which a tree of considerable size formerly stood. There are four others forming eight angles and running from one centre."

All these mounds and other evidences of aboriginal occupancy were early investigated and removed, so there is not a trace today of the Indians occupying the plain, unless the roads and streets were old Indian trails. It would have been very natural for the settlers to adopt the old trails for their paths, and what were originally paths became the streets and by-ways of the present.

When the Pequawkets left the village on the Saco for St. Francis and Canada is not recorded. The disaster to the tribe in the fight with Lovewell's force in 1725 must have been a terrible blow, as it removed forty men of the tribe.

These extracts from the journal kept by Walter Bryant, who ran the line between Maine and New Hampshire in 1741, are interesting as they pertain to Fryeburg:

March 22, Sunday. Remained in my camp, and about nine o'clock at night the camp was hailed by two Indians (who were within fifteen rods of it) in so broken English that they called three times before I could understand what they said, which was: "What you do there?" Upon which I spoke to them, and immediately upon my speaking, they asked what news? I told them it was Peace. They answered, "May be no." But however, upon my telling them they should not be hurt, and bidding them to come to the camp, they came and behaved very orderly, and gave me an account of Ossipe Pond and River, as also of a place called "Pigwacket", they told me the way to know when I was at Pigwacket was by observing a certain river, which had three large hills on the south-west side of it, which narrative of said Indians respecting Ossipe &c I found to correspond pretty well with my observations. They also informed me of their names, which were Sentur and Pease. Sentur is an old man, was in Capt. Lovewell's fight, at which time he was much wounded, and lost one of his eyes; the other is a young man.

They informed me their living was at Ossipe Pond. They had no gun, but hatchets and spears.

Our snow-shoes being something broken they readily imparted wherewith to mend them. They would have purchased a gun of me, but could not spare one. They were very inquisitive to know what bro't English men so far in the woods in peace, whereupon I informed them. And upon the whole they said they tho't it was war finding English men so far in the woods, and further, that there were sundry companies of Indians a-hunting, and they believed that none of said companys would let me proceed if they should meet with me.

23, Monday. Parted with the Indians and went to Ossipe River, which is fifteen miles from the head of Salmon Falls, which number of miles I marked on a pretty large Tree, that lay convenient (And on my return I found on said Tree a sword handsomely formed grasp'd by a hand) One mile from Ossipe River came to a mountain from the top of which I saw the White Hills. Traveled over five large mountains. Camp't.

26. Thursday. The Weather fair and clear, and in my travel today saw the White Hills which were West and by North from me and about seven miles distant, as near as I could guess. I also saw Pigwaket Plain or Intervale Land, as also Pigwaket River which runs from the North West to the South East and cuts aforesaid Intervale to two Triangles, it lying North and South, about eight miles in length, and four in bredth.

About two or three miles beyond Pigwaket I saw a large body of Water three or four miles long and half a mile broad, but whether River or Pond I do not know.

When the settlers came in 1762 and '63 there were no Indians, but they began to come back. In 1767 when Joseph Knight came to the settlement he found "a great many Indians in the region, who were perfectly peaceable." About 1770 Jonathan Dresser, who lived a near neighbor to Rev. William Fessenden on the slope of the hill, was a friend to the Indians, and they frequently came to his house, and would camp in his kitchen, twenty at a time; they would cook over the fireplace, and spend the night there, sleeping on the floor, a confused mass of Indians—squaws, papooses, and dogs.

These visitors were peaceable enough except when they had too much liquor to drink. Then they were noisy and quarrelsome. At one time when the Indians were having a drunken spree at the Seven Lots, they learned of some fine moose killed by settlers in what is now Stow, which irritated them exceedingly, and they threatened to kill Mr. Knight.

On the retreat of the American forces from Canada, in 1777, three stockaded forts were built for the defence of the townspeople. One was near the Weston's bridge, one near Mr. Charles Walker's, and one near the Joseph Colby Place.

Fryeburg, however, never suffered from any Indian hostilities during the early years, when raids were not uncommon elsewhere, yet it was not entirely free from Indian fears, as while the town was furnishing men for the Continental Army to the limits of its ability, an alarm came to the town August 3, 1781, from Bethel, or Sudbury-Canada as it was then called, that a small band of Indians from St. Francis had attacked Shelburne, N. H., and leaving a bloody trail, attacked the outlying farms, had killed three men, plundered several homes, and with three men as captives had started back to Canada.

The story of this affair was handed down through the last century, as it was taken down from the telling by Mr. Joseph Knight, at Stephen Farrington's, in Fryeburg, August 18, 1836.

In his centennial address at Fryeburg, in 1863, Rev. Samuel Souther said in testimonial to the Fryeburg men who went to help their neighbors:

"For promptness and expedition, this night march into the forest, will compare favorably with anything done by communities in the Mother State at the Lexington alarm; while there are circumstances which make it still more worthy of admiration. At the call to repel the British, the whole country sprang to arms. From every quarter thronged the minute men, sure of each other's countenance and support, and following their enemy in the broad day light. Here a little band, raised at an hour's notice, grope their way in the darkness, through a dense forest, directly away from all hope of assistance, and after a hard night's march, follow the trail of a hidden, wily foe that had marked his track with devastation and blood, and give up the pursuit only when convinced that it will be an injury rather than a benefit to those whom they would succor.

"A small company of soldiers, mostly from this town, was stationed at Bethel during the remainder of the season, and also the next year."

The Roster of those men who went to the relief of Bethel is as follows:

Stephen Farrington, Captain; Isaac Walker, Lieutenant;

Privates:

John Walker,   Joseph Knight,

John Farrington,	Jonathan Hutchins, Jr.,
Abraham Bradley,	Barnes Hazeltine,
Peter Astin,	Isaac Abbott, Jr.,
Abner Charles,	John Gordon,
Samuel Charles,	John S. Sanborn,
Nathaniel Walker,	John Stephens, Jr.,
James Parker,	Joseph Greely Swan,
Benjamin Wiley,	Oliver Barron,
Jesse Walker,	Hugh Gordon,

Simeon Abbott.

The archives of Massachusetts preserve the pay-rolls of the detachments who served on the Androscoggin. That of Farrington and his men, is in the handwriting of Moses Ames, signed by himself, Richard Kimball and Samuel Walker, Selectmen of Fryeburg. This detachment cost the Commonwealth of Massachusetts, but £21, 6s, 4d.

The most famous of the Pequawkets was Paugus (the Oak), who was among the killed at the fight with the Rangers from Massachusetts under Captain John Lovewell, and whose body was found buried when Colonel Tynge and a squad visited the place some days later. He was a chief well-known in the surrounding country as being revengeful and a fighter. His sub-chief was WaWa (Wild Goose). A poet has thus referred to Paugus:

> 'Twas Paugus led the Peq'kt tribe.
> As runs the fox would Paugus run;
> As howls the wild wolf would he howl,
> A huge bear-skin had Paugus on.

Others of the tribe who were known to the early settlers of Fryeburg were Watora-Nunton, Hegon, Scawesco, Adeawando, Nathaniel, Tomhegan, Philip, Swarson, Sabatis, Moll Ockett, Moll Sussup. Three Pequawkets signed the treaty of Falmouth, September 29, 1749, they were: Ooneez, Marcuso, Marcagit. Others who were known were: Old Natullack, Squando, Polan, Assacumbit. The last had the reputation of having killed 140 English, and for this service to the French cause was knighted by Louis XIV. Sentur and Pease were mentioned by Walter Bryant. Swarson at the beginning of the Revolutionary War went into the Continental Army and became an officer; he was made much of, and was presented with a sword. He called himself a "Whig" Indian. Tomhegan was in the attack on the settlers of Bethel.

Perhaps the most noted Indian, locally, was Sabatis. He was

captured while a boy by Rogers in the attack and massacre at St. Francis in 1759. As there were several men from Pequawket in that affair, it was natural that this boy should have gone with them. This Indian is not to be confounded with "Old Sabatus" who was in Arnold's expedition to Canada.

Sabatis was a common character around the Seven Lots. There are a few stories told about him. He was noted for his fondness for liquor, and when under the influence of spirits slept out of doors with his feet in water. He used to enjoy swimming among the cakes of ice in the river, when it was breaking up in the Spring; he would dive down among them and come up, and raising his dripping head, would shake himself, and say for the amusement of his spectators, "See otter, see otter."

Sabatis had two wives, Moll Ockett and Moll Sussup. Their domestic relations were more or less mixed, and resulted in quarrels, each claiming to be the lawful wife. Sabatis, adroitly referred the matter to them to fight it out, the winner to take the husband. Moll Ockett won.

Under the shadow of Jockey Cap are several pieces of the cliff which by the action of frost have been detached from the rock. In one place two pieces have fallen in such a way that one rests above the other, forming a space beneath large enough to permit several people to occupy it. This has always been known as "Moll Ockett's Cave", and the tradition, reasonably well-founded, exists, that this last of the Pequawkets, was accustomed to occupy the cave when in the vicinity.

Be that as it may, Moll Ockett was a real person, who was accustomed after the Indians left the land of Pequawket to visit the place and was well-known among the early settlers, in whose families she was often well-received. She lies today in the cemetery at Andover, Maine, where a simple grave-stone, placed through the generosity of Henry Varnum Poor, tells the short and simple annals of her life, as follows:

MOLL LOCKET.
Baptized Mary Agatha,
Died in the Christian Faith,
August 2d, A.D., 1816.
The Last of the Pequakets.

The variation in her name from the name given her when baptized in the Catholic faith is explained by the fact that in many

Indian dialects the letter r was represented by 1, which with the broad a caused her name to be represented in the Indian language as Mali Agat, which through careless attempts to represent the Indian expression by the English-speaking people became Mollocket, and the best rendering is as two words, "Moll Ockett".

No one knows when or where Moll Ockett was born. Quoting from a careful article published in the Oxford Democrat, Jan. 2, 1863, by Dr. N. T. True of Bethel: "She was born on a point of land on the Saco river below the Falls, where is now Saco village. It appears, however, that she spent her earliest years at Fryeburg, and she was wont to say that she could remember when the pine trees at Fryeburg were not taller than herself." This was her own account of her birth. She often boasted of her noble descent, her father and grand-father both being prominent chiefs of the tribe.

"A woman who knew Mollyockett as far back as 1779, described her as a pretty, genteel squaw. She possessed a large frame and features, and walked remarkably erect even in old age. When allusion was made to this latter trait, she would quaintly though not very aptly reply, 'We read, "Straight is the gate".' She wore a pointed cap, but in other respects dressed in Indian style.

"She was easily offended. She made her appearance one Monday morning with a pailful of blueberries at the house of her friend, the wife of Rev. Eliphaz Chapman of Bethel. Mrs. C. on emptying the pail, found them very fresh, and told her that she picked them on Sunday. 'Certainly', said Molly. 'But you did wrong!' was the reproof. Mollyockett took offense and left abruptly, and did not make her appearance for several weeks, when, one day she came to the house at dinner-time. Mrs. Chapman made arrangements for her at the table, but she refused to eat. 'Choke me,' she said. 'I was right in picking the blueberries on Sunday, it was so pleasant, and I was so happy that the Great Spirit had provided them for me.' At this answer, Mrs. Chapman felt more than half condemned for reproving her as she did. Who could possibly judge this child of nature by the same law that would condemn those more enlightened?"

One of her feats of curing in Fryeburg was remembered. When Mrs. Evans, wife of the old Ranger and hunter, John Evans, was suffering from a felon on her finger, Molly said she could cure it, and immediately went to Jockey Cap Ridge, and picked the roots of Solomon's Seal, which she pounded and applied to the felon, and it effected a cure.

She spent the later years of her life making baskets, moccasins and wampum and such Indian trinkets. She was industrious as long as she could see. When taken to Capt. Bragg's during her last sickness she did not wish to be carried into the house. She said she wanted to die in a camp where she could smell cedar. So a small camp was made for her near the house, and when she was moved into it, she said, "This is the place for poor Indian." She was very grateful to those who cared for her to the last, and would say, "I ought to be thankful only for a little water." When asked if she was prepared to die, she replied, "Me guess so. Me hear people read in the Bible, 'Straight is the gate,' and me try to walk very straight for good many years."

Dr. True said that "she possessed more than ordinary ability among those of her sex and people. She gained the respect and even the love of the whites at the time of life too when the mere mention of an Indian was wont to kindle up in the breasts of white men anything but pleasing emotions."

II

THE BATTLE AT THE POND

> Of worthy Captain Lovewell I purpose now to sing,
> How valiantly he served his country and his King;
> He and his valiant soldiers did range the woods full wide.
> And hardships they endured to quell the Indians' pride.
> —*Author Unknown.*

We at this distance may not fully appreciate the sentiments of the Indians, who saw the settlers as interlopers. They could not recognize that the country was large enough, the wilderness still afforded food for all, and that the settlers were well-disposed. Trouble between the races developed into bloodthirsty attacks on the settlers, who defended their homes and families even at the expense of killing the savages, which only added fuel to the fire of their rage.

The early history of the settlement of New England is filled with instances of the growth of the evil spirit of the Indians, and the corresponding hatred of them by the settlers. Between 1675 and 1710 there had been many raids; among communities that suffered, some from several attacks, were: Bridgewater, Deerfield, Dunstable, Haverhill, Lancaster, Rehoboth, Massachusetts; Concord, Dover, Exeter, Kingston, Vernon, N. H.; Berwick, Falmouth, Wells, York, Maine.

Following the Peace of Utrecht in 1713, a peace of ten years was enjoyed. Meanwhile the growth of the settlements increased into the wilderness, and Father Rasle, the French missioner, working among the Indians, began to stimulate attacks on the whites. Finally, exasperated by a series of attacks, in August 1724 Harmon and Moulton with 211 men and 17 whale boats set out from Fort Richmond for Winslow, Maine. From there they marched to the

Indian town at Norridgewock, the nest of Father Rasle. They killed eighty persons without regard to age or sex. Father Rasle met his end at this time.

Dunstable, Mass., the home of the redoutable John Lovewell, had suffered frequent attacks, and the account was not settled. He emulated the attack on Norridgewock, and knowing the region of Pequawket, whose tribe had dabbled their hands in blood along the border, he raised a company of men and ranged the woods, making captures of a few Indians.

The next year he raised another company and set out for Pequawket, where in spite of the large loss of life to his little company, they inflicted such punishment on those Indians as to compel them to quit the country. In the modern fashion of debunking, some have claimed that Lovewell's expedition was merely a mercenary attempt to get the bounty for scalps. Without doubt such bounty would be very helpful in those days of scarce money, but the array of facts regarding Indian raids on the settlements shows this return for the danger involved to have been a minor consideration.

Only eight days after the battle, May 16, 1725, Rev. Thomas Symmes, minister of the church in Bradford, Mass., delivered a sermon on the engagement. In that time Mr. Symmes had obtained such information as warranted his discourse. This historical sermon was printed, but the edition was soon exhausted, and a second edition was issued that summer. This account was extended and improved, and was repeatedly reprinted. It was printed as a booklet by Russell, proprietor of the printing office at Fryeburg, in 1799, and in 1818 A. & J. Shirley, of Portland, formerly of Fryeburg, issued "A Brief History of the Battle which was fought on the 8th of May, 1725, between Capt. John Lovewell, with his Associates, and a Body of Indians under the command of Paugus, Sachem of the Pigwacket Tribe." Rev. Amos J. Cook wrote some "Preliminary Remarks," descriptive of Fryeburg, to introduce this account of the battle, the opening sentence of which was:

"The principal design of the present edition of this manual is to preserve the History of a Battle; which, however inconsiderable in itself, has, in its consequences, been justly deemed of great importance. It is an event, worthy of being recorded in the annals of New England."

In the many printings, it suffered nothing in loss, except perhaps accuracy, and gained through the addition of plausible interpretations, traditionary rumor, possible incidents, and the ideas of the writers, until it is uncertain, what was true and what was fiction.

In 1865 an edition was issued by Frederick Kidder, printed in Boston. It was carefully compiled, and reproduces the sermon of Mr. Symmes with great care. It has seemed wise, in consideration of the many versions, to reproduce the wording of the sermon as printed in Mr. Kidder's edition.

Mr. Kidder says in his preface:

> Among the various conflicts with the Indians of New England, since the first settlement of the country, perhaps none has created a greater or more lasting sensation than "Captain Lovewell's fight" in 1725. Certainly, no event, from that time to the Revolution, had taken so strong a hold of the feelings of the people, or had so constantly been the theme of the fireside and of the soldier. It will be hard for the present generation, who have spent their youth in villages or cities, to realize the anxieties and feelings of the families who inhabited the frontier towns of our country at that period.
>
> But there are lingering among us a few aged persons who well remember, that, in the days of their childhood, while the family were gathered for a winter evening around the ample hearths of that period, some old man told the story of the brave Captain Lovewell and his company, their successes and misfortunes, till it awakened such an intense interest in their breasts, that the listeners were almost carried back to the scene of the encounter, and started as the wild blast swept round the house, almost expecting to hear the whoops of the savage, and to see the forms of Paugus and his warriors. They can also call to mind how they have listened to hear their grandmothers sing one of the rude songs of that day, of which those heroes were the theme.
>
> But the Battle of Bunker Hill, and the succeeding events of the Revolution, threw Captain Lovewell and Paugus into the shade, and they are now only on the pages of history.

Mr. Kidder's volume was the result of the expressed desire "that further searches should be made, and, with Mr. Symmes account and sermon, be embodied in a book that should embrace everything that could be found relative to the event, and those connected with it". He says, "The present readers of history love details, and Pigwacket fight is one of those events that will be read with interest as long as the contests of Thermopylae and Bunker Hill continue on the pages of history."

Mr. Symmes gave in the introduction of his address, the following explanation. The sermon, copied in part, is reproduced with the spelling and emphasis as given in Mr. Kidder's book:

Tho' I at first proposed only to Reprint the Relation of this Action, given us in the Public News Papers; yet having been favoured with a more particular account from the Valorous Capt. *Wyman*, and some others of good Credit, that were in the Engagement; I hope it will not be unacceptable to *any*, and I am sure it will be very grateful to *some;* to have the story published with some Enlargements.

Here begins the story:

'Twas then about the 16*th* of *April,* 1725, that the Brave LOVE-WELL began his March from *Dunstable* for *Piggwacket,* with *Forty-Six* Men under his Command.

WHEN they'd Travell'd a little way, *Toby,* an *Indian* falling Lame, was obliged to return, with great Reluctancy.

WHEN they came as far as *Contoocoock,* one *Wm. Cummins* of *Dunstable* was so disabled by a Wound he'd Receiv'd from the Enemy some time before, that the Capt. dismis'd him, with a Kinsman of his to acompany him.

THEN they Travell'd as far as *Ossipy,* and there one *Benjamin Kidder* of *Nutfield* falling Sick; the Capt. made a Halt, and tarried while they built a small Fortification, for a place of Refuge to repair too, if there should be Occasion. Here he left his Doctor, a Serjent and seven other Men, to take care of *Kidder,* and of a Considerable Quantity of Provision, here left to lighten the Men, and facilitate their March, and for a Recruit upon their Return.

WITH his Company now reduc'd to *Thirty-Four* Men with himself. the Capt. Travell'd to *Pigwacket,* which is about *Forty* Miles from said Fort.

THEIR Names that made up this Company (excepting his that started from them in the beginning of the Battle and ran back to the Fort, which I'd be excused from mentioning) were as follow.

Capt. John Lovewell, Lieut. Josiah Farwell, Lieut. Jonathan Robbins, Ensign John Harwood, Serjent Noah Johnson, Robert Usher, Samuel Whiting, all of Dunstable. Ensign Seth Wyman, Corpo. Thomas Richardson, Timothy Richardson, Ichabod Johnson, Josiah Johnson, all of Woburn. Eleazer Davis, Josiah Davis, Josiah Jones, David Melvin, Eleazar Melvin, Jacob Farrah, Joseph Farrah, all of Concord. Mr. Jonathan Frie, Chaplin, of Andover. Serjent Jacob Fullam, of Weston. Corporal Edward Lingfield, of Nutfield. Jonathan Kittridge, Solomon Kies, of Billerica. John

Jefts, Daniel Woods, Thomas Woods, John Chamberlain, Elias Barron, Isaac Lakin, Joseph Gilson, of Groton, Ebenezer Ayer, Abiel Astin, of Haverhill.

FROM the *Thursday* before the Battle, the Company were apprehensive they were Discover'd and Dog'd by the Enemy: And on *Friday* Night, the watch heard the *Indians* about the Camp and Alarmed the Company, but it being very Dark, they could make no further Discovery.

SATURDAY the Eighth of *May*, while they were at Prayers, very Early in the Morning, they heard a Gun; and sometime after spy'd an *Indian* on a Point, that ran into *Saco Pond*.

THEY now concluded that the design of the Gun, & of the *Indian's* Discovering himself, was to draw them that way; And expecting without fail to be Attack'd; It was now proposed, whether it were Prudent to venture an Engagement with the Enemy, (who they perceiv'd were now sufficiently Alarmed,) or, endeavour a speedy Retreat. The Men Generally and Boldly Answered, "We came out to meet the Enemy; and we have all along Pray'd *God* we might find 'em; and we had rather trust Providence with our lives, yea Dy for our Country, than try to Return without seeing them, if we may, and be called Cowards for our Pains".

THE *Captain* readily comply'd to lead them on, though not without Manifesting some Apprehensions;—And (supposing the Enemy were a Head of 'em, when as it prov'd, they were in the Rear) Ordered the Men to lay down their Packs, & March with greatest Caution, and in utmost readiness.

WHEN they'd March'd about a Mile and Half, or two Miles, Ensign *Wyman* spy'd an *Indian* coming toward them, whereupon he gave a Sign, and they all squat, and let him come on: presently several Guns were Fir'd at him; upon which the *Indian* Fir'd upon Captain *Lovewell* with *Bever*-Shot and Wounded him Mortally (as is supposed) tho' he made little Complaint, and was still able to Travel, and at the same time Wounded Mr. *Samuel Whiting*: Immediately *Wyman* Fir'd at the *Indian* and Kill'd him; and Mr. *Frie* and another Scalp'd him.

THEY then March'd back toward their Packs, (which the Enemy in the mean while had seiz'd) and about Ten a Clock, when they came pretty near where they laid 'em, on the North East end of *Saco Pond*, in a plain Place, where there were few Trees and scarce any Brush; the *Indians* rose up in Front and Rear, in two Parties, and ran toward the English Three or Four Deep, with their Guns Presented: And the English also Presented in a Moment and ran to meet them; and when they came within a few Yards, they Fir'd on both sides, and the *Indians* fell amain, but the English (most if not all) 'scaped the first Shot, and drove the *Indians several* Rods, both sides Firing three or four Rounds. But the *Indians* being more than double in Number to our Men, & having soon Kill'd Captain *Lovewell,* Mr. *Fullam,* (only Son of Major *Fullam* of *Weston,*) Ensign *Harwood, John Jefts, Jonathan Kittridge, Daniel Woods, Ichabod Johnson, Thomas Woods,* and *Josiah Davis:* and wounded Lieutenant *Farwell,* Lieutenant *Robbins* and *Robert Usher,* in the place where the Fight began, and striving to Surround the rest; The word was given, to Retreat to the Pond, which was done with a great deal of good Conduct, and prov'd a vast service to the English (in Covering their Rear,) tho' the *Indians* got the Ground where our Dead lay.

THE Fight continu'd very Furious & Obstinate, till towards Night. The *Indians* Roaring and Yelling and Howling like Wolves, Barking like Dogs, and making all Sorts of Hideous Noises: The English Frequently Shouting and Huzzaing, as they did after the first Round. At one time, Captain *Wyman* is Confident, they were got to Powawing, by their striking on the Ground, and other odd Motions, but at length *Wyman* crept up toward 'em and Firing among 'em, shot the Chief Powaw and brake up their Meeting.

SOME of the *Indians* holding up Ropes, ask'd the English if they'd take quarter, but were Answer'd Briskly, they'd have none but at the Muzzle of their Guns.

ABOUT the middle of the Afternoon, the Ingenious Mr. *Jonathan Frie,* only Son of Captain *James Frie* of *Andover,* a Young Gentleman of a Liberal Education, and who was Chaplain to the Company, and greatly Belov'd by them, for his Excellent Performances and good Behaviour, and who fought with Undaunted Courage till that time o'Day, was Mortally Wounded. But when he could Fight no longer, He Pray'd Audibly several times, for the Preservation and Success of the Residue of the Company.

'Twas after Sun set when the Enemy drew off, and left our Men the Field: And it's suppos'd not above *Twenty* of the Enemy went off well. About Midnight the English got together, and found *Jacob Farrah,* just expiring by the Pond, and Lieutenant *Robbins* and *Usher* unable to travel. Lieutenant *Robbins* desir'd they'd Charge his Gun and leave it with him, (which they did) for says he, *The Indians will come in the Morning to Scalp me, and I'll kill one more of 'em if I can.* Eleven more that were Wounded, who were Lieut. *Farwell*, Mr. *Frie*, Serjent *Johnson, Timothy Richardson, Josiah Johnson, Samuel Whiting, Elias Barron, John Chamberlain, Isaac Larkin, Eleazar Davis,* & *Josiah Jones,* March'd off the Ground, with the Nine that received no considerable Wound, who were Ensign *Wyman, Edward Lingfield, Thomas Richardson,* Two *Melvins, Ebenezar Ayer, Abiel Astin, Joseph Farrah,* and *Joseph Gilson,* who did not perceive they were way-laid or pursued by the Enemy, tho' they knew our Men had no Provision, and must needs be very faint. Four of the Wounded Men, viz. *Farwell, Frie, Davis* and *Jones,* after they'd Travell'd about a Mile and Half, found themselves unable to go any further, and with their free Consent, the rest, hoping for a Recruit at the Fort, and to come back with Fresh Hands to relieve them, kept on their March. But one Morning as they were passing a thick Wood, they Divided into Three Companies for fear of making a Track, by which the Enemy might follow them. One of the Companies came upon Three *Indians,* who pursu'd 'em sometime; And *Elias Barron* one of that Party stray'd from the rest, and got over *Ossipy River,* by the side of which, his Gun Case was found, & he has ne'r been heard of since.

ELEVEN in another Party recover'd the Fort, and to their great surprize, found it Deserted. For in the beginning of the Battle, the man that I promised not to Name, ran directly to the Fort, and gave the Men Posted there, such an account of what had happen'd, that they all made the best of their way Home. There came in also to the Fort, One *Solomon Kies,* who having fought till he'd received three Wounds, & lost so much Blood he cou'd not stand, He crawl'd to Ensign *Wyman* in the heat of the Battle, & told him "He was a Dead Man; But (says he) if it be possible, I'll get out of the way of the *Indians,* that they mayn't get my scalp." This *Kies* Providentially found a Canoe in the Pond, & roll'd himself into it, & was driven by the Wind some Miles toward the Fort; when being Wonderfully Strengthen'd, he got to the Fort, as soon as the Eleven aforesaid; & they all came in to *Dunstable,* May 13th. at Night. *O that Men would Praise the Lord for His*

Goodness, and for His Wonderful Works toward the Children of Men.

May 15th. came in at *Dunstable* four more of our Soldiers, whereof Ensign *Wyman* was one; who says, "They'd no sort of Food from *Saturday* Morning till *Wednesday* following, and yet scarce felt at all Hunger-bitten." They then caught two Mouse-Squirrels, which they roasted whole, & found them a sweet Morsel. Afterward they kill'd some Partridges and other Game, & were Comfortably Supply'd till they got home.

Eleazar Davis came in at *Berwick*, & reports, (as I'm Inform'd) that He and the other Three left with him, when they'd wait'd some Days for the Return of the Men from the Fort, & at length despair'd of their coming, tho' their Wounds Stank & were Corrupt, & they were ready to Dy with Famine; yet they all Travell'd several Miles together, till Mr. *Frie* desired *Davis* & *Farwell* not to hinder themselves any longer for his sake, for that he found himself Dying, & so lay down, telling them "He should never rise more:" Charging *Davis*, if it should Please GOD to bring him home, to go to his Father, & tell him, that he expected in a few Hours to be in Eternity; and that He was not afraid to Dy. Whereupon they left him; and this Hopeful Gentleman Mr. *Frie,* who had the Journal of the March in his Pocket, has not been heard of since.

Lieutenant *Farwell,* who has been very much & no doubt Deservedly Applauded, was also left by *Davis* at a few Miles distance from the Fort & not heard of since. But *Davis* getting to the Fort and finding Provision there, tarried and Refresh'd himself and recovered strength to Travel to the place mention'd. *Josiah Jones* another of the Four, came in at *Saco.*

Since the Action, Col. *Tyng* with a Company, have been on the spot, and found and Buried Twelve of our Men. They also found where the *Indians* had Buried Three of their Men, and when they were dug up, One of them was known to be the *Bold PAUGUS,* who had been such a Scourge to *Dunstable;* but if he be gone to his own place, He'll cease from Troubling.

BUT thus I've related the Story of the Action at *Piggwacket,* according to the best Information I cou'd obtain; and hope that there no *Material,* I'm sure, there are no *Willing* or *Careless* Mistakes in it.

AND I've only to add,

THAT whoever Considers the Distance our People were at from an English Settlement, in a Howling Wilderness, and very far in the Enemies Country, who were at Home, & more than double the Number of our Men; Their Fighting from Morning to Night in a Long, Hot Day, without any Refreshment; The Number Kill'd and Wounded, amongst whom were some, that were Persons of Distinction on both sides; will doubtless grant that this Action Merits a Room in the History of our *New-English* Wars, whenever a Continuance of it shall be Publish'd If any judge, I've observ'd some Circumstances in this Action too Minute, I've only to say, if some such Persons or their Relations had been in the Action, it's possible they would not have been of this Opinion. However, those who I am firstly Obliged to Gratify, wont easily come into their Sentiments in this matter. And I must beg of the others to forgive me this Wrong, and that they'd only consider, the Different Taste of Readers, & consequently the extreme Difficulty, if not Impossibility of pleasing every Body, in a Performance of this Nature. And yet none would be more willing to do it, than the Unworthy Author, who is a Hearty Lover of His Country, and of all Good Men of every Denomination.

—*T. Symmes.*

An Attestation

We whose Names are hereunto Subscrib'd having had the Preceeding Narrative carefully Read to us (tho' we can't each of us, indeed, Attest to every particular Article & Circumstance in it) yet we can and do Aver that the Substance of it is True; and are well Satisfy'd in the Truth of the whole:

> Seth Wyman
> Ebenezer Ayer
> Abiel Asten.

While this account may lack certain details that other historians and writers have incorporated in their accounts, the fact of the attestation of three men who were in the engagement closes all mouths as to the other details.

In the edition of 1818 Mr. Symmes says in his preface, "Having been favored with a more particular account from the valorous Captain Wyman, and some others of good credit, that were in the engagement" the edition contains some additions. These changes are in the wording and minor details, such as the spelling of the name of the Chaplain, FRYE, instead of Frie, who, Mr. Symmes also stated, was a college graduate in the Class of 1723. The story of the death of Paugus, is included as follows:

"Several of the Indians, particularly PAUGUS their Chief, were well-known to Lovell's men, and frequently conversed with each other during the engagement. In course of the battle, PAUGUS and Chamberlain discoursed familiarly with each other; their guns had become foul, from frequent firing; they washed their guns at the pond, and the latter assured Paugus that he should kill him; Paugus also menaced him, and bid defiance to his insinuations: when they prepared their guns, they loaded and discharged them, and Paugus fell."

Nathaniel Bouton, of Concord, N. H., in 1861, issued an edition of Mr. Symmes' account in which he followed the edition of 1818, with some additional notes. He gives the name of the man who ran away, Benjamin Hassell, who told his story of the fight until he left, which practically substantiated the account by Mr. Symmes.

Some careful historical writers have given this engagement a place among the notable Indian fights, and have included it among the historic affairs of the kind in all New England history. In his "A Half Century of Conflict" Parkman said, "The story of Lovewell's Fight is one of the most interesting in the early history of our Country."

The present generation may well remember that the existence of the town of Fryeburg was dependent in great measure on the result of Captain Lovewell's fight.

The Society of Colonial Wars, in the Commonwealth of Massachusetts, considered the marking of the site of the battle within their jurisdiction, since it was then a part of the Massachusetts Bay Colony; and June 17, 1904 placed a bronze tablet on a monument of local stone, at a point where it would be easily seen by the passing public. The ceremony was attended by a number of members, and the event was made a special Field Day.

The exercises at the unveiling of the monument were brief, but were followed in the afternoon by a special meeting in the Fryeburg Congregational Church, at which addresses were made by Mr. A. J. C. Sowdon, Governor of the Massachusetts Society of Colonial Wars; Orin Warren, M.D., President of the Lovewell's Fight Memorial Association; Hon. James Phinney Baxter, Mayor of Portland, President of the Maine Historical Society, President of the New England Historical & Genealogical Society; Emerson

Leland Adams, Principal of Fryeburg Academy; Hon. William Warren Towle, Ex-Senator Massachusetts Legislature; Walter A. Robinson, Master in the Boston Latin School; John Stuart Barrows, Commander of the National Lancers, of Boston.

The souvenir of the occasion was a reprint of the Second Edition of Rev. Thomas Symmes's Sermon, as printed, "By B. Green, Jun., for S. Gerrish, near the Brick Meeting-House in Corn-Hill, 1775."

The tablet on the monument bears this inscription:

TO MARK THE FIELD OF LOVEWELL'S FIGHT
ON THE 8TH DAY OF MAY 1725 BETWEEN
A COMPANY OF MASSACHUSETTS RANGERS OF 34 MEN AND
80 WARRIORS OF THE PEQUAWKET TRIBE LED BY
PAUGUS IN A CONTEST LASTING FROM EARLY
MORNING UNTIL AFTER SUNSET THE
INDIANS WERE REPULSED
AND THEIR CHIEF
KILLED

TO THE MEMORY OF

CAPT. JOHN LOVEWELL OF DUNSTABLE	THESE
LIEUT. JONATHAN ROBBINS OF DUNSTABLE	12 KILLED
ENSIGN JOHN HARWOOD OF DUNSTABLE	ON THE
ROBERT USHER OF DUNSTABLE	FIELD
SERGT. JACOB FULHAM OF WESTON	OF
JACOB FARRAR OF CONCORD	BATTLE
JOSIAH DAVIS OF CONCORD	WERE
THOMAS WOODS OF GROTON	FOUND
DANIEL WOODS OF GROTON	AND
JOHN JEFTS OF GROTON	BURIED
ICHABOD JOHNSON OF WOBURN	BY
JONATHAN KITTREDGE OF BILLERICA	COL. TYNG

LIEUT. JOSIAH FARWELL OF DUNSTABLE
JONATHAN FRYE, CHAPLAIN; OF ANDOVER
ELIAS BARRON OF GROTON
WERE WOUNDED AND DIED BY THE WAY
9 OTHERS WERE WOUNDED

THE SURVIVORS LED BY ENSIGN SETH WYMAN
BEGAN THE HOMEWARD MARCH AFTER MIDNIGHT

ERECTED BY THE SOCIETY OF COLONIAL WARS
IN THE COMMONWEALTH OF MASSACHUSETTS
17TH JUNE 1904

The Centennial of Lovewell's Fight 1825

The story of Lovewell's Fight is one of the nursery tales of New Hampshire, there is hardly a person that lives in the eastern and northern part of the state but has heard incidents of that fearful encounter repeated from infancy.

—*North American Review.*

Many of the earliest settlers from Concord and other New Hampshire towns, and towns in the northern part of Massachusetts, to whom the story of Lovewell's Fight was a household tale, kept it alive since it happened during the early years of the lives of their parents, and had been told to the children.

With such historical associations, the residents of Fryeburg, in the centennial year, observed the day with appropriate ceremonies.

"Paugus Day", May 19, 1825 dawned favorably, and according to this report published in the Portland Argus, it was a day long to be remembered by those who enjoyed it:

"At 10 A.M. a procession was formed at the Village, consisting of a numerous assemblage of carriages, which moved to the Battle Ground. * * * *

"When the front of the procession reached the pond, minute-guns were fired from two nearly opposite points, which are memorable from one of them being the place where Lovewell's party first discovered their approach to the enemy, and the other, that where an Indian hunter was shot.

"When the procession had wended its way to the beach of the pond it formed in a convenient position to listen to an address by Colonel Samuel A. Bradley, who drove his horse into the shallow water, and from that position addressed the company. He gave a vivid description of the engagement, pointing out the places which have been made familiar by the historians and related facts and anecdotes.

"Enoch Fessenden read a ballad appropriate to the occasion, and then the return was made to the village, when reached, a new procession was formed at Major Eastman's, and with the orator and poet moved to the meeting house.

"Here the exercises were begun by Prayer by the Rev. Carlton Hurd, which was followed by the oration by the Rev. Thomas Davies.

"Following the oration Enoch Lincoln read a poem appropriate to the occasion.

"Returning from the meeting house, a dinner was provided by Maj. Philip Eastman, which was presided over by Hon. Judah Dana, assisted by Colonel Bradley, General Ripley and Enoch Fessenden as vice presidents. At the after-dinner exercises toasts were presented; an ode was read by H. W. Longfellow, and original songs were rendered by Mr. Lincoln and by Mr. Willis of Portland.

"The day closed with a grand ball at the Oxford House."

While it is impossible to give the names of those who responded to the toasts offered, their lofty sentiments and spirited expressions are worth preserving:

1. The day we celebrate. A brilliant link on the bright chain of our Country's History. As we deliver it to posterity unsoiled by the rust of a century, let our successors of 1925 take care to renew its polish and increase its lustre.
2. The 8th of May, 1725. Its morning beamed on the unbroken power of the savage; its meridian witnessed their dreadful conflict; its evening beheld the fall of their chieftains and warriors. May its commemorations be as lasting as time.
3. The memory of Captain John Lovewell and the thirty-three invincibles whose achievements we celebrate this day. Eloquence can add nothing to the character of their enterprise, perseverance and valor.
   "Sleep soldiers of merit; sleep gallants of yore;
   The hatchet is fallen, the struggle is o'er.
   While the fir-tree is green, and the wind rolls a wave,
   The tear-drop shall brighten the turf of the brave."
4. Jonathan Frye, the chaplain and the journalist of the heroic company, whose feats in the battle we celebrate. These plains once listened to the pious strains of this devoted hero, and although his bones may still be mouldering in some distant spot or whitening the field of the cottager, his piety and heroism shall live in the hearts of his country-men through distant ages.
5. Ensign Seth Wyman, the commander of the remnant of that little band of heroes who fought and bled to redress the wrongs of an injured people. Recollection will dwell with grateful feelings on the prowess and sufferings of the valorous spirits through the long tracks of future time.
6. John Chamberlain, whose superior dexterity leveled in the dust the undaunted Paugus; his courage and bravery will be handed down to posterity from century to century.
7. The remnant of the Pequawket tribe; although expelled from these plains, where civilization has erected her standard, may they in happier climes experience the fostering hands of the American Republic.

8. Pigwacket, the favorite abode of the sons of the forest, the chosen residence of their chieftains and kings; the scenes of their triumph and the cemetery of their dead; thy meandering Saco for an hundred years has not rolled to the sound of the war-whoop or listened to the yell of the savage.
9. The first settlers of Pequawket: Enterprising, resolute and intelligent, no difficulties could impede or dangers appal them. Their spirit was as noble as the mountains around them, as firm as their foundations, as pure as the breeze on their summits. May their successors imitate their virtues.
10. The Progress of Improvement. The tomahawk and the scalping-knife have been converted into the plowshare and the pruning-hook; the warwhoop softened into the strains of melody. On the spot where the wigwam stood, now stands the temple of God, and the hall of Science.
11. The days of Pocahontas and the New England Pilgrim: a glorious era in the history of man.
12. The American Revolution: a practical commentary upon the divine adage, "The race is not to the swift, nor the battle to the strong".
13. The Memory of Washington. It lives in the hearts of his countrymen, and his character will shine with increased splendor through the successive ages.

Ode written for the Commemoration at Fryeburg, of Lovewell's Fight, by Henry Wadsworth Longfellow, then a student at Bowdoin, who came to the celebration to read his ode, as related in The Life of Longfellow by his brother.

> Many a day and wasted year
> Bright has left its footsteps here,
> Since was broke the warrior's spear,
>   And our fathers bled.
> Since the tall trees, arching, shake
> Where the fleet deer by the lake,
> As he dash'd through birch and brake,
>   From the hunter fled.
>
> In these ancient woods so bright,
> That are full of life and light,
> Many a dark, mysterious rite
>   The stern warriors kept.
> But their altars are bereft,
> Fall'n to earth, and strewn and cleft,
> And a holier faith is left
>   Where their fathers slept.

The Battle at the Pond

From their ancient sepulchres,
Where amid the giant firs,
Moaning loud, the high wind stirs,
    Have the red men gone.
Tow'rd the setting sun that makes
Bright our western hills and lakes,
Faint and few, the remnant takes
    Its sad journey on.

Where the Indian hamlet stood,
In the interminable wood,
Battle broke the solitude,
    And the war-cry rose;
Sudden came the straggling shot
Where the sun looked on the spot
That the trace of war would blot
    Ere the day's faint close.

Low the smoke of battle hung;
Heavy down the lake it swung,
Till the death wail loud was sung
    When the night shades fell;
And the green pine, waving dark,
Held within its shattered bark
Many a lasting scathe and mark,
    That a tale could tell.

And the story of that day
Shall not pass from earth away,
Nor the blighting of decay
    Waste our liberty;
But within the river's sweep
Long in peace our vale shall sleep,
And free hearts the record keep
    Of this jubilee.

III

COLONEL FRYE'S GRANT

>No vale with purer peace the spirit fills
>   Than thine, Fryeburg the fair, Fryeburg the free.
>   Dear are thy men and maidens unto me;
>Holy the smokeless altars of thy hills;
>   Sacred thy wide, moist meadows, where the morn
>   Delays for very love; divinely born
>Those drooping tresses of thy feathery elms,
>   That lisp of cool delights through dreams of noon;
>   Gentle thy Saco's tides, that creep and croon,
>Lapsing and lingering through hushed forest realms
>   Which love the song-bird's boon.
>   —*Henry Bernard Carpenter.*

Pequawket was the region in which Colonel Joseph Frye, of Andover, Mass., found the place satisfying his ideas for a township, an extensive valley in the eastern foot-hills of the White Mountains, through which ran the Saco River. The Saco had its rise at the foot of Mount Willard, at the gateway of the Crawford Notch, received all the waters of the Notch, and also of the southern slopes of the Pinkham Notch, with the small tributaries through Bartlett and Conway. In prehistoric times it had found a place for a lake in the Pequawket valley, and the remains of the river flowed in a large bend around that valley.

The formation of the land shows great hydraulic action in the past. A large portion of the township is alluvial soil, and the southern section, including the Village, is a sandy plain, a second deposit of the great waters. The combination affords a diversity of farming lands, and where forested, bears trees favorable for the habitation of man.

The mountain ranges around the Pequawket valley are sources of a water supply. The system of the Kezar Lakes in the town of Lovell drain into the Saco, as do the many ponds in the valley. The high ground and foot-hills of Pleasant Mountain in the east, separate the area from the lakes and streams of the more eastern section of the state.

This formation makes an arable territory greater than at any other point along the whole course of the Saco and its tributaries. At no point North or South of this valley does the land spread out to as great an extent, or offer land better suited for a farming community.

It was, then, to such an attractive wilderness that Colonel Frye turned to find a desirable homestead grant. He had led a hard and exciting life since his young manhood, having gained distinction by his efficiency during years in the military service of the Crown. He had encountered hardships of campaigns in the wilderness, dangers of battle and from Indian enemies, from both of which he had experienced remarkable escapes. Now, with the Colonies at peace with their French and Indian enemies, Colonel Frye sought, in the language of the Massachusetts motto, "quiet peace under liberty"; a life that would provide him an income and a home for the rest of his life. Inured to hardships, he did not fear the labors and dangers of hewing a home out of the pathless forest.

The valley of the Saco appealed to him, so he made a journey to it, examining it carefully for present and future advantages. From his observation of the territory and his study of its possibilities, this area seemed to be provided with all the natural advantages to be expected of a land suitable to be occupied by home-makers. As he overlooked it from the high hill in the south-west corner of the desired grant, he gained a general idea of the extent and variety of the land. His practiced eye recognized the possibilities, and he was making no uncertain selection.

The attractions of the valley to this intelligent New Englander included besides the agricultural possibilities the great proceeds to come from lumbering, as the forests of virgin pine and hemlock covered the plains and hillsides. Dense forests of huge trees invited the lumberman. These forests were comparatively free from underbrush, as the foliage and height of the trees had disposed of such small growth. The trees indigenous to the locality were: white, red and pitch pine; white, yellow, black and gray birch; white and hard maples filled lowlands and the higher ground; spruce, hemlock and fir occupied the swampy grounds and clothed the mountains; white and red oak throve in the fertile upland soil; ash, poplar, elm, bass, hackmatack were plentiful; the nut-bearing trees, oak, beech, oil-nut, hazel produced supplies of mast sufficient for feeding swine.

In ravines and low ground berry-bushes abounded, such as high and low-bush cranberries, blueberries, blackberries and raspberries. The ground was favorable to apple and pear trees, and any kind of vegetable indigenous to the latitude could be raised in abundance.

Wild-flowers in great profusion were to be found in the forests. In the years between 1835 and 1844, Mr. Amos Richardson, preceptor of the Academy, catalogued 400 different species.

Accordingly Colonel Frye prepared his application for a grant of this area for a township, based on his veteran military service to the Colonies. He was politic enough to strengthen his personal application by representing the probability of further colonization of the adjoining country, once it was opened, thereby making the wilderness more valuable to the Commonwealth than merely wild forest lands. He intimated that his military service entitled him to the free gift of the grant, though he offered to pay a reasonable sum. His application is given herewith:

Province of the Massachusetts Bay.
    To his Excellency, the Governor of said Province; To the Hon. His Majesty's Council & House of Representatives, in General Court assembled, Nov. 11th, 1761.

The Petition of Joseph Frye humbly sheweth that your Petitioner having been informed if your Excellency & Honours should see cause to dispose of any of the wilderness lands belonging to this Province it was probable it would be by sale, takes leave to inform you that between the uppermost settlements on the Saco river in the County of York, and the Mountains above Pigwacket there are sundry Tracts of land not yet disposed of which (in the opinion of your Petitioner) would make considerable good settlements for husbandmen, & as a settlement pretty well advanced up the said river would naturally bring the rest of said lands into the esteem of such men & consequently render them more valuable to the Government. He humbly offers to bring forward the same & if your Excellency & Honours see fit to approve the offer of your Petitioner He humbly prays you will please to grant him liberty to purchase a tract of land sufficient for a Township in some place between a river running into Saco river, called Great Ossipee & the Mountains above mentioned, with liberty to make his pitch within said limits & to return to your Excellency & Honours a draft of the same in such a term of time as you shall think proper to order him, but inasmuch as your Petitioner has spent the prime of his life in the defence of his Country, viz. the last war from the beginning of the year 1745 until the settlement of Peace, and the present war from the year 1754 last December (saving a suspension of eighteen months occasioned by his falling into the hands of the Enemy, when Fort William Henry was taken & by which he suffered a heavy loss), He humbly hopes your Excellency & Honours will please to grant him such lands upon something easier terms than other wise he could have flattered himself with.

      (signed) Joseph Frye.

Upon the Petition of Joseph Frye, Esq., praying for a grant of lands the following order passed, viz.—

Voted and resolved. That the prayer of the Petitioner Joseph Frye, Esq., be so far granted as that he have liberty to lay out a Township of the contents of six miles square, in some place on the other side of Saco river between the river called Great Ossipee & the Mountains above Pequawket, & to make his pitch within said limits where it may not interfere with any former grant & that he return a plan of the same in six months after the first day of March instant, if the General Court be then sitting or at the first time of their sitting thereafter to have it confirmed, & that he also do give Bond with sufficient security to the Province Treasurer or to his successor, to settle the same with sixty good families each of which in the term of five years from the grant to have built a good house of twenty feet by eighteen & seven feet stud, have cleared for pasturage or tillage seven acres each & that they also out of the premises grant one sixty-fourth part to the first ordained Protestant Minister, one sixty-fourth part for the use of a Parsonage forever, one sixty-fourth part for the use of Harvard College in Cambridge forever, & one sixty-fourth part for the use of a school forever within the said Town & further that the said Joseph Frye give Bond with sufficient security to the Treasurer to pay to him or his successor for the use of the Province one hundred pounds lawful money within twelve months from the date of the confirmation of the grant & that the said Town shall within ten years have a Protestant Minister settled among them.

Sent up for concurrence,
    James Otis, Speaker.
In Council, March 3d, 1762, Read and concurred,
        A. Oliver, Sect'y.
Consented to Fra Bernard
   Copy examined,
     per John Cotton,
      Dept. Sect'y.

February 24, 1763, the plan having been returned, the grant was confirmed to Joseph Frye, Esq., with the following defined bounds, viz.: Beginning at the South Corner at a Spruce tree marked, from thence North 45° West (by the needle) 2172 rods to a beech tree marked; thence North 45° East, 2172 rods to a maple tree marked; then South 45° East 2172 rods; thence South 45: West 2172 rods. (The township lying on both sides of the Saco River, and the grant subject to all the conditions and reservations specified before).

Colonel Frye gave fifty deeds to prospective settlers dated May 2, 1763, (consideration twenty pounds sterling each), conveying one sixty-fourth of the Township, and specifying the conditions upon which the grant was made to him, as well as the conditions upon which the deed was to be valid which were as follows: To erect a house of the dimensions provided for, in four years; to have cleared seven acres pasturage, and to have a good family settled thereon to the acceptance of Colonel Frye, or a majority of the Proprietors of said Township; to afford each his proper quota for land for a house of public worship; for a burying-place, a training field and all necessary roads. In default of fulfilling these conditions, the land to revert to Colonel Frye.

When Colonel Frye was surveying the grant, he occupied a camp on the ridge east of the present road from the Canal Bridge to the settlement of the Center. It was near the geographical center of the area he intended to make his claim, but he later chose a higher hill, to the west of his camp. This hill was the highest in that vicinity, and was a natural point for the chief proprietor and grantee of the township to occupy.

In the full expectation that his hill would be the center of his town, Colonel Frye went on with his preparations. The lot for the minister was close by; a field for a cemetery and a training-field were indicated on the lower slope of the hill; the first meeting-house was located about a mile eastward from the Frye Hill.

The original Town Line was through what is now Fryeburg Village. It ran north of Pine Hill, at the left or south of the road from Fryeburg Village, over the shoulder of Pine Hill, to the Saco River, and continued about two miles on Green Mountain. Colonel Frye thought he was safe in thus starting his first line on ground he considered entirely in the Province of Maine. He laid out his grant to be a little more than six miles square, but three rods in every hundred rods was allowed for the sag of the Gunter's chain, and the township was so understood by the authorities of Massachusetts until 1764, when Captain Harry Young Brown, a veteran of the French and Indian War, was granted a township six miles square above Colonel Frye's grant, on the Saco River.

Captain Brown, in the belief that he was building on his own land built and lived in a house formerly standing on the bluff above the Saco, where John Weston built the present house. (The main part of the Brown house was moved to the corner of Smith and Warren streets, in the village.)

This grant of Brownfield, caused the lines to be run according to the line of Fryeburg, as a base. In 1765 the Town of Conway, New Hampshire, was granted, and controversy regarding the Province line broke out again. In March, 1766, the commissioners from Massachusetts and New Hampshire ran the line between the Province of Maine and New Hampshire. By their survey they found that 8544 acres of Capt. Brown's grant proved to be in the Province of New Hampshire; and 4144 acres of Colonel Frye's proved to be in the same Province. Thus it is plain why the North West corner of the Fryeburg township was taken off.

To make up for the area lost to New Hampshire, the General Court of Massachusetts granted to Colonel Frye of the unappropriated land, north of the north line of the township, by the line of New Suncook, now Lovell, to the line of Eastman's and Bradley's grant on Cold River, and by this latter line to the Province line, and on this line, to the north corner of Fryeburg, about 7,000 acres known as the Fryeburg Addition. Later this area and Eastman's and Bradley's grant were incorporated as the Town of Stow.

Colonel Frye deeded that part of his grant which had been proved to be in New Hampshire to the Province of Massachusetts and the deed was recorded in the York County Records.

Other changes were made in the area of Brownfield, and in 1802, a triangular shaped piece of land, beginning at the south corner of Fryeburg, at a stake and stones, thence running N. 46½ degrees West, 1175 rods on the Fryeburg line to a pine stump on the line of New Hampshire thence S. 6¼ degrees West, 910 rods to a beech tree marked H.Y.B.; thence N. 76 degrees East, 985 rods to the first mentioned bound, coming to a point where the Province line crossed the town line on the intervale near the monument between the two states, containing about 2600 acres, was annexed to the Town of Fryeburg.

IV

JOSEPH FRYE

> He was a man, take him for all in all,
> I shall not look upon his like again.
> —*Hamlet.*

Joseph Frye, was born in Andover, Mass., March 19, 1712. He married Mehitable Poor, also of Andover, and they had nine children, two dying in infancy. He was by profession a civil engineer, and was able to run-out his grant himself.

Frye early joined the militia forces of his state, and was an Ensign in the company commanded by Lieutenant Caleb Swan, a graduate of Harvard College who married Frye's sister. He passed rapidly through the grades of an officer, and was Major in General Winslow's force that was sent to reduce the inhabitants of Acadia to subjection to the English Crown. He was obliged to assist in the transportation of the Acadian peasants from their homes, and he burned their houses, over two-hundred and fifty, a task which was very distasteful to him.

In 1757 Gen. Lord John Loudoun was given command of the British forces in North America, and a vigorous campaign against the French and their Indian allies was contemplated. A council of the New England governors with Lord Loudoun was held, and troops were voted in accordance with Loudoun's apportionment plans. On account of the death in 1756 of Lieutenant Governor Phips of Massachusetts the work of preparation there was delayed. On the date for assembling the forces, March 25, no troops were ready, and the whole plan was interfered with. To quote from a book published in 1933.*

"Fortunately most of the preparations were already completed through the energy of Colonel Fry(e), 'a sensible man'; by the

* "Lord Loudoun in North America," p. 217.

middle of May the seventeen companies of Massachusetts troops were at Albany." Colonel Frye* was in command of a regiment of Massachusetts and Connecticut troops. The campaign was directed to the capture of Crown Point, and the troops occupied Fort William Henry, where later they were besieged for six days. During the siege a council of war of the commanding officers was called to consider the situation. Colonel Frye was one in this council; he opposed the surrender, and proposed to Colonel Monroe, who commanded the forces at the Fort, to go out and fight the enemy with his single regiment rather than capitulate; but this was not permitted, and articles of capitulation were executed.

In Hoyt's History of Indian Wars is this reference to Colonel Frye:

"He went to the war of 1755 and was at the siege of Louisburg. He was in the unfortunate capture of Fort William Henry by Montcalm, in 1757. La Come, who had great influence among the savages, sent for Colonel Frye, commanding the Massachusetts regiment, and informed him that he well remembered the humanity he had shown to his country-men in Nova Scotia; that he should embrace the present opportunity to express his gratitude, and reward his humanity, and that neither he nor any of the Massachusetts troops should receive insult or injury from the Indians.

"But during the whole transaction he kept at a distance, nor did he send a party to afford the promised protection, nor use his influence to moderate the vengeance of the Indians.

"In the confusion consequent on the attack upon the defenseless troops, an Indian chief seized Col. Frye, plundered and stripped him of his clothes, even to his shirt, and then led him into the woods in a direction and manner which left no doubt as to the design of the ferocious chief. Arriving at a secluded spot, where the Colonel expected to meet his fate, he determined to make one effort for his life, and roused by desperation, with no other arms than nature gave him, he sprang upon the savage, overpowered and killed him on the spot, and fleeing rapidly into a thick wood, he eluded the search of the Indians.

"After wandering in various directions for several days, subsisting wholly on whortleberries, he reached Fort Edward, and joined his suffering companions."

His grandchildren recalled that he kept a fast each year in

* No record has been found to show when he became Colonel.

memory of his suffering from insects and the lack of clothing and food.

Military experience with men taught him how to handle them and secure obedience to his orders. In fact, he was much respected and beloved by the men under his command. On his return from the expedition to Acadia, a distressing experience to him and to the men under him, he was presented with a silver tankard, as a testimonial of their regard and appreciation of his conduct of the campaign. It bears this inscription:

>To Joseph Frye, Esq.
>Colonel and Commander-in-Chief of
>the forces in the services of the
>Province of Massachusetts Bay
>and late Major of the Sec-
>ond Battalion of General
>Shirley's Provincial
>Regiment.
>This Tankard
>From a just sense of his care and conduct
>of the Troops while under his command
>at Nova Scotia and a proper appre-
>ciation of his Paternal Regard
>for them since their return
>to New England is
>presented by
>His Most Humble Servants
>The Officers of Said Battalion.
>Boston, Apr. 2d, 1757

This tankard descended through the family till it came into the possession of the late Judge Frye's family of Bethel.

Colonel Frye continued in the service during the war, and retained his title. He returned to his home and a quiet life, but Nov. 11, 1775 The Provincial Congress chose him to command the forces in the County of Cumberland, in the Province of Maine. His duty was outlined as follows:

>Watertown, Nov. 14, 1775.

Sir:

You are directed upon receipt of the commission inclosed, immediately to repair to Falmouth to take command of all the men in the County of Cumberland raised for the defence of the sea coasts and if you find it necessary for the safety of said town and county you are directed to call together their militia or part thereof and to take command of them also, and discharge them as soon as the service will admit, you are also directed to do all in your power to prevent the enemy from making any further depredations in that county, and to that end you are ordered to fortify such advantageous parts as in your opinion will most conduce to so salutary a purpose.

In the name and by order of ye Council,

James Otis, Pres'd't.

It was evident from this charge, that the Congress thought well of Colonel Frye and his abilities as a soldier. This assignment came after Mowatt's attack on Falmouth, when the business part of the town was burned. Colonel Frye was in Falmouth that winter.

The next year, 1776, the House Journal records: Jan. 1. Jos. Frye Esq. chosen Colonel and appointed to command the Forces to be stationed at Falmouth. Pay, £16 per month.

He arrived in Falmouth November 25. January 6, 1776, he wrote to a member of the Legislature at Watertown concerning the situation in Falmouth, and showed good sense and judgment in regard to housing the troops, as there was a scarcity of places due to the burning of the town the year before. He also asked for provisions for the force to be sent, as there was a shortage. The danger of an attack on Falmouth having passed, on November 23 the troops were disbanded. Meanwhile Frye on February 14 had been appointed by the General Court a Brigadier General in the Continental Army, and in the spring he received the pay of a Major General in the Colonial Army, £41, 7s.

This rank was one of the reasons for General Frye resigning from the Army. He felt that he had been slighted, having been overslaughed by the appointment of other men as Major Generals, who lacked his military experience. He also was at variance with some of the plans of General Washington, which made service under him disagreeable. General Frye, like Cincinatus, resigned from the army and retired to his plantation in Pequawket. He had built his house on the hill near the center of the grant in 1768. It was a two-storied building with a gambrel-roof, and was 40 by 60 feet in dimensions. The barn stood near, in the rear.

The road which he had laid out turned at a right angle from the main road from the Seven Lots and passing up the hill by his house continued West of Bear Pond, to a ford in the river; thence up "Willow Meadow" to the North Fryeburg road to the house once occupied by Charles Gordon, and later by Clarence Kimball, as far as Nathaniel Frye's. From that point a road went to the Center and along the East side of Bear Pond until it connected with a road from the one that passed over Frye Hill. It was along this road that several houses were built, but the change of the course of the river made their position inconvenient. The cellars of those houses may still be traced.

The house and store of the General were burned in 1812; a house was built on the same site by his sons Samuel and Richard, though but one-storied. The General's grandson Isaac Frye, lived in a one-story house across the road from the General's house.

While no trace of a building remains on the hill, the site is now a town park, the right of way and two acres covering the house lot having been deeded to the town by the descendants of General Frye. Interested persons marked the site by a bronze tablet on a boulder with the following inscription:

HOME SITE OF
GENERAL JOSEPH FRYE
FOUNDER OF THE TOWN OF FRYEBURG
WHICH WAS GIVEN TO HIM IN 1762
BY THE
PROVINCE OF MASSACHUSETTS
FOR DISTINGUISHED SERVICE IN THE
FRENCH AND INDIAN WARS

This memorial stands opposite the site of the General's house, in a position where it can be seen easily. The old road to the houses near the river and Bear Pond passes between the memorial and the site of the General's house, the cellar of which can still be seen.

Colonel Frye was a man of strictly business-like methods, in his daily life as well as in his dealings with the public. There is a little book about 6 by 7½ inches square, home made, the pages discolored with age, the cover of heavier brown paper showing the results of exposure from hanging on a window frame. On the front cover, in carefully printed penwork is this title:

A D 1773
MEMORAND^m BOOK
of the Loan of Tools
&
CONTINUED TO 1783 & to 1784

The first entry on the first page is this:

February 24th 1773

Mr. James Osgood borrowed my Crosscut Saw which he is to return to me the 10th Day of March next—

(used 3 Days)   March 10th punctually brought home

                              March 15th 1773
Mr. John McMilan borrowed my Hand Saw which he is to return home the 18th Inst
                                          Punctually brought home

                              March 24th 1773
Mr. Nathll Merril borrowed my Crosscut Saw which he is to return home the twenty ninth Inst as good as he received it (the unavoidable wear Excepted, with an acct. how many Days he used the same—
Used 1½ Day to be
Divided between Majr
Osgood & Mr. Nathall Merril   Punctually brought home

                              March 28th 1774—
Mr. Aaron Abbot borrowed my Crosscut Saw and is to bring it home the 29th of the same month as good as he rec'd it the unavoidable wear excepted.

                              March 29th; 1774
Mr. Isaac Abbot borrowed my Crosscut Saw which I allowed him to take from Aaron Abbots, and is to bring it home the 31st of the same month as good as he recd it the unavoidable wear excepted
                                          Punctually brought home

                              June 21st 1774—
Mr. Daniel Farringtons Son Putnam borrowed my broad & Narrow Chizells, and is to bring them Home as soon as he has Framed his Barn as good as recd them, the unavoidable wear excepted—   Punctually brought home

October 26th 1774. Mr. Samuel Bradley borrowed my Breaking up Plow and is to bring it home the 31st Instant as good as he recd it, the unavoidable wear excepted
                                      brought home after a while

    March 6th 1775 Mr. Jona Hutchins borrowed my Crosscut Saw and is to bring it home the 13th Inst as good as he recd it the unavoidable wear Excepted
                              brought home in Pretty good Season

    These are a few entries showing the peculiarities of the system. He closed the last page with this statement:

Before I made this Book, People borrowed tools of me and would not bring them home by means whereof I lost tools and was at great expence oftime to look up those I save. and after I made this Book

to remember who had them (I am told) it made some very angry, and
pleased none very well, however it brought them into a habit of bring
home my tools so that I often lent and did not enter the loan of them
till neglegt obliged me, and as by my ommission I have lost an iron
wedge and a breakingup hoe I am obliged to begin again to enter the
loan of my Tools.
1784 Jany 2d, Benj Dresser borrowed my narrow chizeel for
one Hour. his words were "will you lend our Folks your
narrow chizzel one hour? so lent it to him accordingly
Jany 5th brought home
Novbr 10th 1774 Lent Nathll Fryes History of Sir Francis
Drakes voyages &c to Mr. Heza Astin who is to bring it
home at expiration of two months from this day
          Punctually brought home

That was the last entry. The quaint book shows his meticulous care in even the little things of his life.

Colonel Frye was untiring in the development of his grant. He devoted himself unremittingly to the interests of the settlers, and saw to it that all dealings should be fair and honest. He spent money and time in assisting the forward movement of the township in every way, as will be seen from an examination of his accounts with the Proprietors which he kept scrupulously.

It is not surprising in a municipality of such youth and slender establishment that municipal money would be scarce, and until organized to assess and collect taxes it might be hard to pay bills. At least, Colonel Frye found it so, and after advancing considerable money and giving his time, he felt obliged to appeal formally to the Proprietors for a settlement of his account, as follows:

The Proprietors of Fryeburg to Joseph Frye, Dr.

May 1763

To Cash paid at Boston to Capt John Googins for ½ Barrel of Pork
 for the use of Surveyors while Surveying Land in said Fryeburg,
 2£s, 6d.

To truckage and Freight paid Capt. Googins for carrying said Pork
 from Boston to Biddeford 2s, 8½d.

To Cash paid Mr. John Waldo for 3½ Galls Rum and the Keg the
 Rum was put into, which was sent by Capt. Googins with the
 aforesaid ½ Barrel of Pork and for the same use the Pork was
 sent for, 14s.

Sept.

To Cash paid Robert Miller for Pilotage in Serch of a Road from Phillipstown over to Saco-Plains on Saco River and from thence towards Fryeburg Six Days at 3s p Day, 18s.

To Cash paid Robert Miller for piloting Mr. Harbard from Phillipstown to great Ossapee River (said Harbard being bound to Fryeburg on the Proprietor's Service) 2 Days at 3s pr Day, 6s.

To Cash paid Mr. Willard of Phillipstown for a Horse to carry Mr. Robert Miller on his Journey with Mr. Harbard, 6s.

To Cash paid Robert Miller for the Service his Son did for said Proprietors by himself & Team in building a Bridge over Swan-Pond-Creek, and other work at little Ossapee River, 11 Days at 6s per day, 3£, 6s.

To Cash paid Mr. John Stanyan for Rum for the use of those who built the Bridge over Swan-Pond-Creek, which was for the Service of said Proprietors, 1£, 18s, 8d.

To adjusting and Settling Accots with Messrs. Jeremiah Page, Timothy Clements & Benjamin Stevens for their service in Surveying Lands in Fryeburg in A.D. 1762, & making the Rate for paying for that Service, 1£, 6s, 8d.

Dec. 1763;
To Planning and drawing the writings Necessary for drawing for the House & Intervale Lots of the first division in said Fryeburg, 1£.

To a new Batteau wore out in the Service of said Proprietors in carrying the Mill-Irons from Biddeford to Fryeburg, and in carrying other Stores & things from one to the other of said Places which were Necessary to enable the first Settlers in Fryeburg to begin their Settlements, and consequently of Service to the whole of said Proprietors, 6£.

Nov., 1771
The Proprietors of Fryeburg having suffered great hardships for want of a Road to Falmouth, which is the most convenient Sea Port Town for them;—In consequence of the desire of Several of said Proprietors and my own inclination to serve the Interest of us all, I went there to see if I could obtain help from my Friends in Falmouth to open a Road from Pearsontown (thro' a Tract of Wilderness-Land belonging to the Government) to the great Falls in Saco River which would open our way to that Sea Port; and obtained encouragement that they would try to raise money by Subscription to do it.—but let me know at the Same Time, that if I would join with them in application to the general Court, for a grant of the said Tract of Government Land to the Subscribers, it would so encourage subscriptions that there would be no doubt but a Sufficiency of money would be Subscribed to

do the business;—Upon which I promised to do it, and accordingly entered upon the business and by exerting myself at the expense of Time, Money for the Support of my Self and Horse the first Journey;—

For writings to the General Court which I did repeatedly, and for other writings & Journeys which that affair occasioned, I obtained of my Friends the opening the Road as I proposed to them, to the great advantage of said Proprietors, without any expense to any one of them (except my Self) for all which Service & expense of Time, Money & writings, I look upon my Self, justly deserving from said Proprietors, £6.

To my Service in the Office of said Proprietors' Clerk from the 23d Day of June 1766, to the 15th Day of Sept., 1777, eleven years & near three Months—The Service of which Office was of such a complicated Nature, and of such long continuance as renders it impossible to particularize the Same any nearer than by saying in General Terms, That after the first legal Meeting of said Proprietors when I was chose into said Office, It was a Service of drawing Petitions for Proprietors' Meetings, drawing warrants for warning the same; Composing of votes and Recording them, which was rendered very arduous by re-laying out their Lands, &c. And frequent attendance upon one & another of said Proprietors in the course of eleven years in looking into the Records &c &c.—In which Service I have also included the Task of keeping Journals of said Proprietors' proceedings in clearing Roads from Phillipstown to Fryeburg, &c—

Examining the Same and drawing out the account of what each Proprietor did on that business, either by himself or others, and bringing all into one general Account, in order to an equitable adjustment of the work among them. (the Sheets containing said general account are now in the hands of said Proprietors' present Clerk), Likewise my Service at Dunbarton in assisting Jeremiah Page, Esq., in drawing a Plan of Fryeburg and in laying down therein all the Lots of the first and Second Divisions of Land and Meadow Lots which he had laid out in said Township in A.D. 1766.

For all which services & expenditures I deserve three dollars from each of the 60 Rights in sd Township that have been always Taxed since formed into a Propriety, amounting to £54.

Errors excepted pr Joseph Frye,

N.B. the foregoing Accot is charged in Silver money—Dollars at Six Shillings each—Total 98, 4s, 10½d.—Joseph Frye.

May, 1766, To drawing three Warrants for the first legal meeting of said Proprietors, at 3s each, 9—To Journey of my Self and Horse to Judge Lynd at Salem to get him to Sign them, 6/8—To Cash paid the Judge for Signing the Same, 6/8. Total 1£, 2s, 4d.

Dec. 1768. To cash paid Mr. Grindal Rawson in part pay for his

Preaching in Fryeburg in 1767, 3£, 14, 0.
1769
April 22. To Cash paid Mr. Grindal Rawson in full pay for his Preaching in said Fryeburg in said year 1767, 15, 10, 0. Total, 19£, 4s.
Contra
By Cash Subscribed by the Proprietors & others in Fryeburg to pay Mr. Rawson for Preaching in said Place in A.D. 1767, part of which has been collected by Mr. Ezekiel Walker, and part is yet due, the whole subscribed is £12.12.
By Cash Recd of Capt. Brown towards paying Mr. Rawson for the same Preaching 3.18.

[Rev. Grindall Rawson is mentioned in a foot-note in Spragues' Annals of the American Pulpit, Vol. 1, Page 160, where it is stated that he was a native of Milton; was graduated at Harvard in 1745 (the Harvard catalogue gives him as in the Class of 1741). He was a Congregational Minister.]

The proprietors "allowed" parts of the account but "negatived" freely, various such negatived items footing up to £17.6, in addition to the balance due for Mr. Rawson; and on the long account of £54., settlement in full was made for £18. So Colonel Frye seemed to be left "holding the bag."

Colonel Frye, having built a large house, opened in it the first store in the township. In 1770 he sent this petition to the Massachusetts civil authorities:

Petition of Joseph Frye, 1770, Province of Massachusetts Bay, to the Honorable Thomas Hutchinson, Esq., Lieut. Governor and Commander in Chief, to the Honorables His Majesty's Council and House of Representative in General Court assembled, the petition of Joseph Frye humbly showeth; that under patronage of this government your petitioner has settled upward of fifty families in a new township (at present called Fryeburg) in the county of York, which is at such a distance from any seaport town that the inhabitants thereof have it not in their power to procure sundry of the absolute necessaries of life, through short periods which nature often called urgently for, and they being unable to purchase so many of them at a time as to answer nature's just demands through the year, they often suffered for want; that as your said petitioner is determined with all possible speed to move himself and family into said township, and for remedy of that inconvenience open a store there, he presumes he may say it is necessary he should be legally authorized to sell spiritous liquors there, as such liquors are what laboring men stand in need of; that as said township is not incorporated there are no selectmen to recommend any person in it to the Court of General Sessions of the peace for the county wherein it lies (which is what the law requires) he can not obtain license from thence. Wherefore your petitioner your

honorable and honorables would please to empower him to sell spiritous liquors at his dwelling house in said township by such a method as you shall judge proper, and as in duty bound prays.
      Joseph Frye.

In the House of Representatives, Oct. 30, 1770.
 Resolved, that the prayer of the foregoing petition be so far granted, as that the Court of Gen'l Sessions for the peace for the County of York, are hereby empowered to Grant the petitioner license to Retail Spirituous Liquors in said Township of Fryeburge at their next Term & until the time for Granting Licenses in said County by Law shall commence.
Sent up for Concurrence, T. Cushing, Sp'k'r.
In Council Oct. 30th 1770, Read and Concurred, Jn'o Cotton, D. Secr'y.
   Consented to, T. Hutchinson.

 Colonel Frye lived in a sort of baronial style in his home, sitting in his own room, rarely occupying the same room with the rest of his family, which was increased by the addition of seven children. In his solitary grandeur he was attended by his negro slave man, whom he had brought from Andover where it was the custom for men of means to keep from one to three slaves. These slaves were held until freed by statute in 1780.

 Isaac Abbott, son of one of the early settlers, recalled in his adult years calling as a boy on the General, and complaining about the lack of school advantages in the town. The General took an interest in the lad, and told him, if his father would consent, he would teach him. He taught Isaac arithmetic, and in eight days the boy could cipher in the "Double Rule of Three."

 General Frye was a power in the community during the active years of his life, as shown in many ways. He was efficient as a penman and as a drafter of legal documents and petitions to the General Court. Among his varied talents must be included poetical ability, and though not a prolific writer, these verses of his, written May, 1770, give him a place among the early Maine writers.

Calm Content

No more the court, nor martial themes
 Delight me like the verdant groves,
When I concert my rural schemes
 Midst singing birds and cooing doves.

These sylvan songsters' tuneful lays
 In innocence and free from fear,
So smoothly chanted on green sprays
 Both sooth my mind and charm my ear.

> I would not change these rural scenes
>   For what in Court is to be found,
> Nor quit these groves and purling streams
>   For highest rank on hostile ground.
>
> But thus retired I'll spend my days
>   In hymning praise to God on high,
> Joining the birds' sweet warbling lays
>   To honor Heavenly Majesty.
>
> And when from hence I take my fleight,
>   My sins; O God through Christ forgive,
> And bring me to the realms of light,
>   In endless peace and bliss to live.

General Frye's remains are buried in Pine Grove Cemetery at the Village, and the monument to him and the Frye family records his name and deeds as follows:

> General Joseph Frye,
> Born at Andover, Mass., March 19, 1712.
> Died at Fryeburg, July 25, 1794.

Gen. Frye served his town and state with fidelity in civil life and his country with distinction in the field. In recognition of his military services as Colonel at the surrender of Fort William Henry to Montcalm, 1757; commander of the forces of Massachusetts Bay at the capture of Louisburgh, 1758; Major General by appointment of the Provincial Congress, 1775, he received from Massachusetts a grant of this township which bears his name.

While we give much credit to the men who founded Fryeburg, for their high character and integrity, their determination in enduring the privations of the early years in the wilderness town; while we praise their sturdy lives, we must not ignore the fact that they were accompanied by women in every way as courageous and enduring as they were. The wives of the first settlers of Fryeburg are entitled to the praise and honor given to their husbands, for they sustained them by their love and fortitude, in the trying times encountered.

General Frye was fortunate in his companion, Mehitable Poor, of Andover, Mass., sister of General Enoch Poor, a soldier of the Revolution. She knew some of the distresses of early life in the times when Indian raids were frequent, and she grew up in the atmosphere of disagreement with the Royal rule. When she came with her husband into the wilderness, she came well-knowing what life would be away from home and relatives, enduring privations while building a new home and establishing a town. But Mrs. Frye met the situation with the bravery of her kindred, and brought up a family that were a credit to her in character and uprightness through succeeding generations.

A remarkable fact that shows the value of inherited good family is that two famous Senators in Congress were direct descendants of the two great men of Fryeburg in its earliest days: William Pitt Fessenden, Secretary of the Treasury, in 1864, grandson of Rev. William Fessenden, and William Pierce Frye, President of the Senate, great-great-grandson of Joseph Frye, the founder of the Town. The strain of blood and breeding has continued to the grandson of William P. Frye, Senator Wallace H. White.

General Frye's oldest son, Joseph, was brought up in his father's foot-steps, and became a worthy son of a noble sire. He went into the Colonial service in the Revolutionary War, where he served as a Captain, commanding a company at the Battle of Monmouth. After the war he returned to Fryeburg and settled with his wife, Mary Robinson, his college sweetheart, on the north side of his father's hill. It was said of them, they were the handsomest couple that entered the church.

He was prominent in town affairs, serving as Town Clerk for many years, also as Selectman. He was as skilful a surveyor as his father, being instrumental in surveying and plotting several of the neighboring towns. He had the reputation of being the most polished gentleman in town, and was called, "Gentleman Joe".

A few extracts from his Journal will give an idea of the man, of his occupations and of the difficulties of travel.

1792. Sept. 20. Being the day appointed by Gen. Goodwin for reviewing Col. Kinsman's regiment or rather that part comprehending Fryeburg, Brownfield &c., we attended and returned to Swan's at night.
Lord's Day, Nov. 12. Set out on a journey to Standish, traveled to Mr. Moses Parker's—In the small-pox camp Nov. 13 to Nov. 17—Sat. 18. found our enoculation did not take and quit camp, and Mond Nov. 20 travelled to Fryeburg the devil to pay about s—1 p-x &c.
Nov. 24 went to and lodged at Col. McMillan's.
Nov. 25, very unwell at the Col's—at evening was informed Christopher Howe's enoculation rec'd at Standish had taken, which determined me that was the cause of my complaint.
Nov. 26. went to Mr. Sam'l Stark's, James Walker and John McMillan with me where we all remained till the 25th Dec., 1792 and underwent

the operation of the small pox—then we were liberated.

1793. Feb 15. About Lt. Webster's all day. set Card to cut out drawers and trousers.

Feb. 17. This night And. Pierce Card departed this life at Mr. John Dolloff's.

Apr. 24. Attended the exhibition at ye Academy.

Dec. 14. After breakfast at Swan's set out for Conway—after calling on sundry persons some on business & some to say howde &c—arrived at Mr. Stephen Dinsmore's at evening.

1794. Lord's day, Jan. 26. attended public worship at the Academy.

March 10—this day Billey began boarding at Mr. Merrill's in order to go to school at the Academy.

June 27. Travelled to Fitch's in Flint'stown.

1795. Jan. 26. The evening of this day Mr. Wm. Steele's house was burned with three children in it.

Sept. 26. attended the muster in Fryeburg yesterday.

1796. Apr. 27. after breakfast at brother Nat's went to 7 Lots to see the Trustees of the Academy—then went to and lodged at Dr. Chase's.

Apr. 28 Went to the raising of the republican meeting house in Conway, lodged at my son Stephen Densmore's.

Monday, June 13. At Mrs. Foster's (Boston) till after dinner, paid my bill there which was 13 dollars, Then waiting for a wind to sail for Portland with Capt. Wm. Freeman, and wind not serving put up with Capt. F. at Capt. Wilder's.

Tues. June 14. Wind not serving still at said Capt. Wilder's.

Wed. June 15. on board Capt. Freeman's schooner part of the day & part on shore—lodged on board.

Thurs. June 16. Wind not serving still in harbor at Boston—tarried on board all day—lodged on board.

Fri. June 17. On our passage to Portland—at sea all night.

Sat. June 18. Arrived at Portland about 4 o'clock—hauled alongside Deering's Wharf. Went to Capt. Davis' & lodged there.

August 17. Went to 7 Lots to forward a letter to Joseph by Mr. Morris Witham to Mr. Boothby who is going to the Ohio.

Wed. Oct. 12. After breakfast at Swan's went to 7 Lots—Exhibition Day at the Academy &c. Lodged at Lt. Jas. Osgood's.

Thurs. Oct. 13. Went to brother Nat's and lodged there—they began raising the Bridge at the lower end of the town this day.

Wed. Oct. 19. Attended the ordination of Mr. Smith—lodged at Stephen Densmore's.

Friday, Sat. & Sunday, Nov. 11, 12, 13. At Portland quartering at Davis's.

Mon. Nov. 14. Still at Portland waiting for the wind to convey us to Boston—yet at said Davis's.

Wed. Nov. 16. Wind in our favor. Settled my account at my friend

Davis's—due to him 24/3—did not pay it, left a desire for Mr. Philip Eastman to pay it—then went on board Delano's packet at 8 o'clock. Thurs. Nov. 17. Arrived at Boston at 3 o'clock, put up at Mrs. Foster's.
1797. Thurs. Jan. 26. At Portland—went on board the stage & travelled to Rice's at Kittery—lodged there.
Friday Jan. 27. Dined at Portsmouth, then proceeded on and lodged at Newbury.
Sat. Jan. 28. Proceeded on for Boston & arrived there about sun set, put up at Mrs. Foster's. My expenses for fare in the stage 8 dollars & 1 dollar per day for my living in a general way and sometimes more.
Thurs. March 16. At Boston waiting for a passage to Portland, at Mrs. Foster's.
Fri. March 17. As yesterday.
Sat. March 18. As yesterday. Settled with Mrs. F. this day for all my board up to and including this day.
Lord's day March 19. At Mrs. Foster's as the packet was not ready.
Mon. Mar. 20. Capt. Briggs not yet ready to go—still boarding at Mrs. F's.
Tues. Mar. 21 Wed. Mar. 22. Thurs. Mar. 23. Each "As yesterday."
Frid. Mar. 24. At 11 o'clock came to sail on board s'd packet commanded by Capt. Briggs—brisk wind, weather looking likely for bad—stood for Portsmouth—between 8 and 9 o'clock struck on a ledge called the Whale's Back. beat over that, then run on the westerly part of Wood Island, so called. After the tide left us we got on shore 15 in number, with some small part of passengers duds &c—a very dark and stormy night.
Sat. March 25. Capt. Briggs went up to Portsmouth town. I tarried by the wreck with several others, the principal part of the passengers went off in the morning, in the boats that came to our relief. Capt. B. returned toward night after which we went to Mr. Bell's on Great Island and lodged there.
Lord's day March 26. After breakfast & paying 7/10 expenses went to Portsmouth in a boat with Mr. Osborn and Mr. Bell, put up at Mr. Greenleaf's.
Mon. Mar. 27. Capt. B. was up to town. I was with him &c. &c.
Tues. Mar. 28. After breakfast went over the ferry—at 1 o'clock set out in the stage, travelled to Maj. G's. lodged there.
Wed. Mar. 29. After breakfast proceeded on for Portland, arrived there a little after sun set, put up at my old friend Davis's. Paid 4 dollars for stage fare. expenses on road 4/9.

THE OLD WESTON HOUSE
The ell was Harry Young Brown's house, p. 33

THE CHASE HOUSE
On Lot 6, see page 53

V

THE FIRST SETTLERS

> There may be, and there often is, a regard for ancestry, which nourishes only a weak pride. But there is also a moral and philosophical respect for our ancestors, which elevates the character and improves the heart.
> —*Daniel Webster.*

The first white people to pass a winter in Pequawket were John Stevens, Nathaniel Merrill and Limbo, a Negro slave, who in the winter of 1762 pastured cattle on the great meadows, feeding them on the hay which they cut and stacked the summer before. At the beginning of winter they drove 105 cattle and 11 horses from Gorham to Pequawket, and camped with them on the high land and fed them all winter. Much hay was cut on the meadows near where Capt. Brown built his house, in what was first to be Brownfield, now East Conway.

These men lived on hasty-pudding, cream and maple sugar. Having many cows they had milk in profusion, enough so that they said of it, "it ran down hill." Merrill is said to have made his breakfast on two quarts of milk, thickened with fifteen partridge eggs.

The first settlers began to come in 1763, more followed in 1764. They came on horses and in ox-carts and afoot, driving their stock before them. They forded the small streams, and the larger ones they crossed in ferry-boats and on rafts. Colonel David Page and Timothy Walker built a ferry-boat at the crossing of the Great Ossipee, near where is now the bridge between Cornish and Hiram. This was the line of travel from Phillipstown (Sanford) to Francesborough (Cornish), across the Ossipee to the falls in Hiram, then through what is now Brownfield, to Pequawket.

In 1763 came Nathaniel Smith and his wife (Betty Fitzgerald), who settled in what is now East Conway. He was a mill-wright, and built the mill on the outlet of Walker's Pond, in what was called, "Sodom". Late that fall came Samuel Osgood, Jedediah Spring, David Evans, Nathaniel Merrill, John Evans, Moses Ames, most of them with families. Their route was by Berwick and York, then to the crossing of the Ossipee, where they camped, November 20, when they had to use snow-shoes and hand-sleds. They crossed the river in turn, using "a tall horse." The women rode astride, or as Mrs. Evans said, "We rode the strongest way." James McMillan came at the same time, and helped the party. By that time a foot of snow had fallen, but they pushed on the other seventeen miles, and when they reached Pequawket the snow was two feet deep. There was one log house, which they occupied until they could build houses for the families. They suffered, but endured the privations of that winter and until they could start their first crops.

Probably the conditions of daily life of the early settlers of Pequawket were no different from those of any of the pioneers of this country. The privations were greater when they came to the settlement than later, and the living was in proportion to the supplies they brought with them. As travel conditions were so poor, transportation resolved itself into carrying into the wilderness the absolute necessities for the immediate needs and the gun and the axe were the principal requirements of the man, while the housewife had to get along with a kettle and a frying-pan, until they had a house over their heads and a place to keep the articles they could bring from their former homes. All their provisions other than what forests and streams provided were brought from Phillipstown, Me., or Concord, N. H. The trails were poor, marked only by spotted trees. The means of transportation were horses, which could carry on their backs but a limited quantity of supplies of any kind. In the winter men went from Pequawket to Concord, 70 miles, on snow-shoes, and dragged hand-sleds, on which they brought back sometimes about 400 pounds of supplies.

Indian meal porridge was the chief staple food. This was made more appetizing with moose and bear meat, peas and sometimes beans. In the spring they had sap porridge thickened with meal; occasionally they had fish and pork which they brought from Saco. The customary drink was water unless they had a cow. They drank tea on Sunday mornings. Only the older women drank coffee. A great luxury was a broiled beaver's tail; it was fat and juicy. Doughnuts were fried in moose suet and bears' grease. For vegetables they boiled the roots of the bracken. Mrs. John Evans brought with her a quantity of potato eyes for planting. They planted onions and other vegetables as soon as they had gardens.

The next year from Concord, N. H., came Aaron Abbott, who has the distinction of being the only first settler to become one of the first members of church.

A number of pioneers came that year (1764) from Andover, Mass., among them being Simon Frye, a nephew of Colonel Frye, Isaac Abbott, Daniel Farrington, John Farrington, and William Howard; these last two families went to Stow.

In 1766 Caleb Swan and William Wiley came from Andover, Wiley by way of Newburyport to Saco. He crossed the Ossipee on a raft. He took a grant on the West side of the township. The families that came later that year from Andover—Bradford, Atkinson and Crawford—crossed the Ossipee at Waterboro. Joseph Knight and a dozen more families came in 1767.

Lieutenant Caleb Swan, above mentioned, was a graduate of Harvard College, a classmate of John Adams, second President of the United States. He served in the French and Indian Wars. He settled at the Falls, having first drawn a lot at the northern part of the township, but could not reach it for the high water. He came with three cows, a yoke of oxen and a horse. Naamah, his daughter, died in April, 1770, and the snow was so deep that it was necessary to use a hand-sled to move her body.

In 1767 the settlers used batteaux to bring grain from Saco. These boats would carry eight or nine barrels. These supplies were paid for with beaver and sable skins.

It was told that after Thanksgiving that year five men went to Saco by boats for supplies. They were gone longer than they expected, and their anxious families were quite alarmed at the delay. One evening when they were gathered at the house of one of the families, it was proposed that they go to Lovewell's Pond to see if there was any sign of the voyagers. While waiting on the beach, they heard the sound of oars and paddles, and so anxious were some of the women, that they ran along the shore to meet them. It was said the men's shoulders were almost worn to the bone from their labors in making the numerous carrys.

In 1768 Rev. Paul Coffin of Buxton visited the settlement. He made a friendly visit, preaching and baptizing among the people. There were then, in addition to the names of settlers already given, John Webster, Stephen Knight, Moses Day, Capt. Henry Y. Brown, the grantee of Brownfield, Joseph Walker, Supply Walker, Ezekiel Walker and Asa Buck. Jonathan Drew, another Andover man came in 1770.

Joseph Emery, M.D., the first physician in the town, came in 1768 from Andover, and built his home on the "Drift Road" at the village.

Some idea may be obtained of the life in the township at this time, from a bill in Colonel Frye's handwriting:

> To my Battow (batteau) £3
> To mending pair of shoes and making moccasins, 1, 9, 0.
> July 1769, To five days battowing 15.
> March 1771, Dr.
> To One Hundred thirty-seven pounds Moose meat
> To one Journey to Saco, to myself and oxen 1, 18, 4.
> To my oxen to Parsonstown
> To battowing for James Osgood, 10 days
> To battowing &c &c 14 days
> Conway September the 16, 1766.
> This day reckoned with James Osgood and ballanced all accounts, and is due me Thurty Eight Pounds—Old Tenor.
> Fryeburg, October 1766. Colonel Frye Dr.
> To carrying a hide to Saco, and ploughing irons, for 3½ bushel of Salt, 2, 2, 0.
> July 1767
> To battowing half a barrel of Molasses. 10, 0.
> Going to Phillipstown with your team, nine days, 1, 16, 7.
> June 1767 To journey to Steep Falls a battowing 4 days, 16.
> To my battow to Steep Falls 4.
> Two Journeys to Parsonstown

Jedediah Spring settled on the "Drift Road," at a site between the land now owned by Dr. Cohen and Loren Brown, where the cellar-hole was visible for many years. His daughter Betty was the first white child born in the township, Sept. 28, 1764.

One of the earliest acts of Colonel Frye was to lay out on the plains and, in the part of the township nearest the Province Line, a series of lots of forty acres each. He began at the town line and running parallel to that line made seven house lots, which occupied the whole space from the town line along the high bank above the intervales to where the bank, following the course of the river, turns north-west, and where the road to Swan's Falls now begins. Unconsciously he limited the area of the Village. These lots extended south easterly to the vicinity of Lovewell's Brook, which is known also as the "Mill Brook."

To help in locating the approximate limits of the "Seven Lots," this description may be of assistance:

Lot No. 1, drawn by John Evans, (later transferred to Capt. Timothy Walker) began at the Town Line, which ran near the house built by Captain Vere Royce. The other side was bounded by a parallel line, about opposite the "Drift Road." This lot was occupied later by Dr. Griswold, Asa Charles, Gerry Morgan, and lately Loren Brown.

Lot No. 2, Samuel Osgood's Grant, was bounded by the Evans line, and extended to Portland Street. It included the site of the first tavern, later of the Oxford House and the "Oxford" Hotel. Here Col. Osgood built the first framed house in the Seven Lots. The site is now occupied by C. E. Mulford and C. E. Fox. A by-way separated it from Lot No. 1.

Lot No. 3, David Page's Grant, extended from Samuel Osgoods lot, to about where the Congregational Church now stands.

Lot No. 4, drawn by Moses Ames, was from Page's lot to a little below the place where he built his house. The Memorial stone to Rear Admiral Peary marking the meridian line stands near the site; a blacksmith shop stood in the rear.

The next lots did not extend quite so far as the first four, but the difference in extent and area was made good by other small lots near by, the numerical order of which was changed.

Lot No. 6 came next. It was that of Nathaniel Merrill, extending from Moses Ames's line to the by-way to the intervale, beyond the "Chase House," and crossed what is now the Bridgton Road. It included all the present holdings of Fryeburg Academy. Merrill began the house occupied by Major C. W. Pike.

Lot No. 5, the Grant of James Clements, extended from Merrill's line to about where is a by-way to the intervale, below the house built by Charles Tibbetts, and occupied for many years by his daughter, Miss Fannie Tibbetts. This way was supposed to have been originally an Indian trail, and possibly led to a ford of the river. James Clements built a frame house on his grant.

Lot No. 7, which was David Evans', began at Clements' lot, and extended about to where now is the road to Swan's Falls.

The general limits of these lots were governed by the turns of the plains land, at the foot of the hill of Bradley Park, on the south-west, to the turn of the same plain toward the north-west. They constituted what was referred to for many years as "The Seven Lots," the only name by which the locality was known until January 1777 when the Town of Fryeburg was incorporated. Even after that the old name clung in the minds of the older settlers.

In the progress of time, these seven lots became many more, as they were cut up and sold to the incoming residents. Some of the present division lines between house-lots are near, if not exactly the same lines of the original grants to the first settlers. New streets have cut them, and caused new boundaries, but the extreme limits of the Seven Lots can still be indicated.

John Evans drew No. 1 in the division; later he exchanged this lot for one about three miles away, which for many years was known as the Major Evans Place.

John Evans also acquired the "Mill Lot" near the Seven Lots, which included Lovewell's Brook, the line of march of Capt. John Lovewell coming into Pequawket, in 1725. On this brook John Bucknell had built the first grist mill in the township, which was carried on for many years. Evans made his home there, and there the majority of his children were born.

On the shore of Lovewell's Pond in the area owned by John Evans is a large rock at the water's edge. It is known as "Moose Rock." The story is, that one evening Evans was after his cattle that had strayed, and near the shore of the pond he was chased by a large moose. He took refuge on the rock, and picking up a stone threw it at the moose, striking its horns, and frightened it away.

John Evans was the father-in-law of James Osgood, "Uncle Straight-hair" as he was called, because his hair was very curly, who built the Oxford House in 1800. He was born in November 1757, the son of Samuel Osgood, one of the first settlers of the township, who occupied lot No. 2, at the Seven Lots.

As soon as they were financially able, the early settlers throughout the township built substantial houses; those spared by fires are still standing, showing how people lived in a more generous day. Little hamlets and neighborhoods grew up, which with the passing years have become more attractive.

Naturally the settlers took places near Colonel Frye's location, and near neighbors were Joseph Frye, Jr., and Ezekiel Walker toward Bear Pond, the sites of whose places are now in the channel of the river, following the changes caused by the Canal. William Russell occupied a place on the road to the river, the cellar of which was visible in recent years.

Rev. William Fessenden occupied the "Minister's Right," opposite the road to Colonel Frye's. David Page occupied the farm next, which was later the home of Albion Page, Franklin Shirley, and more recently is owned by the "Indian Acres" camp for boys. His son Ebenezer Fessenden built across the road, and that house, occupied by Jacob Powers and later by Dexter Wiley, was burned.

Jonathan Dresser lived on Frye Hill, on the side below the site occupied by Ebenezer Fessenden. He was in business there for some years, and when he died was buried in the old Town Burying Ground, which was in the seven acres, across the road, appropriated for a Training-Field and Burying Ground.

From the "Center," the roads extended in several directions, and farms were developed along them. Isaac Abbott settled on the site on the east side of the road, and the ell of the house, was built into the present house on the site.

Along the road that was known as "Fish Street" were: Ebenezer Day, on the farm in later years occupied by Thomas Day. Nathaniel Frye occupied a farm opposite the road to "The Harbor." Captain Vere Royce after removing from the Village, built a house in this neighborhood. William Eaton established himself here, as did also Abraham Bradley.

These and other settlers, who occupied farms at the Center, along Fish Street and in what is now North Fryeburg, and along the road to the river at "Toll Bridge" and who have populated these areas with their descendants were: Solomon Charles, Moses Knight, Simeon Charles, Isaac Charles, Ebenezer Stevens, Bliss Charles, Nathaniel Walker, Samuel Stevens, Jonathan Stevens, Abner Charles, Joseph Charles, Charles Walker, Benjamin Wiggin, John Walker, James Wiley, Daniel Chandler, Jabez Day, Joseph Knight, Oliver Knight, Caleb Knight, Jeremiah Eastman, Joseph Chandler, Moses Chandler, John Gordon. They acquired good farms which have been held by their descendants through several generations. Richard Eastman settled on the east side of what is now known as the "Old River," at the Toll Bridge. He conducted a ferry there until the bridge was built. His house was several rods below the location of the bridge.

Benjamin Barker occupied a farm some distance farther along the road to Lovell, from the Bridge, and this farm has been occupied by three generations of the family.

Deacon Simon Frye, a nephew of the Colonel, settled in the eastern end of "Menotomy" district, near the river. In September 1767 he cleared the land, built a house and occupied it. He conducted a ferry at that place for a number of years on the trail to Bridgton from Fryeburg Village.

John Bolt Miller settled at what is known as "The Island" in Saco river, near Lovewell's Pond. This farm was later occupied by Morris Witham, and is now owned by the second generation since Col. James Walker who followed Witham in ownership.

The early settlers on the west side of the river were: John Webster who occupied a lot between the Province Line and the "White Lot" brook, owned later by his son Colonel David Webster; among the others who settled along the trail, whose locations it is difficult to place today with any accuracy were: Barnes Hazeltine, Hubbard Carter, Ezra Carter, Edward Shirley, Robert Colby, where the Colby house now is, Edward Carlt, Nathaniel Hutchins, Stephen Farrington, James Parker, Isaac Walker, Hezekiah Astin (Austin). John Charles, on the north side of the river, John Stevens, Samuel Charles, Samuel Ingalls, near the brook which was given his name.

William Steele, supposing he was in the Frye grant, settled on what has been known for many years as the "Woodward Farm."

Some of the early settlers made clearings on the east slopes of Green Mountain, where above the frost-line they were able to cultivate corn-fields with success. Some of the old fields are still known by the old names, such as: "The White Lot," where is the head water of the Fryeburg Water Company; the "Sargeant Opening," the "Kelly Opening" and similar identifications. While these lots are largely grown up to forests they are recognized in old deeds and in boundary lines.

The importance of locating the first Proprietors is to show dispersion throughout the township and to give the reason why the area is so well occupied today.

Among the early inhabitants of Pequawket was Lieut. Hugh Stirling of the British Army, who came from Scotland to America, and settled in Derryfield, (now Manchester) N. H., where he met

Isabel, the sister of John and William Stark. He said he found in her the only woman he ever loved.

Hugh Stirling first saw Pequawket in the summer of 1758, coming here with William Stark. He cleared several acres, in preparation for a home-site. Later he returned with his wife, Isabel and two children. He burned the fallen trees, planted corn, built a log house, and his corn being abundant, remained as a settler.

The site on which Stirling located, while in the bounds of Col. Frye's grant, was later set off into New Hampshire, but he was to all intents and purposes a resident of Pequawket. His cabin stood about a mile south-east of Stark's Hill.

Once when Stirling was laid up with an attack of rheumatism he said to his wife:

"Belle, I wish I could have some venison steak to eat." To which his wife replied,

"We have had several white frosts this month, and the acorns have been falling fast. The deer are very fond of them, and there are plenty of oaks, on the banks of the Saco, about a mile from here. I will take the gun, and go there, and before sun-set I'll bring back venison enough for you and the children."

Isabel Stark Stirling was of a family that feared nothing. She was a real frontiersman's wife, and did not hesitate to go gunning for deer or any other beast that might be of use. Accordingly she went where she expected to find a deer, and after four o'clock, when the shadows were beginning to grow long, she saw several deer coming toward the place where she was concealed. She fired and killed a fine buck.

Having reloaded her gun, and dressed the deer, taking a supply of steak, she was about to return to her family, when she heard the snarls of a catamount. She took cover at once in a tree, and waited. Presently she saw a bear come down the bank of the river, and cross, closely followed by a large catamount.

The bear came within three rods of where Isabel was hidden, and waited. The catamount at once sprang on the bear, fastened his teeth in its throat, and tore it. But the bear was not idle. It held the cat by the neck, and with the claws of its hind feet tore the body of the cat. The result of this terrible duel was the death of each of the participants.

Isabel waited on her perch, until she was assured the two animals were dead, then climbed down and went home, arriving about dark. She served Hugh and the children a savory venison steak for supper.

The next morning, she went to a neighbor, who lived about a mile away, and together they went to the scene of the deadly duel. They found the bear and catamount undisturbed, and the bear-meat and venison in good condition. They took what they required, and the skins of the three animals were valuable additions to the comfort of the Stirling family that winter.

The conditions which governed the location of the "Seven Lots," three miles south-west of Frye Hill, and which were influenced by the natural conformation of the surrounding country, worked contrary to Colonel Frye's plans and expectations. More settlers came to the town-nucleus formed by the occupation of the "Seven Lots," and a neighborhood grew faster there than at the chosen center of the township. At the time of the settlement of the village there was no thought that there would be a highway through the White Mountains to the Connecticut valley, or even along the old Indian trail to Lake Memphremagog, to the River St. Francis, and the paths traveled by the Pequawkets, but the discovery in 1773 by two hunters, Nash and Sawyer, of the great defile and their report to Governor Wentworth of New Hampshire that it would not be difficult to build a road through the "Notch," interested the whole Saco valley, and the neighboring towns of Bartlett, Conway and Fryeburg took measures to see that such a road was constructed. The condemnation of the rights set apart to Captain William Stark, who remained a Loyalist when the Revolutionary War began, caused them to be sold, as was all his real-estate in the township, and the funds were devoted to the construction of this road.

Later a Toll Corporation was formed, some of the stock of which was owned by Fryeburg people, which improved the road, and established toll-gates in Bartlett, on the east line of Hart's Location, and at Fabyan's, putting the whole road under toll conditions.

The opening of this road brought new conditions to the country beyond the mountains, and brought the inhabitants nearer to the markets of Portland. The business in winter reached large proportions, as the farmers' "Lumber Boxes," large pung-sleds, carried the produce of the farms to Portland, and returned with supplies of salt, molasses, fish and rum.

This trade was a benefit to the "Seven Lots," since Fryeburg afforded a convenient stopping place for the teams going and coming, as it was about half way between the Upper Coos and the sea-board. Within the recollection of a recent generation, trains of red Lumber Boxes, perhaps half-a-mile long passed through the village, some of them stopping at the two taverns. During the first thirty years of the establishment of the village, this trade did much to develop the settlement, and to bring other people in, both tradesmen and professional people. Stores thrived, and a steady commerce was carried on between Fryeburg and Portland and points further remote. The palm of authority and business passed from Colonel Frye's little capitol on the hill, never to return. Since those days, the "Seven Lots" merged into Fryeburg Village, and has been the largest populated portion of the whole town.

VI

EARLY LIFE AND CUSTOMS

> We're flowing from our native hills
>   As our free rivers flow:
> The blessing of our Mother-land
>   Is on us as we go.
> We go to plant her common schools
> . . . .
> And give the Sabbaths of the wild
>   The music of her bells.
>   —*John G. Whittier.*

We who live when almost every imaginable convenience for house and field is available, do not stop often enough to consider the hardships of our forefathers and foremothers. Let us turn back to those early years after the first settlers began to come to Pequawket, travelling seventy or eighty miles afoot, often through the snow, and camping at night in the woods. That experience was enough to complete the toughening process begun often in their early homes, and by the time they arrived at the new township, they knew what was before them.

The first thing to be done on arrival was to get up shelter for the women and children. The first habitations were lean-to camps, before which the great fire kept them fairly comfortable day and night. The first houses were built of logs cut from the trees felled on ground that was to be the farm. These logs, in the round, were cobbled together, and the spaces between were filled with mud, moss and anything that would stick, to keep the heat in and the cold out. The windows were few and small, filled with greased paper, which let in some light. The doors were of split logs, closely fastened together with wooden pins, and hung on wooden hinges, which only a woodsman knew how to make. The art is lost today. These doors were fastened by a long latch, hung on a pivot at the end, which swung across the door and into a chock cut in the log of the doorway, or into a piece of wood made to receive it. When the latch was down no one outside could come in, unless a cord through the door hung outside. "The Latch-string is out," was a familiar invitation for a visitor.

The houses were roofed with hemlock bark, or with split slabs, fastened by wooden pins to the purlins that lay across the few rafters. The single room of the cabin was kitchen, living room, dining room and bed-room for the family. A loft was built under the roof, and was reached by some kind of a ladder, perhaps made by cutting notches deeply into a log. Here the children slept, as it was the warmest part of the house. The older members of the family slept on such bedsteads as they could make from the materials at hand; the beds were filled with dry grass until they had straw.

The floor of the first cabins was the earth. Split logs furnished a better footing until a more permanent floor could be laid.

The next step in the progress of building was the hewn-log house, which was a great advance over the simple log house. The logs being straight and well-hewn, fitted closer, and required less pointing with mud or mortar. Such houses lasted longer and in some instances were finished outside and inside and lasted a century or more.

As soon as sawmills were established and producing boards and timbers, frame houses succeeded the log houses. The general method of construction of house and barn was similar. The building was framed on the ground; four corner posts were arranged, with plates and girts to bind them together. Then the frame was raised, and in such a way as to bring tenons and mortices together, and the frame thus set up was fastened with dowels through the connections, making a firm building, stronger than a nailed frame.

Between the four corner-posts was the studding, and the boarding outside and frequently inside completed the strong structure. The living room was generally sheathed with wide, clear boards, of which the settlers had plenty, the forest being of large, original growth, and so boards were sawed that were from two to three feet wide, without a knot in the entire length. The old houses to-day show the corner posts, sheathed over, but telling the story of the construction. The roof was made with four rafters, connected by purlins, on which the roof-boards were nailed, up and down, instead of at right angles to the rafters as in the case of modern "balloon-frame" construction.

Nails in those days were hand-made, so as much as possible dowels and wooden pegs were used in fastening the frame of a house. The art of nail-making was well understood, and creditable products were available, from small nails to large spikes.

Shingles and clapboards came as soon as the mills could produce them. Until then they were hand-riven and shaved. To insure regularity in size it was necessary to choose a town officer, a "Culler of Shingles," whose duty was to examine the products and throw out those that were imperfect or of wrong size. There was no need to use anything but clear lumber, so no knots were allowed. The clapboards were chamfered at the ends, and laid to overlap about two inches.

While some the earliest cabins built a fire in the center, and a hole in the roof let out the smoke, it was too barbarous a style to last long. For a log house the fire-place was built of field-stone, and the chimney above, at first was made of small logs, cobbled together as those used in the house, and the inside and the cracks plastered with clay. The wooden chimney was often catching fire and endangered the whole house. Field stones were used until hand-struck bricks were made.

In the fire-place was a wooden "lug-pole" from which the kettles and pots were hung by chains or withes. It was liable to be burned out and was an inconvenient arrangement. When the iron crane was hung, the family was supposed to be established, and so the event was made a ceremony by the neighbors. On this crane were iron "pot-hooks" and "trammels" by which the height of the kettle from the fire could be adjusted. The "Dutch oven," was a convenient utensil for baking, being a kettle set among the coals and the cover heaped with live coals, which gave a high and steady heat.

The first houses were usually one story, with low walls, for comfort in winter. The fire-place and brick-oven took up as much space on one side of the room as was deemed necessary. The fire-place was large enough to take four-feet sticks of wood, and then have space enough at each end for the children to sit and keep warm. At night they could see the stars by looking up the large straight chimney flue.

It was something of an art to build a fire properly. First the "back-log" was placed against the back of the fire-place; then in front and resting on the andirons, or on stones, was laid the "forestick," upon which and against the back-log the light wood and kindling were piled. Under this construction was laid birch-bark or pine cones, and the light applied. The light was produced by the flint and steel, or by fire from the pan of the musket, or from coals saved buried from the night's fire. When every means failed, a child was sent to the nearest neighbor to borrow a brand or a few live coals. The memory of this task was fresh in the minds of many old settlers.

The architecture of the dwelling houses of early Fryeburg conformed to the circumstances and climate of the locality. The heavy snows of winter were expected to slide off the roofs, so the majority of houses and barns were built with slanting roofs, the "square pitch" predominating. Barns were generally of a less pitch than dwellings. The style affected in the earlier settlements of New England, where the second story overhung by several inches the lower story, and the rear slant of the roof extended to the top of the first story, was out of date, because of different living conditions, so the majority of the first frame houses were substantial, two-story, square buildings, with the large chimney in the centre, the roof being either with two slopes, or perhaps the "Hip roof" was preferred. In this respect the buildings followed the Colonial type of dwelling, so common in the Bay State.

The large chimneys were built to have a fire-place in each room, usually eight to a house, with the fireplace in the corner of the room. If a house had but four rooms on the two floors, the fireplaces were on one side of the rooms. These old chimneys were so built that the first floor room, usually the kitchen, though sometimes the living room, contained a brick-oven attached to the chimney by a flue, so that a fire was started in the oven on baking-day, and allowed to burn steadily until time to bake, when it was withdrawn, all the coals and ashes being cleared, and the various dishes —brown-bread, beans, rye bread and whatever required length of time to bake—were put in, and the door closed tightly. Pies and foods requiring less time were put in later. The heat, thoroughly incorporated in the brick walls, was sufficient to bake everything in the oven to the proper degree, and give that characteristic taste desired in brown-bread and baked-beans. The housewife tested the heat of the oven by putting her bared arm in as far as she could reach and the heat was regulated accordingly. For boiling, broiling and frying the utensils fitted for the fire-place did the work, but the brick-oven did the baking for the week, except such bread and biscuits as could be baked before the fire-place in the tin "baker." The "tin kitchen" roasted the joint or the fowl to perfection; the spit was made with a prong on one side near the outer end, which fitted into holes at regular intervals. As the roast progressed it was turned, the prong of the spit holding it in place, securing evenness of cooking. Before the introduction of the tin-kitchen, a roast was hung by a string before the fire and the dripping was caught in a dish on the hearth.

Furniture at first was made by the settlers themselves, owing to the limited means of transportation from their old homes. Tools were essential for such cabinet work, though for building a log house an axe, a saw and an auger were sufficient. The skill in the use of these rudimentary tools was remarkable. A man who lived in Fryeburg said, "Give me an axe, and I'll make a pianer."

"X-tables" were the principal form, benches and stools were the seats. A "settle" was a most desirable seat in the draughty houses, its high back and close finish below kept off the cold o'nights, and being set facing the fire, the heat was reflected until it was a very cozy corner.

Table furniture was reduced to the lowest terms; pewter was the earliest form of ware, and the plates were large; some known in Fryeburg were used later to cover a barrel. Wooden trenchers were used for holding large quantities of food, and some tin ware was available. These dishes were kept on shelves against the walls called "dressers." Heavy table-knives and two-tined forks were in common use.

In the same room were the utensils so essential to house and home-keeping in those days, the flax and wool spinning-wheels, and in many homes a loom for weaving the required cloth. As the people prospered and transportation from their former homes became easier the supply of furniture and utensils increased.

To occupy the early dwellings winter and summer required proper clothing for the settlers. The winters were cold as now, and with the scarcity of foods, and living in chilly houses, the suffering during the winter of 1766 and '67 was not surprising. The settlers had to keep warm. The men wore outer garments of skins of animals they killed in the forests. They wore breeches and long stockings of wool which came to the knees, and for winter comfort they wore moccasins of leather. In fact, the dress of the men was anything to keep them warm.

Good food, when they could get it, was the best protection against the changes of the weather. As soon as they began to cultivate their cleared and burned-over land, the crops were bounteous, for the land was virgin soil. The Indian corn gave them meal for porridge, mush and bread. They raised peas and beans, which were staple articles of food, boiled, baked and in porridge. They had cows early, so milk provided desirable food for children, and bread and milk or mush and milk was a common diet. Molasses was obtained occasionally, which varied the foods. Maple syrup they made themselves. Rye-meal with Indian-meal made the best of bread. Few potatoes were raised at first, ruta-baga turnips being used as we use potatoes. The forests and streams supplied meats and fish; pork products came from the swine they raised, which got their living in the woods from the roots and nuts.

For drinks the early settlers had plenty of pure water. Tea was a common drink, and "a dish of tea" is frequently mentioned in old diaries. As soon as orchards were bearing, cider was a common beverage. Coffee was reserved for special occasions. Alcoholic liquors were common, rum predominating. It was considered almost a necessity, and was used as medicine and stimulant as well as for conviviality. It was a common drink among the men, and even the clergy were not averse to its comfort. Drunkenness was not common among the settlers.

There was little idleness in those days. The men were busy from daylight till dark in work in the forest in winter, and in their fields with their crops in the summer and autumn. The women certainly had no spare time. There was the house work, the children to care for, which included their instruction in elementary knowledge as well as the religious training which was zealously attended to. Then between the necessary daily preparation of the food, the manufacture of yarn and fabrics was enough to fill any other time. Books they had in very small numbers, even the minister's library was limited. They all had the Bible, which served as the first primer for the child. There was nothing to distract from the routine of daily toil. What rest they had was at night around the fire-place, and then early to bed and early to rise. Candles, their only light, were "dipped" from the beef tallow, and a capable woman could dip 200 candles in a day.

The preparation of the raw materials from which the clothing of the family was made, was no small labor. The wool had to be sheared from the sheep, washed, carded, spun into yarn which was but the beginning. The yarn was dyed, with the extract of butternut hulls or with indigo, then it was knit into hosiery and other useful garments, or woven into cloth, the design of which depended on the artistic sense of the weaver.

Flax, the source of the linen for many clothing and household uses, was raised by the farmers as a regular staple crop, an acre being a regular planting. It grew sometimes four feet tall, and was pulled at the proper time in August. In this work the women assisted. The processes of fitting the flax for use as a fabric fiber required much work, and crude apparatus was used, but once the fiber was reduced to a spinable degree the work went on rapidly. It was spun on a small wheel into yarn sufficient in size for making thread for sewing, or for weaving. Woven with a mixture of wool it produced "linsey-woolsey," a common form of cloth for working garments. In the early days, when materials were limited, the women carded together cattle's hair and floss of flax or tow, or wool and hair, and spun it into yarn used for making stockings for their families. The linen produced from flax was a common material for summer garments and for bed and table linen. Even the tow was turned to some good use in family life.

The flora of the woods and fields furnished a number of dyestuffs, and a still greater variety of household remedies was derived from the roots and leaves of many plants. Much was learned from the friendly Indians regarding medicines from the wild plants, and effective cures were made from such simple remedies, and the roots and herbs were gathered each year and dried and hung in the garret for future use. "Old-wife's remedies" originated in this way, and undoubtedly relieved many trivial ills.

The work on the farms was laborious. The implements in use were heavy and crude. Plows were made of wood, the shares covered with iron plates. All hand implements were strong but unwieldly, which added to the labor. All mowing of hay was by hand, and the "hang" of the scythe was not always accurate. The hay was raked by hand, and later by a "Revolver Horse Rake," which was an implement made of a timber, through which were run the teeth, the points on each side being opposite. It was hauled by a horse, and guided by the driver who walked behind. When the rake was full, he raised the handles which brought the teeth against the ground, causing them to turn the raking contraption over, dumping the hay, and bringing the teeth on the other side into operation. It was cumbersome but it served. The work in the woods was done with the axe. The logs were chopped apart; the crosscut saw was unknown.

The farm buildings consisted, besides the small home house, of as large a barn as could be afforded, without cellar; around were cart-sheds, hen-houses, smoke-house, corn-crib, tool-house and whatever building was necessary to the work required. Every farm was its own repair shop and a thrifty farmer saved time and expense by mending and making his own implements.

With the increase of farms the necessity for blacksmiths developed, and a shop was to be found at frequent intervals. Horses required shoeing, oxen were shod in a "sling," which held the animal immovable for the time. The smith always was in demand to repair tools, and to make accessories and necessary parts to vehicles and utensils.

From the first, the thoughts of the settlers centered around the Meeting House, as the town formed the Parish. The people generally were religiously inclined, and were glad to have a settled minister. But while the meeting each Sabbath gave them an opportunity of seeing neighbors from the more remote parts of the town, it was by no means the only time or place of social gathering. If a man was sick or incapacitated for work the neighbors got together and looked after the crops or whatever was imperative. The women brought their dinners, and a social time was enjoyed at noon. "Bees" were common, when the people assembled to perform any public work that was necessary, with similar social relations. Farmers "changed works," one man working for a day for a neighbor, who in turn helped him a similar way. The "Raisings" were occasions of interest, when the men gathered to raise the frame of a neighbor's building, a barn, for example. They framed the timbers into form, and by main strength, aided by pick-poles lifted the frame into place, and pinned the parts together. Such occasions were tests of human strength, and cider was freely supplied, which often excited the men to greater efforts.

The women had their social affairs, such as "Quiltings," when a group gathered at some house and all proceeded to sew the quilt and lining and wadding between into a comfortable bed-quilt. As this occupied an afternoon, the husbands came in time for supper, and after a social evening took their wives home. It was often customary to raise the new quilt on its frame to the ceiling of the room, and have a regular "kitchen break-down" under it, with music furnished by a fiddler.

Among the young people evenings were enjoyed at which the entertainment consisted of the regular old-fashioned games, and kissing games were always popular.

Later, when village life was more possible, friends used to meet and spend the evening in singing rounds and glees and hymns that were well known. The fresh natural voices joined in melody, the pitch for the tune being obtained by a "Tuning-fork," as musical instruments were not common until the middle of the nineteenth century. The people were trained in vocal music, through the choirs at meeting and the singing schools which were conducted every winter by men well qualified to instruct. Jeremiah Eastman from Concord and Joshua Gamage from Cambridge were popular.

Hospitality was not lacking, and friendships were maintained among the settlers, even when distance was considerable between homes. Transportation was on foot or horseback; in the latter case the woman rode on a pillion behind the man in the saddle. Mounting blocks were essential. The first roads were mere paths following old Indian trails, wide enough for one person or horse; these trails were marked by "spotted trees," and therefore travel by night was reduced to the most necessary cases. The first wagons were crude and without springs. The early carriages were two-wheeled chaises, the body being hung on thoroughbraces in place of springs. The single-seated gig was used until late years by professional men on their travels. As oxen were the principal motive power, horses being kept for riding and single work about the place, the first carts were heavy, with large wheels and axles of wood, to which the wheels were fastened by "lynch-pins." It was with such crude and slow-moving vehicles that the first settlers carried their goods to market, and brought their supplies from store or mill. In winter ox-sleds were used entirely and people occasionally went to meeting or visiting on such conveyances, well bundled in skin robes.

When the Sabbath came, there was no work done except the essential. When a minister was in the vicinity, as occasionally some one visited the Seven Lots, the people attended his service at a central home, Caleb Swan's home being a frequent place of meeting. The families were strict in their attention to their religious duties; their children were always baptized when a minister was available. The Meeting House was at first as crude as the homes, and was a place of no creature comforts. The seats were hewed planks; there was no heat in the building, the sermons were often long, but no sleeping was tolerated. The men sometimes used to stand up to keep from going to sleep. Two sessions of the service were customary down to the 1860's.

The pulpit in the South meeting house was a high construction, with a sounding board, typical in meeting houses of the period. The minister reached the exalted position by a flight of narrow stairs. The elder men used to sit near the front, in order to hear the preacher, and there was a seat reserved for the deacons. The pews were square, straight-backed, and were uncomfortable to sit in; that, with the absence of heating, made the service an uncomfortable experience, but it was considered the necessary "mortification of the flesh," which was a part of their understanding of religion.

The absence of heat, was to some extent compensated for by the use of "foot-stoves," little frames inclosing an iron box, with perforated sides, in which was a dish of metal holding a pint or more of live coals. This little heater, when a number were in use, moderated the somewhat frigid temperature of the great room. It was customary to get it refilled between the services, and by this means the women keeping their feet on the "foot-stove" would manage to be more comfortable.

There was a quaint custom in the service—at the singing of the last hymn, the entire congregation arose, turned around facing the gallery and the choir, their back to the pulpit, and sang the hymn. Then they turned again for the benediction.

After the schools were established, the children were taught politeness, being expected to bow and courtesy to the teacher and to visitors at the school. The result of this instruction with the wholesome training in respect to parents and elders at home was to make the youth of those days polite in all circumstances.

Under such conditions the first settlers of the Pequawket Valley increased in number and in wealth. The farms were cleared, stone walls built, cattle increased, crops were bountiful and farmers who were thrifty became wealthy, and left their children a valuable legacy in the farm and forest property.

VII

FIRST PROPRIETORS

Fryeburg township was granted to Colonel Frye as his own property. There were no other grantees considered. The township was for him to sell in such sized lots as he chose.

He divided the area into sixty-four rights. As has been said, besides the personal rights there were four public rights set apart: One for the first ordained Protestant minister of the Gospel, and one for the Ministry; these two being known as the "parsonage lots;" one for Harvard College; and one for the Common Schools. The remaining sixty were disposed of as follows with the number of rights to each proprietor:

Hezekiah Astin	1		Stephen Farrington	1
Moses Ames	1		Simon Frye	1
Aaron Abbott	1		Daniel Farrington	1
Abraham Bradley	1		Joseph Frye	8
Benjamin Barker	1		Joseph Frye, Jr.	1
Capt. John Chandler	1		James Haseltine	1
Ezra Carter	1		Samuel Ingalls	1
Lieut. Caleb Swan	1		Andrew McMillan	3
James Clement	1		Nathaniel Merrill	1
Abial Chandler	1		Samuel Osgood	1
John Charles	4		Lieut. Oliver Peabody	2
John Chandler, Jr.	1		David Page	1
Ephraim Colby	1		John Russell	1
Moses Day	3		Capt. William Stark	2
James Osgood	1		John Stevens	1
John Evans	1		Mark Stacy	1
William Eaton	1		Capt. John Stark	2
Phillip Eastman	1		Timothy Walker	1
Obadiah Eastman	1		Ezekiel Walker	1
Richard Eastman	1		John Webster	1
David Evans	1		Isaac Webster	1
John Farrington	1		Total	60

Not all the Proprietors who took rights in the new township became settlers. They held shares as investments, or with possible intention of settling later. Those who did not settle were: Ezra Carter, of Pennacook (now Concord, N. H.). His share was occupied by Ezra Carter, his son; Lieut. Oliver Peabody, who took grants in several new townships, but never occupied them; Captain John Stark, afterward the General who won the battle of Bennington; Capt. William Stark, brother of John, who continued a loyalist and left the colonies. Mark Stacy and Andrew McMillan did not occupy their grants, but McMillan's son settled on the grant.

The rights allotted to each settler by Colonel Frye at the beginning of the occupancy of the township were actually merely tentative; and as the settlers pledged themselves and families to live in the township the rest of their lives, it was necessary that the division of rights should be made permanent and legal.

On February 2, 1766, sixteen of the Proprietors made application to Hon. Benjamin Lynde, a Justice of the Peace in Salem, to call a meeting of the Proprietors, to be held in the dwelling house of Ezekiel Walker, in Fryeburg, on June 23 at 9 o'clock in the forenoon, to have a legally called meeting, and to do certain acts enumerated in the petition, as follows:

Province of the Massachusetts Bay, Andover, Mass., Feb., 1766
The Petition of the subscribers hereto sheweth:

That your Petitioners are some of the Proprietors of a new township lying on each side of Saco River at a place called Pigwacket in the County of York, of which Joseph Frye was originally sole proprietor, and as there are two other new Townships lately laid out adjoining thereto, it is commonly distinguished from them by the name of Fryeburg. That as the grant of this township directs that it is to be settled with sixty families and that four sixty-fourths parts thereof be appropriated to public uses, the Division of it into sixty-four rights seems pretty clearly implied. That in A.D., 1763, your Petitioners and the rest of the Proprietors of said Township without being legally assembled to pass any votes with respect to the settlement thereof, laid out upon their upland fifty-seven house lots of forty acres each. And assigned to each and every right in said Township a twenty acre intervale lot, and to fifty-seven of said rights, each of them a forty acre house lot, to open the way for beginning the settlement of the place, which is called the first division of said Township, though not complete, there being seven of the rights to which no house lots have yet been laid. That as the greatest part of the lots in said first division have been found to answer the end for which they were designed, it's requisite that all such lots should be confirmed to the rights to which they were assigned and the rest allowed to drop and others laid in their stead. Also that said first Division should be completed by laying out seven forty-acre house lots to the seven rights to which no house lots have yet been laid out as above mentioned.

All of which with sundry other things, concerning said Township necessary to be acted upon agreeable to the law, as well as the nature of the affair in its first principles, renders a legal meeting of said Proprietors highly necessary, wherefore your Petitioners pray your Honor would please to call a meeting of said Proprietors to be held at the dwelling of Ezekiel Walker in Fryeburg aforesaid on the twenty-third day of June next, ensuing the date hereof at nine o'clock in the forenoon,—there and then to proceed on the business of said meeting which your Petitioners take leave to arrange in the following to wit:

1,ly To choose a Moderator of said meeting.
2,ly To choose a clerk of said Proprietors.
3,ly To choose a committee for laying out lands in said Township from time to time as the Proprietors shall legally direct.
4,ly To confirm to the right to which they were heretofore assigned as many of the forty acre house lots and twenty acre intervale lots laid in said Township, A.D., 1763, as the Proprietors thereof shall think proper and to allow the rest to drop.
5,ly To direct the committee laying out lands in said Township to lay out to each right therein allowed to drop their first Division house lots and Intervale lots, a forty acre house lot and a twenty acre Intervale lot in lieu of each forty acre house lot and each twenty acre Intervale lot, so dropped. And a forty acre house lot to each of the seven rights to which no house lots have yet been laid out, whereby the first division may be completed.
6,ly To give the committee directions for the rules of their conduct in laying out the lots mentioned in the preceding article.
7,ly To direct the committee to lay out meadow lots in said Township now fit for mowing, into forty-four shares of equal value.
8,ly To fix the time when the meadow shall be laid out.
9,ly To determine the manner by which a sixty-fourth part of a share of said meadows shall be confirmed to each right in said Township.
10,ly To direct that a second Division of both Upland and Intervale land be laid out to each right in said Township.
11,ly To determine how much Upland and how much Intervale land shall in said second Division be laid out to each of said Rights.
12,ly To see if the said Proprietors will direct that such allowances be made among the house lots of the first Division as are necessary to make the house lots of equal value—And that the same be done among the Intervale lots of the same Division.

13,ly To give the committee directions for the rule of their conduct in laying out the second Division in said Township. And also with respect to the allowances to be made among the lots of the first Division as mentioned in the article preceding this.
14,ly To empower the committee to employ surveyors and chainmen at the cost and charge of said Proprietors to assist them in laying out said lands in said Township as they are or may be legally directed so to do.
15,ly To determine what pay the committee for laying out lands in said Township as they are or may be, legally directed so to do.
16,ly To determine what pay the Proprietors' clerk shall have for the duties of his office.
17,ly To see if the Proprietors will raise money to pay the aforesaid committee, surveyors, chainmen and clerk for the services they, (in their respective capacities) do for said Proprietors, and determine how the same shall be raised.
18,ly To fix the place in said Township whereon the meeting-house shall stand.
19,ly To determine what quantity of land shall be laid out for the meeting-house to stand upon and for necessary room around the same.
20,ly To fix the place and how much land shall be laid out in said Township for a burying-place.
21,ly To fix where and how much land shall be laid out in said Township for a Training Field.
22,ly To pass such other votes relating to the affairs of said Township as the Proprietors thereof in said meeting shall think necessary.
Lastly. To determine how Proprietors' meetings shall be called for the future.

Andover, Feb'y 2d. 1766.
Signed by:

Joseph Frye	10 rights.	James Swan	1
John Wilson	1 "	John Chandler	1
Daniel Farrington	1	Ezra Carter	1
John Russell	1	Timothy Walker	1
Ebenezer Day	1	Stephen Farrington	1
Oliver Peabody	1	Philip Eastman	1
Thedore Carlton	1	Eben'r Frye	1
Hezekiah Austen	1	Caleb Swan	1

One right represented one sixty-fourth part of the Township.

According to the warrant, this meeting of the Proprietors was held June 23, 1766, when it was decided that each Right's share of the meadows in said Township should be ascertained by a lottery. (This vote was reconsidered at the Proprietors' meeting held in 1767, and validity was declared void and of no effect.)

It was then voted that the ten meadow lots laid out in the easterly part of the great meadow be confirmed and assigned to the ten rights in the Township belonging to Joseph Frye. Other meadow lots within the great turn of the river were assigned to the said Proprietor thereof. The remainder of the Rights in the Township should have their respective shares in the meadows and should have them assigned and confirmed to them by lot, and a committee was chosen to manage the assignment. This committee performed its duty, and later reported to a meeting of Proprietors, that the assignment was satisfactory.

At this same meeting it was voted to lay out one acre of land near the easterly side of Bear Pond, for a Meeting House. The Proprietors also voted to lay out four acres adjoining the Meeting House lot as a Burying Ground.

Having laid out the township into lots and assigned them to the settlers, it became necessary to have roads for the Proprietors to reach their lots, and the routes followed by the incoming settlers needed improvement.

Accordingly at a town meeting held July 27, 1767, it was voted to lay out two open roads, the first to begin at the most suitable place on the Town Line, south of the River, and to run by the most convenient courses on the same side of the river, to Daniel Farrington's intervale land, being the land later occupied by Caleb and Fred N. Frye; the whole length of this road to be about six and one half miles.

This road through the Seven Lots followed the course of the high ground of the plains-land above the intervale, and passed about between the house and barn of the Captain William Evans' place, later occupied by his descendant, Samuel Evans. From this point a branch road was later made to Caleb Swan's, now known as "Swan's Falls."

The course of the original road continued, and is still to be seen, on the north-easterly course passing the grounds of the West Oxford Agricultural Society, past the site of the former Chautauqua grounds and across "Moosehorn" Brook, up the Page Hill, where it turned abruptly to the left, north-westerly, to the site occupied by Colonel Frye.

The second road was to begin at the most suitable place on the State Line, on the North side of the River, and running on the north side, down the river by the most convenient course to the house lot of Andrew McMillan, the residence of the late Deacon John Charles, being about five miles. This is the road through West Fryeburg and Birch Hill sections, to a point where later it was continued through North Fryeburg, and still following the north side of the river, around through the Harbor.

Three kinds of roads were established by the Proprietors: Highways, the principal lines of communication between the settled areas; By-ways, roads for accommodation of individuals, between farm-lands, especially on the intervales, so the lots could be reached without trespass. (There are several such ways in the town); and Drift Roads, to accommodate any one who wished to use them. At this meeting, July 27, the first vote in relation to building a grist mill was passed. This provided that the mill-privilege on Lovewell's Brook and 60 acres of pine land, also 40 acres of adjacent pasture land should be given to the builder of the mill; bonus also was voted to be paid in cash or in work, the same to be raised out of each Right in the township, except the four Public Rights. This was not large remuneration for building a dam on the brook, and making and setting a mill-wheel and the necessary machinery for grinding grain. The mill which was built later remained in operation for many years subject to repairs and changes from time to time. The site is now deserted, but the water-supply has rarely failed.

It was also voted at this meeting to lay out a Training-Field on the ground originally designed for a Meeting House, and seven acres was appropriated as sufficient for that purpose.

Joseph Frye was chosen Treasurer, and Ezekiel Walker Collector of the Proprietors.

There was plenty to trouble the Grantee and the Proprietors in getting the township into shape, and procuring a fair allotment of the land, especially that all the land be of equal value either as intervale or upland, and accessible for settlers. On June 26, 1772, this petition was drafted, and sent to the Massachusetts Commonwealth authorities:

A Petition of Joseph Frye—Setting forth—That on the North Corner of the Township at Pigwacket in the County of York which was granted and confirmed to him in 1765 there lies a quantity of intervale land seperated (by low sunken Land) so far from any Upland in said Township, except a small strip as renders the settlement of any Families in that part of it impracticable and the improvement of said intervale very inconvenient. And praying that he may be allowed to drop 4147 Acres of the Land in the west Corner of s'd Township and to lay out the same quantity in the Province Lands adjoining to the Northwardly part of said Township, in lieu thereof, to accomodate the said intervale Land with Upland.

This petition was considered favorably by the General Court, and the petitioner was granted the right to return to Massachusetts the acreage that he described, and receive in place of it the same quantity of Government Land adjoining to the Northwardly or Northeastwardly part of the township, not to interfere with any other township, and that he should return a plan of the area within a year's time. It was also stated that Mr. Joseph Noyes was appointed to make a plan of the land in question, with "two Chainmen under Oath," and return the same to the General Court.

The changes due to the determination of State lines raised new problems of division of land, both upland and intervale. In 1774 the Proprietors voted to re-lay all the first and second divisions so that each Proprietor should have eighty acres of upland and sixty acres of intervale.

After that, between 1787 and 1825 there were a third, fourth, fifth and sixth division, making the town plan like a crazy quilt.

Colonel Frye was anxious to have communication with Portland as soon as possible, to relieve the settlement from the task of hauling provisions from Concord, and to open a line of trade with the sea-board. But there was much work to be done on roads and highways in the town and the near-by communities, and so it was not until 1772, nine years after the settlers occupied the township, that he took active measures to that end. He prepared the following document, which was submitted to the General Court of the Commonwealth of Massachusetts:

Province of the Massachusetts Bay.
To his Excellency the Governor, To the Honorable His Majesty's Council and House of Representatives of said Province in general Court Assembled.

The Petition of Joseph Frye humbly sheweth—
That under the patronage of this Government He undertook the settlement of a new Township (now called Fryeburg) at Pigwacket, in the County of York, which being so far in the wilderness as to render the getting a passage thereto, that would make a Road for Wheel Carriages exceeding difficult, It cast a very gloomy aspect upon the Undertaking.

But as such a road must first be had, or it would be in vain to attempt the settlement of the place, your Petitioner and his Associates exerted themselves to the utmost of their Power to find a Passage that would answer that Purpose. Made two expensive trials on different courses, and carried each Road the greatest part of the way through the woods, and there met Insuperable Impediments in the way, by means whereof Their Labor on those two routes was entirely lost, and They almost Discouraged.

However your Petitioner used means which revived the Courage of his Associates to abide by Him in a Third Trial: Pitched upon a time when he would go (with two men only) to look out the way and Accordingly went; and thro' much difficulty found a Passage thro' the Wilderness which He thought might Possibly answer, and made report thereof to His Associates, who thereupon went with Him, clear'd, Bridg'd and Causeway'd the same where it wanted (except great and Little Ossipee Rivers); Then measured the Road and found, That from the Town then called Phillipstown [Sanford] (which was the Place of their Departure) to Fryeburg was fifty-four miles. And also found the Cost they had been put to in getting said Road (Including the two fruitless Attempts) amounting to upwards of four hundred Pounds Lawful Money—Having then got a road for Wheel Carriages (tho' a very Rough one in Some Places) They proceeded to the Settlement of the Place with all Possible Speed, and in about five years after got upwards of fifty Families Settled therein.—That tho' your Petitioner believes the People Settled there, are in general, as Laborious a Set of People as have undertaken the Settlement of a Plantation in the Wilderness for many years past; yet it's certain That their Task in Subduing Their wild Land, Building Mills, clearing Roads, building Bridges &c. &c. &c., within Their own Department is as great as in Their Infant State They are able to bear,—

Notwithstanding which, as Their Lands will not produce all the absolute Necessities of Life, They have been Obliged to maintain the greatest part of a Road of fifty miles in length to get to the Sea-Coasts for those Necessaries that are lacking: This is such a great addition to the Difficulties They Labor under within Their own Place as will, (except Relief from This Court Prevents) Terminate in Their Ruin.—

Your Petitioner and Associates having Labored under this Difficulty for upwards of eight years, and finding They were no Longer able to Support Themselves under it, and that Falmouth (tho' fifty miles distant from Fryeburg) is the most Convenient Sea-Port Town for them; your said Petitioner (hoping to obtain some speedy help from thence) set out for Falmouth, where He arrived on the 15th of November, A.D., 1771; and on the then next Monday evening was favored with the Company of a Number of the Gentlemen of that Town, when he laid before them the Difficulties His Remote Plantation Labored under for want of a Road to them, Showing Them at the Same Time, That the way to get the most Convenient Communication opened between Falmouth and Fryeburg, was to open a Road from the North end of Pearsontown [Standish] (Steering about Northwest thro' a tract of unappropriated Wilderness Land belonging to the Province) to the falls in Saco River, called the Great Falls; and then there would be only the width of said River to get into the Road your Petitioner and Associates had opened to Fryeburg as above Related:—upon which the Gentlemen, for the immediate Relief of said Young Plantation, and in Consideration of the Prospect of advantages arriving therefrom to the Publick, opened a Subscription for Raising Money to Clear, Bridge and Causeway a Road, the way your Petitioner had Proposed to Them; and immediately Chose a Committee to Seek a Passage thro' the woods for that Purpose:—This Committee went on the Business for which they were Chose, and after finding the way where the Road must unavoidably go, they measured and found the length of the Road from the north end of Pearsontown-Road to sd. Falls, would be fourteen and a half miles, and that it would go the greater part of the Distance on sd. Tract of Province Land.—

The Subscribers being soon informed by their Committee what length of way They had to make sd. Road, They proceeded with all Possible Speed to opening the same, and (at great expense) have Cleared it two rods wide, and altho' there are many bad Brooks and miry Places in their way, They have Bridged and Causewayd the same, so that a Number of Loaded Teams that went from hence Traveled so Comfortably thro' sd. Road, it has much Revived the Spirits of the (almost Discouraged) Inhabitants of this young Plantation for the Present—But here your Petitioner begs leave to observe, that said Tract of Province Land turns out very Different from what sundry Persons have heretofore Conceived of it; It having Lately been found to be such a Mountainous, Boggy, Ponded and broken Fragment of Land, That none who had grants of Land to lay out in that part of the Province would accept of, but Chose to go many miles further into the Wilderness than take it; It's likely to lay (no one can tell how long) a grievous Stumbling-Block in the way of the back Settlements as there is no Prospect of it's ever being made a Township of whereby the Road may be kept in Repair.

So that the kindness of the Subscribers will not be of that lasting advantage to the back Settlements They Really Stand in Need of, Except your Excellency and Honours would be pleased to grant said Tract of Land to Some persons or other, upon such Terms as will Induce Them into an Obligation to Maintain the Road thro' it—And as the said Subscribers, In Consideration of the Danger of the Roads not being kept in Such Repair as to Answer the good Design of it, Have (since They open'd Their Subscription) manifested a willingness to bind Themselves to keep said Road in good Repair, Provided They might have a Grant of Province Land to Defray the Charges of it, your Petitioner begs leave humbly to Pray Your Excellency and

Honours, would (on Their Request) be pleased to grant to them for that Purpose.—

And as in Duty bound will ever Pray
                                    Joseph Frye.

To His Excellency and the whole Court,
   To whom the Foregoing Petition is
   Addressed.

We, the Subscribers, who are Associates of the above Petitioner, Proprietors and Inhabitants of the said Township of Fryeburg, beg Leave to Declare, That the foregoing Petition contains a True and just Representation of the Expense and Difficulty of getting a Road to this Place, and of the Expense and Difficulties we have been put to, and Still Labor under within our Department. And upon the whole That our Sufferings for want of help to maintain a Road to the Sea-Coasts have been such as Constrains us to make known to your Excellency and Honours, we are no longer able to Support ourselves under Them.

And as the Subscribers mentioned in sd. Petition have been so Compassionate to us, as to open the Road for our Relief, as therein justly set forth; and from their Knowledge of our inability to maintain said Road in that Repair which is absolutely Necessary, are willing to bind themselves to do it, Provided They may have a Grant of the Tract of Province Land the Road goes thro' to Defray the Expense of Such Repairs, We beg Leave humbly to Subjoin our Prayer, That the Prayer of sd. foregoing Petition may be Granted.

And as in Duty bound will ever Pray.

Ebenezer Farnum, Isaac Abbott, Timothy Walker, Caleb Swan, Hugh Stirling, Samuel Osgood, Nathaniel Smith, Stephen Farrington, Rachel Walker, David Evans, Simon Frye, Joseph Greely Swan, Jedediah Spring, Joseph Frye, Jr., Ezekiel Walker, John Bucknell, Jonathan Dresser, Richard Kimball, Benjamin Russell, James Swan, Isaac Walker, Nath'l Merrill, Ezra Carter, Samuel Walker, John Evans, Moses Ames, Hezekiah Asten, John Farrington, Samuel Ingalls, Peter Asten, Nathan Ames, John McMillan, John Stevens, Henry Gordon, Joseph Pettingill, Joseph Walker, Stephen Knight, Ebenezer Day, Abner Charles, Joseph Kilgore, Aaron Abbott, Abraham Bradley, Benjamin Kilgore, Timothy Bradley, John Webster, John Walker, Peter Chandler, David Page, William Wiley, Moses Day, John Charles, Jr., Samuel Walker, Jr., Daniel M. Cross.

VIII

THE CHURCH

The people in their capacity as citizens regarded the cooperation of ministers and churches as essential to their success in asserting and maintaining their civil rights. The churches in general followed the leadership of the ministers, though at the first in many of them there were two parties, one favoring the royalists and the other the cause of liberty. The influence of Congregational churches was not less potent in shaping the new government than in throwing off the yoke of the old. Congregationalism was in its nature a democracy.
—*Rev. A. E. Dunning, D.D.*

One of the conditions governing the grant of territory in Pequawket to Colonel Joseph Frye was that within ten years there should be a settled Protestant Minister in the township. The proprietors were desirous to have this condition complied with as soon as possible, for the families were all accustomed to religious associations and had come from churches in their home towns.

It was difficult to meet the situation, for a minister, much as one was needed, was an added expense, and money was scarce. They were obliged to delay longer than they naturally desired.

In less than a year and a half from the arrival of the first settlers, Rev. Timothy Walker of Concord, N. H., from whose parish several families had come to Fryeburg, visited the town in the wilderness. His visit, while of parochial nature, was also a tour of exploration, and he brought to his former parishioners the latest news of their home-town and of their friends and neighbors.

Parson Walker left Concord, Sept. 19, 1764, and arrived in Pequawket Sept. 22. It was a distance of over 70 miles from Concord, over a poor trail, stopping where night found him. His old friends were ready to hear him, and he preached twice, Sept. 23, and 30. He left after a week's visit. While in Pequawket he baptized Elizabeth, daughter of Jedediah Spring, who came to the Seven Lots, with others in November, 1763. He visited Lovewell's

Pond, also paid a visit to Nathaniel Merrill who was building a grist mill at "Sodom."

Parson Walker had a son Timothy, who although he later became a judge, was educated for the ministry, and preached frequently. In the summer of 1765, then a young man of twenty-eight, he went to Pequawket where were many of his former neighbors. He visited on week days and preached Sundays, remaining some six weeks.

His journal of the visit contains some interesting entries:

July 20, Visited Capt. Brown, A.M.; Col. Frye, P.M.
" 21, Preached all day.
" 22, Took a view of the Intervale.
" 23, Dined with Col. Frye. Drank tea at Mr. Day's.
" 24, Col. Frye dined with me. P.M. I drank tea at Capt. Brown's with Col. Frye.
" 27, Took a view of Pigwacket from Stark's Hill with Capt. Eastman and Mr. Page.
" 28, Preached all day.
" 29, Lieut. Frye visited me. A.M.
Aug. 1, Dined with Lt. Frye. Visited Mr. Charles. & L'd at Capt. Walker's.
" 3, Went to lower end of Lovell's Pond.
" 4, Preached all day.
" 6, Took a view of Pleasant Pond. Killed 2 ducks.
" 8, Capt. Walker and company arrived with battow from Saco.
" 9, Went to Lovell's Pond and took account of the stores brought in ye battow.
" 11, Preached all day.
" 14, Went after pigeons.
" 17, Breakfasted at Mr. Ames. Visited Lt. Smith. P.M. Went a pigeoning.
" 19, Attended the errection of Lt. Smith's house.
" 21, Took a view of the place where Col. Lovell had his fight, with Mr. Ingalls.
" 22, Visited Mrs. Brown, A.M.
" 23, Visited Mr. Evans.
" 25, Preached all day.
" 28, Mr. Spring returned from hunting Masts.
" 30, Dined with Capt. Walker. Drank tea at Mr. Day's & lodged at Capt. Walker's.
" 31, Returned A.M. with Capt. Walker. P.M. wrote a deed for John Evans.
Sept. 1, Preached all day. P.M., Mr. Ezekiel Walker and company arrived from Rumford. (Concord)
" 2, Drank tea at Capt. Brown's.
" 3, Set out with Lt. Frye and company for Rumford.

It would seem from these incidents, which were typical of every day, that young Mr. Walker enjoyed himself, and yet was busy and helpful among the people.

In 1767, as has been said, Rev. Grindall Rawson preached, being engaged by Colonel Frye. In October, 1768 Rev. Paul Coffin, the minister at Buxton, made a "pilgrimage" to Pequawket, preaching, baptizing and visiting. His visit is fully described in his journal. In the summer of 1774 Rev. William Fessenden, a friend and fellow minister, who had preached in Mr. Walker's church in Concord, was influenced to visit Pequawket, and preached several times, evidently with satisfaction to the people. He found the field well-cultivated, Parsons Walker and Coffin having kept the faith alive in the hearts of the people. The Town took action Oct. 5, 1774,

> To see if they will give to Mr. William Fessenden a call to settle in the gospel ministry in said township, and if so, to see what they will give him as a settlement and yearly salary.
> Article 3: To see if they will sell some of their timber on the common and undivided lands in said township for the purpose of paying such a settlement as shall be voted.

These articles were acted upon favorably, as they voted to call the minister, and a letter was sent inviting him to come by the next May, if agreeable to him.

At a Proprietors' meeting January 10, 1775, a letter from Mr. Fessenden was read, accepting the terms of the call, which included a salary of forty-five pounds for the first year, reckoned to begin October 11, 1775. His salary was to be increased five pounds each year, until it reached the sum of seventy pounds, where it was to remain, during his pastorate. This salary was to be paid, one-third in Indian corn and rye, at three shillings lawful money per bushel for the first six years of his ministry.

Mr. Fessenden began his pastorate in May, 1775. That August a church was organized, and the new minister was ordained October 11, of the same year.

The ordination called together a number of ministers from the neighboring towns, including Rev. Paul Coffin of Buxton; Rev. Mr. Merrill of Biddeford; Rev. Mr. Thompson of Standish; Rev. Timothy Walker of Concord, N. H., and Rev. Nathaniel Porter of New Durham, N. H. Mr. Porter two years later was installed at Conway, N. H.

As there was no meeting house at that time it is thought that the ceremony was held in Lieut. Samuel Osgood's house, since a bill was rendered by Lieutenant Osgood, for "making provision for the council that ordained the Rev. William Fessenden. £13, 7s and 6d." This bill was not paid, for some unknown reason, until ten years later.

Mr. Fessenden boarded the first summer with Hezekiah Austin in the "Birch Hill" neighborhood. As soon as possible the Proprietors built him a house on the right set apart for the minister, on the hill next to Colonel Frye.

The first steps toward building a meeting house were taken in June, 1767, when the Proprietors chose a committee "To center the Meeting House." This committee measured from the old townline to Samuel Walker's, whose house was the farthest north at that time. The exact center of the township was found to be at the accepted "Center," about where Hon. E. C. Buzzell lives, and construction was started directly opposite, south of where the old Gammage barn stands.

After the town was incorporated, in 1777, there was dissatisfaction expressed by the townspeople with the site and the house that had been started; so the Town voted to buy the house.

The construction of a meeting-house was an important item of town business, and February 16, 1778 the Town voted "That the place to build a meeting house should be on a height Ridg of Land Between Bogg Pond and Bare Pond, and on the Easterly side of the main Road Leading Threw s'd Town, said Ridg is on the Lot called the Pitch lot."

The dimensions of the Meeting House were set as follows: "fifty-four feet in length, and forty two feet in width, and to have a gallery, and the length of the Posts to be in Proportion to the Bigness of the House."

They voted to raise "One Hundred Pounds, Lawful money to Bring forward the Building of s'd Meeting House." They chose a committee and directed them "to Bring forward the Building said Meeting House as they shall think Proper, they being accountable to the Town for their Conduct." This committee was Isaac Abbott, Stephen Farrington, Ezekiel Walker, Moses Ames, Stephen Knight, John Charles, Samuel Walker.

At the town meeting held April 13, it was "Voted to Chuse Seven men as a Comitee from the Different Parts of the Town to consider the Distance the Remote famalys are from the Place where the Town voted to set the meeting house at their meeting the 16th of February last Past and to look out the most Convenient and Suitable Place for Building said Meeting house at or as near the Place where the Town voted as they think Best and make Report to the Town for their acceptance at the ajournment of this meeting or some Later Day."

June 25, the Town held another meeting, this time at the house of Mr. Isaac Abbott. The report of the committee on location of the Meeting House was as follows:

Your Com. have taken the Matter under Consideration and Report that the Senter Between Mr. William Steel and Mr. Samuel Walker is where Mr. Isaac Abbott's Barn Lately stood, and that a Senter Between Mr. John Bolt Miller's and Mr. James Murray's is at the same Place. But it is our oppinion that the Place for Building said House ought to be about seventy rods farther to the Southward to the east side of the main Road upon the Lot commonly called the Pitch Lot for the following Reasons:

1st. Mr. Samuel Walker Liveing Better than Two Miles Below Mr. William Wiley's a Lone and it appears to us just and equitable that the house ought at the Place above Mentioned.

2ndly Because the Most Famalys will come in to the main Road Southward of the Place where we think the said House ought to Stand When they Attend Public worship and also the Most Rates.

This report was signed by the committee.

The Town voted not to accept the report of the Committee.

Then the Town voted to buy an acre of ground from Isaac Abbott, on the ridge for the site of the meeting-house, which is a little south of the present Odd Fellows' Hall.

The house was built facing the west, the gable end toward the road. The entrance was on the west. The pulpit was on the north side, about middle way, a high pulpit with stairs on each side. No galleries were ever finished, and the inside never was finished. The seats were made of white-pine plank.

It was never possible to use the house in the winter, there being no heating accommodations, and the town paid Isaac Abbott $25 a winter for the use of a large heated room in his house, in which to hold meetings. Here Mr. Fessenden preached. The room still exists as a part of the house occupied by Francis Buzzell.

In 1795 a meeting house was built at the Village, to accommodate the growing population in that end of the town. It was known as the "South Meeting House," and served until 1850.

While the church affairs went on quietly under Mr. Fessenden, and he was a man of influence in the town, for some unknown reason a number of his parishioners in the north part of the town became dissatisfied, and in 1788 they invited Rev. Zebediah Richardson of Sanford to come and conduct services. Mr. Richardson was a Baptist, but the people who sent for him were not known to have had any proclivities in that direction.

Those who aligned themselves against Mr. Fessenden were: Deacon Samuel Charles, John Charles, John Stevens, Jr., Lieut. Nathaniel Frye, Joseph Chandler, Benjamin Wiley, Hugh Gordon, Ebenezer Stevens, Samuel Stevens. These men were large taxpayers, and they felt the injustice of being obliged to pay a town tax in support of one faith, when they were followers of another. The Baptist Society was formally incorporated by the Great and General Court of Massachusetts, in 1790 and the supporters of the Baptist minister refused to pay the town minister's tax, claiming that they were entitled to a certain percentage of the minister's tax, according to their property valuation.

The matter had come before the town meeting of April 6, 1789, in the second and third Articles in the warrant, as follows:

Art. 2nd. To see if the town will direct their selectmen to give orders to those petitioners who call themselves of the Baptist persuasion, on the Treasurer, to take the sums they are assessed (in the tax called the Minister's Tax) to support the Gospel in that way, which in conscience appears to them to be most agreeable to the word of God.

This article failed of passage.

Art. 3rd. To see if an accommodation with those who call themselves the Baptist Society, can be effected in such a way and manner as will prevent a lawsuit, if a lawsuit should be found unavoidable, to raise money for defraying the charges thereof.

In 1790 Rev. Mr. Richardson began suit against the town to recover the salary he claimed was his due. The suit dragged along for several years, and the feeling between the Congregationalists and the Baptist Society became marked.

An effort was made in the town meeting of June 19, 1795 to relieve the Baptist Society in this article in the warrant:

To see if the town will vote that the Baptist Society shall not be taxed in the ministers' tax any more than their paying up all the taxes that are now assessed in said minister's taxes, and take out the cost of court that is depending between Mr. Zebediah Richardson and the town of Fryeburg, each paying their own cost.

This article was passed over.

In September, 1796 a town meeting was called, and Article 5, was of especial importance to the established church of the Town. The article was:

> In compliance with the request of Lt. James Osgood and others— As a number of the inhabitants of Fryeburg are desirous the Rev. Mr. Fessenden should preach some part of the time in that part of the town called Seven Lots, the petitioners pray their request may be taken under consideration and order taken thereon, and the term of time pointed out, that said Seven Lots may be accommodated with preaching agreeable to their desires.

This article was not acted on at the meeting.

The church establishment was more or less of a trial to the townspeople, as they were having to consider matters pertaining to it frequently. This article in the warrant for a town meeting for Oct. 1796 is an illustration:

> Article 5: To determine by vote which is most agreeable to a majority of the town of Fryeburg, viz., A meeting-house at each end of the town, or one meeting-house in the center of the town.
>
> The Clerk's record says: Nov. 7, 1796. 5-ly. It appears by a clear vote that a majority of the town of Fryeburg are in favor of a meeting-house at each end of the town of Fryeburg.

Whether the Town grew weary of sectarian wrangling is not recorded, but at a town meeting Nov. 7, 1796, the vote was passed as follows:

> Voted: That this town will make no further provision for the support of the Rev. William Fessenden in the ministry of the Gospel except that the said Rev. William Fessenden will make some contract with the town therefor, and the town clerk be directed to present him with an attested copy of the vote and preamble thereof.

In less than a year and a half, the inhabitants decided without any help from the municipality, that they would have a meeting-house at the Center, for in the records of March 5, 1798 is this statement: "Town meeting adjourned to Apr. 2, next, to meet at the new center meeting-house."

At a meeting the May following, the Town voted:

That the old meeting-house should be sold at vendue, when Moses

Ames, Esq., was appointed Vendue Master, to sell the same. The conditions of the vendue is as follows:

1st. The old meeting-house is to be set up vendue, and to be struck off to the highest bidder.
2nd. The security to be given to the town treasurer.
3rd. The money to be paid the first day of Dec. next, and to be appropriated to pay the debts of the town.
4th. 25 cts shall be received as a bid.

The above conditions were accepted by the town, and the house bid off by Robert Page at $18.50. That the matter was not entirely ended there, is shown by the action of the Town on Sept. 14, 1798, when this item was found in the warrant for the meeting:

4th. To see if the town will appropriate the money that the old meeting-house was sold for, to buy glass, and said glass be equally divided to the two meeting-houses now in said Fryeburg.

The clerk's record says the 4th article passed in the Affirmative.

At the town meeting, April 7, 1800, the Town chose a committee to confer with Rev. William Fessenden to settle a law suit commenced by him against the Town.

This committee interviewed Mr. Fessenden, and their certificate of appointment and duties bore this indorsement back to the Town:

Fryeburg, April 8th. 1800. The subscriber has agreed with the committee of the town named in this paper; that if the town suffer themselves to be defaulted in the action commenced by myself against the town, I will stay execution for the term of three months from the default.

William Fessenden.

Mr. Fessenden made this statement of his position:

The subscriber viewing with grief the broken and divided situation of the town with respect to supporting public worship of God here, and sincerely disposed, as he conceives he has ever been, to promote the best interests of the town, both spiritual and temporal, the same disposition actuates the subscriber in making the following proposal. viz.: to give up my civil contract with the town and proprietors as far as respects my annual salary from and after the eleventh day of October next; that is, if the town will pay up my annual salary to the eleventh of October next the town as such and the proprietors in their corporate capacity will by these presents be discharged from said civil contracts. The subscriber does not mean nor would he be understood to give up his pastoral relations to the church of Christ in this place, but means to be at liberty to preach the word and administer the ordinances of the gospel when, where and at such seasons as to him shall be thought to be best. Perhaps at this time it will be inconvenient for the town to pay up the present year's salary. The subscriber is disposed to wait for the same, provided the town will pay him interest after three months from this date. The subscriber suggests to the inhabitants of the town that he has no idea of ceasing to preach the Word in this place so long as he conceives preaching may be to your peace and happiness.

I am with the utmost sincerity a friend to the town of Fryeburg.
William Fessenden.

The Town disposed of the lawsuits against it by Rev. Mr. Richardson and Rev. Mr. Fessenden, and voted that each person should draw from the town treasury the amount of his minister's tax and pay it to the minister whose preaching he attended. As only seventy pounds was the required tax, the matter was thus fairly settled, but the Baptists being many of them large tax-payers, drew from the treasury about one half of the seventy pounds.

Mr. Fessenden continued to preach at the South Meeting House. After his death in 1805 the pulpit was supplied by occasional clergymen until 1809, and there was criticism of the desultory way in which services were maintained, so that at a town meeting in that year, the Town appointed Joseph Chandler as agent to defend it against the indictment of neglect of preaching. This aroused the Town to the careless condition into which it had drifted. It was voted to call Rev. Francis Whiting to be settled over the church and parish, and he accepted, remaining from 1809 till 1814.

He was succeeded by Rev. Nathaniel Porter, D.D., a classmate of Mr. Fessenden, who was pastor at Conway; he preached at the South Meeting House for several years.

The same year that Mr. Whiting came, a Universalist faction presented this petition to the General Court, asking incorporation as a religious society:

To the Honorable Senate and House of Representatives of the Commonwealth of Massachusetts, in General Court assembled, May, 1809:

The subscribers, Inhabitants of Fryeburg and Fryeburg Addition, in the county of Oxford, being of the denomination of Christians called Universalists, humbly represent to the Honorable Court that they labor under many Disadvantages in raising and appropriating monies for the support of a public teacher of piety, morality and religion, and being desirous of associating for the support of a teacher on whose Instruction they can conscientiously attend, humbly ask that they with such others as may join with them may be incorporated into a religious society by the name of the First Universalist Society in Fryeburg, that they may enjoy all the privileges to such societies belonging, and be enabled to raise funds for the maintainance of such teacher and other like purposes, and as in duty bound will ever pray.

Inhabitants of Fryeburg.

Solomon Charles	Ebenezer Stevens
Moses Knight	Samuel Stevens
Samuel Charles	Jno. Stevens
Bliss Charles	Natha. Walker
Abner Charles	Ebenezer Day
Joseph Charles	Charles Walker
James Charles	Benjamin Wiggin
John Charles	Stephen Farrington, Jr.
John Charles, Jr.	John Walker, Jr.
John Walker	Mason Wiley
Henry D. Hutchins	John Wiley
Jabez Day	Ebenezer Day
Daniel Chandler	Joseph Knight
James Wiley	John Knight
Benjamin Wiley	Jacob Farrington
Moses Chandler	Putnam Farrington
Joseph Chandler	John Swain
John Gordon	Thomas Day
Isaac Abbott	Jerem'h H. Eastman
Oliver Knight	Caleb Knight
Simeon Charles	Thaddeus Bemis
Isaac Charles	

A number of the petitioners had formerly been associated with the Baptists.

With the separation of the District of Maine from the mother-state of Massachusetts in 1820 many changes in the state management followed, among them the ending of the "Town Parish", and no longer was the Town obliged to appropriate money for the support of public worship. By that time, 1821, the South Meeting House was in frequent, if not constant use, and the Church of the Second Parish was formed; the Town having been the First Parish, and the Universalist society the Third Parish.

In 1823 the Rev. Carlton Hurd was called to the Second Parish, and he continued in the pulpit of that church until his death in 1855. He was an able man, and was recognized by Dartmouth College with the degree of Doctor of Divinity.

Mr. Hurd began his pastorate in the South Meeting House. It

was built in 1795 at the junction of the Main road and the Mill Road [later the Bridgton Road]. It was a large house, two storied, with two rows of windows, and a gallery on three sides. The pulpit was set high on pillars, well above the congregation. It faced southwest, and the entrance through a porch was on that side. It was told that Mrs. J. B. Osgood, who lived in the house on the hill at the south-west end of the village, could stand in her front door and with a spy-glass see directly into the door of the meeting house a mile away. This was a typical meeting house of New England, but without a steeple.

In 1824 a revision of the church creed was made, introducing new articles of faith. These changes produced discussion and dissention, the more liberal-minded members not being satisfied with the changes. The disagreement becoming serious, a number of the dissenting ones left the Congregational church and took measures to establish a Unitarian society.

The movers in this action held that as the church had changed its covenant, it was no longer binding on any who did not agree with the new form. Other issues in the community were brought in, widening the breach, until the effort to form a Unitarian society crystalized, and services were held in the old Academy building. Among the occasional ministers who preached there was Ralph Waldo Emerson.

This breach in the Congregational church served to unsettle many persons, and the Unitarian cult throve for a time, but as it was supported financially by a limited number, it gradually lost ground. In 1828 another denomination began to develop, which that year resulted in the establishment of a Methodist Episcopal church; this absorbed the remainder of the Unitarians, and that society disappeared entirely.

The Methodists held their service in the Academy building, and the Rev. David Copeland conducted services there, serving also the people of that faith in Conway and Bartlett.

Judge Judah Dana was active, after leaving the Congregational church, in fostering the Methodist movement. He was followed by other influential families. He and Col. E. L. Osgood gave to the Methodists a lot of land between Main Street, and the Old Burying Ground, where in 1845 a church building was erected and was occupied during the next forty years. After preaching there was abandoned, owing to the decrease in the membership of the church, the interest of the Methodists turned to the north part of the town, the village church was sold and became the Parish-house and hall of the Church of the New Jerusalem (Swedenborgian).

The Methodist interest developed steadily at the new field, and a commodious chapel was built near the old river, at the "Harbor", where an active church has become established.

The building of a Universalist chapel in 1838 at the junction of the two roads from Birch Hill and West Fryeburg and from Fish Street and the Center, met a long felt want for religious services, and there was a strong organization for a long time. During the recent past the interest and attendance has waned, only occasional services being held. At the present time (1937) a ministerial supply is located at North Fryeburg, and inter-denominational services are conducted in that neighborhood and in an adjoining town.

A religious movement which originated in East Fryeburg, developed into a Free Will Baptist organization. It throve for a time as the community was isolated from the rest of the town and was homogeneous, but it had no influence on the various religious movements in the village and in time passed away.

In 1831 the State Conference of Congregational Churches was held in Fryeburg, which was a factor in the religious movement that was manifest in the country, and 91 members were taken into the church during the years 1832 and 1833. From that time during Mr. Hurd's pastorate the Church made marked progress.

A movement began for a better church building. It crystalized in 1848, when work was begun on the site of the house of Dr. Eliphalet Lyman, on Main Street. This new building was of classical design, of the Doric order. Its stately portico is surmounted by a graceful steeple, whose vane is one hundred feet above the street. The building contained 80 pews, each pew representing a share subscribed for. At one end was a handsome pulpit on a rostrum; at the opposite end a gallery for organ and choir. This building, like its predecessor, was built entirely by voluntary offerings. It was dedicated the first Sunday in July, 1850, and has been in constant use ever since. The Town Clock is in the steeple. It is a conspicuous feature of Main Street, and is one of the finest church edifices in the County of Oxford.

For four years Mr. Hurd enjoyed the new building in which he was so vitally interested. He died in 1855, and was succeeded by

Rev. John Q. Peabody, who was installed pastor in 1856. For three years he served the church, and was followed by Rev. David B. Sewall, a member of a leading family in the denomination.

Mr. Sewall became closely connected with the interests of the community. He was made a member of the Board of Trustees of the Academy and served some time as Secretary of the Board. He bought the house formerly occupied by Mr. Hurd, and for fourteen years ministered to the church. In 1873 he left the pastorate for a new field, and though urged to remain he accepted a call to the church in York.

The pulpit was then occupied by the Rev. Baman N. Stone, who continued as pastor for three years, during which period, in August 1875 the Centennial of the establishment of the church was celebrated for several days. The exercises were interesting and impressive.

In 1877, Mr. Stone having accepted the theological beliefs of Emanuel Swedenborg, the pastoral relation was severed, and he was dismissed with a number of members. A church of that denomination was formed, and a church edifice was built on Oxford St., dedicated August 31, 1879. Mr. Stone continued to minister to that church until his death, April 7, 1918. Since then the church has been under the pastorate of the Rev. E. C. Hamilton, and more recently of the Rev. Louis A. Dole, who resigned in the summer of 1937, to accept a call to Bath. He was succeeded by the Rev. Wilfred G. Rice, who came in the summer of 1937 from the Humbolt Park church, Chicago, Ill.

In January 1933, a number of people in the village who were interested in the tenets of the Christian Science denomination, formed themselves into an Association, holding services each Sunday. While the organization is small, it is composed of sincere and consistent people who follow the teachings of their church.

Following the Swedenborgian separation, the Rev. Javan Knapp Mason, D.D., served as pastoral supply for the Congregational Church until the fall of 1886. In the spring of 1887 Wallace Nutting was acting pastor for the summer. He was succeeded by William F. Livingston, who was ordained and installed pastor in the autumn of the same year, continuing in the pastorate until 1889.

Albion H. Ross served the church during the year from March, 1890 until the autumn of 1891, when he was succeeded by Rev. Charles S. Young, who remained until May 1896.

In 1896 Ernest H. Abbott came to the church, and was ordained and installed pastor. He continued till 1901, and was followed by Rev. George B. Spalding, who acted as pastor until 1903.

From that time until the present (1937) no pastor has been installed, their services having been limited to short acting pastorates, the succeeding clergymen and their terms being: Rev. Edgar T. Pitts, 1903 to 1905; Rev. Stephen T. Livingston, temporary supply; Rev. Edwin P. Wilson, 1905 to 1910; Rev. William G. Mann, who supplied during the summer of 1911; Rev. John B. Carruthers, 1912 to 1915; Rev. Solomon T. Achenbach, 1915 to 1920; Rev. Edwin W. Wild, 1921 to 1931; Rev. Harold G. Booth, 1931 to 1937; Rev. Wesley U. Riedel, 1937.

IX

PARSON FESSENDEN

> A man he was, to all the country dear,
> And passing rich with forty pounds a year.
> Remote from towns, he ran his godly race,
> Nor e'er had changed, nor wished to change his place.
> * * * * * * * * * *
> E'en children followed with endearing wile,
> And plucked his gown, to share the good man's smile.
> —*Oliver Goldsmith.*

Rev. William Fessenden came to Fryeburg as a possible candidate in the summer of 1774. The parish considered him favorably, and the next year he was given a call from the Town, and accepted.

Something may be learned from Parson Fessenden's Diary about the beginning of his work at Pequawket. The diary is written on small pages, about 6 by 3¾ inches, containing about 400 words to a page. The writing is very fine, and a magnifying glass is required to read it with ease. It is written with ink that still holds its color, although it is brown from age.

The quotation begins with the date of his starting on his journey to Fryeburg:

May ye 18th, 1775. set out on a Journey to Fryeburg. Mr. Aston in company. got to Col. Badger's and lodged there. the weather warm. 19th. pursued my journey. dined at Capt. Sinclair's. lodged at Mr. Lara's. the weather not so warm as yesterday. 20th. pursued my journey and arrived safely, in Fryeburg at evening. for God's mercies through the journey I hope I shall be thankful. the weather something poor. 21st. Preached at Fryeburg, may God of his mercy sanctify the word preached both to speaker and hearers. the weather warm. 22nd. at Mr. Stephen Farrington's, my lodging being appointed there. P.M. Went over to see the people who met to see whether they were willing to let me join the Army. they voted for me to stay, and but one that was contrary minded. returned to my lodging in the evening. Rainy in the afternoon and evening. 23d A.M. at my lodgings. P.M. visited Col. Frye. returned at evening. very warm. 24, A.M. at my lodgings. P.M.

went to seven lots, preached a Lecture to men who are going to the American Army. may God of his mercy sanctify what was delivered agreeable his will, both to speaker and hearers. 25. Went to Capt. Brown's. lodged at Capt. Page's with Moses Charles.

(The doings of the 26th are obliterated by the condition of the paper.) went and supped with Mr. Cotton . . . returned to my lodging. ye weather warm at evening. 27th. A.M. at my lodgings. P.M. went to view some land that was designed for me as a building place. did not like it. pitched upon another place. returned to my lodgings at evening. a thunder shower. some hail. 28. A.M. preached at Fryeburg. may God of his mercy set home upon the hearts of both of speaker and Hearers what was delivered agreeable to his will. very hot, a smart thunder shower, heavy thunder. 29th. A.M. at my lodgings. P.M. went to Conway to visit Col. McMillan the . . . (obliterated) . . . 30th. A.M. at Cotons . . . P.M. returned to my lodgings, . . . 31st. A.M. at my lodgings. P.M. went on a visit to Joseph Walker, returned before night to my lodgings. June 2nd. had company, Dr. Emery. ye weather . . . (whole line obliterated)

3rd. A.M. at my lodgings. P.M. went to view an I . . . (obliterated) . . . 4th. Preached at Fryeburg. may the divine spirit Opperate with ye preached word for ye spiritual good both of speaker and hearers. there was a frost this morning, it did much damage, ye Day was warm. 5th. Visited and dined at Mr. Nath'el Merrill's. drank coffee at Mr. Moses Ames. supped at Major Osgood's. 6th. Went with ye committee to lay out a house lot. dined at Mr. Ezekiel Walker's, returned to my lodgings at evening. Capt. Royce lodged with me. 7th. A.M. visited. P.M. visited. The weather for three days past warm and pleasant. 8th A.M. went to meet ye committee for laying out roads. P.M. Attended ye funeral of Mrs. Nason's son about two years of age, who fell into ye fire and burned his inwards so yt he was seized with convulsion fits and died in about eight and forty hours from ye time he was burnt. O may I be quickened by such instances of mortality to be preparing for my own death. returned to my lodgings. a fine shower in ye evening. 9th A.M. about my lodgings. dined at Mr. Abr Bradley's. P.M. went to Mr. Joseph Walker's to see a barn raised. returned to my lodgings, a little after sunset. Doct' Emery and Major Osgood supped with me. fine weather. 10th. at Home at my studies. ye weather fair and warm. 11th Preached at Fryeburg. May ye divine spirit   with ye preached word upon ye   of preacher and hearers. a fine shower in the morning, very hot weather. 12th, visited and dined with Mr. Daniel Ingalls. P.M. visited. returned to my lodgings before night. the weather pleasant. 13th. A.M. visited. P.M. went to Brownfield to meet the committee from Conway, Fryeburg, and Brownfield. lodged at Capt. Brown's. Rain in the morning., in the afternoon the wind from the Northwest high and very cold. 15th. Breakfasted at Capt. Brown's, dined at Major Osgood's, returned to my lodgings at evening. the day very cold, more moderate toward evening. something of a frost. 16th. Had fifteen people plowing land for my house. Very warm.. 17th. had some men to work out a House Plot. Dined at Mr. Samuel Walker's. P.M. Went to Conway, lodged at Capt. David Page's. The weather very warm. 18th. Preached at Conway. May God's blessing accompany the word for the good both of the speaker and hearer. After meeting went to Col. McMillan's, lodged there very hot, a fine shower in the evening. 19th. Set out on my journey homeward in company with Mrs. McMillan, Capt. Brown, wife and daughter, Mr. Gammage, Nathaniel Merrill and Abial Lovejoy.

Mr. Fessenden brought to the infant town his bride, Sarah Clement, a native of Haverhill, Mass. She met Mr. Fessenden at her home in Dunbarton, where he preached, and there they were married, August 4, 1774.

The first years of their married life were those of all the early settlers, full of hardships, toil and privation. Their house stood on the "Minister's Lot", a little lower on the hill than Colonel Frye's residence. It was on the east side on the height of land, about ten rods from the main road, opposite the present home of Mr. Wiley. It was built in the usual custom, two rooms and an entry on the front, and a large kitchen and a small bed-room in the rear. The kitchen with its huge fire-place was the living-room, where the house work was done, and the minister worked on his sermons. It was a hard place for the young woman of twenty-two, but she met her life with heroism.

In this plain home Mrs. Fessenden bore nine childen and reared them, doing her housework and helping her husband in his parish. She taught the children the rudiments of an education. It has been written of her: "Though not having the early mental training and education of her husband, her excellent sense, native good taste and great intellectual powers soon made her a woman of cultivated mind, while her strong character made her a fit helpmate for a pioneer clergyman".

Mrs. Fessenden taught her children the fundamental truths of the catechism in the home, as it was too far for them to go to the meeting house, over the trails of the imperfect roads. The children learned to sing from her repetitions of the hymns used in the public worship. In fact, there was little in the way of the instruction of the times that she did not impart to the growing family.

The Parson's house was open to every one who came for help,

and regardless of the needs of the family, they gave of the little they had to relieve the wants of others less fortunate.

Mr. Fessenden was a man of ability. A native of Cambridge, Mass., he was a graduate of Harvard College in 1768. He was faithful to his profession, visiting his parishioners regardless of the weather, going to the bedsides of the sick and dying, attending funerals on snowshoes, and this without regard to the church affiliations. He was a man who took his duty with full consciousness of the responsibility. He was at all times, the pastor of his people, and did not fail to do his duty as he understood it. He was sincere, and in the subjoined letter, unfortunately incomplete, he states clearly his understanding of the duty of the church and his position relative to restrictions put upon him.

Fryeburg, April 5th, 1803.

To the church in Fryeburg—an address from their Pastor.

Brethren: When I requested the Church in this place to meet two years ago last fall, one object of the meeting was to enquire of the church why Provision had not been made the summer preceeding for the administration of the Lord's supper, & whether the church would make provision for the celebration of the Gospel ordinance; the Business at that time was overruled by some of the church so that no provision was made; After the Council convened at this Place & Peace was apparently restored, still there was not any Provision made; & when some of the church were uneasy at our continued neglect & a request from some members of the Church came to me to call a meeting of the Church last fall I supposed the meeting was called to know whether the church would make provision for the administration of the sacrament of the Lord's supper. how was the Time of our meeting taken up? if I remember Right principally in a recrimination from Judge Frye upon my conduct after the setting of the Council in this place. What were his charges? one was that I had preached on the Fast-Thanksgiving Days at the South Meeting House in this Town; another was that I had not joined with Wm. Russell Esq, at his & at the request of some others to answer a publication in a public print, of which Publication I had no concern directly or indirectly; these were the things alledged against me after the sitting of the Council; still no provision was made for the celebration of the ordinance of the Lord's supper in this place, now my Brethren supposing I had nothing to offer in vindication of my conduct as it respects the two things alledged against me by Judge Frye, would they have rendered me unworthy to have administered the sacrament of the Lord's supper to the church? were they sufficient to justify the Church before the Lord their Redeemer for the neglect in the matter? let every honest hearted Person as in the Presence of Deity answer the above questions—I have been enquired of by some of the church what ought to be done in existing circumstances. I think we ought to be humble before God that we have been so cold in our affections toward him as to cause him to suffer us to be troubled with any Roots of Bitterness which have sprung up among us; let each one of us ever act & conduct as under the Eye of an all seeing Judge to whom we must give an account. Let no Man nor Body of men hinder us from doing our Duty. let us be on Guard not to be deceived by spurious appearances of zeal for Religion; especially when such appearances are not accompanied with marks of true holiness in those who profess them; let each aim at the Glory of God & the Peace & prosperity of his Church; in this way we may humbly Hope God will be pleased to restore his Favorable Presence amongst us & cause Peace to dwell in his Church in this Place."

The remainder of the original manuscript was lost, but apparently Mr. Fessenden had reached the end of his letter. The year before, Mr. Fessenden by one vote, had defeated Judge Frye in the election for Representative to the General Court in the Commonwealth of Massachusetts, for the third time. He had been obliged to bring legal action for his salary against the Town some years before, which he settled amicably. He had also experienced the Baptist defection; and the closing years of his life were not the happiest of his service. In this case there might have been an element of jealousy in the attack on him.

Mr. Fessenden showed his kindliness, in the following letter to the first preceptor of the Academy. The "sin which too easily beset" was overindulgence in liquor, not an uncommon failing for men who had served in the army during the Revolutionary War, as had he.

Fryeburg Oct. ye 13th, 1792.

Dear Sir

I shall make no apology for the following as it springs from the purest Friendship to you and your Family—You are about to undertake a journey to visit your Hon'd Parents and other relatives; I wish you to go because I think it is a duty you owe to them, but Sr. I wish you to go and I pray, set a double watch and guard against yt sin which too easily besets you; I have many reasons for this advice & yt which ought ever to influence you I shall mention the first; a sense of the divine displeasure against sin of every name & Nature; you are under engagements, the most solemn engagements to God to guard against sin; it is a duty you owe to yourself, to your honor, your Peace, your Comfort & your happiness both here & hereafter; it is a duty you owe to your Family, for their comfort in their life is closely connected with your virtuous conduct; it is a Duty you owe to your aged & honored Parents whose hearts are rent with any things yt wounds ye reputation of a child: it is a Duty you owe to the Academy whose Honour reputation & usefulness in a great measure depend upon the exemplary behaviour of its Preceptor; it is a Duty you owe to me and other of your Friends whose reputation in some sort depends upon your virtuous conduct; I was last July amongst your friends & acquaintances, I was publicly enquired of by some who have your Interests at Heart, respecting your life. I gave them such an account as I thought consistent with Truth; my dear friend let your conduct be such all times as not to put me to the Blush should Providence lead me to see the same persons again; I would not dictate but let me intreat you at all Times to be careful as to the Company you mix with; avoid as you would the most fatal Poison those who would Tempt you to turn aside from the paths of Sobriety; I beg leave to caution you against an indiscretion which has once & again escaped you; what I mean is, your threatening to leave the Academy upon some supposed offense; you hurt the feelings of your friends, & you discourage some who think it is for your interest, as well as for the interest of the Academy, for you to be its Preceptor; I am sensible you have many things to try your Patience, but let me intreat you never give a loose rein to your passions, so as to wound your own Interest, or the feelings of your friends; I can assure you with the strictest Truth as to myself, & I firmly believe it to be the sentiments of the rest of the Trustees, that we want no better, no other Preceptor than Mr. Langdon, when his Reason is on the throne, & O! it is my devoutest wish it might ever be there—I sincerely wish you a good journey. I wish you to go out and return home under the guidance & safe Conduct of the good Spirit of God, who is able to keep your feet

from falling, and He will do it if you avoid Temptation, & trust in him, you dont know neither can you know how much I have your honour & happiness at Heart, but this you may be assured of that I am your sincere friend
Wm. Fessenden

No one who reads this outpouring of a friendly heart, can fail to think it a letter that could be read with advantage by every young man, starting on any journey.

It was said of Mr. Fessenden: "The memory of Mr. Fessenden is precious. In his public duty as minister, and in private relations as father of a large family he was a model. Dignified in bearing, generous in spirit, fearless and uncompromising in the maintenance of the right, yet eminently courteous and forbearing, he left to his descendants that 'good name' rather to be chosen than great riches."

Mrs. Fessenden survived her husband thirty years. After his death, she lived with her daughter, Mrs. Oliver Griswold, until her children were well-grown. She removed to the home of her son General Fessenden in Portland, where she died in 1835. The monument erected to her memory bears this tribute:

SARAH CLEMENT FESSENDEN,
wife of the Rev'd William Fessenden. Born at Haverhill, Mass., April 6th, 1752, O.S. Died at Portland, Maine, April 7th, 1835. Endowed with an admirable understanding and warm affections, early impressed by religious truth, and trained in the practice of Christian virtue, she afforded through life a bright example of all that is excellent in woman. A blessing to her husband, her children and her children's children, loving and beloved to the last, she left of herself only the most refreshing memories,
Indulgent memory wakes, and lo, they live.

A dignified monument in Pine Grove Cemetery at the village, marks the place of burial.

X

THE NEW TOWN

> These old and friendly solitudes invite
> Thy visit. They, while yet the forest trees
> Were young upon the unviolated earth,
> And yet the moss-stains upon the rocks were new,
> Beheld thy glorious childhood, and rejoiced.
> —*William Cullen Bryant.*

Having successfully developed the First Settlers, with no form of government, into a working body of lawfully appointed Proprietors, who created a Republic, it became evident that further organization was necessary to form a proper Town. Under the simple system of living as Proprietors the settlers were unable to raise money for the various necessary purposes by taxation, and as it was impossible to develop the township into a Town, without a firmly established form of government, it was seen that the time had arrived when the town must be incorporated, to take its place among the border towns of the Province of Maine.

Accordingly the petition to the General Court was drafted and signed by forty-eight residents, and forwarded to the General Court in session in the winter of 1776 and '77, at Watertown, Mass.

Here follows the Petition and list of names affixed thereto:

Colony of the Massachusetts Bay.
To the Honorable General Court, convened at Watertown, the 22 day of Nov. Anno Domini 1776:
The Petition of the subscribers, Inhabitants of a New Township formerly granted by the General Court of said colony, to Joseph Frye, Esq., humbly sheweth that we have fully performed the conditions of said Grant in every respect—having at least sixty-three families settled on said Grant, who have lately called and settled a Learned & Orthodox Minister of the Gospel according to the usages of the Churches of this Colony. That we labor under various difficulties and disadvantages, for want of a Legal Incorporation being unable as a

corporate society to provide for the support of our said Minister, In the manner usually practiced by the several Towns and Parishes in the Colony, or to provide a school for the instruction and education of our youth. whereby the rising Generation among us are in danger of growing up a wild uncultivated race, much to the publick damage as well as grief to their parents; as also Incapable of establishing and repairing necessary Highways as well for the publick as our own use; as also doing many other Corporate Acts necessary for the well ordering of Society, We therefore humbly pray that the Honorable Court would be pleased to take our case into consideration and afford us relief by Incorporating us according to the limits of our Grant or Grants thereby, vesting with the Privileges which other Incorporated Towns in this Colony do by Law enjoy and your Petitioners shall as in duty bound ever pray.

Non Proprietors.	Proprietors.
Joseph Walker	Richard Eastman
Aaron Abbott	Hezekiah Asten
Joseph Emery	William Wiley
Jonathan Hutchins	Daniel Farrington
Samuel Bradley	Joseph Frye
Job Eastman	Stephen Knight
Samuel Walker	James Swan
William Eaton (2)	John Farrington
Peter Allen	David Evans
Abraham Russell	Moses Day
Edward Cutler	Samuel Osgood
James Parker	Stephen Farrington
John Stevens	Ezra Carter
Jonathan Dresser	Isaac Walker
John Chandler	Timothy Walker
Stephen Dresser	Abraham Bradley
John Bolt Miller (2)	John Charles
Jacob Colby	Abner Charles
John Becknell	Benj'n Russell
John Becknell, Jr.	Simon Frye
	Ezekiel Walker
	Ebenezer Day
	Samuel Charles
	Moses Ames
	Nat'l Merrill
	John Evans
	David Day

As the Township had conformed to the requirements set by the General Court in issuing to Colonel Frye the answer to his petition for a Grant of land, the action of the General Court was favorable to granting an Act of Incorporation, endowing the new Town with all "The Powers, Privileges and Immunities which other towns in the Colonies do enjoy".

This was the charter of Incorporation:

AN ACT TO INCORPORATE THE TOWN OF FRYEBURG

An act for erecting a tract of land (called Fryeburg) of two thousand, one hundred and seventy-two rods square, lying in the county of York, which was granted a township to Joseph Frye, Esq. Anno Domini seventeen hundred and sixty-two, into a town by the name of Fryeburg. Whereas the inhabitants of that tract of land, consisting of proprietors and non-proprietors promiscuously settled thereon, having lately been united in ordaining a minister of the gospel among them and desirous of a unity in the expense of his support of building a meeting house and other public charges of that place, but cannot lay a tax themselves for these purposes till said tract of land is incorporated into a town. Therefore, be it enacted by the Council and House of Representatives in General Court assembled and by the authority of the same that the aforesaid tract of land originally bounded as follows; viz: At the south corner to a spruce tree marked; thence north forty five degrees west, two thousand one hundred and seventy-two rods to a beech tree marked; thence north forty-five degrees east; two thousand one hundred and seventy-two rods to a maple tree marked; thence south forty five degrees, east; two thousand one hundred and seventy-two rods to a pine tree marked. Thence south forty five degrees west; to the first bound, be and hereby is erected into a town by the name of Fryeburg, excepting and reserving therein about four thousand, and one hundred and forty seven acres of land lying in the west corner thereof, which the Great and General Court in compliance with a petition of the above named Joseph Frye resolved to receive back and in lieu thereof granted him the same quantity of government land, with liberty to lay it out adjoining the northward or northeastward part of his township, as said resolve dated June twenty-fifth, seventeen hundred and seventy-two will appear, and the inhabitants of said tract of land excepting as above excepted, be and hereby are invested with all the powers, privileges and immunities which other towns in the colonies do enjoy.

Be it further enacted that Tristram Jordan, Esq., be and hereby is empowered to issue his warrant directed to the principal inhabitants of said town requesting him to warn the inhabitants thereof who have a free hold according to Charter to meet at such a time and place as shall be therein set forth. To choose all such officers as are or shall be required by law, to manage the affairs of said town.

In the House of Representatives, January 10. 1777, this bill having had three several readings, passed to be enacted.

Samuel Freeman,
Speaker P.T.

In council January 11, 1777, this bill having had two several readings, passed to be enacted.

John Avery,
Deputy Secretary

Consented to by the major part of the Council.

Warrant For First Town Meeting—

To Lt. Samuel Osgood, Gentleman: Greeting: Pursuant to an act of the great and general court of the State of Massachusetts Bay for erecting a tract of land called Fryeburg of two thousand one hundred and seventy-two rods square, lying in the country of York, which was granted as a township to Joseph Frye, Esq., Anno Domini seventeen hundred and sixty-two, and confirmed Anno Domini seventeen hundred and sixty-three, into a town by the name of Fryeburg, and said tract of land being erected into a town by the name of Fryeburg by the authority of the State aforesaid, in the year of our Lord 1777. Excepting and reserving therein about four thousand one hundred and forty-seven acres of land lying in the west corner thereof, and whereas in and by said act, I, the subscriber, am appointed to issue a warrant to some principal inhabitants of said township to notify the inhabitants of said town qualified by law to vote in town affairs, to choose all such officers as shall be necessary to manage the affairs of said town. These, therefore, in the name of the Government and people of this State, to require you to notify the inhabitants of said town qualified as the law directs to meet at the dwelling house of the Rev. William Fessenden in said town on Monday, the 31st of March instant, at ten of the clock in the forenoon, to choose a clerk and other officers by law required and to do any other business relative to the well being of the town which the qualified voters of said town shall at their meeting see fit. Given under my hand and seal, Pepperellborough, this eleventh day of March, Anno Domini one thousand, seven hundred and seventy-seven.

Tristram Jordan,
Justice of the Peace.

In accordance with this warrant, Samuel Osgood, being the inhabitant named therein, issued the following notice:

Fryeburg, March 15, 1777.

By virtue of the above warrant to me directed, I do hereby notify the inhabitants of said town qualified as the law directs to meet at the time and place and for the purpose herein mentioned.

Samuel Osgood.

The following is the record of the First Town Meeting: Fryeburg, March 31, 1777.

Agreeable to the foregoing warrant the town being legally assembled, they proceeded on the business of said town meeting:

1. Chose Deacon Richard Eastman moderator of said meeting.
2. Chose Richard Kimball town clerk for the year ensuing.
Then the meeting was adjourned for two hours.

The Town reassembled agreeable to adjournment, and chose the following officers: who were sworn whenever there was an oath required by law:
Deacon Richard Eastman, Isaac Abbott, Nathaniel Merrill, Deacon Simon Frye, Ezra Carter, Selectmen. W. Wiley, Constable. Richard Kimball, Moses Ames, Stephen Farrington, Ezekiel Walker, Benjamin Russell, Committee of Safety, etc. Fence viewers; Samuel Walker, Nathan Ames, and David Evans. Field Drivers; John Farrington, John Charles, Jr. and John Bucknell. Sealer of Weights and Measures, Isaac Abbott. Surveyors of Highways; John Evans, Moses Day, Peter Astin and Benjamin Russell. Tything Men; Moses Ames and Daniel Farrington. Wardens; Ebenezer Day, Hezekiah Astin, Nathaniel Merrill and James Parker. Sealer of Leather, James Parker. Hog Reeves; Isaac Walker, Abraham Bradley, and Benjamin Russell. Deer Reeve, Deacon Simon Frye. Town Treasurer, Ezekiel Walker. Pound Keepers; Isaac Abbott and Peter Astin. Surveyors of Lumber; John Walker and David Evans.

"Then the town voted to have swine go at large the year ensuing." Following this important act, this meeting was adjourned to Friday, the third day of April, next.

The selectmen and committee of Safety proceeded to establish prices, to give every worker his just dues, as follows:

In pursuance of an act of the great and general court of the State of Massachusetts Bay entitled an act to prevent monopoly and oppression, the selectmen and committee of safety of Fryeburg set and affixed the following prices herinafter enumerated, which are to be taken and deemed to be the prices of all such goods and articles in the said town of Fryeburg and all not hereinafter enumerated to be in proportion.

	£	s	d
Day's labor of a man finding himself in July and Aug.	0	3	9
Being found in the above month and at other seasons of the year in proportion.	0	3	0
Good marketable winter wheat at 6s 9d, 66 lbs per bushel	0	6	9
Good marketable spring wheat at 6s, 66 lbs, per bushel,	0	6	0
Good rye at 4s 4d per bushel,	0	4	4
Good Indian Corn at 3s 4d per bushel,	0	3	4
Good sheep's wool at 2s 3d per lb.;	0	2	3

Good well-dressed flax at 1s per pound,	0	1	0
Good well-fatted pork by the hog at 5d per lb.,	0	0	5
Good salt pork, clean of bone at 9d per lb.,	0	0	9
Good grass feed beef at 2½d per lb.,	0	0	2½
Best stall feed beef at 3½d per lb.,	0	0	3½
Good peas at 6s per bu.,	0	6	0
Good potatoes in the fall of the year at 1s per bu.,	0	1	0
Good potatoes in the spring of the year at 1s 4d per bu.,	0	1	4
Good oats at 2s per bu.,	0	2	0
Good yard wide tow cloth. at 2s 3d per yard,	0	2	3
English hay of the best quality, 1s 9d per c. w. lbs.,	0	1	9
Sugar called maple sugar of the best quality, 8d per lb.,	0	0	8
Good Mercht. tobacco raised in this state, 9d per lb.,	0	0	9
Good butter at 9d per lb.,	0	0	9
Good tryed tallow at 8d per lb.,	0	0	8
Work for one yoke of oxen a day in seed time,	0	2	4
Imported salt of the best quality, 15s 5d per bu.,	0	15	5
House Carpenters at 4s per day,	0	4	0
Joiners at 3s 4d per day,	0	3	4
Brick layers at 4s per day,	0	4	0
Shoemakers for making men's and women's shoes,	0	2	7
West India Rum, merchantable at 8s 10d per gal.,	0	8	10
New England Rum at 5s 8d per gal.,	0	5	8
Molasses at 5s 2d per gal.,	0	5	2
Molasses by the quart, 9½d.,	0	0	9½
Best Merchantable Sug at 9½d per lb.,	0	0	9½
Good merchantable Coffee at 1s 6d per lb.,	0	1	6

     Richard Eastman,
     Nathaniel Merrill,
     Simon Frye,
     Ezra Carter,
     Isaac Abbott,
       Selectmen of Fryeburg.
     Richard Kimball,
     Moses Ames,
     Stephen Farrington,
     Ezekiel Walker,
     Benjamin Russell,
       Committee of Safety.

Having adjourned the town meeting to April 3 the record states:

"Met according to adjournment and adjourned to the 17th instant at eleven o'clock in the forenoon at the same place as the last adjournment."

"April 17th. Met according to adjournment and David Evans was chosen Culler of Shingles. Voted then that this meeting be disolved and it was disolved.

Richard Kimball,
Town Clerk."

Meantime a warrant, with eight articles, had been issued for the same date at twelve o'clock, following the brief morning session:

Fryeburg, April 17, 1777.

Agreeable to the foregoing warrant the freeholders and other inhabitants met at the place mentioned in the warrant (the dwelling house of the Rev. William Fessenden) and after the warrant being read:

1-ly. Chose Deacon Richard Eastman moderator.
2-ly. Voted that this town accept the Rev. William Fessenden as our minister.
3-ly. Voted. that the Rev. William Fessenden's salary be forty-five pounds for his first year's service in the ministry beginning the 11th of October, 1775, as agreed on by the proprietors of this town at their meeting Oct. 5, 1774.
4-ly. Voted that the Rev. William Fessenden's salary be fifty pounds beginning Oct. 11, 1776, and ending Oct. 11, 1777.
5-ly. Voted that the Rev. William Fessenden's salary shall rise five pounds lawful money a year until the said salary shall come to seventy pounds like money which is to be stated and given as the said Mr. Fessenden's annual salary, to be annually paid to him so long as he continues in the pastoral relation to the Church of Christ in this place.
6-ly. Voted that one-third part of Rev. William Fessenden's annual salary be paid in Indian corn and rye, Indian corn at 3s lawful money and the rye at 4s like money, per bushel for the first six years of his ministry to be reckoned from Oct. 11, 1775.
7-ly. The seventh article to empower the selectmen to hire money to purchase a standard of weights and measures and a town book for the town; the question being put, it passed in the negative.
8-ly. Voted to chose three men to examine the accounts that may be brought against the town by a former committee of safety, and others that may have any accounts against the town. Then the town made choice of Messrs Benjamin Russell, William Wiley and Lt. Isaac Walker as their committee.
9-ly. Voted that one pound lawful money be paid by the town to any person or persons that shall catch or kill any grown wolf in this town; he or they making oath before a Justice of the Peace that the said wolf was catched or killed within the bounds of this town; he or they bringing a certificate under said Justice's hand, with the head to the selectmen and constable.

Voted that this meeting be disolved.
A true entry. Attest:
Richard Kimball,
Town Clerk.

At the town meeting of September 11, 1777, the first action was taken for a valuation of the property held in the Town, and the Selectmen were instructed "to go to the several inhabitants & take the valuation of their estates both Real and Personal."

It was also voted to raise "sixty pounds Lawfull money for a School, and other necessary charges".

The Town held a meeting December 15, and voted to allow the Accounts brought against the town for various services rendered for travel to different places on town business; for seven and a half day's work in "Numbering the People", all of which amounted to 14 pounds, 7 shillings and 10 Pence.

In 1778 the town held its March Meeting on the 2nd of the month, and transacted the usual routine business, and met again on April 13, when they voted: "That the Annual March Meeting shall be held for the Futer on the First Monday in March", which has been the custom ever since.

At the same April meeting they voted that the location of the school houses be left to the Selectmen. They took the first action as to the allowance for "working out a highway tax", setting the sum at seven shillings a man, and four shillings for a yoke of oxen, a day.

They voted to raise two hundred and fifty pounds for the support of the Town Schools and other necessary charges of the Town. On April 10, 1779 they considered whether the Town should give the selectmen directions how the Town School should be kept, but voted in the negative.

At the meeting held September 16, 1779, the Town declined paying Lieut. Samuel Osgood for providing for the Council that ordained the Rev. William Fessenden.

The year 1780 was marked in town affairs by the necessity of providing and equipping the quotas of soldiers for the American Army. April 27 the town voted "That the Selectmen write to Col. Cutts representing the state of the town, pleading to be exempt from raising the six men requested, to man the lines at Casco, and it was further voted that Captain Joseph Frye should proffer the representation of the Town to Colonel Cutts. May 15 they voted to send five men to the lines at Casco. It was also voted to pay a bounty, and to complete the equipment of any soldier not able to equip himself.

In June 1780 they voted that if the Selectmen could not fill the quota by enlistment by the 9th inst. they should proceed to "Detaching" men, as prescribed by law. On June 23 the Selectmen ordered the Train Band Soldiers and the Alarm List to appear armed and equipped "on the neighest piece of ground to the House appropriated to public worship that is suitable for them to parade on, in order to raise two men by Draft, Lot or Voluntary Inlistment."

The Town also voted to raise the necessary money for the purchase of beef for the army, but on November 29 the committee reported that they could not procure the beef.

Similar conditions obtaining during the next year, the Town did its best in raising money for enlisting and paying a bounty to men for the army. Rev. William Fessenden donated fifteen pounds from his salary to assist the town in carrying on the war.

An instance of the town's parsimony and charity was demonstrated at the meeting March 4, 1782, when the Selectmen exhibited their accounts for the service they did immediately for the Town (exclusive of extraordinary service on account of the distressed inhabitants of Amosascoggin River) the sum total of which amounted to 24, 4, 6. Put to vote it was "passed in the Negative".

On the article in the warrant relating to the application of Daniel Farrington as to two children found on his door-step, upon Mr. Farrington's offering to take one to support on the condition that the child be bound to him, it was voted "to pay said Farrington one shilling and four pence per week he shall or has board the other child"; and the Selectmen were directed to proceed with the other child as the Law directs.

It was not until December, 1780, that the townsfolk were ready to enter the political field. Choosing a Representative to the Great and General Court was not a mere formality, as on December 5, 1780, "A meeting was called to chuse some suitable person to represent the Town in the Great and General Court of Massachusetts —and a Committee to be chosen to draw up necessary instructions". Deacon Simon Frye was elected, and the Committee was Lieut. R. Kimball, Lt. I. Walker, Messrs W. Wiley, M. Ames, Steph. Farrington.

On December 28 this committee reported their instructions to the Representative elect, as follows:

To Dea'n. Simon Frye, Sir, You being chosen to represent the Town of Fryeburg in the General Court of the Commonwealth of Massachusetts, your Constituents highly approving of the Constitution of Government under which we are settled, and finding in the 19th Article of the Bill of Rights it is our privilege to give our Representative Instructions; and to request of the Legislative Body by way of Addresses, Petitions and Remonstrances for redress of rongs and grievances—Your Constituents are ever ready and willing cheerfully to contribute to the support of government and defence of the United States.

You are instructed to use your endeavours that Publick faith be kept Inviolate. You must be sencible that the Taxes laid on us, A.D. 1780 greatly exceeds our ability, and which we can not pay without our Famileys greatly suffering for the Necessarys of Life. You are therefore Instructed to use your best endeavours that the Locality of our Town with its circumstances be duly Represented. You are further Instructed by Addresses, Petitions or Remonstrances to request of the General Court an abatement of the Taxes already laid on us. Furthermore, that you use your best Endeavours for an Act to oblige the owners of Land unincorporated to make and maintain proper Roads through their sd. Lands.

These instructions were reported to the Town Meeting, and, as there were no comments recorded, the meeting was disolved.

To give instructions to the Representatives was a regular custom, as they were given to the representatives of 1786 and 1787 and to the delegate to the Constitutional Convention of 1787. In those constructive days the citizens of Fryeburg took a lively interest in the processes of making a new Nation and of developing a State.

These instructions were given to Moses Ames, Representative to the General Court of the Commonwealth of Massachusetts, on his attendance on the legislative session, May 31, 1786:
Sir:

As the end and design of all Government is the happiness of the community, it is therefore the indispensable duty of the Legislative authority of every State at all times to preserve a due balance of power between the various interests within the same, but is rendered more particularly requisite in the present day of perplexity and distress for want of a circulating medium. You will therefore endeavour to have such Regulations adopted and Laws enacted as may have a tendency to relieve us from our present embarrassments; and we conceive that one essential measure thereto will be to have our Ports open to all foreign Powers, which will have a tendency to introduce money and advance the price of Lumber, Fish, Cattle and the produce of the earth, and to reduce the price of English goods which are necessary for cloathing, especially in this and other places which have not the means of manufacturing them for their own use.

Another necessary step will be to reduce the excise and imposts, and appropriate the money arising from the remainder of the payment of the foreign debt.

You will endeavor that Paper Money sufficient for a currency be emitted for the purpose of redeeming a part of the State securities, which money shall be received in payment of executions, and which shall be redeemed by a tax annually laid for that purpose, and so continue till the whole of said securities shall be redeemed.

You will endeavor to encourage and promote agriculture, which is the chief support and dependence of a nation, and in order that you will (by bounties and other ways) encourage the raising of Wheat, Peas, Flax and Hemp, and the keeping of sheep, and the manufacturing of Pot and Pearl-ash.

You will endeavor to prevent excessive usury, and that no undue advantage of distressed Debtors might be taken by purchasing property under its value, which is a discouragement to industry and trade, you will endeavor to make Real and Personal Estates receivable for the payment of all debts, by an appraisment of judicious men; provided that a paper currency shall not be emitted.

As a multiplicity of Officers and Dependents on Government with large salaries and fees is burdensome and oppressive to the People, you will endeavor to reduce their number and the salaries and fees.

We are of the opinion that our Courts of Common Pleas are unnecessary and burdensome, and so great a number of Lawyers are oppressive to the community; therefore you will use your influence to discontinue the former and reduce the number of the latter, and regulate practice of the remainder, so as to render it less oppressive to the people.

You will use your endeavors to have the Proprietary Laws revised and to prevent the sale of more lands than what is necessary for the payment of Taxes for the charges of bringing forward the settlement of the same, and that all their meetings and advertisements respecting the Eastern Lands be published in the Cumberland Gazette, and in the town where the lands lay; and that in five years after the grant all Proprietary meetings be held in the Townships where the lands lay, and the Inhabitants be impowered to raise money to make and repair Roads for the Public good.

You will oppose the monopolizing the Public Lands, and will encourage the Cultivation and Settlement of the same.

These appear to us to be the most important articles of a public nature to which your immediate attention is required. You will give such attention to the other concernments of this Town as your own knowledge together with the information you shall receive of them will enable you to do. But you are instructed to prefer a Petition that the expenses this Town were at in the year 1777, after the retreat out of Canada, in erecting three Fortresses within the same as a defence against the Incursions of the Enemy into this part of the State may be reimbursed them.

The foregoing Report is submitted by the Committee,

Paul Langdon, Chairman.

June 6, 1786.

Town voted to add the following to the instructions:

That if it shall not be found expedient to issue paper money in the way above proposed, you endeavor that it be emitted in some more suitable method. You are likewise instructed to use your endeavors to remove the General Court from Boston to some more convenient place.

Moses Ames being the representative of Fryeburg at the Convention in Boston in 1787 called for the ratification of the proposed Constitution of the United States of America, he was given to understand the sentiments of his constituents from these instructions:

Sir:

As this Town have made choice of you to represent them in the proposed convention, they have thereby reposed confidence in your integrity and abilities to answer their expectations on this important occasion, and as you will have opportunity of attending to every argument which probably can be adduced either in favor of or in opposition to the proposed convention this Town do not pretend critically to consider every objection that may be made to, or point out the merits of the same. But the duty they owe themselves and posterity constrains them to express their disapprobation of some parts of the Constitution.

They conceive that the term and mode of appointment of the Senate has a tendency to render that branch of the Congress perpetual.

That the Legislative power of Congress will supersede, and in its consequences entirely vacate the Constitutions of the respective States. That the power of making treaties should have been vested in the Congress collectively. And it appears highly absurd to propose an oath of affimation to the officers of Government of whom no religious test is required.

The foregoing are the most material objections which you are instructed to make to the Constitution proposed. We would not wish that it should be entirely rejected, as we esteem it with proper amendments to be well calculated to promote the welfare of the Union.

These instructions were prepared, December 2, 1787 by the committee composed of: Simon Frye, Esq., Paul Langdon, Capt. Joseph Frye, Lieut. Stephen Farrington, Lieut. John Webster, Mr. Nathaniel Merrill and Capt. John Evans.

Moses Ames attended the convention, as one of the forty-six men from Maine, of the 355 delegates who formed the convention at Boston. He is recorded as voting in opposition to the ratification of the Constitution as presented. The 46 delegates from Maine were divided on the question, twenty-five voting in favor of ratification to twenty-one opposed.

Fryeburg was insistent that its patriotism was above question during the Revolutionary War, meeting as far as it was financially able the requisitions for men, meat and clothing, but it did feel that it was unjustly treated in having to bear such heavy taxes, too heavy in proportion to those of other towns more fortunately conditioned.

In 1780 this petition was sent to the Great and General Court of the Commonwealth of Massachusetts:

Commonwealth of
Massachusetts   To the Hon'l. the Senet and House of Representatives

The Petition of Simon Frye in behalf and by the Direction of the Inhabitants of the Town of Fryeburg, humbly sheweth—the said Inhabitants were at great expence in looking out by different routes for a road to said Town and Clearing Fifty four Miles through an uninhabited Country in order to move their families that the unseasonable Frosts have cut of their crops for many years so that they were obliged to transport great part of their provisions from Boston—that they were at great expence on the Roads to Falmouth and Saco which together with many other expences and Difculties must have broke up the Settlement had it not been for the Vigorous Exertions of some of them and the assistance of their friends by reason of s'd Frosts and Freshets which have so frequently proved hurtful to our grain we have scarsely even been able to raise a sufficiency thereof for the Town notwithstanding they have been obliged to part with grain at some seasons, for Salt and other Necessaries it always is wanted in the Town before the year comes about—that the Transportation from Falmouth which is the nearest market Town (by reason of the badness of the road and extraordinary blocking Snows was not less than five shillings pr. Hund'd. wt. in lawful silver money before the present war—that said Town is under great disadvantages on account of keeping sheep which is so necessary for Clothing in these times: for altho we have much exerted ourselves in that matter we are disapointed and have suffered much Loss in them as well as in other young Cretures, by reason of the wild beasts of the wilderness—our Plantation being new and many of the Inhabitants very Indigent when they went thither, have not been able to procure themselves Houses comfortable to live in—that their unavoidable Expence as a Propriety & a Town are very great: these and many other difficulties incident to new Towns renders us incapable of paying so large a Tax as those Towns that lye better Situate and more improved said Town by order of the Honorable Court is Assessed—May 15th 1780 in the sum of £ 8400 0 0. In Oct. 24th 1780 in the sum of £8400 0 0. In a silver money Tax of the sum of 108 0 0, another of 6915 lb wt. at 30/ pr pound £10372 10 0. Sum Total of said sums is £32680 10 including the Silver money Tax in the value of Silver.

The charges arising in the Town for hiring Soldiers the year past, and other Necessary Charges is £12910 0 0. The aforesaid sums yet remain Due the Town have not been Able to Discharge any of them and think themselves intirely unable to pay the whole thereof in their Circumstances—

Notwithstanding our Indigent Circumstances we feel ourselves as willing to Exert ourselves for the support of Government and Carrying on the war as any people in the Commonwealth (according to our Ability—But we humbly Conceive we have more laid upon us than our due proportion with other Towns Comparing Abilities and Circumstances—wherefore humbly pray the Honorable Court to take our Case into their Consideration and make such abatements of said Taxes as they in their wisdom shall think just and Reasonable—and your Petitioner as in Duty bound shall ever pray

Simon Frye.

In response to this petition the Assessors of Fryeburg were instructed by the General Court to stay all proceedings upon the last tax act till a revision of the valuation should take place. The treasurer of the Commonwealth was also instructed to stay execution for taxes until further orders. The Resolve had the concurrence of the Senate, and was approved by the Governor, John Hancock.

The Town had no use for Loyalists, or "Tories" as they were commonly called, as this communication showed:

Resolve of the Town of Fryeburg, June 2, 1785. This Town after taking under consideration the alarming intelligence they have lately received from the Town of Boston, of the late attempt of a number of the obnoxious Refugees, to land at Dartmouth, and the report that interest was making for the return of others to their estates &c in this Country again, are of the opinion that the admission of such persons as have taken refuge under the British King during our late struggle in defence of our just rights and liberties, and thereby been instrumental of protracting the late Barbarous and cruel war against their own country, and as far as in their power, been the means of the expense of much blood and Treasure of their late fellow citizens, would be attended with dangerous consequences to the United States of America—Therefore, Resolved: That it is the opinion of this Town, that all persons in that predicament, and have been declared Traitors to their Country, ought never to be suffered to return and dwell in it again, but be entirely excluded therefrom. And the Selectmen are hereby requested to inform the Committee of Correspondence of the Town of Boston, of this Resolve, as soon as may be agreeable to their request in their letter accompanying a Resolve of said Town of Boston, dated April 7th, 1785.

A true entry
Attest, Joseph Frye, Jr., Town Clerk

From the phrasing of this document, it was evident that it was the democratic expression of one town to another town, and that Boston was not considered a city by the people of the little settlement.

Life in the new town moved steadily and slowly toward better conditions. Farms were prepared for planting and good harvests were secured. Hay-fields became productive, and more live stock was raised, and in twenty years, the little municipality had grown in ability to support itself, and in self-respect.

One feature of the locality that was not considered at first, was the frequency and ease with which the Saco River overflowed its banks. The rapid rises of water from the drainage of the White Mountains flooded the intervales and brought affliction on the settlers. The condition became so intolerable that the Town decided to approach the General Court of Massachusetts, and inform them of the losses by water. Paul Langdon, who was an educated man, drew a petition, telling the conditions and praying for relief. This is the document as presented:

To the Honorable Senate and House of Representatives of the Commonwealth of Massachusetts in General Court Assembled.

The Inhabitants of the Town of Fryeburg in the County of York humbly beg leave to represent to the Honorable Court, that a valuation of said Town was taken and returned to the Honorable Court, in the year 1784, in obedience to their orders; but that from a misapprehension of the contents of said Town a very material mistake was made in said return, with regard to the number of acres of land contained in said Town; which mistake has been unnoticed in former valuation, but has proved injurious to this Town, and must have still continued so, had not your Remonstrants, by carefully examining the Original Grant and confirmation of said Town searched out the error, which they request liberty to point out to the Honorable Court, Viz.; That the said Town was originally ordered to be laid out six miles square, but from a view of the situation of the country being almost encompassed with steep and lofty mountains. There was found to be many bogs, morasses and waters which rendered it impossible to comprehend within the six miles square a quantity of improvable land sufficient for a Township according to the original intention. It was therefore Surveyed at 2172 Rods Square being 252 Rods Square more than Six miles, and was confirmed by the Honorable Court; the Said 252 Rods Square being allowed for the great abundance of Bogs and Waters Including 3 Rods in a Hundred for Sag of chain; yet this allowance 4957 acres though to appearance large, did not amount to the quantity covered with waters, which from actual Survey amounts to 5452 acres, wherefore the Town really contains by the confirmation of the Original Grant but 22,545 acres of Land; Improvable and Unimprovable. out of which should have been deducted 4147 acres granted to Joseph Frye, Esq. In lieu of the same quantity resigned back to Government and which is not yet Incorporated with the Town, but has through Inadvertency hitherto been estimated in our valuations; which deductions would leave but 18,398 acres as the total contents of Said Town, from which last number there should be 1149 acres Subtracted for publick Rights which are exempted from Taxes, and 5421 acres of unimprovable Land and the remainder after deducting 240 acres for Roads will amount to 11,588 acres and is the exact quantity of Rateable Land at which in justice we ought to have stood in that Valuation.

We beg leave just to hint another mistake in the above mentioned return which we conceive arose from a misapprehension of the order and Intentions of the Honorable Court—viz.; that the Buildings therein returned as dwelling Houses, excepting Eighteen only, were not of the value of five pounds and were nothing more than Huts, hastily put together for the immediate shelter of the Settlers, who are as yet unable to erect more commodious habitations; our circumstances in general being much reduced by great and frequent "freshes" which have often prevented the sowing and planting our lands in proper Season, whereby our crops have been greatly shortened and our losses have several times almost urged us to address the Legislature for some abatement of our Taxes, but the abundant Rains in October last have rendered the Circumstances of this Town more peculiarly distressing by the destruction of Buildings & fencing, carrying away and otherwise entirely ruining a part of our most Valuable Lands, and destroying the produce, not to mention the damage sustained by destruction of Bridges etc. A short schedule of the Damage thus Sustained we beg leave to lay before the Honorable Court as follows:

    1 Grist Mill carried away
    9 Houses carried away & rendered untenable

The New Town

```
    2 Barns    do.
    4 Oxen     drowned
   12 Cows     do
    3 Heifers  do.
    4 Calves   do.
    4 Sheep    do.
    8 Swine    do.
  148 Tons English Hay destroyed
  572 Bushels Indian Corn     do.
   10 Bushels Wheat
   70 do.     Peas
   50 do.     Oats
 1750 do.     Potatoes
  400 lbs.    Tobacco
```

About 33 miles of fencing according to the most exact calculations we have been able to make, 153 masts of the Dimensions of 17 inches to 34 inches diameter were carried out to sea, besides Logs, Boards, Clapboards etc., etc., to the amount of one hundred and five pounds; 174 acres of land washed away and covered with sand to the depth of five or six feet, 149 acres of which was cleared tillage and mowing Land. Our humble Petition therefore is that the Honorable Court would be pleased to take into consideration the mistakes made in the above Valuation, that they may not operate Injuriously to this Town in the apportionment of the present depending Valuation; and likewise would consider the distressing Circumstances of this Town and Grant us such Relief as they in their Wisdom shall think proper, and In Duty Bound Shall Every Pray

In behalf and by order of the Town

       Paul Langdon, Clerk P.T.

Fryeburg, Feb. 1st 1786.

It was evident that the Great and General Court saw the justice of this petition, for on March 20, 1786 they passed a resolution abating the Tax laid upon Fryeburg nearly 200 pounds, which though comparatively small, was so much relief, and paid the Town for acting in its own behalf.

XI

THE COMMON SCHOOLS

> History records the fact that the Congregational churches of New England gave to this country its magnificent system of public schools; so the determination of our forefathers that their children should be able to read the Word of God and that the pastors of their churches should be educated men, brought into being the free-school system of this country.
>
> —*Rev. James Tompkins, D.D.*

In the earliest years of Fryeburg the settlers had too much to do in establishing homes and in making a living to give proper attention to education. This was not from lack of appreciation of the necessity for education of the youth, for the men of the community were educated, several having had the instruction of Harvard College; others less fortunate had the training of rough life, which they were determined their children should not be obliged to go through.

Those children who could be assembled at some home were given instruction in common school subjects by Hugh Gordon, who began keeping a private school in 1775. As early as 1769 a rather desultory effort had been made by William Frost in Caleb Swan's home. Mrs. Dolly Frye, a daughter of Mr. Swan, told that while she did not go to Mr. Frost's school, he taught her to write, in writing books made from birch-bark. Simon Colby for a time kept a little school in what later became East Conway.

The matter of organized instruction was presented at a town meeting in September, 1777, and after careful consideration, the sum of sixty pounds was appropriated for the maintenance of schools, and Hugh Gordon was the first officially authorized schoolmaster in Fryeburg. The success of the school was evident, as it was continued the next year (1778) under Mr. Gordon, but it was kept in a dwelling house as no appropriation had been made by the Town for building a schoolhouse.

Common Schools

November 19, 1778 the Town raised two hundred and fifty pounds toward the support of the town school. The succeeding years saw an increased sum raised, and September 6, 1784, it was voted to build four schoolhouses in different parts of the town, the same to be eighteen feet square, seven feet posts, and finished in such a manner as to make them comfortable in cold weather.

The school system developed during the succeeding years, until in 1825 schools were conducted in fourteen school districts and 490 scholars were in attendance. Since that time the number of districts has changed from time to time, and schools have been discontinued because of the scarcity of pupils in certain districts.

The highest number of districts reached seventeen, located as follows:

No. 1,	Village,	No. 9,	Birch Hill,
No. 2,	Village,	No. 10,	North Fryeburg,
No. 3,	"Fellows" Neighborhood,	No. 11,	Center Fryeburg,
		No. 12,	"Fish Street",
No. 4,	Menotomy,	No. 13,	Toll Bridge,
No. 5,	The "Island",	No. 14,	"Nebraska" (Haley Neighborhood),
No. 6,	East Fryeburg,		
No. 7,	"Mount Tom" Neighborhood,	No. 15,	"The Harbor",
		No. 16,	Smart's Hill,
No. 8,	West Fryeburg,	No. 17,	Hemlock Bridge.

In the course of the years the district school buildings felt the wear of time, and became untenantable, lacking room for increasing numbers of pupils in some districts, and becoming too roomy in others where the population had diminished. In some schools but two or three pupils could be enrolled, and yet the schools were carried on, with unwarranted expense and untrained instruction. This condition became uneconomic, and it was decided to transport the pupils of such districts to other near-by schools. The old, unused schoolhouses fell into decay, and being occupied only by squirrels, were disposed of by sale, or torn down.

There are now in use in the town seven schoolhouses: one at the Village and one each at North Fryeburg, East Fryeburg, West Fryeburg, Center Fryeburg, Toll Bridge and The Harbor; in all the eight grades are taught. Instruction in Drawing and Music is included in the higher courses. Especial attention is given to the general health of all, much benefit being received from the services of a State Field Nurse.

The first step toward a definite union came with the grading of the two Village schools, and the discontinuance of the district system, the management of the schools being in the hands of the Supervisor of Schools. Districts No. 1 and 2 were graded; the Primary, which was the larger, being established in the "Stone Schoolhouse" of District No. 1; and the Grammar grade in the wooden building of District No. 2.

In 1902 the Town decided to build a modern type of schoolbuilding at the Village, for the Graded Departments, which had outgrown their accommodations. The "Peter Walker Lot", so called, from one of the early residents on that site, was bought at the corner of Main and Pine Streets. The building was designed by Carl S. Hatch, a Fryeburg boy who had become a capable architect. It met the requirements for the first eight grades, but a few years later the building was enlarged to accommodate the increase of pupils entailed by the transportation from abandoned districts.

The schoolhouses in the town were then fitted to accommodate the total number of pupils reported between the ages of five and twenty-one years, which by the last school census was 271 boys and 226 girls, Total 497.

The old time system gave an "agent" in each district authority to hire the teacher for that school. Abuses were easily possible and educational standards could not be high.

In 1877 a Supervisor of Schools was elected by the Town. During the forty years following, B. Walker McKeen, Rev. B. N. Stone, and Fred W. Powers held the office for half that period, their individual terms being not consecutive, however. Shorter terms were those of N. O. McIntire, Rev. G. C. Andrews, T. W. Charles, C. C. Warren, Prin. R. C. Clark of the Academy, Drs. A. C. Ferguson and F. H. Jordan. Only one woman has held the position, Mrs. Lucia M. Lougee, who resigned after four years service.

In the 1890's a "Supervising School Committee" of three members was chosen, and instead of Supervisor, the title of Superintendent of Schools appears in town reports.

In 1918, in connections with Brownfield, Denmark and Stow, a Union Superintendent was employed. Each of these towns elects a School Board of three members, and these Boards choose the Superintendent. Under this plan Charles L. Clement was chosen and served till 1923, when Charles A. Snow, the present Superintendent, succeeded him.

This system raises the standard of the incumbents, assures cooperation of the School Board, and gives a uniformity of instruction and conduct of the schools which fits the pupils better for the Academy or other schools of similar grade.

When the township was laid out by Colonel Frye, one sixty-fourth was set apart for the common schools. This was divided into nine lots, and a town committee leased them by auction prices to the highest bidder. The lowest bid which brought a lot was $31.50, and the highest bid was $759. These lots were leased for a term of 999 years, the rental to be paid annually. The committee accepted in lieu of money the notes of the lessees, with securities. The whole sum resulting from this transaction amounted to $1,329.85, exclusive of interest.

These lots were held, subject to the leases until 1833, when they were sold for approximately $1,440. The money obtained is supposed to have been invested in the Town Farm, on the road from the village to Center Fryeburg.

"Hind-sight is always easier than fore-sight", and the town authorities had not unusual prescience. Had they been able to consider the possible growth of the township, with settlers in the various neighborhoods requiring school privileges at some future time, they might have held the lots as leased for thirty or forty years, which would have been good business for the lessees, and a source of income to the Town, to be set aside for the schools. Had they done this, the sum accruing by that time would have formed a large fund for the support of the schools, and a great relief in the taxes avoided.

This splendid arrangement was not destined to develop, however. The valuable lots fell into the hands of those who made money from them, and have been productive of good timber. The Town has no fund for the schools and continues to pay for the limited view of their townsmen of the past.

There have been a number of efforts to consider the establishment of a high school, but it has been wisely recognized that the expense of building and maintaining a suitable schoolhouse would be a burden; that the instruction possible would be less efficient than that offered by Fryeburg Academy; and that the annual tuition charged was a better investment than could be made by the Town operating for itself. Consequently a good number of pupils are turned over to the Academy each year, being well-prepared students, able to take up the more serious work of the higher grades.

The year of 1936-1937 found seventy-one students from Fryeburg enrolled at Fryeburg Academy. In June 1936 twenty-three pupils completed the courses of the Grammar schools, and of these, eighteen were at once enrolled in the Academy. Of the other five, two were attending high schools elsewhere. A fair average of the town school scholars win honors each year at the Academy. At the date cited, fourteen students from Fryeburg common schools were attending higher institutions.

As a result of the present system of conducting the common schools and the Academy, the number of illiterates in the town is comparatively negligible, confined to those drifting persons whose condition and circumstances contribute to the list of families aided by the Town. Progressive methods of instruction and care of the health of the pupils, with medical and dental supervision, are steadily building a class of young people who are an asset rather than a liability to the communities from which they come to the schools.

XII

FRYEBURG ACADEMY

> Long live the good School! giving out year by year
> Recruits to true manhood and womanhood dear:
> Brave boys, modest maidens, in beauty sent forth,
> The living epistles and proof of its worth!
> —*John G. Whittier.*

As has been told in the previous chapter, the common schools were started in 1777, with a growing attendance. In 1791 the desire for further education of their children, especially in more advanced English studies and in Latin and Greek, moved people in Fryeburg, Conway and Brownfield to consider the establishment of a "Grammar school," which would give a broader education. They discussed the proposition with such earnestness that they immediately obligated themselves to go ahead with the undertaking, and subscribed sufficient money to build a schoolhouse, equip, and support it. This school was enlarged, and Fryeburg Academy was established, and incorporation sought.

It was necessary in such an important undertaking to have the sanction of the General Court of Massachusetts; accordingly a petition was addressed to that body as follows:

To the Honorable Senate and House of Representatives of the Commonwealth of Massachusetts in General Court assembled—Jan'y, 1792.

The Memorial of the Subscribers humbly sheweth—

That the Proprietors of Fryeburg in the year 1763 penetrated through the wilderness fifty four miles distant from any civilized inhabitants to Pigwacket and by great labor, and expense and having encountered many difficulties and endured numerous hardships, they effected a settlement at that place; and have now the pleasing satisfaction to see not only the wilderness through which they passed, in some degree settled, and cultivated; but also which affords the most agreeable ideas that this part of the Commonwealth will soon, by its increasing population, add to the wealth and security of the State: But amidst these pleasing contemplations, the disadvantages this part of the Commonwealth are under for want of proper schools, cannot but excite an anxiety for the instruction of our rising youth, in such branches of literature as may render them virtuous, useful and ornamental to society; and which from the scattered situation of our settlements and other difficulties, cannot be obtained as in the more populous and opulent parts of the State. Yet in some measure to remedy the evil consequences of such a want of proper instruction, We your Memorialists and Petitioners, Inhabitants of Fryeburg and some of the adjoining Towns, have exerted ourselves and formed a society for the purpose of setting up a Grammar School in the Town of Fryeburg—have completed a building for that purpose sufficient for the reception of about eighty scholars, employed a proposed Instructor, and admitted about fifty Students. We have also chosen Trustees and established rules and regulations for the Government of the School, but our abilities will not admit of our establishing a fund sufficient for supporting and continuing the said institution. We therefore humbly ask the Aid of the Honorable Court, that by a grant of unappropriated land in the County of York, or by some other way, as they may see best, the said institution may be supported, and rendered extensively useful to many generations—likewise that said institution may be incorporated and vested with the powers and privileges of an Academy. So that the place which hath been in times past the seat of a Savage Nation that were a scourge and terror of the Eastern Country, may henceforth become the seat of Knowledge and Virtue and prove a blessing to rising generations and millions yet unborn—as in duty bound shall ever pray.

(Signed)

Paul Langdon
Ezekiel Walker

William Fessenden
Henry Young Brown
David Page
Simon Frye
Nath'l Porter
John Osgood
Moses Ames
James Osgood
James Osgood, jun'r.
David Evans, jun'r.
John Merrill
William Evans
John Evans
Abraham Bradley
Nath'l Merrill

This respectfully worded petition succeeded in obtaining both desired forms of assistance. The Fryeburg Academy Grant was a great aid in establishing the school on a good financial basis and helped through the years that followed.

This grant was of twelve thousand acres of land, north of Fryeburg, in Oxford County, a liberal gift even at that time. In after years it was valued at nearly $1,000,000, and had it been carefully conserved would have been of great assistance to the institution, but it was disposed of by the trustees to meet expenses.

The first Board of Trustees included Rev. William Fessenden, the first minister, who was a prime mover in the undertaking, Rev. Nathaniel Porter of Conway, N. H., David Page and James Osgood of the same town, Moses Ames, James Osgood and Simon Frye of Fryeburg, and the Preceptor of the Academy. The meeting for organization was held in November, in Brownfield. At the second meeting the Board was increased by the election of Rev. David Little of Kennebunk, and Rev. Paul Coffin of Buxton, whose regard for Fryeburg had occasioned his visits in the past, and who was chosen President. Paul Langdon was elected Preceptor, at a salary of fifty-two pounds sterling a year.

Mr. Langdon was the son of Rev. Samuel Langdon, who was President of Harvard College at the time of the Revolutionary War; he made a prayer before the troops as they left Cambridge for the fortifications on Bunker Hill. Paul Langdon received a fine education, and served with distinction in the Continental Army. His service in Fryeburg Academy was notable for the rare skill he showed in rousing his pupils to their best endeavors. He was a born teacher, possessing high intellectual powers. He was especially noted for his knowledge of the classical languages, and his pupils said of him, "More Greek and Latin in Master Langdon's forefinger than in most men's heads," that long finger being so often used to point out a way to better translation or to emphasize some important derivation or rule. He lived in a house near the Academy, near Pine Hill, traces of which lasted for more than a century. He retired from the preceptorship in 1799, but remained in Fryeburg until 1816, when he removed to New York, where he died in 1834.

There was difficulty in securing a fit successor to Mr. Langdon, and during the ensuing year, Daniel Weston, John P. Thurston and Rev. William Fessenden served as teachers. For a few months in 1801 Mr. Fessenden continued in charge, among his assistants being Enoch Lincoln, afterward Governor of the State, Samuel Fessenden (father of William Pitt Fessenden), William Barrows and Bezaleel Cushman, afterward an honored lawyer.

Mr. Fessenden taught the fall term of 1801, and then the trustees secured Daniel Webster, a recent graduate of Dartmouth College, as Preceptor, who assumed charge January, 1802.

Mr. Webster brought to the school an earnest endeavor to awaken the students to their opportunities, and made a favorable impression. His salary was not large, and to increase his earnings he copied deeds in the office of the Registrar of the Western District of the County, securing the employment from Lieut. Osgood with whom he boarded. When Mr. Webster finished the school year he was presented an honorarium of five dollars by the trustees. Fryeburg Academy was the only school of any size that he taught.

He was followed by Rev. Amos Jones Cook, a man of ripe culture and with progressive ideas. He was given a salary of fifty pounds a year.

At this time the trustees voted, "That as the cultivation of Music has a direct tendency to soften the ferocious passions, ameliorate the manners &c., instrumental and vocal music be attended to by those students who have talents and indication to improve therein." Mr. Cook was appointed teacher of music and "two good flutes and two good violins" were provided by the trustees; also at this time, mathematical and philosophical instruments including a telescope and a thermometer were purchased. Mr. Cook began the collection of articles of curiosity and interest, forming a Museum, which was not excelled in the State. He was ambitious for the Academy and introduced new methods. The school grew in numbers and reputation, and outgrew the original limited quarters.

In 1803 the trustees voted to build a new and commodious building, 55 feet long, 36 feet in width and 23 feet posts, being two storied. Mr. Cook planned the inside arrangement. The location of the new building was a matter for consideration and argument, as some desired the building to be placed on Fessenden Hill, nearer the center of the township; others preferred the location under Pine Hill. The larger number preferred a new site, and the building was finally erected on or near the present site, and was completed in 1806. It was a superior building for the times. In the belfry was hung a bell, the gift of Hon. John Phillips, Jr., of Boston, the first bell to sound over the Pequawket region.

This new Academy was dedicated June 4, 1806. Rev. Nathaniel

Porter delivered a scholarly address, whose prophetic peroration is here given:

"I close this discourse, with the short benediction, that you and your children may enjoy and improve all offered advantages for instruction in the knowledge of God, and useful literature. That generations successively rising up in their fathers' stead, may be the exemplary patrons of truth, the firm friends of education and order, the props and ornaments of civil and religious society, till the sun shall rise and set no more."

Mr. Cook continued in the Preceptorship until 1833, when age and ill health compelled his retirement.

Owing to an unfortunate disagreement among the trustees, due to different religious and political sentiments, two factions formed, and two schools were carried on at the same time in the building, one under Amos Brown, a graduate of Dartmouth, and the other under Henry B. Osgood, a graduate of Bowdoin. The school under Mr. Brown grew in numbers until it was obliged to move from the Academy to a hall in the village, until peace was restored. About this time the trustees sold the ground on which was the old Academy to Samuel A. Bradley, Esq.

Mr. Brown having accepted the principalship of Gorham Academy, the year of 1834-1835 began with John S. Wallis, a graduate of Yale, who continued one year in the Academy. He was followed by James H. Merrill, a graduate of Dartmouth, who gave such satisfaction that he remained two years. In the spring of 1837 Amos Richardson, a graduate of Dartmouth, came for a year, but remained until 1844. His administration was one of the most successful in the history of the Academy. In 1842 the Semi-centennial of the foundling of the Academy was celebrated.

Judah Dana, a student at Dartmouth, was in charge from the fall of 1844 until the spring of 1845, when he was succeeded by Joseph McGaffey, a graduate of Dartmouth, for a year; followed by William R. Porter, a Bowdoin graduate, for a year. Joseph C. Pickard, another graduate of Bowdoin, followed for the year 1847-1848. The next Preceptor was John Haskell, also a Bowdoin graduate, who did not complete the year, it being finished by Thomas Souther, a Dartmouth graduate.

Alvin Boody, a graduate of Bowdoin, followed as Preceptor in 1850. His administration is marked as one of the saddest in the history of the Academy, for on the night of May 28, 1851, the beautiful building with its contents was burned, by an incendiary who was the tool of some disaffected students. Investigation resulted in the matter being dropped, and no prosecution was made, though the instigators were strongly suspected, but no positive proof was obtainable. The school immediately occupied the "Old Meeting House" during the summer; then moved to the Stone Schoolhouse (now occupied by the Woman's Library Club), and afterwards to the Congregational Vestry, until the new building was completed in the fall of 1853. This was of brick, from designs by Gridley J. F. Bryant, a Boston architect, and built by Ammi Cutter. It was dedicated in August, 1853, Rev. John Wilde being the orator of the occasion.

Mr. Boody continued until the fall of 1855, when he was succeeded by his assistant, Henry Hyde Smith, a Bowdoin graduate, who carried on the school until the summer of 1858, when Alfred B. Dascomb, a graduate of Dartmouth, was engaged for the summer term.

The next two years, 1858-1860 saw Isaac M. Wellington, a graduate of Dartmouth, in charge.

The year of 1860-1861 was disturbed by the Civil War, and the following Preceptors officiated until the summer of 1861: Sewall Charles, a graduate of Bowdoin, the fall term; John M. Pease, a graduate of Bowdoin, the winter term, and Ebenezer Knowlton, a graduate of Amherst, the spring term.

From the fall of 1861 to the Spring of 1862 the Academy was closed.

School was resumed with Benjamin P. Snow, a Bowdoin graduate, continuing in charge until the fall of 1864. He was succeeded by Edwin F. Ambrose, a graduate of Dartmouth, who remained till the fall of 1865, when Charles D. Barrows, also a graduate of Dartmouth, conducted the school for the next two years.

The fall term of 1867 began with Usher W. Cutts, a graduate of Bowdoin, who remained three years.

About this time the school year was changed to begin with the fall term, as it has continued. Caleb A. Page, a graduate of Bowdoin, came to the Academy in 1870, and his administration continued until 1873.

Graduates of Bowdoin College were the Principals for the next four years, and included: Frederic A. Wilson, 1873 to 1875, Augustine Simmons, 1875-1876, Walter A. Robinson, 1876, until the spring of 1877, when he went to another academy. The year was finished by Arlo Bates.

In the fall of 1877 John W. Fiske, a graduate of Amherst, conducted the school for one year. Wendell H. Adams, a graduate of Bates, followed for a year.

The fall term of 1879 began under the charge of Prof. George H. Ricker, a graduate of Dartmouth, a teacher of wide experience, who made improvements in the course of study, establishing a system which served as a basis for future development. Under Professor Ricker the first formal graduating exercises were held, at the close of his incumbency in 1883.

Albert F. Richardson, a graduate of Bowdoin, became Principal in the fall of 1883. He at once began to increase the number of students, further developing the courses of study. Under his administration the attendance of students reached the highest number to that date in the history of the Academy. Mr. Richardson closed his connection in 1889.

Again the prestige of Bowdoin graduates was shown to warrant their employment and the succeeding years saw these men in charge of the Academy: John E. Dinsmore, 1889-1892; John C. Hull, 1892-1895; Ernest R. Woodbury, 1895-1900; Charles G. Willard, 1900-1903; Emerson L. Adams, 1903-1906; Charles G. Willard, 1906-1910; Ridgely C. Clark, 1911-1916; Ernest E. Weeks, 1917-1918; Edwin K. Welch, 1919-1922.

In 1922 Elroy O. LaCasce, a graduate of Bowdoin, was secured as Principal and gave such satisfaction and showed such progressive ideas that he was retained for an indefinite period. Mr. LaCasce developed the courses to a practical degree, and the large classes graduated each year showed the reputation of the school. The numbers of students attending increased each year, until the capacity of the buildings was taxed.

In the summer of 1924, through the efforts of the friends of the Academy, assisted by the donation from Col. Harvey D. Gibson, of the Board of Trustees, a graduate of the Academy and a New York banker, a commodious and convenient Gymnasium was built on the grounds of the Academy. Mr. E. S. Converse, of New York, gave $100,000 which at once put the institution on a firm basis, establishing a fund which has increased.

Due to the interested generosity of Cyrus H. K. Curtis, the Philadelphia publisher, two buildings were attached to the building of 1853. These were in harmonious style, and added strength and dignity to the institution. They were given the names "Curtis" and "Cutter" Halls, perpetuating the names of the donor and his wife. The cost of these two buildings, and of the improvements to "Academy Hall," was over $105,000.

The buildings of the Academy, beside the three Halls of Instruction include: Gordon Hall, the Manual Training School; the Harvey D. Gibson Gymnasium; the Houses of Residence—Alumni House, Frye House, Langdon House.

The grounds of the Academy have been extensively enlarged by purchase and gift, having a frontage on four streets, with area for athletic fields and for enlargement by the increase of buildings. Recent years (1937) have seen the attendance over two hundred pupils each term. The corps of teachers is always kept at a high point of excellence and ability.

From the first, Fryeburg has been noted for the educated men and women among its citizens. The especial mention in this chapter of the college from which each Preceptor was a graduate was to show the determination to have men of high education at the head of the school. Almost without exception the Preceptors of Fryeburg Academy have gone on to success in after life, winning distinction in some profession—teaching, law, medicine, the ministry,—looking back to the days in Fryeburg as being influential in their lives.

It was recognized after occupying the second Academy building, that more attention should be given to the special instruction of the girls of the school, and on April 23, 1806, the trustees passed this vote:

"That a committee of three be appointed to consider the expediency of employing an Instructress for the summer months."

The committee were of progressive minds, and on the 26th of the same month, they made this report:

"The committee are of the opinion that it will be expedient to employ a Preceptress for the two summer quarters next ensuing, the expenses of which to the Trustees will not in our opinion exceed $30. That it would be the duty of a preceptress to instruct in needlework, embroidery and painting, and likewise to assist in the instruction of reading, writing and English grammar."

Later in the year, in December, the trustees voted,

"That an agent be appointed to petition the General Court for a donation of lands or otherwise, for the purpose of establishing a fund for the Education of Female Youth."

That the innovation of a woman as a teacher, was a success, was evident by the testimonial which the Trustees voted to Miss Isabella Child for her success as an Instructress of Females.

The list of women who have been assistants in the teaching of the Academy is long. That their assistance to the Principal was recognized is proved by the fact that in several instances a Principal has taken the Preceptress away, to preside over his life as his wife.

It is impossible to list here more than the names of those holding the highest position for the women teachers, and unfortunately that list is not complete. The title given has varied from "Principal of the Female Department," "Associate Principal," "Preceptress," usually, to the present "Dean of Girls." In some cases length of tenure rather than title gave first place. The larger number of "assistants"—teachers of music, drawing and special branches—while deserving recognition, will live in the memory of their pupils until the full history of the Academy is written.

The list is as follows:

1806, Isabella Child
1814, to 1816, Hannah M. Spring
1817, Maria P. Austin
1818, to 1827, Eliza Chamberlain
1829, and 1830, Mehitable J. Cook
1839, Barbara B. Hall
1840, Elizabeth Dunlap
1841, Hannah T. Church
1842, Huldah P. Fessenden
1843, Elmira Hanscom
1847, and 1848, Frances L. Carter
1851, Judith Walker
1852, to 1854, Mrs. S. E. Boody
1855, and 1856, Ellen A. Barrows
1857, Martha A. Pike
1858, Hannah B. Jewett
1860, Ellen A. Barrows
1861, School closed
1865, and 1866, Marion Merrill
1867, Mrs. Wentworth
1871, Helen Morrell
1872, Hannah M. Huntress
1873, M. Augusta Wade
1874, Helen Sewall
1876, Florence Warren
1878, Alice M. Emerson
1879, to 1883, Hattie G. Ricker
1884, Katherine F. Stone
1885, to 1887, Helen M. Staples
1888, Laura E. McIntire
1889, to 1892, Mary E. Buzzell
1893, to 1895, Mary F. Farnham
1896, and 1897, Margaret E. Merrill
1898, to 1903, Sara M. Locke
1904, to 1906, Anastasia M. Walton
1906, to 1910, Mrs. Sara Locke Willard
1911, and 1912, Susan M. Walker
1913, to 1922, Mrs. Ella F. Hasty
1923, to 1932, Nancy B. Farris
1933, Mrs. Elsie Files
1934—, Ruth Piper

It would be difficult even to impossibility to estimate accurately the number of persons who have attended Fryeburg Academy to date. There have been many thousands and they have gone forth the better for the instruction and association. It is possible to mention a few of those who have attained prominence in the country in the various walks of life, and among them are: Albion K. Paris, third Governor of the State of Maine; John W. Dana, three times Governor of the State; Alpheus Felch, Governor of Michigan; Abiel Chandler, founder of the Chandler Scientific School at Dartmouth College; Rufus Porter, founder of the *Scientific American;* James W. Ripley and Samuel C. Fessenden, both Members of Congress; Rufus Ingalls, Quartermaster General, U.S.A., during the Civil War; Paris Gibson, U. S. Senator from Montana; Mary Pierce Andrew, Mother of Gov. John A. Andrew, of Massachusetts; Caroline E. Farrar, mother of "Artemus Ward"; James R. Osgood, publisher; Kate Putnam Osgood, poet; Stephen Henry Chase; Seth C. Gordon, M.D.; Judge William G. Barrows; Judge Henry C. Peabody; Col. Harvey D. Gibson; Major Clayton W. Pike; Clement A. Walker, M.D.; Rev. Samuel Souther; George B. Barrows; Thomas Souther; George P. Bradley, M.D., Surgeon, U.S.N.; William Stickney; Moses Evans, M.D.; Rev. Prentice H. Evans; S. Wilson Evans; Simeon A. Evans, M.D.; Clinton B. Evans, Chicago Editor; Gen. Samuel Fessenden and Thomas Fessenden, lawyers; Rev. Joseph Fessenden; Rev. Caleb Page; Horatio Nelson Page, M.D.; Capt. John Page, U.S.A.; Rev. Samuel Osgood, D.D.; Henry B. Osgood; Nathaniel Frye.

XIII

SACO RIVER

From a lake where rugged mountains tower high on either hand;
Over ledges, pebbled shallows, 'round broad sweeps of shining sand;
Under banks ablaze with wild flowers, shaded deep by maple trees,
Flows the Saco, kissed by shadows, rippled by the summer breeze.
—*John Stuart Barrows.*

As the Land of Egypt is called, "The Gift of the Nile", so Fryeburg is the Gift of the Saco River, for it was the wide expanse of intervale land through which the river ran that attracted Colonel Frye to the locality.

At that time the Saco ran through the primeval intervales, making a course of thirty-two miles to gain three between the point where it entered the area and where it left to proceed in a generally direct course to the ocean. The course through the ten thousand acres of intervale was unusual among the rivers of New England. Other rivers of Maine flow in more direct routes from the sources to the sea, the Connecticut and Hudson are straight-flowing rivers, indicating the tremendous forces of Nature, that at some time in the formation of the Earth made valleys that afterward became the courses of the rivers.

The formation of the lands in the valley of Fryeburg, seems to show the work of water in motion. The sandy plain on which so much of the town rests, especially the Village, seems to show that a current, whirling into this valley, encountered the barrier of the hills and deposited the sand it carried, until the whole western section of the township was filled with a terrace or bench twenty feet or more thick. From the hills on the southwest of the town, to the rampart of Pleasant Mountain, this sand lies in a huge beach, which resembles the shores of ponds at present.

The soil of the plains and that of the intervales is quite different. The plains are a yellow sand, lacking in fertility, but with a top soil that contains the humus of years from the decay of vegetable matter, and bears a heavy growth of pines and other trees. The intervale land is alluvial soil, with an indefinite depth. Beneath this soil is a sub-soil of clay, in which lie buried tree trunks and fragments of trees, which shows the great age of the land. These remains of an earlier growth have not been examined as to their age, but they are older than any modern growth, and that the waters of a great lake deposited the clay and mingled with it the parts of trees, was the natural course of Nature.

Readers will take great interest in the technical description of the work of Nature in forming the Fryeburg valley, as written for this sketch by Prof. Richard J. Lougee, of the Geological Department of Colby College, Waterville, Maine. Professor Lougee is familiar with the town of Fryeburg and its physical formations, and his estimate covers the situation so that any one studying the area can understand readily the geological conditions. Professor Lougee writes as follows:

The present peculiar winding course of the Saco River can be ascribed to a succession of events which have their beginnings in the dim geologic past. The region through which the river flows is one of complex crystalline rocks consisting of two principal types—an old series of banded mica gneisses and schisto which may have originated ancient sediments, and which have been altered by later intrusions of granite and pegmatite. During the ages since these rocks were formed they have been profoundly eroded. Lowlands such as the Saco Valley are largely attributable to stream erosion in the past etching out the areas of least resistant rocks. In the Fryeburg region intrusive rocks of a coarse granitoid type form the principal hills or mountains bordering the Saco Lowland and projecting as conspicuous isolated elevations within it.

An unknown amount of additional erosion on hills and valleys alike is ascribable to the ice of the Glacial Period, but the thick deposits left within the Saco Valley following the glaciation have had more effect than other factors in determining the present course of the river.

Judging by deposits of fine clay that occur in several low parts of the valley, it appears that the glacial ice gave place to a glacial lake which overspread much of the Saco Lowland. Several glacial deltas at Stow and North Chatham, N. H., mark the water level. Due to post-Glacial elevation and tilting of the land, in common with all the rest of Maine and also perhaps due to the cutting down of local barriers further down the valley, this lake in the Fryeburg region was drained. The newly-formed post-Glacial Saco River, possibly still fed by melt-water from ice in the headwaters of the valley, spread immense deposits of fine sand into the lowland, burying the clay beds and any pre-Glacial river channels in the bed rock, and building up a widespread sandy flood-plain. Eminences like Jockey Cap and Mount Tom were surrounded by this sand which also forms the broad plain on which Fryeburg Village is located. Reentrants of the valley not along the direct line of the river escaped complete aggradation, and form today the depressions of Kezar Lake, Kezar Pond and Lovewell's Pond.

Eventually the river ceased building the sandy flood-plain and commenced to dissect it. In its wide meandering and downward cutting it has removed vast quantities of the sandy fill from the valley, leaving terraces at various levels. So widely has the river meandered in dissecting the glacial debris that at many places it has been superimposed on ledges far off the line of its pre-Glacial course. Falls in the profile of the river have thus been produced.

The modern flood-plain of the river, known as the intervale, is two miles wide at Fryeburg, and about thirty feet lower than the high sandy plain. Its surface is scarred by swampy depressions and old channels, formed by the meandering river, but is so flat and susceptible to overflow at flood periods that local residents in 1817 were able to greatly shorten the course of the river by digging an artificial cut-off. The high bluff separating the Fryeburg sand-plain from the intervale marks the southernmost recent migration of the meandering Saco River in this locality.

Here in the broad intervales the Saco makes the "great bend", referred to in the early transactions of the settlers. It flowed around the valley searching for an outlet, but taking its time through the charming scenery, as if loath to leave such beautiful environment. For thirty-two miles, according to Colonel Frye's surveys, it flowed through farming lands and received the waters of brooks and the drainage of a number of ponds. It flowed unvexed and unchallenged, until the ravages of its almost annual freshets robbed the farmers of stock, products of their farms, and even the farms themselves were damaged by erosion, and at times made useless by standing water as described in an earlier chapter. At last patience ceased, and measures were taken to relieve the situation. A canal was opened through the ridge east of Bear Pond to relieve the intervales in a measure from the water in that vicinity. This drain made a difference in that locality, but the evil continued in other parts of the town.

June 6, 1812, a meeting of the town discussed the project intelligently. A committee was chosen to see on what they might agree with those persons through whose land a canal might pass, and make an estimate of the probable cost of opening the proposed canal.

At a meeting held May 10, 1813, it was voted to petition the General Court of the Commonwealth to open a canal from the Saco river near William Russell's place, which was a short distance north of General Frye's hill, to Bog Pond. It also was decided to petition the General Court for permission to conduct a lottery, or for a grant of land for financing the enterprise, and to build necessary bridges.

The undertaking dragged along for almost two years, during which sentiment was cultivated in favor of the canal, and steps were taken to secure the rights to invade private property and dig the canal.

In March, 1815, the General Court passed an act to incorporate the proprietors of the Fryeburg Canal. This act was approved March 15, and a strong board of more than thirty proprietors was appointed by the Legislature. These were permitted to open the canal, following this course: Beginning on the northerly bank of the river, formerly owned by Joseph Frye; about fifty rods south-westerly of the dwelling house of William Russell, and running through the lands of Ebenezer Fessenden, Jr., Peter Walker, Isaac Abbott, Stephen Abbott, to Bear Pond, and from said pond through the canal to Bog Pond, and thence eastwardly to Saco River near the dwelling house of Simon Frye.

That this did not help matters as fast as desired, is evident from the petition to the General Court, by Joseph Chandler and thirty-six others:

The Honorable Senate and House of Representatives of the Commonwealth of Massachusetts, in General Court assembled at Boston, on the second Wednesday of January, A.D., 1816

The subscribers Inhabitants of Fryeburg in the County of Oxford respectfully represent that the Saco River runs thirty-three miles in its course through said town, that a large part of the lands in said Town are intervale and meadow and liable to be annually overflowed; thousands of acres of said intervale and meadow remain in a state of nature, and can never be cleaned and cultivated; that part of said Intervale, which has been hitherto cultivated can rarely be planted or sown in the spring of the year with convenience and safety before the first of June in consequence of the water remaining upon them; and the products of the cultivated parts of said Intervale are thereby limited in quantity and value, and those products are frequently injured and sometimes nearly destroyed by Summer freshets. To remedy these evils and to render the great body of said intervales productive, the Inhabitants of said Town, for a number of years past have contemplated the opening of a new channel for said river, so as to limit its course to about eighteen miles within said Town, said new channel has been partially opened by the water in times of freshets and by the labors of various Individuals, with a view to the completion of an object so desirable and important to the Inhabitants of said Town, to obtain what has deserved the requisite authority and to provide the means of indemnity to those who might be injured by the opening of said new channel a petition was presented to your honorable body, signed by Robert Bradley, Joseph Chandler and many others for an act of Incorporation. Conformable to the prayer of said petition, and on the second day of March last an act was passed "incorporating" Robert Bradley, Joseph Chandler and others, by the name of the "Proprietors of the Fryeburg Canal"; which act is deemed essentially defective and calculated to defeat the object of those who petitioned therefor, in as much as the Individuals composing said corporation are made liable in their Individual as well as corporate capacity to make good all damages sustained by any person or persons in consequence of opening said new channel, and the real estate holden by the Individual members of said corporation, whether in common or severally, is also made subject to be taken and set off on Execution to respond any damages which may be recovered by any Individual by reason of opening said new channel, thereby attaching a perpetual and indefinite incumberance to the real estate of every member of said corporation, as there is no period prescribed by said act, when claims against the members and their lien upon their real estates shall cease; and the mode prescribed by said act for determining questions of damages claimed by Individuals against said corporation is also deemed unnecessarily burthensome and expensive; and on the other hand, the said act does not contain a single provision vesting said corporation with any immunities or privileges or powers except the right of organizing themselves, and opening said new channel *at their own expense.* Wherefore your petitioners humbly pray the Hon. Legislature so to amend said act and to make such further provision by law relative to the same, that the said corporation be authorised and allowed to purchase and to hold and improve for their benefit any real estate on or adjoining said new channel and river within said Town and also to erect and improve all such mills and other works thereon as they may deem expedient, and that the time may be defined and limited by law when all claims for damages against said corporation which may be sustained by Individuals in consequence of opening said new channel as well as against the several members thereof and their estates shall be barred and cease, that a standing committee may be appointed to appraise all damages claimed by Individuals against said corporation; and that several members of said corporation may be authorized to have and maintain actions of contribution against the other members thereof to indemnify themselves for such damages and costs as they shall have been subjected to in consequence of the payment of Executions which may be recovered against said corporation.

Fryeburg January 26, 1816.
Joseph Chandler and thirty-six others.

Commonwealth of Massachusetts.
In the Senate February 13th 1816.

On the petition aforesaid ordered that the petitioners cause an attested copy of their petition with this order thereon to be posted up at two or more public places in the Town of Fryeburg, and also to be published in the Portland Gazette for three weeks successively the last publication to be thirty days at least before the second Wednesday of the first session of the next General Court, that all persons interested may then appear and show cause if any they have why the prayer of said petition should not be granted.

Sent down for concurrence
In the House of Representatives, Feb. 14, 1816.   John Phillips,
Read and concurred,   President.
A true coppy,   Timothy Bigelow, Speaker.
Attest
S. F. McCleary, Clerk of the Senate.

In the session of the General Court of the Commonwealth of Massachusetts, of June, 1816, the following Act was passed:

An Act in addition to an act entitled "An act to incorporate the Proprietors of the Fryeburgh Canal."

Sec. 1. Be it enacted by the Senate and House of Representatives in General Court assembled, That the Bear Pond, situate in Fryeburgh, and which lies in the course of the New channel, pointed out and authorized by an act, entitled "An act to incorporate the Proprietors of the Fryeburgh Canal", shall be deemed and taken to be the Pond intended by said act, notwithstanding the same is denominated "Bean Pond" in the first section of the act aforesaid.

Sec. 2. Be it further enacted, That any person who shall be damaged in his property by the opening of said new channel, and who shall claim damages of said corporation, shall exhibit and deliver his claim in writing to the Clerk of the said Proprietors, and shall therein name the sum, so claimed by him; and the said Corporation shall have and be allowed the term of ninety days, from and after the delivery of the written claim as aforesaid, to their Clerks, to settle with the person so claiming damages; and no application to the Circuit Court of Common Pleas, nor the Supreme Judicial Court, for the appointment of a Committee to estimate the damages so claimed as aforesaid, shall be made to and sustained by either of said Courts, until after the expiration of said term of ninety days.

Sec. 3. Be it further enacted, That the said Corporation may purchase and hold real estate, on said river and new channel, within said town of Fryeburgh, not exceeding the value of ten thousand dollars, and may erect such mills and other works thereon as they may deem expedient; and may also be lawfully possessed of and hold personal estate not exceeding ten thousand dollars; And they are hereby vested with all the powers requisite to enable them to manage and improve the same.

Sec. 4. Be it further enacted, That all claims or right of action which individuals may or shall have against said Corporation, or the Members thereof, by reason of opening the said new channel, shall be barred and cease at the expiration of four years from and after the time the cause of action shall have accrued.

Sec. 5. Be it further enacted, That the several Members of said Corporation are hereby authorized to have and maintain actions against the other Members thereof, to recover such sum or sums of money as shall idemnify the Member commencing said action, for all damages and costs he may have sustained or been subjected to in the payment of any execution recovered against said Corporation, or any monies due from said Corporation.

(Approved by the Governor, June 20, 1816.)

Being thus protected by the law, the proprietors went ahead, and the canal into Bog Pond was made operative. As soon as this canal became of any size through the washing of the water running through, it drained Bear Pond, and in the freshet of 1820 the immense volume of water passing through turned the whole current of the river in the new direction.

The change of the current and the shortening of the whole course of the river quickened the current, and thereby washed the bottom out of the whole course of the river, from the rapids at Swan's to the change of direction at Bear Pond. The river cut a channel through Bear Pond, and thereby lowered the bottom of that body of water, until it was completely drained. The same depth of channel continued through Bog Pond, and whereas this body of water was larger in area than Lovewell's Pond, it was drained.

The Bear Pond area being left higher than before became well drained, and is now valuable farm land, a part of the area of the Town Farm on one side, and good land on the other side of the river, in what was known as the "Day Farm."

The great effect was on the farm lands to the northward of the town, where the river having lost its power, and become nothing but a series of little pools of water, ceased to be the menace to the farmers, and their farms steadily improved, until now they are splendid areas of the best farming land in the country, and producing thousands of bushels of potatoes and sweet corn in abundance annually.

The first method of crossing the Saco was by fords and ferries. The fords were made when the river was low and at points where it was shallow. The ferries were established by the Proprietors of the township where the roads seemed to require them. The town voted to establish a ferry where the "lower leg" of the river passes through the Toll Bridge district, near where Deacon Eastman had established his claim. The ferry business was given to Deacon Eastman and his family and heirs and assigns forever. He was to keep a ferry boat capable to carrying four horses at one time. The rates of ferrying were:

> For ferrying a Man, 6d.
> For ferrying man and horse, 1s, 6d.
> For man and horse and cart, and lumber or goods, in proportion to above prices.

John Stevens was allowed to keep a ferry opposite his dwelling house, on the north side of the river in the Birch Hill district, if he kept under constant repair a ferry boat twenty-four feet long and twelve feet wide, over all. His rates for ferrying were set at:

> For a Man and Horse, 2d.
> For a Man, 2/3d.
> For a Yoke of Oxen, 2 2/3d.
> For a yoke of Oxen and empty Cart, 4d.
> For a half-ton weight, 2d.
> For a greater or less weight, in proportion.

Barnes Haseltine was allowed to keep a ferry where is now Swan's Falls, subject to the same regulations that governed Stevens' ferry. A ford was possible below Weston's Bridge, in early times.

When a road was opened from Menotomy to Long Pond in Bridgton, Deacon Simon Frye and son conducted a ferry until the Bridgton Road was opened in 1834, further south, crossing the river the other side of Mount Tom, below Cat Pond.

Fryeburg has been rather overloaded with bridges, owing to the surrounding river, having had no less than seven covered bridges, and three open shorter bridges.

The first town action recorded as to bridges was in 1786, to build an open bridge across Kimball Brook, at North Fryeburg.

The first bridge built across the Saco was in 1790, at Swan's

Falls. In October, 1794, they began raising a bridge at the lower part of the town, between Fish Street and North Fryeburg.

Most of these early bridges were of the type called "pier bridges" and were easily swept away by the high freshets. The picturesque covered bridges were a later invention, and the needs of the town required good strong structures that would withstand high water, and would last indefinitely. They were maintained until the State began to take charge of certain trunk lines of roads, when the concrete bridge took the place of the covered.

The type of covered bridge was devised by Paul Paddelford of Littleton, New Hampshire. It was popular throughout New England, and copied elsewhere, so might be called the typical American Bridge. The designer was employed in 1844 to build "Weston's" bridge, across the river close under Pine Hill. This bridge originally was 250 feet long; later it was lengthened.

In 1846, Mr. Paddelford built the "Canal" bridge, which was 272 feet long. This bridge was taken down in 1932-1933 and a concrete, open structure was built to replace it, a large part of the expense being borne by the State.

In 1848 the bridge on the Bridgton Road, known as the "Walker" bridge, was built in the same style as the two earlier. This was 164 feet long and was built by Paddelford. In 1935-1936 it was replaced by a modern steel bridge, and the grade changed.

"Hemlock" bridge on the road from Toll Bridge to East Fryeburg, 116 feet long was built in 1857.

The "Island" bridge on the Denmark Road, now discontinued, was built in 1862, and was 110 feet long. This bridge was over the rapids in the river, and was swept away in the great freshet in March, 1936. At the same time the "Island" was completely isolated by the washing away of the small, open bridge on the other side of the island.

The bridge 87 feet long over Charles River, the tributary of the Saco that brings the waters of Charles Pond into the river, was built in 1856. This bridge was replaced by a modern structure.

An iron, open bridge over the old river was built in 1894 for the highway from Fish Street to the "Harbor," 87 feet long.

In the summer of 1827, we find measures taken by four citizens of the town to build a grist-mill at Swan's Falls, and they entered into the following agreement:

Articles of agreement between Messrs Abraham Andrews, Samuel Swan & Caleb Swan & their Heirs all of Fryeburg in the County of Oxford & State of Maine, Husbandmen, on the one part, and Mr. Joseph Quimby of Fryeburg, county and state aforesaid on the other part, respecting the said Quimby; tending a gristmill, intended to be erected at Swan's Falls in Fryeburg—

We the subscribers, hereby agree & consent, that the aforesaid Joseph Quimby, may tend the aforesaid Gristmill, during his abilities to do the same, with general satisfaction to the owners & customers, That he make the repairs that is customary for a millar to make, viz. to put in a cog or lade-board when wanted, at his own expense, and to keep said mill clean & in good order for grinding, whenever the water will serve for grinding, And that he the said Quimby, have liberty to carry by water a grindstone, also a Joiner's Lathe, & also a circular Saw a mecanical Shop for his own use and convenience, & have priviledge of water to try & prove other machinery, and that he have one half of all the toll he shall collect by grinding, as a compensation for his services as above.

Abraham Andrews
Samuel Swan
Caleb Swan
Joseph Quimby

Dated at Fryeburg this
25th day of June, A.D., 1827.

This mill was built on the east side of the river, and the traces of the flume where it was dug along the bank are still in evidence. The mill operated until the next year, when a rise of water carried it away. The mill-stones still lie on the bank above the river. Two sets show the size and shape of the granite stones.

There is one relic of Indian times which has come down to the present—the cruise along the Saco, from the Village to Lovewell's Pond. The Pequawkets had the benefit of the long course following the current, making calls into the many ponds and "Poke Lokens" along the way, spending as many days in the trip as were fruitful in fish and game; coming at last to the outlet of Lovewell's Pond, where they would paddle into the pond, and coming across the waters, would make a landing at "Moose Rock," and from thence to their village was about two miles. The road now used to reach the pond at that point is without doubt the old portage, as it is in a straight line between the two points.

This hunting trip has been turned into a pleasure excursion by the people of Fryeburg, and every summer sees canoes and small boats going "Around River." Until the building of the dam at Swan's Falls, it was easy to start at Weston's Bridge, and either to run the falls, or to make a portage by them. Otherwise, the start can be made at the falls, when it will be uninterrupted smoothness until the little rapids at the Denmark Road give an element of risk or excitement to the journey. The rest of the way is as unhindered as it was for the aborigines.

When Robert E. Peary was a college boy, before he had made Fryeburg his home, he took great pleasure in this trip. Of it he wrote: "I had a small, light boat well fitted with comfortable seats, a pair of long wide oars and a good paddle and I could put it just where I wanted to. The first three or four miles I had to stand up a la Indian while paddling, in order to keep off the sand bars. After that, it was the ideal of laziness. The river ran deep and strong between two dense fringes of trees and all we had to do was to sit and let the river take us along. Occasionally we would come to snags or a fallen tree would jut into the river, but two or three strokes of the paddle would send the boat skipping by, and then all would be lovely again."

Of course the trip is materially shortened from Indian times. The Canal has reduced the journey to about seventeen miles, but it is long enough for a summer day. The trip can be made in five hours with plenty of water, but the ordinary summer pitch of water is best; then the canoes can slip along lazily, the occupants enjoying the changing scenery. The sights include eagles, ducks, herons and other wild fowl; the farms and fields are beautiful in colors, and the over-arching trees turn the river channel into a shady bower.

There is probably no other locality than Fryeburg that can offer such a unique and enjoyable excursion as the trip "Around the River."

> "Dear Saco's stream winds clear and bright
> Through verdant vales, a silvery thread,
> Emerald and blue, in shade and light,
> The circling hills in beauty spread."
> —*Carolyn E. McMillan.*

XIV

MOUNTAINS, PONDS, BROOKS

"I pity people who weren't born in a vale. I don't mean a flat country, but a vale: that is, a flat country, bounded by hills."
—*Thomas Hughes.*

By no means a trivial possession of Fryeburg is the scenery. In the foot-hills of the White Mountains, the town is yet far enough away from the higher peaks to soften the outlines and give the whole landscape a beauty impossible in nearer views.

The mountain range begins in the west with Chocorua, which has been styled "the most rugged peak east of the Rockies." As the eye turns northward, next is the long rampart of Moat, which looms above the Conway valley. Nearer is the rough outline of the Rattlesnake hills, a row of little peaks like the knuckles of the hand. Here is the location of the Redstone quarries, which have furnished the pink granite for many important buildings throughout the country. The huge mass of Green Mountain comes next. The water supply of the Village is taken from brooks on the low hills of the southeastern side, three miles away. Next, standing between Green Mountain and Kearsarge, is Hurricane, which in recent years has been opened to travel, by a road between South Chatham and Kearsarge Village.

Dominating the whole view from Fryeburg is Kearsarge, whose symetrical cone is a wonder in the natural architecture of mountains. Although only 3,200 feet in altitude, half the height of Washington, it is the most conspicuous elevation in the locality, and completely blanks Washington from the view of the Village.

This mountain has been known as Kearsarge from the earliest times; only in later years has the mountain in Warner, N. H., been put forward to claim the honor of being the mountain that gave the name to the U.S.S. Kearsarge, the corvette that fought and sunk the Confederate sloop of war, Alabama, off Cherbourg, France, June 12, 1864. The writer heard Hon. Gustavus V. Fox, state that the vessel which won that engagement was named for the mountain in Chatham and Conway. As Mr. Fox was Assistant Secretary of the Navy during Lincoln's administration, it would seem that his statement regarding the name should be conclusive.

Following along the range, the next conspicuous object is Doublehead, twin peaks of not great height. Sable is the next mountain, its rounded top being a harmonious figure in the landscape. The next is Baldface, 3,600 feet high, a double-headed mountain. From Fryeburg the southern peak is the more conspicuous, its sharp cone a striking feature, behind which the northern and higher peak is just visible over the left shoulder. At the foot of this mountain is seen the low top of Eastman.

Almost directly in the north are the long ranges of Royce, which is in two distinct mountains. "Evans Notch", named for John Evans, a Fryeburg settler, and a noted hunter, runs along the side of Speckle Mountain, a road, east of Royce, built by C.C.C. enterprise, in 1933-1934. This road runs over the shoulder of Speckle Mountain from Stow to Gilead, Maine, striking the Androscoggin valley between Gilead, Maine, and Shelburne, N. H. A tumbled range of blue hills in North Lovell and Stoneham fills the northeast, with Sabatis in Lovell, the last eminence of any size in the landscape.

The only mountain between Mount Tom, in Fryeburg, and the hills of Brownfield, is Mount Pleasant in Denmark and Bridgton, whose great bulk, extending over a large area, divides the Saco valley from the ponds of Bridgton.

These mountains, like the plains of the Saco valley, have given the locality a reputation for the lumber industry, which has been important since the first settlers built their log houses and cleared their rights, throwing the cuttings into the river until they blocked it and made it necessary to clear a channel. Capt. Samuel Osgood and James Osgood were employed by Saco lumber men to clear the river of this drift-trash from Cat Pond for almost a mile, for which they received $500., and a price for every log they turned through. They sent more than a thousand down the river.

Fryeburg does not boast a single mountain of height like those of the neighboring towns, but it has a number of gentle hills, that afford good farm and orchard lands and give diversity to the scenery.

The highest elevation is Mount Tom, 1,040 feet altitude above sea level. It is near the geographic center of the township, and is a prominent feature of the landscape, its precipitous southern side being picturesque, bearing trees and shrubs that seem to hold in the crevices, and give it more beauty. The northwestern side is a gentle slope, and at one time an easy carriage road made it possible to drive nearly to the summit.

In the southwest, near the State boundary line, is Stark's Hill, so named from Capt. William Stark, one of the first proprietors, in whose right it was. It is 1,020 feet high, and it gave Colonel Frye an excellent view of the Saco valley to the northward. Rev. Paul Coffin in 1768 rode on horseback to the top, claiming to be the first to attempt such a feat. Covered with forests, it is a ridge of solid granite of good quality, and has been worked by quarries. It is the location of fine ski coasts.

In continuation of Stark's Hill is Long Hill, to the southward, 800 feet high; then Bald Peak about the same altitude. These make the three hills, sometimes called the Pequawket Hills, which the Indians told Walter Bryant would indicate the Pequawket land.

Across the intervening pine plains from Starks Hill is "Jockey Cap", a strange form of outcrop of the underlying stone. Its altitude above the plain is about 200 feet, and it is conspicuous from any point. It has been called a huge boulder, but it is too similar to other hills through the surrounding country to be anything but an outcrop. Its rough face toward the southwest is a sharp precipice, and was covered with a crop of rough lichens, that gave it a black color. Its sides and contour seem to suggest that it was originally a pinacle, and that the glacial movement broke off and transported the top seems probable. The wide view of the distant mountains, from Sandwich Dome, N. H., in the southwest, around to Baldface in the north, and then the rolling lower mountains in Maine, is well worth the climb by an easy path to the summit.

Toward the northeast from Jockey Cap is the hill of "Highland Park," an old farm-site that Dr. John Buzzell, a Portland physician, developed into a sanitarium in the early '80s. It is a commanding position from which to view the whole surrounding valley. Its height is about the same as the other hills of the town, 640 feet. It was formerly known as "the Major Evans Farm".

In the southeast from the Village may be seen "Oak Hill," a long rangy height, 640 feet, with the southern face a precipice of fine granite. It helps to confirm the theory advanced here that Jockey Cap belongs to the local arrangement of hills. The face is broken in a few places by distinct trap dikes of different widths; one so disintegrated that a pathway can be found in it, the walls of granite on either side.

A little hill, nearer the Village than any of the others, marks the probable site of the Indian village. It lies close to the Saco, and from the rocks that show in the river channel the Indians could launch their canoes. Until the Province Line between Maine and New Hampshire was run it had no name other than "Brown's Hill", so named from Captain Harry Young Brown the grantee of Brownfield. After that, ownership gave it the name "Mount Bradley," which was not so permanent a name as "Pine Hill". It is now included in "Bradley Memorial Park", and will always so remain.

The outside boundaries of the town have a few hills. They are: Birch Hill, in West Fryeburg, a large sprawling height, 740 feet, covered with forest; Smart's Hill, 547 feet high, on the border of the town next to Sweden; Carter Hill, 720 feet high, in East Fryeburg, looking down on Kezar Pond and surrounding country; Stanley's Hill, in the eastern part of the town, 620 feet high. Frye Hill has been mentioned earlier. A shoulder, a little lower, was called "Fessenden Hill" from the fact that Parson William Fessenden occupied a homestead thereon; and a little below, where a shoulder makes a suitable place of a farmhouse, is "Page Hill", so called from David Page, a farmer who passed his life there.

The figures given of the heights of the hills, unless otherwise stated, are those above the sea level. As the bench mark in the Village gives the altitude of Main Street as 429 feet at that point, the height above the locality can be estimated by simple subtraction. Thus, Pine Hill is above the surrouding streets but 171 feet, Stark's Hill, but 591 feet, and others in similar proportions.

The number of ponds is less today than when Colonel Frye looked out over the valley. The number grows less as the natural course of nature is to fill the smaller ponds until they become meadows, then disappear, except at times of freshets. Instances have been given of such changes in different parts of the town.

The largest pond is Kezar, which lies between the east part of the town and Bridgton. It is irregular in shape, and has extensive meadows around it. It was to these meadows that the people of

Gorham came to cut hay, and then drove their cattle to be wintered. This pond is near the channel of the old river, into which it drains. It is less subject to sudden rises of water than are the other ponds along the present course of the river.

Bog Pond was the second largest sheet of water until it was drained, changed by the river. It formerly extended from the Menotomy Road to Fryeburg Center, and covered more area than Lovewell's, but the canal changed the flow of the river to such an extent that it drained this pond, and filled much of it with sand washed down from the intervales above. It holds the name merely by inheritance.

Lovewell's Pond, on whose shore occurred the baptism of blood that gave it its name, is a beautiful sheet of water, of rectangular shape, about two and one-half miles long and three-fourths of a mile wide. Its shores are rocky, with occasional sandy beaches at the northern end. The southern end is meadow, and the outlet is pushed into the pond by the deposit of matter brought down by the river at high-water.

This pond is deep, soundings at mean low water being thirty feet and more. It is so situated that squalls are frequent; when the wind comes over the plains from the northwest, in a few moments the surface is thrown into waves, white capped and boisterous. On such occasions it has been the scene of serious accidents, and in the summer of 1876 claimed the life of John Jay Bradley, son of A. R. Bradley, grandson of Robert Bradley.

Lovewell's is a famous fishing pond. The waters are stocked with black bass, white perch, and the native fish abound, such as pickerel, yellow perch, sun-fish, chubs and hornpouts.

Two islands rise from the waters. Pine, the larger, near the eastern shore is wooded; Loon is a barren islet, frequently submerged. A huge rock or ledge appears at very low water, on the eastern side of the pond, a menace to boats. Many camps of considerable size and convenience are along the shores of the pond.

Other ponds of good size are located on the borders of the township. They include Kimball, on the Chatham border; Charles, in the northern corner, which outlets into the Old River; Pleasant, on the southeasterly side, partly in Denmark.

In the southern corner of the township are several small ponds, "kettles", relics of glacier action. Near the Porter Road several; "Davis", a round pond under the shadow of Oak Hill, has no visible inlet or outlet, yet its waters are pure, and the sandy beaches are clean; Clay Pond, is farther along this road, of a somewhat similar nature to Davis. It is larger and is long; its shores are reedy and bushy. It has an outlet into a brook that runs easterly to the Saco.

Under the line of the "Pequawket Hills", are Black and Peat ponds, both of them kettles, like Davis. Black Pond's outlet is from Stark's meadow, Lovewell's Brook, which near the village makes the water-power for Ward's Mill, and thence runs to Lovewell's Pond, the only brook flowing into Lovewell's that ever turned a mill.

There are instances in the town of ponds becoming filled with the wash from the hills and the deposits of the river: "Cat" pond near the Bridgton Road, and "Goose" pond south of Lovewell's, both of which, in the memory of older inhabitants, from sheets of water, have become meadowy marshes, the resort of wild fowl.

It is not surprising that with so few hills in and around Fryeburg the number of brooks of any size is limited. While there are numerous ravines among the hills, which at certain seasons of the year are water courses, the number of steadily-flowing small brooks is few. From around Stark's Hill one on the south side flows across the "Nebraska", or Haley Neighborhood Road, under the railroad track, and under the highway from Fryeburg to Conway close to the State line; on the northeastern side is Choat's Brook, a little stream that begins in the morass at the foot of the hill and crosses the road at the foot of a little rise on the edge of the village.

Another brook that empties into Lovewell's Pond is known as "Fight Brook", because it is mentioned in the historic account of the fight between the Rangers under Lovewell and the Pequawket Indians. It has its rise in the height of land between Jockey Cap and Highland Park Hill. It crosses three highways, and at times of freshets easily overflows.

From Jockey Cap Ridge, in a little dismal swamp on the height of ground, comes a little stream, that weaves its way northwestward, across the main road to Lovell, emptying into the Saco. It is known as the "Moosehorn" brook, and as the old town way crossed through it, it became a familiar watering place for horses. It furnishes a boundary between a meadow and the tract of land known as "The Moosehorn", where for a number of years were the Maine Chautauqua Union Assembly grounds.

One of the largest brooks is "Ballard", formerly "Ingall's" Brook, which has its rise in the hills northwest of West Fryeburg, flowing to Saco river. It was a mill brook from early times, as there John Webster and Edward Shirley built a saw and grist mill in 1793. In more recent years it was familiarly known as "Locke's Mill," from a large saw mill built by S. B. Locke. This is now an active scene of lumber-sawing.

At the north part of the town is Kimball's Brook, which drains Kimball Pond, in Chatham, into Charles Pond, just on the border of Stow, but comes into Fryeburg at the village of North Fryeburg, near the Corn-packing establishment.

In the eastern section of the town is Elkins' Brook, the boundary between Fryeburg and Bridgton, which cuts off the corner of the area originally expected to be in the grant and empties into Kezar Pond. Another brook emptying into Kezar Pond, on the east side, is Dock Brook, which rises in Sweden.

Two small brooks have a place on the map, though of no great importance; Pray's which flows from Lovell into the Old River, below Toll Bridge; and Popple, which rises in Sweden and flows into Kezar River, thence into the Saco.

There are many physical characteristics in the township which time has changed or even obliterated. Among them, more noticeable because in the village the open spaces are more common, is the old water course that made a little pond southwest of Oxford Street, where a saw mill stood originally, later the first building of Isaiah Warren's tannery. This little pond was sufficient to float the logs that were used in the saw mill, and afterward it furnished water to the tannery. For many years after the tannery was gone a swampy pool remained, supporting a luxuriant growth of rushes.

This same water course was in evidence on the other side of Oxford Street, near the second tannery building, where it stood for years as a stagnant pool. No outlet was visible in continuation of this brooklet, but that there still are underground springs along this vein appears from the water that flows in a small stream near the corner of Portland and Warren streets. It is a part of the water system which flows into Lovewell's Brook, above the mill pond, and keeps the "Death Hole" still an active bog.

A little thread of a brook which has its rise in the wilderness between the railroad and Smith Street crosses the street and flows toward Lovewell's Brook, under Fair Street in a swampy channel.

It is evidently from a spring beneath Stark's Hill, as it never dries in summer.

During the occupation of the Moosehorn area as Martha's Grove Camp Ground, a driven well in the grounds revealed a source of spring water, having its origin in the hills to the eastward, which proved remarkably cool and was a source of much enjoyment to those who occupied the grounds. This spring, used only in the summer, proved never-failing, and it had a more than local reputation for its purity.

Edwin F. Vose, M.D., of Portland, in 1885 called attention to the needlessness of going from Maine to noted springs of Virginia, Arkansas, or Saratoga, N. Y., when Maine has springs whose water is as valuable in correcting internal disorders. He wrote of this spring in part,

> The writer has had repeated opportunity to test the curative action of the Martha's Grove spring water on mucous membranes particularly, and finds those of stomach and bladder peculiarly susceptible to its influence. Nervous dyspepsia and nervous irritability of the bladder come within its sphere of action to a marked degree.

A chemical analysis of the water was made by the State Assayer:

> One U. S. gallon contains 4.13 grains of mineral matter. This consists of
>> Sodium Sulphate.
>> Sodium Chloride.
>> Iron Bicarbonate.
>> Magnesium Sulphate and
>> Calcium Bicarbonate,
>
> Only the slightest trace of vegetable matter was found. A large amount of dissolved carbonic acid and air is present. Its effect on the system would be that of a mild tonic and laxative. It is remarkably pure water and one of the best for drinking.
>
> S. K. Hitchings, State Assayer.

The site of the spring could be found probably without much difficulty. It is one of several springs which underlie the area, and flow to or under the river. Another course of an underground spring made an outlet into the river, where the water was exceedingly cold to a bather, and undermined the bank. This spring supplied the kitchen and dining room, during the Assemblies.

An undeveloped mineral spring of indeterminate qualities is known to exist on the Hutchins farm, in West Fryeburg. A spring that never has failed exists near the house of the late Thomas Abbott, on Pine Street, in the Village.

It has been stated, on the authority of some of the older inhabitants, that prior to 1840 there were two "runs" across Portland Street, one between the present residence of Mrs. Weeks and Mrs. Warren and the Isaiah Warren house, and the other beyond the Warren house. There are still evidences of these runs on either side of the street, but at the period mentioned it was possible for any one sitting on the piazza of the Eastman store, on Main Street, opposite Portland Street, to see the stagecoach coming from Portland on the rise of ground after crossing the brook by Ward's Mill, and then to lose sight of it twice, in these two runs, before it reached Main Street.

The fact that a four-horse coach could go out of sight in those runs shows their width and depth.

While at some time all these water courses were probably active little brooks, the natural course of events assisted by improvement of the streets, has caused them to become filled, and their places are now known only to the oldest inhabitants. Today, between Choats Brook and the Moosehorn Brook, there is but one active water course in the village limits. That the sub-stratum is filled with little springs of water is evidenced by the condition of the intervales, near the high bank of the village, where the ground is damp and meadowy, needing to be drained in order to produce good crops.

> O mountains, back to your grand fastnesses,
>   As once our fathers, so we turn today;
> Alone unchanged, your mighty brotherhood
>   Watches the generations pass away;
> Yet, all untroubled, in your purple state,
> Ye hold your watch toward the sunset gate!
> Still in your loyal arms ye clasp the valley,
>   And hear the song the murmuring Saco sings;
> Still to the hurtling storms ye bare your helmets,
>   Dashing the hail their scurrying legion flings.
> Calm in your shadow rest our dear departed;
> Sleep sweet, O tender, strong, and loyal-hearted!
>   —*Rebecca Perley Reed.*

XV

FRYEBURG IN THE WARS

"Who dares?"—this was the patriot's cry,
As striding from the desk he came,—
"Come out with me, in Freedom's name,
For her to live, for her to die?"
A hundred hands flung up reply,
A hundred voices answered, "I!"
—*Thomas Buchanan Read.*

That the first settlers were men of strong character and not afraid of Indians or any other enemies in their new location is evident from the number of them who had seen service in the French and Indian wars, especially in Rogers' Rangers, that noted body of men who followed Indian tactics with such success. Like so many of the settlers of New England, "They feared God, and dismissed all other fear".

David and John Evans were both members of Rogers' Rangers, John holding the rank of Sergeant. Both participated in the disastrous expedition sent by General Amherst against the St. Francis Indians, and were among the few survivors of the terrible homeward march through the wilderness, where the greater number perished from exposure and starvation.

John Evans told of his experiences with Rogers: at St. Francis the rangers were ordered to kill all women and children. He went first, and came to a papoose who looked him in the face, and he couldn't kill it, so passed it by. Rogers asked why he did not kill it. Evans told him he could not. Rogers said, "Nits will be lice", and killed the child.

On the march back, for fourteen days Evans ate nothing but roots and herbs. When he got home on a Friday, he went to see all his friends and neighbors, and ate with them; he ate until they told him to leave off. Between the time he arrived and Saturday night, he had eaten twenty-two times. The next day, Sunday he did not go to meeting. Mrs. Evans said "He wasn't very well."

Other veterans of Rogers' Rangers, who saw hard service were: William Stark, brother of General John; Nathaniel Merrill and David Page, these two carried wounds; Daniel Farrington; Nathaniel Hutchins; Samuel Osgood.

Colonel Frye, had extensive service in the French and Indian Wars. Other settlers who served in those wars were: Col. John Webster; James Osgood; Lieut. John Walker; Capt. Vere Royce, a British officer; Simon Frye.

Nathaniel Hutchins was captain of a company in the French and Indian War, and at one time was in command of a fort in Canada which he was obliged to surrender to the French. When his sword was demanded in surrender, he broke it into three pieces across his knee, and threw them away, saying as he did so, "I'll see you damned first". Hutchins and Walker were with Arnold at Quebec. Walker came back with two others through the wilderness to the Androscoggin valley, coming out to civilization at Brunswick. They ran out of provisions, and finding the remains of a young moose left by the wolves, they managed to get enough meat to keep them from starving. They even were forced to boil their mooseskin breeches, and eat them. They were so weakened at the last that they could not get up the bank of the river without help.

Lieutenant Webster was obliged to surrender, and was stripped of his clothes by the Indians. He concealed his watch and silver shoe buckles about his person in such a way that they escaped the observation of the Indians. He feigned lameness, which was made actual by the chafing of his watch. The Indians thought that from the way he walked he had some disease, and avoided him. He was obliged to wear old garments that the Indians cast off, which were shabby and infested by vermin. He managed to make his escape and reached his home. The buckles he had saved were afterward melted with other silver, and cast into spoons, which were handed down through generations of the family.

The War of the Revolution came twelve years after Fryeburg began to be settled. There were nearly sixty families scattered through the township, and the town was called upon by the General Court of Massachusetts to furnish men for the army and clothing for the soldiers. Each town was expected to equip its own quota. Requisitions were constantly made for shoes, stockings, coats, shirts and pants. These supplies had to be made by the people, as there were no factories. The selectmen had accounts with thirty different families for making clothing for the army. This clothing was all made from home-grown wool. The wool required carding into rolls, for spinning into yarn. The yarn was woven in home-made looms, and all the processes of converting the sheep's wool into cloth was done by hand. The labor was by no means small, and it interfered with the supply for the family.

The town had appropriated money as it had been required, and had furnished soldiers and their equipment, without complaint, but when in 1779, the General Court imposed a tax of £5,975, 15 shillings, 9 pence and 3 farthings, the people of the little town felt that too much was being asked of them. A town meeting was called for September 8, 1779, and a committee of five was chosen to present a remonstrance to the Great and General Court.

State of Massachusetts Bay,
To the Honorable the Council and Honorable House of Representatives in General Court Assembled.

The remonstrance of the inhabitants of the town of Fryeburg humbly shows; That we, your remonstrants, being so fully pursuaded in our minds that the war in which the United American States are engaged is just, that we are not only willing but desirous of bearing such a part of the expenses thereof as from a due consideration of our ability in this remote place it shall appear to be our just proportion. But to pay the tax of five thousand, nine hundred and seventy-five pounds, fifteen shillings and nine pence, three farthings, which we are called upon for, and in a tax-act is called our proportion of two millions, eight hundred and thirty-seven thousand, six hundred and thirteen pounds, twelve shillings and eight pence, two farthings, is much greater sum than is our power to pay; and with due submission to your honours, take leave to say that we humbly conceive that had there a true account and valuation of our interest in this obscure part of the State been returned to your honours, it would very evidently appeared our proportion of that sum would not be so great. Such a return would have been made had we ever been called upon for it (as we imagine all other incorporated towns in the State were); but we were not. We thought we had reason to conclude, your honours, have considered us (as we really are) in a state of infancy and at such a great distance from the place at which the return must have been made, that you compassionately spared us the expense of it and concluded to lay such a sum upon us as in your wisdom you should judge such a place could bear; and we are confident you would have so done had not reports (as we are informed) made your honours believe our ability to be much greater than in fact it is; the truth whereof we trust we shall hereby make appear and also that the people who propogated these reports were strangers to the true state of our interest and circumstances in life. And in order to show they must be so, your remonstrants beg leave to inform your honours that, being much surprised at the call for such a heavy tax, they caused a town meeting to be called and when met we chose a committee to take a true account of our estates, which they have done, and we take leave to give your honours a view thereof in the following manner:

1-ly. It having been reported (as we often hear) that there has been a great quantity of bread-corn sold out of this place the present year, and consequently a great deal of money must be among us, we, by our committee, have examined strictly into the affair, and find that all that has been sold out of Conway, out of Brownfield and all the places in the Pigwaket country is reported to be sold out of Fryeburg. What quantity it all amounts to we can not tell, but with regard to Fryeburg alone, we find by the strictest examination which could be made by our committee, that there has been sold out of it, of the last year's growth of every sort of bread-corn we raise, no more than three hundred and sixty bushels, as by said committee's account herewith exhibited will appear, all of which was bartered for salt, cotton-wool, shoe leather, iron and such other necessaries as we can not live without, except 53 bushels were sold for money and that money (which is but a small matter) was carried out of town and laid out for the same sort of necessaries above enumerated, so that there is no balance left in our hands from the sale of bread-corn to help pay the tax.

2-ly. Your honours have exhibited herewith, another paper containing an exact account of all the horses, stock of meat-cattle, sheep and swine we possessed the first day of February last, taken by the selectmen of this town in order to a just proportion among us of the State tax, then laying upon the town, and it is near the same now; for the destruction made by the wolves among our sheep, keeps back the increase of them and there are but very few calves raised among us last spring, so that there can be but very little odds in our stock between that and this time. And as there are sixty-nine families in town and most of their houses replenished with young children, your honours will plainly see that very little compared with the tax in question can be taken from our stock to help pay it without stopping our plows, starving and freezing those young families. And since the States are endeavoring to bring our paper currency into repute (in which it is to be hoped they will have success), may we not rationally suspect that the whole of our stock will fall short of paying the tax? And if the whole stock must be taken from us and more too, the town will soon be blotted out of the book of remembrance, for it will be rendered (to our sorrow) unable to do any further service to the State.

3-ly. Your honours have one more paper herewith exhibited, which contains a true amount of all the lands under improvement in the whole town, which you will find is but 1168½ acres; and that land, with the smiles of heaven on the labor we bestow thereon, is all we have at present upon the face of the earth to draw subsistence from, for our families and stock and to pay all sorts of taxes. For we can not raise a single farthing out of our wilderness-land, we have no market for a stick of firewood or timber so that we can reap no profit from that land till by hard labor we can remove the heavy spontaneous growth thereon, and then by further hard labor bring in some profit; but it's long before we can bring it to be so, compared with what might be made of the wood or timber growing thereon, had we a market for the same, as those have for theirs who live near the sea coast. So that we who are confined to the said 1168½ acres to draw from them subsistence for our families and money to pay every kind of tax; and to pay the aforesaid tax of 5975 pounds, 15 shillings, 9 pence and 3 farthings brings it upon us to pay out of each of those identical acres the sum of 5 pounds, 2 shillings, 3 pence and 3 farthings to raise that sum, besides subsistence for our families and money to pay town and county charges, which is impossible to be done. Wherefore your said remonstrants pray your honours would take the premises under consideration and bring said tax down to such a sum as shall appear by the account of our estates and circumstances herewith exhibited as is our just proportion of the State tax above mentioned and as in duty bound prays.

Fryeburg, Sept. 8th, 1779.

>Joseph Frye.
>Richard Kimball.
>Joseph Frye Jr.
>Moses Ames.
>Isaac Walker.
>>Committee per order of and
>>on behalf of said town.

This remonstrance when presented to the town was considered highly satisfactory, and General Frye was chosen to lay the remonstrance and petition before the Great and General Court.

The Revolutionary War saw under arms again some of those who had previously served; among them were Capt. Nathaniel Hutchins, Lieut. John Walker, Gen. Joseph Frye. Those who served that hard winter at Valley Forge included: Ebenezer Farrington, Trueworthy Kilgore, Peter Coffin, Mason Wiley, Joseph Pettengill, Supply Walker, Timothy Walker, James Kilgore, Stephen Knight, Isaac Abbott.

Abbott had been in the army for some six months, and was full of the vigor of a young and husky man. An incident is told of him, in the *New England Magazine,* in an article about Fryeburg. During the service with Washington of Baron Von Steuben, as Inspector General, he was building an army out of comparatively green countrymen.

When Baron Steuben wanted a special detachment of picked men for a dangerous undertaking, he mustered the army, telling all veterans to put a sprig of green in their hats, and every man to look him in the eye. Abbott was a young man, and had been with the army only a short time, but he was anxious to go, so he donned the green, and looked the stern old Baron in the eye. Steuben passed down the line and, returning, clapped Abbott on the shoulder and drew him out of the rank—the first man of all.

He joined the Army while it was at West Point, one of the two men required from Fryeburg. He served in Colonel Putnam's Regiment, and was the tallest man but one in the regiment.

Others who had various service were: Joshua Gammage, Joseph Knight, Capt. Joseph Frye, Jr., Lieut. Nathaniel Frye, David Pettee, William Eaton, John Fifield, Jonathan Dresser, Levi Dresser, Simeon Dresser, William Evans, David Evans, Jonathan Smith, Daniel Harper, Benjamin Patten.

Stephen Farrington, Isaac Abbott, and John Evans participated in the response to the call of Bethel, in 1781 when the Indians attacked some of the residents, and Evans went twice after that.

Many of these men who lived and died in Fryeburg, lie at rest now in the little cemeteries in the town, and on Memorial Day their graves are not forgotten, but bear a little flag of the United States of America, which they helped to make possible.

In recapitulation, the Honor Roll of the men of Fryeburg who served in the French and Indian and the Revolutionary Wars is as follows:

In Rogers' Rangers,
David Evans
John Evans
Daniel Farrington
Nathaniel Hutchins,
Nathaniel Merrill
Samuel Osgood,
David Page,
  In the Line Regiments,
Col. Joseph Frye

Capt. Nathaniel Hutchins
Lieut. John Walker
Col. John Webster
James Osgood.
Simon Frye.
  Served in other Forces:
Capt. Vere Royce,
               British Army,
Edward Shirley,
               British Navy.

FRYEBURG IN THE WARS 159

Revolutionary War:
Gen. Joseph Frye
Capt. Joseph Frye, Jr.
Lieut. Nathaniel Frye
Capt. Nathaniel Hutchins
Lieut. John Webster
Caleb Swan, Jr.
Peter Coffin
William Eaton
John Fifield
William Evans
Ebenezer Farrington
Jonathan Dresser
Levi Dresser
Simeon Dresser
James Kilgore
Trueworthy Kilgore
Joseph Knight
Stephen Knight
David Pettee
Joseph Pettengill
Supply Walker
Timothy Walker
Mason Wiley
William Wiley
Isaac Abbott
Uriah Ballard

When the issues which led to the War of 1812 with Great Britain began to develop New England in general was not so enthusiastic over the situation as to show much military interest, but as the war went on and employment became less, there was more inducement for idle men to go with the colors. No active enlistment began in Fryeburg before 1814, when the danger of a possible attack drew the military companies from the surrounding country to the support of Portland, and most of the service was performed between the dates of June 24, and September 24, 1814.

This is the roster of the Artillery company raised at Fryeburg for this service:

Captain, James Charles
Lieutenant, Joseph Colby.
Ensign, Benjamin Woodman.
Sergt. Nathaniel G. Jewett.
Sergt. Jeremiah Bradley.
Sergt. Isaac Charles.
Sergt. Hall Chase.
Sergt. Jeremiah Chandler.
Sergt. Nehemiah C. Dresser.
Corp. Benjamin Wiley.
Corp. Seth S. Chase.
Corp. Moses Abbott.
Corp. John Stevens.
Corp. William Stevens.

Asa Abbott
Micah Abbott
Isaac Abbott
Silas Abbott
Amos Bemis
David Bradley
Isaac Burgin
Isaac Chandler
John Chandler
Nathan Chandler
John Charles
Simeon Charles
Joshua Gamage, Jr.
John Gordon
Henry Gordon, Jr.
William Harwood
Joseph Gordon
Samuel Hatch
Amos Hill
Daniel Hill
Samuel D. Huntress
Ichabod Hutchins
Stephen Irish
Andrew Johnson
Samuel Tibbetts
William Thompson
John Walker, Jr.
Nathaniel Warren
America Wiley
John Wiley
Oliver Whiting, Jr.
Samuel Wiley
Job Wiley
Isaac Charles
John Charles, Jr.
Samuel Dutch

Timothy Charles	James Johnson	Philip Farrington
David Coombs	Eliphalet Knight	Jonathan F. Fifield
Job Dresser	Jesse Lewis	William Hapgood
William Eaton	John Marden	Joseph Stevens
Jonathan Evans	John Mason	Quartermaster William
Jonathan Farrington	Joshua Richardson	Russell, and Surgeon
Samuel Farrington	Luther Richardson	Moses Chandler of
Stephen Farrington	Jordon Stacey	the staff of the Artil-
Benjamin Fifield	Oliver Stacey	lery Battalion served
Frederic Frye	John S. Sterns	at Portland, June 13
Ephraim Fox	Asa Smith	to June 24.
John Gammage	Joseph Swan	

At the same time a second company of Artillery went from Fryeburg to Portland, the roster of which was:

Captain Philip Eastman
Lieutenant Ebenezer Fessenden
Lieutenant John Evans
Sergt. Abiel Farnham
Sergt. Isaac Frye
Sergt. Noyes Knight
Sergt. William Shirley

Corp. Thomas Day
Corp. Abel Gibson
Corp. James Atwood
Corp. Thomas Farrington
Musician John Page
Musician Jacob Emerson

Stephen Abbott
George Brooks
Jonas Brown
Samuel F. Carter
Enoch S. Chase
Robert Colby
Jacob Evans
Jonathan Fessenden
William Fessenden
Jacob Farrington
William Frye
Stephen G. Hardy
John Hatch
Ebenezer Haseltine
Asa Head

John W. Heath
Senaca Howe
John Hutchins
Jonathan Hardy
John Knight
Israel Lassells
Ebenezer McIntire
James Osgood, Jr.
Isaac Osgood
Caleb Richardson
Jonathan Shirley
John Sterling, Jr.
Benjamin Walker
Jonathan Ward
Isaiah Warren

Staff officers of the 2nd Brigade who served at Portland were: Brig. Gen. John McMillan, commanding brigade; Joshua B. Osgood, Brigade Major; James W. Ripley, Brigade Quartermaster; Enoch Lincoln, Aide de Camp.

Neither town or state records show how long, these troops served, or how many of them served through the war. John W. Heath is known to have served the entire war, and was at the battle of Sackett's Harbor.

Major Philip Eastman was the originator of the "Eastern Artillery", and was its first Captain, about 1810. The Lieutenants were Eben Fessenden and Obed Kimball. The ordnance was two brass three pounders; beautiful pieces and well mounted. The "Gun House", stood on the ground later owned by Rev. Carlton Hurd, and now the Alumni House of Fryeburg Academy. It was moved several times after the company was disbanded. Other men who later were officers of this Artillery company were: Captain William Fessenden, Captain Isaac Frye, Lieutenant John S. Barrows, (whose chapeau and sword are still preserved).

When this company was ordered to Portland in September 1814, Abiel Farnum, one of the members, set out to notify others, and went by night to Denmark and Bridgton. It was high water over the Island, but he waded across, and at Ingalls' notified Isaiah Warren. Then he went on to Perley's in Bridgton, and notified Eben Fessenden to be at Fryeburg at 6 o'clock the next morning. Isaiah Warren reported for duty, on time, fully outfitted and supplied with rations. The company left about 4 A.M. that day. They stopped at Stickney's tavern in Brownfield, for rest and refreshments. They arrived at Portland where they were stationed at Fort Burroughs, which was situated where now are the shops of the Portland Company.

Regimental, and even Divisional Musters, were held at Fryeburg. The regiment formed near the Old Meeting House, and marched through the street to the muster-field, which at times was on the intervale, back of the Oxford House. Sometimes it was further down on the intervale, near the "Beaver Dam".

The Artillery trained on the open field below Warren's tannery. There is a tradition that they used Jockey Cap as a target at some time.

Since those days Fryeburg has never had a military company, but has maintained its honor in wars that followed by a full quota of those required in the service. The Civil War, the War with Spain, and the World War, were all supported by Fryeburg men with willingness and spirit.

Fryeburg answered the call of President Lincoln for volunteers by a hearty response. Beside those who volunteered in the Maine Regiments, there were a number of Fryeburg men in other states who enlisted in local organizations. Many of those who entered the armies paid the soldier's debt and fill honorable graves.

The list herewith gives the names of those who were in the Fryeburg quotas, and as far as possible the Regiment is given:

Name	Regt.	Name	Regt.
Lafayette Alexander,		George Johnson,	
Charles Andrews,	13th.	Joseph H. Johnson,	
Henry Andrews,		William H. Johnson,	
James Andrews,	11th.*	Andrew Kenison, Jr.,	12th.
George Austin,	12th.*	John Kennedy,	
Edwin Bailey,	16th.	Patrick Lawless,	17th.
Amadel Barbour,	11th.	Harris A. P. Lewis,	23rd.
John P. Barker,	12th.	Nelson Lewis,	23rd.
Webster Barker,	17th.	Hazen Lewis,	16th.
Willard Barker,	12th.*	William Lewis,	23rd.
Henry Battery,		Augustus F. Long,	17th.
Peter Beckley,		Augustus J. Lord,	35th.
Richard Bradley, Lieut.,	23rd.	Charles H. Lovis,	23rd.
Charles H. Bragdon,	12th.	Michael McCarty,	
William Bragdon,		James McGuire,	
John Burke,		John McGuire,	
Levi Butters,	16th.	Asa S. McIntire,	
Humphrey A. Chadbourn,	23rd.	Joshua C. McIntire,	23rd.
		Oliver G. McIntire,	23rd.
Horace Chandler,	23rd.	Samuel F. McIntire,	9th.*
Stephen Chandler,	23rd.	Frank McKay,	
Frank C. Charles,	17th.†	Joseph Mitchell,	7th.
Moses L. Charles,	17th.	Joseph Morin,	
Sewall C. Charles,	12th.	Sidney G. Morton,	17th.
Stephen Charles,	12th.†	William B. Morton,	17th.
Walter A. Charles, Corp.	23rd.	Simon Muckley,	
		James Murphy,	
Enoch S. Chase,	17th.	George W. Nichols,	
Orville Clough,		James L. Nichols,	
Steven F. Clough,		Harry G. Norton,	
Abner A. Cole,	13th.	Michael O'Connell,	
James B. Cole,	16th.†	Albert S. Palmer,	
Thomas D. Cook,	12th.	Francis R. Parker,	
Richard Connor,		Ebenezer Pickering,	23rd.
Sam'l R. Crocker, Comm. Sergt.	23rd.	Daniel Powers,	
		John Quinan,	
William W. Devine, Jr.,	12th.*	Monroe Quint,	17th.
Andrew J. Eastman,	23rd.	Albion Richardson,	17th.
Robert Eastman,	12th.†	John Riley,	
James Eaton,	12th.	John Rose,	

* Died.
† Discharge.

Fryeburg in the Wars

David W. Ela,
Simeon A. Evans,
   Hospital, 13th.
Seth C. Farrington,
   Capt. 12th.
S. A. Farrington, Serg., 12th.
John C. Fellows,
   1st. and 9th.*
William R. Fifield, 23rd.**
Thomas Frazier,
Joseph Frye, Jr., 23rd.
William H. Frye, Corp., 11th.
William Gilman, 10th.
William H. Gordon, 1st.
Angevine Gray, 11th.
Melville Gray, 5th.
Richard L. Greenlaw, 9th.
Isiah Guptill, Cavalry, 1st.
Stephen H. Guptill,
   1st. and 12th.
Gilson A. Hall, 23rd.
Samuel H. Harnden, 9th.
George Harris,
John Harvey,
William S. Heald,
Charles W. Heath, 23rd.
Joseph Heath, 6th.**
John L. Hill, 23rd.
Enoch W. B. Hobbs, 23rd.
Lewis C. Hobbs, 23rd.*
Samuel C. Holden, 17th.
James G. Holt, 17th.
Thomas K. Holt, 9th.
William Holt, 9th.**
James M. Howe, Jr.,
   2nd. Lieut. 23rd.
Simeon C. Howe, 17th.
Samuel Ilsley, Serg., 12th.*
Willard M. Jenkins, 17th.*
James T. Jenner, Corp., 12th.
Daniel Johnson, 23rd.

Leonard P. Rounds, 11th.
Edgar C. Stevens,
Job L. Sanborn, 23rd.
Benjamin G. Seavey, 23rd.
Marcus M. Smart, 16th.
William T. Smart, 23rd.**
Abial F. Smith, 23rd.
Benjamin Smith,
Daniel Smith, Jr., 17th.
James F. Smith, 9th.
Ivory F. Snow, 17th.
Isaac Spiller, 23rd.
John L. Stanley, 17th.
Samuel C. Stanley, 17th.
John P. Stevens, 23rd.**
John Stiles,
Alfred E. Thomas, 17th.
Benjamin Thompson, 9th.
George W. Thompson,
John W. Tibbetts, 23rd.
William C. Towle,
   Surgeon.
Alden B. Walker, 17th.
Dexter Walker,
John B. Walker, 2nd.
John S. Walker,
   Asst. Paymaster. 17th.
Joseph C. Walker,
   Serg. 17th.*
Wiley Walker, 23rd.
James E. Webster, 23rd.
Joseph Wiley, 17th.
Stephen J. Wiley, 23rd.
Sullivan J. Wiley,
   Serg. 12th.
William H. Wiswell,
Lozien Poor, 11th.
Samuel Frye,
Harrison G. Morton,
G. H. Richardson,
Reuben H. Small,

* Died.
† Discharge.
**Rejected for disability.

These men enlisted in other States, and are entitled to be considered among Fryeburg's offering:

John Andrews,	Wisconsin Cavalry, *
Edward Ballard,	Attendant Carver Hospital.
Eckley Ballard,	Attendant Carver Hospital.
George W. Cook,	Massachusetts.
Orland Day,	New Hampshire.
John L. Eastman,	2nd. New Hampshire.
Seth W. Eastman,	Winsconsin Cavalry.
Hazen O. Frost,	Wisconsin.
Daniel V. Gray,	Massachusetts.
John C. Gray,	Massachusetts.
Charles E. Lord,	9th Battery, Massachusetts.
Enoch B. Lord,	9th Battery, Massachusetts.
Charles Mansfield,	United States Army.
Charles Osgood,	8th Battery, Massachusetts.
George Richardson,	United States Army.
Ruben W. Shirley,	9th Battery, Massachusetts.
Samuel Souther,	9th Battery, Massachusetts.
John W. Towle,	Rhode Island.
Isaac Walker,	Cavalry, Rhode Island.
Jonathan Webster,	United States Navy.
John Wiley,	Massachusetts.
William H. Wiley,	Massachusetts.
Samuel E. Gordon,	New Hampshire.
Augustus Lord,	Massachusetts.
E. Pickering,	New Hampshire.
John H. Wiley,	Massachusetts.
William Wiley,	Massachusetts.
Charles H. Powers,	Lieutenant, Pennsylvania, *

These men were drafted under the Call of July, 1863:

Caleb Atwood,	Nathaniel R. Hardy,	Wm. B. Richardson,
Charles R. Blanchard,	Ira T. Jack,	Charles E. Stevens,
Charles F. Barker,	George H. Lord,	Lowell B. Sampson,
Joseph F. Coe,	Isaac W. Lord,	Seth Stevens,
James E. Chandler,	Ivory J. Lewis,	Jason W. Towle,
F. W. Day,	John C. Merrill,	Dean H. Wiley,
Harrison G. Morton,	Edward McIntire,	Samuel Wiley,
Andrew H. Evans,	Wm. W. McNeil,	C. W. Waterhouse, Jr.,
Charles W. Frye,	Charles H. Osgood,	James M. Weeks,
Stephen Farrington,	John J. Pike,	Joseph Wiley,
Caleb Frye,	Thomas S. Pike,	John Ward.
Frank F. Hutchins,	Sewall N. Richards,	

* Died.

In more recent years the veterans of Fryeburg and vicinity organized Grover Post, Number 126, of the Maine Department of the Grand Army of the Republic, with a membership of 130. The usual duties of such a Post were conducted; Memorial Day was strictly observed as long as the comrades were able to meet and decorate graves, assisted by the Sons of Veterans, and after the World War by the members of the Legion.

Through the efficient work of some members of the Post, aided by interested citizens, two obsolete cannon were procured from Fort Knox, and established as memorials "To the Soldiers of Fryeburg", on the land of Bradley Memorial Park at the corner of Main and River Streets, where their grim muzzles point to the two approaches to the village from the southwest and northwest.

The first officers of Grover Post were: Commander, William C. Towle; Senior Vice Commander, John Fox; Junior Vice Commander, Ezekiel W. Burbank; Officer of the Day, Tobias L. Eastman; Quartermaster, George T. Marriner; Chaplain, Caleb Wiley; Officer of the Guard, Joseph J. Johnson; Adjutant, J. F. Stearns.

This Post in 1916 furnished, in the person of Comrade Tobias L. Eastman, the Commander of the Maine Department of the Grand Army of the Republic.

Grover Post is now disbanded, its members having followed one another into the "low green tent whose portal never outward swings", but their memory is honored, and the duties of Memorial Day are performed by the Fryeburg Camp of the American Legion, which built a brick headquarters on Portland Street, and maintains its organization in the Village.

Fryeburg had no distinct unit in the War with Spain, as practically all the volunteers who made up the army were National Guardsmen. The military organizations of the state enlisted as a body, and the increase was from men who volunteered to make up the unit to war strength. But Fryeburg was well-represented in that hundred-days war by several young men, former Academy boys, who enlisted and served in different organizations, some of them in other states, and in the navy. The list is as complete as is known:

Lieut. J. Waldo Nash, 1st Maine; Fred W. Sawtelle, 1st Maine; Earle Brown, 1st Maine; Lieut. Lewis M. Walker, Asst. Surgeon, U.S.A.; Ralph Eastman, Mass. Coast Artillery; Ralph Willey,

5th Mass. Infy.; Philip E. Abbott, 6th Mass. Infy.; Ensign Bertrand R. T. Collins, U.S.S. Scorpion, U.S.N.; James W. Eastman, U.S.S. Montauk, U.S.N.; Owen P. Smith, U.S.S. Montauk, U.S.N.

These men continued through their enlistment, though few went outside this country. After the war Dr. Walker continued in the Government service, in care of insane and injured men; Collins continued in the Illinois Naval Brigade; the others retired to private life. Eastman served in the "Milliken Regiment" as Captain and Adjutant in the World War.

Fryeburg Academy was well represented in the World War by men in this and other state's units, as commissioned officers and enlisted men. Frank W. Shaw, for whom the Camp of the American Legion at Fryeburg is named, went out in the Milliken Regiment, but was transferred to the 101st Engineers, the First Corps Cadets Regiment in the Massachusetts contingent. He died of wounds received in one of the allied drives. He was the son of George Shaw, of North Fryeburg.

Ralph W. Shirley, another former Academy boy, like Shaw, was killed in action at Ravin Gobert, near Lucy-le-Bocage, Aisne. He was not credited to Fryeburg because he enlisted in Massachusetts, from Conway.

When the call to the World War came to Maine, Fryeburg responded as was to be expected. The quota was not so large as for the Civil War, but the town is credited as having eighty-two men in the Military service in various capacities and units. From the eighty-four native-born residents of draft age, fifty-four volunteers responded to the first call to the colors. Of this fifty-four reporting, thirty-five were accepted, including some already in France. Men who are accredited to Fryeburg are as follows:

Andrews, Langdon F.	McElroy, Harry D.
Ballard, Jackson H.	McLellan, Charles S.
Barker, Albion G.	Mason, Oliff E.
Barker, Walter D.	Newman, George B.
Bean, Fred W.	Nute, Philip C.
Bell, Merton L.	Osgood, Carrol M.
Bosworth, Wilfred H.	Osgood, Henry D.
Byron, Parker D.	Pease, Ernest A.
Carter, Donald W., Capt.	Philbrook, Harry I.
Chandler, Thomas P.	Pinkham, Ivory O.
Chapman, John E.	Pitman, Merle W.

Cheney, True P.
Davis, Robert N.
Dyer, Henry L.
Eastman, James W., Capt.
Ekstrom, Frank C.
Ela, Lyman E.
Flint, Henry S.
Forest, Arthur S.
Hale, Truman E.
Hall, Alonzo W.
Hastings, Hugh W., Capt.
Hill, Ralph W.
Hill, Roy W.
Howard, Alfred E.
Hurlin, Arthur M.
Hutchins, Harry L.
Hutchins, Richard K.
Jackson, Harvey L.
James, George P.
Jewett, Norman R.
Kenerson, Percival H.
Kerr, John W.
Kneeland, Victor L.
Knox, Frank E.
Knox, Wendell H.
*Leadbeater, John M.
*Lord, Henry M.
Lord, Herbert P.

Potter, Harold E.
Potter, John B.
Pratt, Harold B.
Ridlon, Preston R.
Robins, Cleveland O.
Roberts, Clifton E.
Roberts, George H.
Rogers, William L.
Sanborn, Lorenzo B.
Sargent, John E.
Savard, Albert J.
Sawyer, Arthur R.
Severance, George F.
*Shaw, Frank W.
Sherburne, Thomas R.
Shirley, Leon A.
Snow, Roy A.
Stone, Ralph
Thompson, Ralph W.
*Thurston, Fred R.
Towle, Howard E.
Walker, Lewis A.
Warren, Benjamin O., Lieut.
Wentworth, Herbert H.
Wiley, Herbert L.
Witham, Bertram L.
Woodbury, Victor A.

*Died in the service.

Many in the list came from neighboring towns, but as they enlisted there, were credited to Fryeburg.

Not all these men served in the Army, as the Navy appealed to a few. Several others were in the service, in units from other states, and so not included in the official returns of the Adjutant General: Erving Bell, George Booth, Herbert A. D. Hurd, Ernest Ridlon, Oramel Stanley, Ralph Webster.

Later residents of Fryeburg who were in the United States service, were Major Clayton W. Pike, Harry Chase, J. Edwin Smith.

It happened, in the formation of the "Milliken" Regiment as the first Maine Heavy Field Artillery, that Hugh W. Hastings of Fryeburg, brought in the company that completed the organization, and made it possible to form the regiment. Mr. Hastings, covering a comparatively sparsely-settled area in the vicinity of Fryeburg, succeeded in finding the required number of men, and was congratulated by the military authorities. His grandfather, Major David R. Hastings recruited an infantry company, in the vicinity of his home-town of Lovell, for the Civil War, and became Major in the regiment.

This company recruited in and around Fryeburg was marked for the stalwart appearance of the men who composed it. Mr. Hastings was made Captain of the company, which was designated by the letter D. In the progress of the regiment from Augusta, it landed at Camp Green, Charlotte, N. C., where in the early part of 1918 it was reorganized, and was made the 56th Pioneer Infantry, in the U. S. Expeditionary force. In this reorganization, Captain Hastings retained his company, which was given the letter I. As the senior captain of the battalion, for a time he was in command. Lieutenant Benjamin O. Warren of Fryeburg was assigned as a lieutenant in Company I, with Donald W. Carter, of North Conway, N. H. Captain James W. Eastman, who went out as Adjutant of the First Battalion, was given command of Company A, which was recruited largely in Portland. This regiment was fortunate in not suffering great losses during its service.

A branch of the Red Cross, was organized in Fryeburg, and did efficient service. The officers were: Chairman, Miss Harriet L. Abbott; Vice Chairman, Mrs. Virginia Perry; Treasurer, Miss Mary Hastings; Secretary, Miss Aimee Ballard; Executive Committee, Mrs. Lillian C. Hutchins, Mrs. Lucy C. Hodsdon.

Among natives of Fryeburg who met death in war, was John Page, who was born February 4, 1797. He entered the U. S. Army in 1818, as Second Lieutenant of the 8th Infantry, and the next year found him a First Lieutenant. He received a Captain's commission 30th April, 1831. He was with the 4th Infantry, in 1846, and while commanding the leading division of the regiment at the battle of Palo Alto, May 8, 1846, was under a galling fire from the Mexican Artillery. General Grant, in his Memoirs, page 60, says: "One cannon ball past through our ranks, not far from me. It took off the head of an enlisted man, and the under jaw of Captain Page, of my regiment." In the History of the War between the United States and Mexico, page 111, it says: "Captain Page of the 4th Infantry, which had been ordered to the support of Churchill's guns, also received a severe wound, under which he lingered for several weeks, but finally expired."

Captain Page built the house in the village, later occupied by Russell Page, for his mother and sisters.

A young man, who honored Fryeburg by his ability and military attainments, was Arthur Dow Newman, son of Mr. and Mrs. Benjamin T. Newman, the noted artist, and a grandson of Colonel Abel A. Gibson, U. S. A. Retired, a veteran of the Mexican and Civil Wars.

Arthur Newman was born in Fryeburg, graduated from the Academy, and entered Dartmouth College. While there he received an appointment to the U. S. Military Academy at West Point, from which he graduated with high honors in 1914. He was assigned to the Cavalry branch of the service, and saw active service with the army along the Mexican frontier in 1915-1917. He was highly commended for his ability by his superior officers. He was duly promoted to First Lieutenant. An unfortunate accident, while in a polo game at the army post at which he was stationed, resulted in his untimely death.

Colonel A. A. Gibson above referred to was a native of Brownfield, a graduate of the Military Academy, and after he retired from the service, for wounds, he spent much of his time in Fryeburg.

>Oh, long the day ere War's dark drops
>   Shall dim our laughing sky!
>Long ere our valley's emerald slopes
>   Shall learn the ruby dye!
>God grant no other blast may smite
>   New England's tossing pines,
>Than when His rolling thunder's might
>   Sweeps down their broken lines!
>
> *From a hymn by Kate Putnam Osgood, sung at the Centennial celebration, 1863.*

XVI

BUSINESS AND INDUSTRY

"My earliest recollections of Fryeburg (early 1800s) are of it as a business center. Fryeburg Corner was the business center for all the country around, and Saturday afternoon the village was so thronged, that we young people did not venture through the crowd, unless there was urgent need."

—*Mrs. Lucia Griswold Merrill.*

Fryeburg never has made any marked effort to be a large business place. The merchants have generally carried on business profitably, making a good living and accumulating something on which to retire. The business has been varied, and the stores have met the chief requirements of the people.

Colonel Frye opened the first general store, in his house on the hill. The first store at the Seven Lots was kept by Dr. Joseph Emery, who married a sister of Rev. William Fessenden. His establishment was on the Drift Road, about where now is the stable of the Fryeburg Tavern. He was charged with selling rum to the Indians who occasionally straggled into the settlement.

Jonathan Dresser conducted a business at his place on Fessenden Hill about 1790.

Robert Bradley and his brother John kept a store on Portland Street about 1800. Isaiah Warren went into partnership with John, later, and the firm did a large business for many years.

Captain Seth Spring of Biddeford came to the village, and in 1802 built a store on Portland Street, which is still in use as a grocery store. He was succeeded by his son Lewis Spring and John S. Chase, and later Chase carried on the business. This store was next occupied by Henry C. Buswell, who bought the building and carried on a general store, being succeeded by Edward Payson Weston, who on his death was followed by H. H. Burbank, and by John C. Harriman, who in turn on his death was followed by E. L. Skillings.

The locality around Main Street at the head of Portland Street was called "The Whirlpool," being the location of most of the trade. At one time Jacob Evans kept a store on Main Street opposite Portland. Major Timothy C. Ward had a flourishing business in a general store on the corner of Main and Portland Streets. His building was burned, and he built a larger building, with room for another store and in the second story for the Pythagorean Lodge of Free and Accepted Masons. After the death of Major Ward, the store was occupied by R. C. Harmon, with the first apothecary store in the town. The same space was used by the Post Office during several administrations. Later it was a store of fancy groceries and when it was vacated by the Post Office, it became a general store, until the building was burned. The adjoining store was originally occupied by E. C. Farrington, with Miss M. E. Gage, as a women's supply store, until he built on Main Street a larger store. This store was carried on later by Mrs. E. G. Fife until burned in August, 1906. The store occupied by Miss Gage became the Post Office after the office on Main Street was burned, and when vacated and enlarged, was the apothecary store of John C. Gerry, followed by the general store of J. T. Whittemore, which after his death was bought by George O. Warren, who kept a select store.

Charles H. Tibbetts had a general store in the Bradley & Warren building until he removed to the opposite side of the street, where later he built a store with a tenement in the second story. He was succeeded in the Bradley & Warren store by Gardiner Walker, with a general store. This same building was occupied by Shirley & Cousins with a grocery store for some time, and when they vacated, John C. Gerry opened his apothecary store on his first coming to Fryeburg. The building was burned later, but when rebuilt with two stores was occupied by the E. W. Burbank Seed Co., and after the fire of 1906 the other store was Mrs. E. G. Fife's millinery and dress goods store until her death. It was since then occupied by the Woodsides in the same general lines.

Eben Howe carried on a general store on Portland Street, which later was enlarged and conducted for many years as a millinery and ladies' supply store by Miss Mary S. Howe.

Following his brother Harry H., Nathaniel Randall kept a store in the building later occupied by Seth A. Page as a hardware and tinsmith business. Mr. Page and his son George carried on the only business of the kind for many years, until on their deaths Elmer Brackett succeeded to the business.

Nelson Gammage in 1853 built a store and tenement on a little lot near the Oxford House. He kept a general store, until he sold to Strout & Higgins, who carried on the business until they sold to Eben Weeks, who first established himself in the Warren store, until he became the owner of the Gammage store, where he did a large business until he sold to John Locke. Mrs. M. B. Barker was the last occupant with a millinery and fancy goods store.

Franklin Shirley, who had been in trade in West Fryeburg with his father, formed a partnership with Alonzo F. Lewis, and opened a general store near the corner of Main and Portland Streets, next to the Buswell store. When they dissolved partnership, Mr. Shirley went to Crawford, Neb., and Mr. Lewis gave his attention to his insurance business, and was engaged in literary pursuits. William Locke kept an exclusive shoe store in the building for a few years, and later Mrs. Sarah F. Ladd occupied it with dressmaking and women's supplies, until she gave up business. In 1935 Mr. Cressey opened a "5 and 10" store, which was enlarged and improved in 1938.

An industry of importance in the early days, common through rural New England, was the production of potash. The ample supply of wood, much of which had to be burned to clear the land for agriculture, produced plenty of ashes, from which the lye was made. When the industry ceased, the buildings used for the manufacture of the potash, being strongly framed, were used for other purposes. The house on Portland Street occupied by Deacon John Evans and destroyed in the great fire of 1906, was a potash built by an Osgood. Philip Page built one near the tannery, which was afterward converted into a dwelling. Captain John Page took one of these buildings for the ell of the house later the home of Russell Page and his daughter, Miss Abby. The buildings occupied by Philip Eastman, and by Peter Walker were originally Potashs.

Another industry was currying leather, and the Howe homestead on Portland Street was originally used in this work. So also, the blacksmith shop of Francis Willey, on Portland Street, which was replaced by the Fire Department building, was originally used in this industry.

For a time Portland Street was dubbed "Leather Lane" because of the number of leather-working establishments on it,—a tannery, currier shops, a harness maker, and cobbler shops.

John Evans had the first harness and saddlery shop in the village, in a building that he erected on Portland Street. The building was burned at the same time Major Ward's store was destroyed, but was re-built on the same site. Wallace R. Tarbox, who learned the trade with Deacon Evans, after his death continued the business for a number of years in an improved store and workshop. Later the business was carried on by Nathaniel Walker. In more recent years the store was taken by a branch of the First National Chain Stores. A Nation Wide Grocery store also is on Portland Street. A branch of the Great Atlantic & Pacific Tea Company opened a large store on Smith Street. On Oxford Street John Locke built a block containing two stores with apartments above. The stores have been occupied by a number of concerns, in 1938 by a shoe store and a shoe repair shop.

Francis A. Wiley, a veteran of the Civil War, opened in his house, which he built at the junction of Oxford and Smith Streets, a small confectionery and tobacco store, which proved so profitable that he built a large general store in the rear of his house, on Smith Street, which he later enlarged by building through to Oxford Street. In the second story he opened the "Diamond Skating Rink." He had a large business in general goods and groceries and as a shipper of potatoes, until he sold his business to William G. Spring and Son, who carried it on for some time. They were succeeded by Frank L. Mark, of Portland, an energetic business man, and he continued the business for a number of years, selling to Tobias L. Eastman & Son, who increased the trade materially. Mr. Eastman retiring from the firm, his son James W. Eastman continued in the business until his health failed, when he turned it over to his son, Robert, who later converted the store into a hardware concern.

James J. Rogers conducted a modest furniture business in his shop by his home on upper Main Street. He also made coffins as they were required. After his death Norman Charles built a store on Smith Street, where he sold furniture and continued the coffin business. He was a competent carpenter and builder and erected several houses in the village. He was succeeded by his son-in-law, Herbert D. Hodsdon, who continued the business until the store and contents were burned. Since then the establishment of Frank

A. Hill & Son, Undertakers, on Warren Street, has provided a Funeral Home, a great convenience to this and neighboring towns.

In the late 1860s Elbridge G. Osgood kept a small general store in the building at the corner of Main and Dana Streets. He was succeeded by Josephus Farrington until the building was converted into a dwelling house.

For many years William Kelly provided clothes for men from his tailor shop on Main Street, next to his dwelling. He also ran a bowling alley, between his shop and the blacksmith shop of the Abbott Brothers. That enterprise not proving a continuous success, Mr. Kelly converted the alley into several cottages, which were established elsewhere in the village. The last section was successively occupied as a meat market, a grave-stone shop, and a barber shop, where Charles T. Ladd, who, beginning with a barber chair in the corner of the Oxford House office, occupied the shop until he acquired the property, when he built a large store on the site with a dentist's office in the second story. Retaining his barber business, he added various lines, and the business was continued until he sold it to Perkins and Pendexter who carried on the apothecary department that had been added, with other branches, until the death of Mr. Pendexter when it was sold to Mr. S. T. Oliver. Meanwhile, barber shops had been opened elsewhere.

The Kelly house was converted into stores with apartments on the second floor. A restaurant was established in the old-time tailor shop, a gift shop and a men's furnishing and clothing were opened. Joseph Solari built a fruit and confectionery store, with a restaurant and dance floor. The livery stable conducted by "Billy" Kelly having gone the way of the horse, the site was completely reorganized.

Isaiah Warren for a number of years owned and managed an iron foundry in the rear of Portland Street, manufacturing castings of various kinds, such as fittings for stoves and ovens, fence-palings, frames for mirrors and many other small articles. Plows were produced, and a good business was carried on as long as transportation from large business centers was prohibitive. For a time the business was handled under the firm name of Allen & Warren. Some time after the foundry was closed it was torn down.

Mr. Warren was concerned in a steam sawmill at the lower end of Oxford Street, which afterward was made into a tannery, and that in time was abandoned for a larger building on Portland

Street. Here Isaiah and Otis Warren, his son, carried on a leather-making business. A constant market was provided for hemlock bark from the surrounding forests, until the manufacture of chrome leather struck the death-knell for the small tanneries. The tannery stood idle until it burned.

After the railroad came, new life was given to lumber-working industry. Sawmills were built in the vicinity of the station. The requirements of the sugar manufacturers made a demand for molasses hogshead shooks and heading, which were manufactured in Fryeburg and Lovell, and shipped through Fryeburg in large quantities. As time went on, the corn-canning business brought a new phase of farming to the valley.

Fryeburg Center in the 1830s carried on considerable trade. There were three stores, kept by Joshua Gammage, Justus Charles, and Moody Merrill. In later years Charles Chandler had an extensive general store.

At North Fryeburg, in the early 1840s, the O'Brien Brothers did a large business. They sold to Eben Weeks, who later moved to the Village. James Hutchins continued the store. Hutchins and Webb carry a large stock of household furnishings.

In West Fryeburg Henry D. Hutchins carried on a small store for forty years. Edward Shirley and Hollis Mansfield had a large business further along the road to North Fryeburg. After Mansfield's death Franklin Shirley entered partnership with his father.

An industry of more than local reputation was the E. W. Burbank Seed Co. Mr. Burbank owned an extensive intervale farm on the west side of the Great Bend of the river, where he raised the best seeds of the best crops. In need of increasing his business, he took Seth W. Fife into the company and they conducted it for some years. After the death of Mr. Burbank, it was carried on by Fife and Son, and the business grew, until boxes of seeds were to be found in stores all over the farming section of New England. This business, with the addition of agricultural implements, fertilizers, etc., was carried on until the death of Mr. Fife.

A necessary business in Lovewell's Pond ice was developed by A. R. Jenness, and later by Charles F. Smith, as long as his health permitted; then it became the property of Elmer Brackett and Son. It is a year-around industry, and has many customers during the summer.

In 1874 a movement was made among the farmers for a cheese

factory. A large number of cows were kept in the town and the quantity of milk available seemed to guarantee a successful enterprise. A corporation was formed and the factory was built the following spring. Alden B. Walker, a native of Fryeburg and resident of the village was engaged to take charge of the enterprise, and he and Mrs. Walker conducted it for two years. The factory was well-equipped, and the cheese produced of good quality but the factory was not remunerative enough to warrant continuing the enterprise, as the haul from farm to factory was too long. Accordingly it was discontinued, and the building was later converted into a boarding house, next became the "Argue Not Inn" and finally an apartment house.

Other businesses cater to the various needs of the citizens; Ernest O. Jewett, was the first to open a restaurant, on Smith Street. Another on Main Street was opened by Mr. and Mrs. McCay. Eastman and Hill have a shop for monumental work. James Hobbs has a flower farm, which produces a great variety of beautiful flowers. H. H. Burnham has conducted for several years a watch repairing and jewelry business on Main Street. Asa Osgood Pike & Son conduct an insurance business on Portland Street. A number of repair garages in different parts of the village do a steady business.

Major Samuel Osgood built the first framed house in the village in 1775. It was used as a tavern, and from that time until 1906 the site was occupied by a public house known as "The Oxford House." About 1800 it was a famous tavern, and Daniel Webster lived there during his service in the Academy. After Mrs. Osgood relinquished the hotel, Philip C. Johnson, afterwards Secretary of State for Maine conducted it for a year. He was the father of Eastman Johnson, one of this country's most talented artists of his time. Capt. Isaac Frye, grandson of General Frye kept the house for a time, succeeded by Mr. Knight in 1850. During the 1860s and in the 1870s John Smith and Horatio Boothby were the landlords. Following them, Otis True kept the house, until 1875, when Asa O. Pike, from East Fryeburg, a grandson of the first proprietor, bought the property and enlarged and modernized the house. He added a hall which was first used by the Superior Court of Oxford County for the fall sitting, and was known as "Court Hall." A. O. & C. W. Pike carried on the Oxford House for several years,

Temperance House   Rear of Bradley & Warren Store
         Stark's Hill in the background

JOCKEY CAP

leasing it later to Gee & Ingalls, then to Gee & Son, who kept a popular house until it was burned in January 1887.

The site was unoccupied until 1893, when a local company, of which W. H. Tarbox was a principal mover, began work on a modern building of four stories. As soon as completed, in 1894, O. A. Kneeland took charge of it, as "The Oxford." The following year, the original owners were bought out by Frank L. Mark and Edward E. Hastings, Esq. They refitted the house, and kept it until 1896, when Frank S. Plummer took charge. It was burned August 31, 1906. From that time the site remained empty until it was purchased for two private residences.

Samuel Souther carried on his trade as hatter—learned from the Appletons of Haverhill, Mass.—until he opened the "Temperance House," a large colonial house on Portland Street. On his death, his son, John W. Souther, occupied it until the early 1870s, when it was sold to George H. Abbott, who kept a tavern, the Fryeburg House, until he sold to William Pingree. After that it passed through several hands: Willard L. Mansfield, Hon. Uranus O. Brackett, W. H. Abbott—then the Pequawket House—and M. P. Johnson. It then was vacant until it was burned in the fire of August, 1906. Later the site was sold to the County of Oxford, and a brick building was built for the Western Oxford Registry of Deeds. Next to it, on the site of the I. B. Bradley mansion, the American Legion erected a brick building for its headquarters, and with a change in administration, the Post Office occupied roomy quarters in the building.

In 1884, Alden B. Walker converted the former cheese factory into a boarding house. He conducted it until his death, when it was occupied by Mr. and Mrs. Frank Thomes, who opened it as a tavern, under the name of "The Argue Not"—the result of an argument over a desirable name. The unique name commended the house to many of the travelling public.

Mrs. Blanche S. Page, in 1922, opened "Ye Olde Inn," the Col. E. L. Osgood house which had had different occupants, including "Uncle" John Smith, who gave the name to "Smith Street," which was opened through his garden.

Following the death of Mr. W. B. Post, his residence was acquired by Mr. William H. Irish, who opened it in 1925 as the "Fryeburg Tavern," a transient hotel. It occupies the site of Dr. Emery's house, the first physician in Fryeburg, and the residence for many years of James McMillan, whose family were influential in the village. It was afterward the summer residence of Mr. S. L. Post, Jr., a wealthy banker of New York, who improved the buildings, and being a fancier of good horses, built a large stable and carriage house.

One of the most important events that ever occurred in Fryeburg was the advent of the railroad in 1873.

Travel to the White Mountains had been increasing after the Civil War; enterprising hotel-keepers and stage-drivers conspired together to bring the summer travel and vacation-seekers into the Crawford Notch and the attractive country leading to it. Portland saw the interest growing in the mountain region and began to talk of a railroad through the Notch, and February 11, 1867 the Portland and Ogdensburg Railroad was incorporated. July 30, 1868 the Town of Fryeburg subscribed for $30,000 of bonds. Work began at the Portland end of the proposed railroad in September, 1869. It went slowly, but by August, 1873 it was extended as far as North Conway, where a turn-table was established making it a temporary terminal. The first train was run from Portland through the Notch to Fabyan's August 7, 1875.

A large area was opened for industry and markets; regions of untold wealth of timber were now available; farm lands that hitherto had been limited to home needs now saw a wider market for products, and the merchants at Portland saw new markets for their stocks. Not only was the business of the country affected by the construction of this road, but it opened a new means of travel to the people.

The June day of 1873 that brought the first passenger train from Portland to Fryeburg was a gala day for the Pequawket valley. The train was received by a throng of people that filled to capacity the platforms of the newly erected station, and when the train discharged its load of a thousand passengers, including a Portland military company and a full brass band, the company of interested persons made the day one of the most notable in the history of the "Seven Lots."

Fryeburg had a sentimental interest in the railroad, for of the early locomotives, Number 5 was named FRYEBURG, and Number 6, PEQUAWKET.

For some time after the establishment of railroad connections with the outside world, there was no telegraph. After many calls for an office at the station and in the village, the citizens, under the leadership of Dr. D. L. Lamson, took on themselves the expense of connecting the main line at the station and Main Street, a distance of about half-a-mile. A manager of the Western Union came with his chief operator and directed the placing of the wires, and in a short time Fryeburg was in contact with Portland and the world. The telegraph was established in the office of Dr. Lamson, who mastered the code, and operated the line to the convenience of the citizens for many years.

Fryeburg Village had the distinction of having in its streets the last horse railroad in the United States, as that institution had flourished for several years, a convenience to citizens and an object of interest and amusement to visitors.

The inception of the enterprise was in the need of the Northern New England Sunday School Assembly and Maine Chautauqua Union, which succeeded the Camp Meetings of the Methodist Episcopal Church that for many years had been conducted at the "Moosehorn," the ancient name of a grove of beautiful sugar maples on the banks of the Saco about two miles below the village.

As the demands for better transportation for the Chautauqua Assemblies increased, a few interested persons put their money at the disposal of a company to construct a horse railroad from the Maine Central R. R. station to the grounds of the Assembly.

The rolling-stock was limited to the requirements of the road, and consisted of three useful if not ornamental horse-cars obtained from the Portland Street Railroad, and a modern open car; with this equipment business began. The first movement of the open car from the station where it was delivered, was most primitive—a yoke of strong oxen drew the car along the track, while village people crowded the seats to enjoy the first ride. This motive power did not continue. Horses were in use, and the road was a great help to attendance at the Assemblies. The road began operation in summer, a short time before the Assembly and the season was expected to close at the time of the exhibition of the West Oxford Agricultural Society, the first week in October.

It was the intention of the management to begin running the cars for Village patronage as soon as the snow freed the tracks, but enterprise went even farther than that. A car on runners was constructed, and hauled by two horses with a veteran street-car driver in charge. It ran through the village all winter, giving transportation to the trains, of which there were four each day.

Seth W. Fife, Esq. took an active part in the management of the road, acting at times as conductor. One of the drivers, who became a regular factor of the road, was James Sutcliffe, a local character. A veteran of the Mexican and Civil Wars, he had served on the Western Plains also. He served the road loyally as conductor and driver for a number of years. The sight of Mr. Sutcliffe leaving the car, to use his hoe, which he always carried, to clear away an accumulation of sand which had washed on the rails during the night, is well remembered. He made the service real, helping the passengers in any way possible; baggage was carried to accommodate, and he even would wait a few minutes to aid a belated passenger.

From being a source of amusement and a butt of ridicule the Fryeburg Horse Railroad became a respected institution. But its support was not equal to the cost of maintenance, and though its convenience was thoroughly appreciated, it could not find enough passengers to meet the expenses. So it quietly ceased its operation in 1911; the cars were left on the switch in the edge of the woods, the motive-power was sold, and the grass and weeds continued to grow on the track, undisturbed.

The Fryeburg Water Company was organized May 20, 1882, and the water was turned on in the mains of the streets, Nov. 10th.

From the settlement of the Village the water used for all purposes had come from wells on every homestead site. These wells supplied all ordinary needs, but occasionally, after a long, dry term, some of the shallower wells would fail. These primitive conditions existed until a few public-spirited persons headed by T. C. Shirley, D. L. Lamson and A. R. Jenness, formed a corporation and capital was secured from those especially interested or having money available. Subscriptions to the stock of the Company were solicited and with a capital of over $12,000 the company felt justified in beginning operations, as it was intended to make the corporation co-operative and a neighborhood affair, with no exploiting of the stock. Accordingly that summer the site was secured, on what was known as the "White Lot" on the side of Green Mountain, and September 23, work on the mains was begun. The spot selected for the headwaters of the system, was at the junction of a second brook with the White Lot Brook. A dam was built across the brook, and the system was inaugurated, with gravity as the sole power for forcing the water into the houses.

The distance from the headwater was a little over two and three-fourths miles. Bradley B. Woodward, of East Conway, N. H., had the contract of digging and covering the trench.

The problem of laying the pipe across Saco River, was let separately. The distance was 438 feet. August 10, 1882 the pipe, which was joined by screw joints, was drawn across the river from the sand-flat where it was assembled, by a team of two horses. Once across, it was settled into the river bottom, by digging under it, until it lay at a depth sufficient to protect it, when it was covered and ballasted with stones.

September 23rd work began laying the pipes in the streets. In six weeks the work of laying mains and service pipes to the houses was completed. This was November 4.

The condition of the pipes as laid was thoroughly satisfactory, and water was turned on in the street-mains November 10. The length of the pipes in the streets and service pipes was four miles and 333 feet. The number of faucets established in houses at first sounds ridiculously small, as all that was required was one at the kitchen sink. Few houses, with a private source of water-supply, had plumbing for the whole house. Fifty years from the time of introducing the water, there is hardly a dwelling of any size but is equipped with bath-room and hot and cold water.

It is of interest to know that the successful effort of the Fryeburg Water Company was not the first attempt to develop a public supply of water for the village, for in 1813 an Act to establish the Fryeburg Aqueduct Corporation was passed by the Senate and House of Representatives in General Court assembled, which was approved by the Governor, February 24, 1813.

This Act gave the incorporators the right "to hold one or more pieces of land, in said Fryeburg or any adjacent town (not to exceed two acres in one place) where there are springs of water, and thence bring water in subterraneous pipes to any place within said Town of Fryeburg, and may construct and erect on said land reservoirs and buildings: Provided the funds of said Corporation shall not exceed twenty-five thousand dollars." The charter contained other conditions for government of the corporation, characteristic of such organizations.

The records do not show the development of the aqueduct system, but the assessments on the stock give evidence of the use of money, and there are references to the raising of money to meet the expenses of the Corporation. One of the By-Laws relative to the use of the water is as follows:

"The quantity of water assigned by the proprietors to each proprietor shall be considered his share of the same, and shall not be altered or increased by said Proprietors, and if any proprietor shall alter or cause a larger discharge of water at his post or trough than was assigned to him, he or she shall pay a fine of five dollars for every such offense."

A fine of one dollar was to be charged to any proprietor who allowed any one not a proprietor to take water from his post or reservoir, without permission of the directors.

The largest proprietor was to be permitted to have preference in selling shares, and that statement affords a reason for the pencil entry in the Treasurer's book, "I have sold one share of my stock to one-eyed John Smith. I. W."

What was done with the funds is not stated in the records, and today there is no trace of any "aquaducts," but the fact that so early in the history of the Village there was an attempt to do something a little more modern than having to depend on wells shows a highly commendable degree of progress. Perhaps at some future date, some one digging in the streets, or around one of the oldest houses, may find a bit of leaden pipe that was one of the "aquaducts" of that ancient concern.

With the introduction of a water-service, attention was at once given to the needs in case of fire. At first a Village Corporation was established as a Fire District, being chartered by the State Legislature. Later this charter was amended to permit other necessary village improvements. As soon as the Corporation was in working order, a Fire Department was organized, and apparatus was purchased. The Fire Department was established later in a Corporation Building on Portland Street, with place for the equipment, and a meeting-room in the second story. A loud-sounding bell was installed which was used for fire alarm until an electrically operated siren replaced it. The apparatus is completely mechanized and is efficiently manned.

This was the second effort in the line of fire-protection, for in 1847 we find that the Village was assessed for the maintenance of a Fire Engine, and Merrill Wyman, the Collector for the Fire Company, turned over to the Treasurer, Samuel Ilsley, Nov. 5, 1847, the sum of "fifty dollars to be expended in procuring apparatus for the Engine &c."

From an undated account we find that a bill of $34.00 was incurred for equipment as follows:

½ Doz Axes and handles,	9.00
8 Ladders, 4 with hooks,	12.00
50 feet 1-inch rope for Engine with tags,	4.00
4 Pike poles with hooks @ 1.50 each,	6.00
1 Dog hook for chain,	1.00
3 Hose wrenches,	.75
1 Jug—1 Gall'n Alcohol,	1.00
1 Lamp filler	.25
Platform for the Engine house	
1 Cheap stove do.	
50 feet gutta percha hose	
1 Cistern that will contain 75 Hhds.	

What was the original use of the building used to house the first apparatus is not known, but it was a small unpainted building, which stood for many years between the Registry of Deeds and the stone schoolhouse in the Village.

This building was used to house the village hearse as well as the Fire Engine.

Fryeburg has had various experiences with propositions for establishing financial institutions. In 1839 an effort was made to resurrect the Oxford Bank, which was organized on paper in Fryeburg, the charter being granted in 1836, but as it had never been accepted by the petitioners, it was dead. In 1839 an attempt was made in Portland to float the notes of the defunct bank. The notes bore the signature of E. W. Appleton, president, and Jas. J. Fenton, cashier. The whole scheme was a swindle. Mr. Appleton was a reputable man, who had been made a tool by some New York swindlers, but their attempt was called to the attention of the people, and while some money was obtained, no bills were circulated in Portland, and presently the bubble burst.

In 1872 an act was presented in the Maine Legislature, to incorporate the Fryeburg Savings Bank. The persons interested in this venture were undoubtedly in earnest and worked in the interest of the community, but the attempt failed to materialize.

On June 10, 1907 there was established in the Village, a branch of the United States Trust Co., of Portland, where that institution had begun business two years earlier. For eighteen years it conducted a banking business in Fryeburg to the great advantage of the community; the branch developed so rapidly that in a few years it was doing almost as much business as the home bank. The management was under the charge of Frank R. Dresser, a competent young man who had grown up in Fryeburg. He was recalled to the home office, and Alvin D. Merrill, a native and resident of Fryeburg, was put in charge, and he so conducted the affairs of the Bank as to win for the company the confidence of the community.

In 1922 the directors were convinced that a more substantial place for the Bank was advisable. A fitting brick structure was built and was formally dedicated and opened for business May 18, 1923. An enterprise of so much convenience seemed entitled to a long career, but it fell as victim of the Depression, the Fryeburg branch suffering with the Portland institution.

The Casco Bank and Trust Co. of Portland, which had taken over the affairs of the U. S. Trust Co., opened a Fryeburg branch June 17, 1935. Small dividends have been paid on funds deposited with the defunct company. In the few years that the Casco Trust Co. has been in operation the business has been highly satisfactory to the Portland management, and it is steadily increasing.

Fryeburg has never been enthusiastic over the maintenance of a newspaper in the town. It has had a few experiments but none has lasted as long as the character of the place seemed to warrant.

The first venture was in the early part of 1798, when Elijah Russell started his paper, "Russell's Echo, or the North Star." The first issue was February 29, 1798, and the first five weeks saw an issue each week; afterward it came at irregular intervals. The news was varied, and not particularly interesting. So small a place could scarcely support a weekly paper and supply local news enough to make it readable. In the third issue, of March 1, the editor says:

"As the post comes titiring on but once in fourteen days, and then but little news; our readers will not expect a sheet full till Congress shall order us a weekly Mail, and thereby put it in our power to give a prompt circulation to those articles of information which may be interesting to every individual need of the Union."

It must have been quite a problem to publish a paper so far from the source of supply of materials, as the lack of paper caused the irregularity of the issues.

On May 17, the editor announces that he intends to issue the "Echo" every week in the future, but he failed, as the next date is July 11, making four numbers issued in five weeks and six days. Two numbers were issued between that date and August 14. From August 28 to November 28 only five numbers. On that date the editor heads an editorial "ECHO—revived," and he says:

"The editor did not calculate TWO eclipses of 'The North Star' to take place in less than six months."

Copies of the "Echo" are preserved in the Library of Harvard University, and in the rooms of the American Antiquary Society, in Worcester. One copy is owned in this town.

Russell's establishment was located near the site of the Congregational Vestry and the foundation stones have been dug out of the writer's garden. Russell lived in the building where he carried on his printing office. So far as known from any issues of the paper extant, that of January 11, 1799 was the last one printed in Fryeburg.

In the early summer of 1887 some of the citizens persuaded R. Fult Wormwood to remove to the Village his printing plant, which included a weekly paper, the "Oxford County Record," from Kezar Falls. This was accomplished with the omission of but one week in the issue of the paper. The establishment was set up in the rear of the building known as the "Shirley & Lewis Store," where it remained during two years of publication, until the paper was sold to the publisher of a paper on the other side of the County.

The "Record" was a newsy sheet, containing items of interest in the surrounding towns, with a reasonable amount of communications and literary matter. It was appreciated by the Fryeburg people, and Mr. Wormwood won the respect of his acquaintances. Among those who were engaged in the office was a man who drifted into the place and was employed as a journeyman printer. He proved not only a competent printer, but a worthy member of the village society. His name was Robert E. Peach, and after a year or so in the Record office, he left to become after a few years Bishop Peach, of the Reformed Episcopal Church, with headquarters in Philadelphia.

In 1898 H. G. Freeman opened a printing office in the village.

and continued in the business until the fire of August, 1906. Since then, the town has been without a printing office.

In 1915 and 1916 a paper was printed in Portland under the name "The Fryeburg Post," and contained local and county news beside important and readable matter. Mr. William Gordon searched the Town records for items of interest on the early settlement of the town, and published his findings in the "Post." That paper after a short existence stopped for lack of financial support.

The publisher of the "North Conway Reporter," moved by the quantity and quality of news sent to his paper from Fryeburg, issues an edition, under the heading "Fryeburg Reporter."

In recent years the principal industry at the Village was the manufacture of lumber into commercial forms. The first saw mill for producing boards and making hogshead shooks for export to Cuba was near the railroad station and was conducted by Shirley & Cousins. This was followed by a Bobbin factory, owned and operated by Jerome B. Fellows. Mr. Fellows introduced an invention of his own which materially helped the handling of the bobbin-lathes and increased production.

The Shirley & Cousins mill having burned, Mr. Cousins later built another mill for sawing lumber, on the opposite side of the tracks of the railroad, which was operated for a number of years.

With the increase of sugar production in this country, and use of bags for sugar in place of molasses hogsheads, the production of shooks ceased and all the mills were closed.

A chair factory in a mill built near the railroad station was conducted profitably for a number of years, but was finally closed and later the mill was burned. Another building was erected on the site for manufacture of boxes, which throve until the change to fiber cartons made the business unprofitable.

More recently Charles E. Fox, of Fox Brothers, of Portland, built a saw mill near the site of the Shirley & Cousins mill, and it produces pine boards in large quantity.

Saunders Bros., of Westbrook, in 1936 purchased a twelve-acre site on the Pequawket Trail, about a mile from the Village, and built a mill for producing the blanks for the manufacture of dowels from white birch. This made a market for the great quantities of birch in the vicinity.

Ingalls Brook, now better known as Ballard Brook, furnished an unfailing water-power near the road on the west side toward West Fryeburg. The first mill there was built by Deacon Ezra Carter, Col. John Webster and Edmund Shirley, 1793-1794. It was a saw and grist mill. They sold it early in the 1800s to Uriah Ballard. David Webster, son of Col. David Webster, bought the mill and right from George Ballard, son of Uriah, in the early 1840s. He built a new mill, separating the saw from the grist mill.

The Webster heirs sold the mill to Osborn Charles in 1858. He repaired the dam and the mills, and ran them until 1869, when he sold the plant to Samuel B. Locke, who took down the mills, and built a large saw mill. It was kept in the family, his son, Frank Locke, carrying it on until it was burned Nov. 20, 1891. Locke sold the site to Edward McIntire, who built a smaller saw mill. Phineas Seavey carried it on for a while. Lloyd Stevens became the owner of the plant, and it still is in operation (1937).

Sampson P. Harriman and Charles Simpson brought to the village their dowel mill from North Chatham, and located on Oxford Street, by Ward's Pond, where they continued the business for a number of years, until the deaths of the two partners closed the enterprise. The mill was destroyed by fire.

Following a year of careful preparation several ski-coasts in the vicinity of the Village were opened for use in the winter of 1936, and many persons found opportunities for exciting slides. On Starks Hill two fast, twisting slides were made, giving the coaster all the thrills desired. On Pine Hill there were shorter slides for novices, and on the southeastern slope of Jockey Cap a lively slide, with a ski-tow.

The winter of 1937-38 was more favorable to coasting on these slides, and again they were well patronized, by hundred of visitors, many coming on "snow trains" from Portland, which gives a delightful day in Fryeburg, with all the slides available.

Nearby slopes are investigated for new slides, which are developed as rapidly as needed. The Winter Sports Committee keeps in touch with conditions at every point, making it possible to find out at any time the best place to ski. Not only do the snow trains bring a good number of skiing enthusiasts, but the surrounding towns send automobile parties over the well-kept highways, to take advantage of Fryeburg's delightful coasts among the hills, and in view of the beautiful peaks of the White Mountains.

XVII

TOWN DEVELOPMENTS

> A rural cemetery seems to combine in itself all the advantages which can be proposed to gratify human feelings, or tranquilize human fears; to secure the best religious influences, and to cherish all those associations which cast a cheerful light over the darkness of the grave.
> —*Joseph Story*

As the village grew, increased cemetery area became imperative. The first burying ground in the center of the village being fully occupied by private lots, on June 6, 1841, these persons agreed to pay ten dollars each for the purchase and fencing with stone, of a lot suitable for a burying ground, which was to be sixteen or twenty rods square: I. B. Bradley, John Evans, Carlton Hurd, Amos Brown, Reuel Barrows, Martha Quimby, H. C. Buswell, Russell Page, William Johnston, Daniel McNeal, Isaiah Warren, Asa Charles, Albion Page, Jonathan Evans, Stephen Chase, James Osgood, David Webster.

August 10th these and others took measures to incorporate themselves as a body having the necessary rights to buy and sell according to the needs of the corporation. Later a committee reported that they had purchased a lot of land from Francis Kidder. The site of the cemetery was on the road from Main Street to the point where the Bridgton road began. It was selected for its remoteness, and at the same time for its reasonable convenience.

The area was well forested with pines, hence its name, "Pine Grove Cemetery." As the cemetery became occupied, and stones and monuments were set, these trees proved a disadvantage, discoloring the marble stones, and the roots overturned the stones. It became necessary to remove the growth, until hardly a pine tree was left.

About 1870 it was found possible to build a substantial fence around the area, and John W. Souther took the contract. The stones were cut in the quarry on Oak Hill, and were seven feet long, a foot wide and seven inches thick. They were set in the ground three feet, and were four feet above ground, set close; the corners and gateposts were large stones taller than the fence, with a stone cap, all requiring neither rebuilding nor repairs, as lasting as the hill from which the stones were cut. Some wit has said, "It did not seem necessary to build so strong a fence, as those inside could not get out, and those outside were not desirous of getting in." The harshness of this row of stones, on the street front, is now relieved by a hedge of arbor vitae.

At a later year an area about the size of the first purchase was acquired on the same line of the street, adjoining the original ground. A receiving tomb, needed in winter, has been built. Every year the grounds are improved, by attractively kept lots and dignified memorials to the dead.

The Town has in its keeping a number of cemetery lots in the various burying grounds with nearly thirty funds bequeathed for permanent care.

The Town Proprietors held a meeting July 8, 1793, and passed this vote:

"That one acre of upland on the North side of the River, upon the East side of the road opposite Lt. Stephen Farrington's second division, be and is appropriated for a burying ground."

That ground is the West Fryeburg cemetery, and many of the oldest families of the town rests on that consecrated ground.

There are still in use thirteen cemeteries, as follows: Village, two; West Fryeburg, two; Birch Hill, one; North Fryeburg, three; Harbor, one; Fish Street, one; Toll Bridge, one; Center Fryeburg, one; Smart's Hill, one; Menotomy, one; East Fryeburg, one; on the road between East Fryeburg and Denmark, one. In various remote places are to be found private burying grounds, containing a few family graves.

Since Fryeburg is an agricultural town, every effort made to increase the efficiency of the land and to improve the knowledge of the farmer, works to the benefit of the whole town.

A meeting was held March 27, 1851, at the home of Samuel Stickney, in Brownfield, to consider organizing an agricultural society which would embrace the towns of Fryeburg, Brownfield, Hiram, Porter, Denmark, Lovell, Stow, Waterford, and Stoneham.

The organization was completed at a later meeting by the choice of the following officers: Gen. Peleg Wadsworth, president; David

R. Hastings, vice president; Thomas Souther, recording secretary; Isaac Spring, corresponding secretary; Samuel Stickney, treasurer and collector; Dr. Reuel Barrows, librarian; Trustees: Edward L. Osgood, Ammi Cutter, Jonathan F. Fifield, Joseph G. Swan, Enoch W. Woodbury, John L. Kimball, Henry H. Miller, Isaac Frye, John P. Hubbard.

A charter was received June 3, 1851, and the first meeting of the society, with a Fair, was held in Hiram, October 23, 1851. The exhibits and interest shown promised well for the future. The second meeting was in Fryeburg, near the Congregational Church, October 21, 1852. The third was at Lovell, October 19, 1853. The fourth was at Denmark near the town-house, October 11, 1854. The fifth was at Porter, near the Methodist Church, October 10, 1855. The sixth was at Brownfield, near the Congregational Church, October 15, 1856. The seventh was at Fryeburg, near the Congregational Vestry, October 21, 1857.

It was then seen that the society should have permanent grounds and buildings, and December 18, 1857, it was decided to establish the grounds on a seven acre lot near Fryeburg Village, and the work of preparing the ground, erecting buildings and cattle pens was begun. Lack of funds delayed the progress, and the means of financing the work became a problem. Many lost interest and withdrew from membership at the prospect of signing notes or pledging money. Others, led by Col. James Walker and George B. Barrows, went ahead with the work, and had the grounds and buildings ready for the next exhibition, October 20, 1858.

The Society occupied these grounds twenty-seven years, till November 26, 1884. During that time the railroad came into the town and so close to the grounds that a section was disposed of to the Town for a street to the station. The railroad helped the attendance and the Society throve and freed itself from debt. The fairs were successful but the area occupied was inadequate. It was voted to sell the grounds and a new site was bought on the main road between Fryeburg and Lovell, a mile from the Village. The area included sixty acres. William Henry Abbott was chairman of the committee that secured the grounds and had charge of fitting them for the society's purpose.

The new grounds were developed rapidly, a half-mile trotting track was made, a large grand stand, cattle sheds, and horse stalls were built. The first fair on the new grounds was held October

6-8, 1885, and was the most successful in the history of the society to that date.

The Society is known for the square treatment of all patronizing it, and its good exhibitions. It has been aided by the "Patrons of Husbandry," their Granges in the surrounding towns presenting large, well-selected exhibitions of their products. The success that attended these fairs put the Society out of debt, and it has gone on from year to year improving its grounds and equipment.

Its limits have been extended, until now it includes the towns of Cornish, Baldwin, and Bridgton in Maine, and in New Hampshire the towns of Conway, Bartlett, Jackson, Chatham, Eaton and Freedom.

The improvement in the exhibits, especially marked in the household and educational departments, is due to the active interest of its secretary through many years on the new grounds, B. Walker McKeen, who was a member of the State Board of Agriculture. He interested the Granges to give their younger members more place in the exhibits, and introduced new features and worked for better conditions in every department of the fair.

The residents of the towns in the Society's limits can not value too highly the foresight and hard work of the men who organized and carried the Society through its early years. Some of them lived long enough to see the progress that was being made, and could imagine what an asset the Society would be in the future.

Since the Spring of 1874, Fryeburg has had the benefit of a "Town Clock". It was due to Miss Sarah Osgood, a member of one of the old families of the village, that the movement resulting in the acquisition of the clock originated.

"Aunt Sally", as she was called with respect and affection, lived her closing years in the family of her niece, Mrs. I. M. Wellington, almost opposite the Congregational Church, which the architect had designed to permit the addition of a tower clock. She left in her will the sum of two hundred dollars for such a clock and in 1874 the required sum to purchase from E. Howard & Co., of Boston, the much desired clock, was raised by individual subscriptions.

The clock has been cared for, first, by D. Lowell Lamson, M.D., who took a lively interest in the mechanism, and wound it and kept it in order gratuitously for many years, until advancing age prevented. After him, James I. Lovis and others attended to the winding, and the present attendant is H. H. Burnham, the jeweller. Through all these years, the clock has done its work well, with occasional cleaning, and slight repairs.

The streets in the Village have increased in the last half-century, with Bradley and Stuart Streets between Main and Pine Streets. Newer streets that have been laid out as town ways are: "Pleasant," from Warren to Fair; "Fair," from Oxford to the entrance of the old Fair grounds; "Cottage," from Smith to Pleasant, as also "Maple," which is a narrow way beside the little brook which crosses Smith Street to the brook that runs into Ward's Pond; "Pond," which is from Fair Street, to Ward's Pond. "Cross," unnamed until recently, is the narrow street from Oxford to Smith Street. The old "Drift Road" from Main Street, to the river is becoming attractive for small cottages, and their number is increasing.

In other parts of the town, the single way which has been in use since early days is sufficient, as the dwellings are located along the way, and the farms are continuous. Access to different parts of the town is as convenient as can be desired since the automobile has eliminated distance.

Those who note the position of some houses on Main Street, in the Village particularly on the upper half, may wonder why the houses were placed so near to the street limits. Several houses stand so close to the street that the door steps are almost on the sidewalk. This was due to the fact that the street originally was three rods wide, but at one time it was decided to widen it to six rods. The work of running out the side line was begun on the southeast side and it was intended to take land off the northwest side, but the abutters raised such strong objections that the authorities had to compromise on a width of five and one-half rods.

This affected the southeast side more than the other, and cut off the front yards ruthlessly. From the old Town Line going northerly, it cut the yard from the house occupied by Robert Tonge, later by Elbridge Osgood, and still later by the widow of C. T. Ladd. The next house, owned by Harrison McNeal, was left so close to the street, that one could touch the windows of the street floor. This house continued in such plight until it became the property of Sidney F. Perkins, who moved it back, giving it frontage.

Across Elm Street, the home of Dr. Ira Towle, also was affected, but cutting the front yard could not have been pushed farther without cutting off the porch at the front door. That remained until in later years the owner moved the whole building farther back.

The stone schoolhouse was left close to the street, also the Registry of Deeds, and then there was no marked change until below Oxford Street, when the enlargement of the street brought William Kelly's house and his tailor shop flush with the sidewalk. Beyond Portland Street, no marked change occurred.

This widening was continued on Main Street beyond the limits of the Village, and was carried on the southeast side as far as the Menotomy Road, at the foot of the hill by Albion Page's farmhouse. The widening was made from the west side of the old settlers' road, which still exists, bringing the Fair Grounds fence close to the limits of the highway.

In 1918, a second automobile trail between Portland and Fryeburg, besides the Roosevelt Trail which goes by way of Naples and Bridgton, was proposed, to follow the highway from Portland through Westbrook, Gorham, Standish, Steep Falls, Baldwin, Hiram, Brownfield to Fryeburg, intersecting the Roosevelt Trail at the junction of Main and Portland Streets. The Portland end was to follow the Ossipee Trail, which was already perfected, but the highway beyond, for the proposed Pequawket Trail, would require considerable rebuilding. The proposition did not meet with complete enthusiasm, as the cost was to be shared between the State highway department and the towns through which the trail was to be laid.

The matter was well discussed in Town meeting in March. It was proposed to raise Fryeburg's share, $3,000, by taxation, $1,200; and by Town bonds, $1,800. When put to vote 91 votes were cast in favor of the plan, and 59 in opposition. Hiram and Brownfield waited until they heard from Fryeburg, having agreed to join with this town if it favored the trunk line. The work was begun at once and finished in the fall. The Pequawket Trail follows the old stage route from the seaboard to the White Mountains, and probably follows part of the route cut out of the forest by Colonel Frye in his desire to reach Portland.

At a special Town meeting, June 5, 1920, the town received the gift of a Memorial Park from Mrs. Charles R. Mattson, of Philadelphia and Fryeburg. This consisted of thirty acres of forest growth, on what has been known for years as "Pine Hill."

The land had been in possession of the Bradley family for many years. It remained for Mrs. Mattson, daughter of Israel B. Bradley, M.D., and Sarah Johnston Bradley, to give the area as a park, to be owned by the Town and controlled by a Board of Park Commissioners; memorializing thereby the site of the first Academy, the Bradley family, and the memory of the soldiers of Fryeburg of all the wars.

B. Walker McKeen was Moderator and Francis D. Swan acted as Clerk. The deed of gift was presented by Hon. Albion A. Perry, of Somerville, Mass., and Fryeburg, who acted as Mrs. Mattson's agent. The gift was accepted with enthusiasm, and resolutions thanking the giver were adopted.

The Park is bounded by Main and River Streets. The contour of the hill admits of much development. At the base and cornering on the two streets is a plain area, on which stood the first Academy, in which Paul Langdon, Daniel Webster and Amos J. Cook taught. At the apex of the triangle, are the two cannon, dedicated to the soldiers and sailors. From the summit of the hill, which is a bare ledge, an extended view of the mountains, the river, and the intervales is obtained, while on the eastern side is a view of the village, the view-point being known for many years as, "Village Rock".

In the deed, Mrs. Mattson stipulated that the park should not be a hunting field, but rather a bird sanctuary; not an athletic ground for adults, but rather a recreation field for children. She reserved the right to place on the Park such buildings, monuments and memorials as should be suitable, if she should so desire at any later time.

The Commissioners, nominated by Mrs. Mattson, consisting of five men and five women representing different parts of the town were accepted as follows: Miss Alice O. Hastings, Miss Hattie A. Pike, Miss Rachael Weston, Mrs. Lucia M. Lougee, Mrs. D. R. Bradley, Albion A. Perry, B. T. Newman, J. W. Eastman, E. C. Buzzell, B. W. McKeen.

Until comparatively recently, the streets of the Village at night were in Stygian darkness, except during the phases of the moon. Dr. D. L. Lamson, whose avocation was inventing something for the betterment of human conditions, devised a street lamp, on a post opposite his home, in front of the store occupied by Mrs. E. G. Fife. In it he placed a kerosene lamp, to the burner of which he attached a small clock, with a cam arrangement, by which a shutter was moved across the lighted wick. The cam was adjustable to the time. The first operation of this light was tested by the Doctor, with watch in hand. At exactly the time set, the shutter turned across the wick. This scheme, while practicable, was too expensive for general use. Several other street lights were set up, the common oil lamp being used.

When the first electric lighting company was established at Swan's Falls, the intent was to supply electricity in the Village for all purposes. The Village Corporation was broad enough in its charter rights to permit the use of electricity in lighting the streets. Lamps were erected at convenient points, and others added as needed.

The first attempt to harness the Saco at Swan's Falls was made by a company of which Dr. Charles E. Harris was a prime mover, and he became interested in it to a large extent financially. The plant was established on the west side of the river, where an island makes a channel with a considerable fall. Here were set the turbine wheels and the dynamos. The current was sufficient at first to supply a limited amount of light, but the demand was increasing, and it became necessary to transfer the ownership to the Maine Power Company, which rebuilt the dam, across the main channel, with sufficient strength to withstand the high water, ice and logs. Since then the current has been supplied in ample quantity and connection made with other power plants, so that in spite of accident the current may be unhindered. In 1937 the power company was sold to the New Hampshire Public Service Company and the lines were extended.

Early in its history Fryeburg took advantage of the postal conditions that admitted the establishment of a Post Office at the Seven Lots, although the facilities for transporting the mails were irregular and at wide intervals. The Post Office was established under the spelling "Fryeburgh", which later was changed to "Fryeburg." The Post Masters, and their terms of office were as follows:

Postmaster	Date Appointed
Moses Ames	January 1, 1798
(First returns)	(Established)

James W. Ripley	October 1, 1808
(First returns)	
Judah Dana	March 9, 1811
Edward L. Osgood	January 4, 1837
Asa Charles	June 7, 1841
Edward L. Osgood	July 3, 1845
John L. Eastman	April 18, 1849
Augustus Abbott	June 1, 1853
William H. Abbott	May 11, 1855
Samuel Ilsley	July 26, 1861
Louise H. Ilsley	January 3, 1862
Mrs. Eunice J. Holt	January 9, 1866
Jane W. Frye	December 16, 1878
Tobias L. Eastman	February 2, 1881
William Gordon	January 11, 1886
Amos C. Frye	September 19, 1889
Changed to Fryeburg	October 23, 1893
William H. Abbott	October 23, 1893
Amos C. Frye	July 27, 1897
Mrs. Mary E. Frye	February 16, 1898
John W. Hutchins	January 4, 1915
John E. Sargent (Acting)	May 1, 1923
John E. Sargent	December 18, 1923
William Gerald Jordan	April 21, 1936

When the office was first established the mail arrived on Wednesday, once in two weeks. The carrier came on horse back from Portland until 1810, when a Mr. McKenny drove a two-horse wagon, which would seem to indicate the increase of mail matter, the quantity becoming too great for saddle bags.

In 1815 Daniel Clement was the carrier, making trips once a week between Fryeburg and Portland, using the original method of a horse with saddle bags. During the last of his service he adopted the more comfortable method of a horse and carriage.

Following him, Edward Weston was the carrier, using the horse and saddle bags.

At some later period Daniel Badger carried the mails from Portland through the mountains to Lancaster, N. H.

By 1826 the "Concord Coaches" had become the regular method of carrying passengers and the mails. The White Mountain Stage left Portland Wednesday and Saturday, at 7 A.M., arriving at Conway, N. H., at 6 P.M. The return trip was made Monday and Saturday, leaving Conway at 5 A.M., reaching Portland by or about 4 P.M. The Stage Coach continued as the vehicle of transportation, until the Portland & Ogdensburg Railroad provided quicker and regular service.

It was forty years before a branch post office was created at North Fryeburg.

The O'Brien Brothers, who were in trade there, conducted the first Post Office. The Post Masters and their terms were as follows:

Postmaster	Date Appointed
Daniel W. O'Brien	January 23, 1838 (Established)
Simeon C. Wiley	October 2, 1845
Marshall Walker	January 19, 1863
Lyman R. Charles	January 12, 1865
Charles H. Tibbetts	February 22, 1865
Charles Nutter	October 13, 1865
Loring R. Giles	September 28, 1874
William H. Hatch	April 26, 1875
William H. Hatch, Jr.	May 12, 1875
Loring R. Giles	July 3, 1877
John J. Greenlaw	June 12, 1882
Joseph Russell	March 17, 1887
Fred W. Spring	November 22, 1887
John Bachelder	May 16, 1889
Changed to North Fryeburg	July 14, 1893
Charles P. Giles	July 14, 1893
Frank F. Giles	June 24, 1897
Burt C. Webb	January 2, 1901

The community at East Fryeburg succeeded in having a Post Office established in the large brick house built by Asa O. Pike. The Post Masters and their terms at that office were as follows:

Postmaster	Date Appointed
Asa O. Pike	June 12, 1854 (Established)
Harmon V. Berry	December 20, 1875
Sherman Hapgood	November 7, 1883

Postmaster	Date Appointed
Harmon V. Berry	September 23, 1891
Judith F. Harnden	September 22, 1896
Harmon V. Berry	November 23, 1897

Discontinued September 15, 1906. Mail to Brownfield.

The last branch to be established was at Fryeburg Center. As in the case of the Village office the Department used the same spelling for the three branch offices.

The Post Masters and terms were as follows:

Henry G. Farrington	July 28, 1857 (Established)
Joseph Chandler	December 2, 1859
Discontinued April 28, 1863	Reestablished May 12, 1864
Justus Charles	May 12, 1864
Charles Chandler	July 17, 1871
Changed to "Fryeburg Center"	December 18, 1894
James E. Hutchins	December 18, 1894
Mrs. Emma T. Haley	June 1, 1909
Discontinued January 31, 1911	Mail to Fryeburg

In these times of an unlimited supply of newspapers and mailable literature, it is of interest to know how Fryeburg stood in 1862 as to reading matter and in following the daily news. There was a lively correspondence carried on between the residents of the Town and their friends outside during the year ending with the first of November, as shown by the number of letters sent from the Post Office in the Village, which was 11,292, and about the same number received. The number of regular newspapers taken was, weeklies, 177; monthlies, 28; semi-weeklies, 9; tri-weeklies, 5; dailies, 25; total, 243. That was considered a remarkably good record, for a village of the size of Fryeburg. The number of polls was about 370.

XVIII

IMPORTANT EVENTS AND ORGANIZATIONS

> Breathes there a man with soul so dead,
> Who never to himself hath said,
> "This is my own—my native land!"
> Whose heart hath ne'er within him burned
> As home his footsteps he hath turned,
> From wandering on a foreign strand?
> —*Walter Scott.*

The Centennial of the founding of the Town was celebrated August 20, 1863, at the foot of Pine Hill, on the site of the first Academy building. A procession marshalled by Dr. William C. Towle and headed by a detail of returned soldiers in uniform, formed in front of the Congregational Church and marched to the place of assembly, led by the North Bridgton Brass Band.

Seats for a thousand were filled when the Chairman, Mr. Asa Charles, called the assembly to order, with words of greeting. He introduced the orator, Rev. Samuel Souther, a native of Fryeburg then a resident of Worcester, who delivered an historical essay covering prominent events in the history of the town. He touched the high points of the work of Colonel Joseph Frye in organizing the settlement into a town; and of the principal incidents and the persons notable during the century.

In the afternoon, because of rain, the exercises were resumed in the Congregational Church, which was crowded to the limit. "Toasts" were read by Hon. George B. Barrows, Fryeburg's candidate for State Senator, introducing the speakers, among whom were Dr. N. T. True, of Bethel; Enoch W. Evans of Chicago, a native of Fryeburg; John A. Andrew, Governor of Massachusetts, a grandson of Fryeburg.

Governor Andrew made an eloquent speech of nearly two hours which was heard with great attention, and received with applause.

In the evening the Webster Association of Fryeburg Academy held a Levee in Academy Hall, which was decorated with mottoes to fit the occasion. Several hundred people attended, and short speeches were made. This closed the celebration.

The sesqui-centennial of the Town and the first town Meeting were celebrated in an Historical Pageant, by Herbert A. D. Hurd, Teacher of Music in the schools. July 13, 1927, the day set for this celebration was all that could be desired, and the spacious campus of the Academy offered an admirable stage for the dramatic presentation. Several thousands of people were present, many of whom were former residents of Fryeburg, or descendants of the early settlers.

Led by the Band of the 240th Coast Artillery Regiment, Maine National Guard, a street parade of the characters of the pageant, marched to the Academy grounds, where Massachusetts and Maine, mother and daughter states, met through their official representatives, Gov. Ralph O. Brewster, chief executive of Maine, and Hon. John C. Hull, Speaker of the Massachusetts House of Representatives, representing Gov. Alvin T. Fuller. It was most fitting that Mr. Hull should be present, as he was a Principal of the Academy in 1892-1895. Rev. Henry E. Dunnack, State Librarian, as Historical Orator of the Day, and Mrs. Susan Walker Merrill, a former teacher in the Academy completed the guests of prominence. Mr. Hurd as Chairman of the Town Committee and Capt. Hugh W. Hastings, Secretary, managed the celebration. Pictured in epitome, by school children, was the history of the town in nine episodes.

When the audience reassembled, after a lunch served on the grounds, Mr. Hurd introduced, to speak for the State of Maine, Governor Brewster, who was accompanied by Mrs. Brewster, and by members of his military staff and of the Council. Governor Brewster said, to impress his thought on the audience:

"It is clear that we may expect men and women from the quiet farms to be responsible for the liberty inherited from the pioneers of such communities as Fryeburg. America must go forward to the new culture sure to emerge from the material prosperity of the present day."

Mr. Hull, in responding for the Commonwealth of Massachusetts, praised the sturdy characters of the early settlers and of the people who make up such a community as Fryeburg, and said, "It is well worth our while to celebrate such anniversaries as these. As we look back to their stirring times, we must resolve to keep alive their ideals and their virtues."

Mrs. Susan Walker Merrill, a descendant of some of the first settlers, read an original poem commemorating the founding of the settlement.

Rev. Henry E. Dunnack brought the exercises to a fitting close with a brief account of the early days of Fryeburg, as embodied in the history of Maine.

The Fryeburg Woman's Library Club held a reception in their club room to Mrs. Brewster and Mrs. Hull.

There has always been a decided sentiment in Fryeburg in favor of temperance, and against the sale and use of spirituous liquors.

In 1840 the best element of the people started an active organization to restrict, if not to stop entirely the sale of intoxicating liquors. This organization took the name of the Fryeburg Temperance Union. The officers were: President, Rev. Carlton Hurd; Vice President, Amos Richardson; Secretary, Asa Charles; Treasurer, John Ilsley. Executive Committee, Dr. Reuel Barrows, Lot Wiggin, William Johnston. The rules centered around a pledge, and 192 names of men and women were signed to this.

> We pledge our sacred honor that we will not make use of alcoholic or intoxicating drinks, except mechanically and medicinally, and never in the latter case unless in cases of extreme and sudden physical infirmity, not having time to obtain medical advice; and to employ all the means in our power, both legal and moral (when practicable) to promote the Temperance Reformation.

It is evident from the meager records, that this society became quiet for a time, but in 1845 the Union was re-organized, with the same pledge as in 1840. It appointed a committee especially to go to the liquor dealers in the place, and remonstrate with them, deciding to use moral suasion to try and get them to quit their injurious business. The report was summarized by the Secretary as follows:

> The committee appointed to remonstrate with liquor dealers, and to get them to stop, reported: that it is the height of folly to think of persuading the rum-sellers of the present day to quit their nefarious business, so long as they can get $70 on a hogshead of New England Rum, and $30 on a barrel of West Indies Rum.

A separate effort was undertaken in 1844, when Dr. Reuel Barrows headed a list of 101 men and women, petitioning the Selectmen, the Clerk and Treasurer of the Town, not to license any person to sell ardent spirits or wine the ensuing year.

August 7, 1865, the Saco Valley Lodge of I. O. G. T. was organized in Academy Hall, by sixteen members who obligated themselves in the cause of temperance. The Lodge was composed of the young men and women of the place, and its influence drew also from the adjoining towns. It was active and its meetings were beneficial. At the time of the meeting of the Agricultural Society, in October, 1865, the committee especially appointed for the purpose, showed an "energetic and successful effort to suppress the sale of intoxicating liquors at the Fair." This organization continued until the spring of 1867. During the two years 138 members were connected with it. Survivors at this time are Miss Jane Sewall, Mrs. Mary Swan Fifield and Mrs. Abbie Powers Tenney.

In the late 1870s there was an attempt to organize a Lodge of Good Templars under the interest aroused by Francis Murphy, who spent some time in Fryeburg, but it died a-borning. Mr. Murphy's influence remained in the village, and his two sons went to school here for a time.

In the 1880s citizens of the village aspired to political office, but it was shown to them that their habits would prevent gaining their desire. Accordingly a meeting was held in the Congregational Vestry one Sunday night, at which the cause of temperance was advocated, and over a hundred persons signed this pledge:

"With malice toward none, and with charity for all, we the undersigned, hereby agree to abstain from all intoxicating liquors as a beverage."

The tide of interest once started, was kept in motion. Monthly meetings in the churches were continued for several years. That they were efficient in keeping a healthy sentiment in favor of temperance was evident.

In October of 1880, Mrs. E. A. G. Stickney of Brownfield and Miss Kimball of Chicago, organized a W. C. T. U. in Fryeburg, of which Mrs. G. H. Ricker, wife of the Principal of the Academy was chosen President. The Union began a quiet, but none the less effective work.

Since that time the saloon has showed its head in the village; but at the dictate of the Town voters it was ordered to close, January 1, 1937.

Fryeburg has always had appreciation of the best in Music, and its citizens have shown considerable musical ability. Before the introduction of the piano, vocal music was common, led by tuning-fork or pitch-pipe, and a usual form of entertainment among the young people was to sing glees, rounds and hymns, when a number were assembled. Singing schools were popular; old letters tell of classes of one hundred in the Vestry, under "Singer Sam" Farrington.

In the autumn of 1810 a number of interested citizens, among whom were Amos J. Cook, preceptor of the Academy, Samuel A. Bradley, and Stephen Chase, lawyers, and Timothy Osgood, formed a musical society, taking for its name that of a native of Denmark, Hans Gram, who was born in Copenhagen, in 1756. He came to this country on business but was so pleased with the environment in which he found himself, that he became a resident. He was a competent musician, and was the composer of some superior pieces.

On the first anniversary of the Hans Gram Musical Society, there was special observance with an oration by Oliver Bray, an Honorary member, which was later printed by the society. The orator referred to the society as follows:

Although situated far in the interior, at a distance from those places where access to science is most easily obtained, to you is reserved the honor of founding the first institution of this nature in the District of Maine . . . May we not hope that others stimulated by your laudable example, will form similar institutions in other places and present a barrier through which the follies and vanities of modern pretenders will never be able to penetrate. Should attempts be made in your vicinity again to defile the Altar, by substituting these sacrilegious effusions for anthems of praise, let the doors of the sacred Temple be closed, and its gates barred.

Fryeburg has sent music teachers from Maine to the Pacific coast; among them, Edward Ripley, William Fessenden Ward, Lizzie C. Shirley, Mrs. Minnie Howe Jordan.

Through the influence of John W. Odlin, of Concord, N. H., who was a talented musician and had relatives in Fryeburg, a Brass Band was organized in the village in the later '60s, which was well sustained for a number of years. Mr. Odlin was an experienced bandsman, having served in a band during the Civil War and was a member at one time of Gilmore's noted band. He secured instruments, and led the band for some time.

Some years later a number of musical persons aroused a new interest in a Band, and under the leadership of Dr. D. Lowell Lamson developed considerable ability. This organization, which began in 1883, carried on for some time, but the changing population, and the uncertainty of the younger element made its life short.

A new generation having developed and there being a nucleus of the previous Band, one was started in 1897 under the leadership of Cassius W. Pike. A band-stand was built at the corner of Main and Portland Streets, and weekly practice was enjoyed by those who listened. A uniform was procured, and this Band throve for some time, until deaths and the changes of residence weakened the organization to such an extent that it ceased to exist. Since then no effort has been made in the village to maintain a Brass Band. An orchestra of considerable merit was organized at one time by Mr. Pike, which played for dances and dramatic performances, and was a decided addition to Fryeburg's musical circle. But that, too, followed the inevitable course.

For a number of years, in the '80s and '90s a capable, uniformed Brass Band was maintained among the residents of East Fryeburg, organized by Mr. E. Warren. This Band was in demand in various nearby towns, and at the Fairs of the Agricultural society. For a time a Band existed in the neighborhood of North Fryeburg.

Besides starting a village Band, John W. Odlin helped the people of the Congregational Church to select an organ—the first in the town. Since its installation in 1862 it has been in constant use at the services of the church and in concerts. Its tone has grown sweeter with the years in spite of being subjected to great changes of temperature.

As might be expected, in a town where the chief industry was farming, the "Patrons of Husbandry" would thrive, and a Grange was organized with headquarters at the Center. It was named "Fryeburg Grange," and grew in membership and influence. At one time it conducted a general store for its members, where they could procure staple goods at a cooperative rate. The Grange continues an enthusiastic organization and is an asset to the town. Its exhibits at the West Oxford Fair are always large.

Some time later than the organization of Fryeburg Grange, a movement began to form a grange in the Village. It found plenty of support, and "Paugus" Grange was the result. This organization is a social body, with many members who are not active farmers yet the time may come, as the tide turns back to the land, that it will be a saving power for the farms in the vicinity of the village.

An active Grange has been maintained for several years, at East Fryeburg. That neighborhood being accustomed to doing community business in a thorough-going manner, has been an excellent location for such an organization, on account of the farming interests and the social life the Grange develops.

One of the most important institutions in Fryeburg is the Woman's Library Club, which occupies as its Club House and Library the Stone School House in the Village. It is now (1938) forty-eight years old, and during its existence, more than any other factor, has been useful in organizing the women, developing better acquaintance, and uniting the village.

In August, 1890 the Club was organized, with Miss Mary F. Bradley, as President. It had as its mission: The maintenance of a Library, for the use of the village; and the Intellectual Improvement of the Community. At first the Club met where it was most convenient, until quarters were obtained on the second floor of the Shirley & Lewis store building. Here it established a library, in January, 1891, and held meetings twice a month until September, 1903, when the stone building was occupied.

When the Town built a graded school building at the village for Districts No. 1, and No. 2, the schoolhouses became unnecessary, and at the annual meeting, in 1903, it was voted to give the Stone School House to the Woman's Library Club. The Club at once went to work to have the interior converted to its needs and uses, and November 13th the building was dedicated to its new service.

The Club is a democracy that believes in everyone having a fair chance at the honors, and so its presidents have been many. With few exceptions the Club has given its Presidents a second election. The first to occupy the office, Miss Mary F. Bradley, held office four years; the others succeeding her have served the usual two years, with a few exceptions.

Others who have held the office since Miss Bradley are these: Miss Hannah C. Osgood, Mrs. Susan Gordon, Mrs. Georgiana S. Barrows, Mrs. Adelia S. Eastman, Miss Alice O. Hastings, Miss Hannah C. Osgood, (re-election), Mrs. Marion Wentworth, Miss Mary L. Gordon, Mrs. Carrie G. Newman, Mrs. Mary Mansfield, Mrs. Cora Charles, Mrs. Lucia M. Lougee, Miss Harriet Abbott,

Mrs. Susan W. Merrill, Miss Mary Woodward, Mrs. Mary Bosworth, Mrs. Mary W. Lord, Mrs. Anita Dole, Miss Alice B. Glines, Mrs. Bertha H. Simpson, Mrs. Blanche Fox, Mrs. Ruth Sanborn, Miss Anna Barrows, Miss Harriet F. Woodward. Others who have been honored with election to the presidency, but declined for personal reasons are: Mrs. E. P. Weston, Mrs. Edith S. Bartlett, Miss Susanna Weston.

Since occupying the club house the Club has gone forward as an influence and as a source of interest among the women. Its library has been enlarged by purchase and gift of many books of value and of popular interest, until the library holds several thousand volumes. By the terms of Mrs. Mattson's gift of Bradley Park, this Club was given the power, after her decease, to make appointments to the Board of Commissioners. Mrs. Mattson has presented the Club with a tract of land, on Main Street, a portion of the land owned by her ancestors. It is a favorable site for the mountain view. One of the monuments set by Robert E. Peary to indicate the true-north meridian is on this lot.

The influence of the Woman's Club was felt in West Fryeburg where the Stirling Literary Club was organized. One of its members, Mrs. Susan F. Ballard, ninety years old, had the honor of being the oldest member of a woman's club in the State. She was the wife of the late George Ballard and mother of Eckley and Dean A. Ballard, both prominent citizens of the town.

The Woman's Library Club was not the only effort made in the village to encourage the habit of good reading and to cultivate a literary atmosphere. In 1850, a subscription was circulated, and twenty-one subscribers, at one dollar each entered into this agreement:

> The undersigned, wishing to form an association for the purpose of mutual improvement, hereby subscribe and agree to pay the sum set against our names, said sum to be expended in the purchase of books for the use of the Associates, said books to be selected, rules and regulations made, at the first meeting of said associates.

Reading Circles were maintained each winter by people in the village who were interested in the best literature. Shakespeare's plays were read, the parts being assigned to different individuals. Miscellaneous readings by the members made the meetings interesting. These circles were continued until the time when the Chautauqua movement began to spread, and the Assemblies each year stimulated the formation of a Chautauqua Reading Circle, which for several years read and discussed the books of the course.

An interesting occasion in the Village, August 9th, 1904, was the observance of the attainment of seventy years by a number of citizens and persons connected with Fryeburg at some time. It was arranged by Alonzo F. Lewis, long a resident of Fryeburg, who received his education at the Academy and taught in the schools of the town. He was a member of the firm of Shirley & Lewis until the firm dissolved, when he carried on an insurance business, and delved into historical matters. He was a trustee of the Academy, and for a time was Secretary of the Board.

Mr. Lewis summoned on this occasion thirteen persons who were born in 1834. Besides himself they were Gen. E. C. Farrington, William Gordon and his twin, Samuel Chase Gordon, Miss Olive J. Swan, Miss Abby N. Page, Mrs. Julia A. (Devine) Page, John Weston, Bradley B. Woodward, Jason Whitman Towle, George F. Booth, Thomas Jefferson Allard, Abel F. Sanborn. The gathering, which filled the room, was in the New Church Hall, and among the special guests present were: Hon. Frank B. Sanborn, the Concord sage and writer on historical subjects; John W. Hutchinson, the last member of the noted Hutchinson Family, who sang to pleased audiences all over the country, and were famous in the Federal camps in the Civil War; Mrs. Hale Jacobs, singer, of Malden, Mass.; L. W. Small, journalist of New York; George A. Thomas and his sister Miss Charlotte J. Thomas of Portland; Atherton Furlong, journalist of Portland; Edward Sherburn Osgood, Editor of the *Portland Eastern Argus;* Dr. Seth C. Gordon, Portland; Prof. Walter A. Robinson, former principal of the Academy, master in the Boston Schools. These all made felicitous speeches, and other speeches were made by Gen. Farrington, Mr. Allard and Samuel C. Gordon. Poems and letters from friends were read, and the program was interspersed with vocal music by Mr. Lewis and Mrs. Jacobs, Miss Lovett, Messrs. Hutchinson, Thomas and Furlong. The daughters of several of the "Septuagenarians" served refreshments, and provided the decorations.

General Farrington referred to conditions in his early years at Toll Bridge. He said, in part:

How well I remember our little old red school house, with its rows of high-backed seats, the stern teacher, with his switch and ferrule; our long walks in wind, snow and rain; the building of fires an hour before school-time, for each big boy had to take his turn at this; our cold hands and feet and chilled body, for no one was allowed to go and warm by the box stove, until the Testament had been read by the school; all these things and many more come to my mind as it goes back to the days when I was a boy; the bare feet from spring till fall, the time when the cobbler came to mend the old shoes and make cowhide boots for winter wear; the neighborhood prayer meetings, where our saintly mothers and grave fathers renewed their faith and hope; the stated call of the revered minister, somber and forbidding in appearance, in his high neck stock and subdued tone of voice—the calling-in of the family, the long prayer, warning us of the wrath of God and the fire that could never be quenched; the long hours of Sunday and its oppressive quiet; how all these things crowd my memory now. And still I cannot forget the brighter side: the warmth of the open fire; the boys and girls of the neighborhood; the games of "hi-spy," base and barn ball; the huskings, with the coveted red ear of corn, and the reward it brought to the finder; the apple-paring bees, the swinging of the long parings; the baked beans and pumpkin pies,—how good they were,—none like them now; the home-coming of brothers and sisters at Thanksgiving time; the sparerib roasted before the open fire; the mince pies, and with raisins in them; the baked Indian puddings from the great brick oven; all these bring the sweeter taste to the mouth, and, notwithstanding the change of today to more liberal thought and greater freedom, I would not, if I could, blot out a single experience of those days, for they were impressive, with the stern lessons that went deep into the soul, and taught us that life was a reality and a trust, and that honesty, integrity, manliness, kindness, patience, hope and reward were the things to be lived for.

That is an excellent picture of country life in Fryeburg, in the days when people lived and were happy though money was scarce and luxuries were not considered.

For a number of years, the Methodists of the Portland District had each summer made use of the maple grove, known as The Moosehorn, for Camp Meetings. From primitive beginnings, under the leadership of Mrs. Martha Nutter, of Portland, an earnest and consecrated woman, the grounds had been steadily improved; new buildings erected; a number of houses for local churches built; and many attractive private cottages added to the equipment of the grounds. The Camp Meetings continued until about 1884, but the interest was waning. To employ the grounds and equipment to a profitable advantage, Mrs. Nutter and others concerned, invited those interested in the Chautauqua Movement, to center the summer efforts at "Martha's Grove." Accordingly the summer Assembly of 1884 met for the first time at that place, and the Northern New England Sunday School Assembly and Maine Chautauqua Union became an active effort.

Until 1902 the Assemblies, with their attractive programs of lectures, classes, concerts and entertainments grew in popularity and numbers of patrons.

The list of speakers included: Rev. Edward Everett Hale, D.D., Rev. Lyman Abbott, D.D., Mrs. Mary A. Livermore, Hon. James G. Blaine, Governor Bodwell of Maine, Rev. J. W. Bashford, D.D., Rev. A. E. Dunning, D.D., Miss Lillian M. Munger, Pres. William DeW. Hyde, Rev. A. T. Dunn, D.D., Mrs. W. F. Crafts, F. A. Ober, Prof. G. H. Palmer, Mrs. Alice Freeman Palmer, Rev. N. T. Whittaker, D.D., Miss Anna Barrows, Miss Belle Libby, Fred Emerson Adams, Mrs. J. S. Ostrander, Rev. R. D. Grant, Rev. R. S. McArthur, Miss Mary F. Farnham, H. W. Kimball, Rev. W. F. Livingston, Miss Hattie A. Pike, Prof. W. A. Robinson, Mrs. L. M. N. Stevens, and many others of reputation. Rev. George D. Lindsay, D.D. was the conductor of the Assemblies with an able corps of assistants. Later Rev. Ernest H. Abbott was the conductor. Entertainers and musical organizations produced good entertainments in the evenings, and the large Auditorium was crowded with appreciative audiences. The C. L. S. C. Graduation each year attracted many who could not go to the parent Chautauqua, N. Y. Diplomas were awarded, and the exercises corresponded to those in the original Assembly. As long as the interest in the C. L. S. C. lasted, the Assembly was a success.

Fryeburg at first was in York County, one of the oldest counties of the Province of Maine. When Oxford County was organized the Registry of Deeds was situated at the shire-town, Paris. But Paris and Fryeburg were thirty miles apart, and it was a two days' journey for people on the western side. So, in 1800 the Western District was established, with a Registry.

James Osgood, proprietor of the Oxford House, was the first Registrar, and it was from his inability to write a creditable deed in the records that he hired Daniel Webster to copy the deeds. The first book of records is an object of interest to visitors today, showing the smooth flourishes of Daniel Webster's pen, as he wrote the formal expressions at the close of a deed, and affixed everything but the signature of Mr. Osgood.

Mr. Osgood held the office of Registrar until 1806. The first deed was dated June 20, 1799, and it was recorded January 13, 1800.

Following Mr. Osgood came these Registrars: 1806 to 1812, John Bradley; 1812 to 1840, Daniel Clement; 1841 to 1842, Ira Towle; 1842 to 1858, James O. McMillan; 1858 to 1873, Asa Charles. In the late years of his life Mr. Charles was assisted by his daughter, Frances, and after his death she was acting registrar until 1873 to 1886 Seymour C. Hobbs filled the office. From 1887 to 1890, Elbridge G. Osgood; 1890 to 1893, Annie R. Osgood; 1893 to 1912, Eckley Ballard; 1912 to 1914 Abby Ballard, who had been clerk to her father carried on the duties until the Governor appointed, to fill out the term, 1914 to 1922, Dean A. Ballard; 1922 to 1935, Abby Andrews; 1935 the present incumbent Mrs. Olive Goldthwait, was elected.

Since 1873 the office has been a political one, and the candidates are from the two political parties.

The County erected a building with a vault for the Registry in 1820. It was a substantial but modest little brick building on Main Street, near Elm Street. The business and the records so increased that in 1918, a new brick building was erected on the site of Samuel Souther's "Temperance House," on Portland Street, where ample accommodations for the recording of deeds and the proper protection of the records is provided.

The Fryeburg Registry contains more than a hundred well-prepared volumes of records, and in the 137 years since the office was opened, the entries have averaged at least one each day. Often old deeds, as well as those currently made, are brought for record.

It seems unaccountable that in a town like Fryeburg, with the amount of historical matter originally available, no interest was taken to conserve it, and to collect historic articles; but as those who know the most history often care the least about preserving the current history of their times, and as generation succeeds generation, the happenings of the times becomes forgotten and lost. The Town has been urged by historic-minded persons to publish a history, but efforts in that direction have failed to materialize, on account of the death of those best qualified to prepare such a document.

In the late 1850s and early 1860s Samuel Souther and James Ripley Osgood, began to collect material for a history, but the death of one and the removal of the other stopped the undertaking. Later, George B. Barrows began the work again, and collected material and laid plans for an extensive history. There were at that time, in the town, persons of age to remember many of the people and events that were historically valuable. The death of Mr. Barrows ended his efforts. Alonzo F. Lewis, collected historical data assiduously, but his sudden death stopped his work. William Gordon, from his knowledge of town affairs, and his acquaintance with many old people of his time, about the beginning of the present century wrote and published in a local paper articles "to give the main facts in the history of Fryeburg, since its formation as a town, in order that they may be in form readily accessible to the young people of today." His death prevented him from continuing his work.

In 1881 the Town voted,

That a Committee be chosen to collect Historical matter relating to the Town of Fryeburg, supervise the publishing of a History of the town; the expense to the town not to exceed One Hundred dollars.

The committee consisted of D. R. Hastings, G. B. Barrows, A. F. Lewis, James Walker, I. B. Bradley. On the death of Dr. Bradley, the next year Joseph Chandler was added to the committee and the Town voted,

To raise Three Hundred dollars for defraying the expense of the history, and if the Selectmen considered it necessary to complete the history, to add Two Hundred dollars to the sum indicated.

There the matter rested.

In August, 1920, Miss Hattie A. Pike and Clarence N. Stone, both born in Fryeburg and interested in the affairs of the town, were in conversation about the wealth of historical material in Fryeburg, and the importance of collecting and preserving it. Accordingly they called a meeting in the Woman's Club house, August 11, to organize a local historical society, to which came about thirty persons, including residents, former residents and interested visitors. Officers were elected, and a code of by-laws was drafted.

The officers chosen were: President, John L. Osgood; Vice Presidents, Clayton W. Pike, Miss Alice Hastings; Secretary, Miss Harriet Abbott; Assistant Secretary, Miss Abby Ballard; Treasurer, Miss Carey Bradley; Assistant Treasurer, Mrs. Mary Leadbeater; a number of committees were appointed for different purposes. About thirty persons signed this statement:

> We express our interest in collecting and preserving material connected with the history of Fryeburg, and in other activities of The Fryeburg Historical Society, in which we hereby enroll.

Of the thirty persons, who signed the roll, at the time of this writing (1937), eleven are dead, sixteen live out of Fryeburg, and three are still residents. No other meetings are recorded in the Secretary's book.

Fryeburg has its share of secret fraternities, which began with Pythagorean Lodge of Free and Accepted Masons, instituted June 13, 1803. It is number 11 in the Maine jurisdiction, so it is one of the old lodges of the state.

This organization had its meeting place, for many years, in the block owned by Major T. C. Ward, on the corner of Main and Portland Streets. Change of ownership brought the block into the possession of Albro R. Jenness, and on his death he willed it to the lodge, of which he was a member. The building remained in the possession of that organization, until it was burned, March 16, 1933. The loss of property of the Lodge was considerable, but the most valuable articles were saved. After the loss of their home they met in the apartments of the Lodge of the I. O. O. F., at Fryeburg Center, until the new building was opened in 1938. The building is a Masonic Temple, solely, no business concerns being provided for in it. It is a large, roomy building, and will provide a home for the Lodge indefinitely, being well-constructed. It stands next to the Legion Building, which contains the Post Office.

Pythagorean Sisterhood is a prosperous organization of the Eastern Star that has been connected with Pythagorean Lodge for years, and serves to bind closer the pleasant relationship between the families of Masonic associates.

In the 1880s Pequawket Lodge, an organization of the Knights of Pythias, was formed, which held its meetings in a hall over the store of E. P. Weston, until it was found possible to erect a building. It has been a popular organization ever since. Mountain View Temple, of Pythian Sisters was formed later as an auxiliary body.

A Lodge of the Independent Order of Odd Fellows was organized at Fryeburg Center which with its auxiliary body of Rebekahs has been in operation for many years. It maintains a lodge room in that neighborhood, as more of its members are from that and adjoining sections of the town.

The establishment at the Village of a Tribe of Red Men found favor with many of the young men, and in March, 1909, the degree of Pocahontas was administered to a number of women, thereby forming Washtela Council of Pocahontas, an auxiliary to the Tribe of Red Men. There is a Tribe of Red Men at North Fryeburg, but in the Village none exists.

A Kiwanis Club was organized and received its charter dated January 31, 1929. Since then it has organized as the Kiwanis Club of Fryeburg-Lovell, the neighboring town. The joint form of membership has been a beneficial influence in drawing together the two communities, increasing acquaintance, and giving each the benefit of the progressive spirit of Kiwanis.

August 31, 1932, came Fryeburg's opportunity to win a temporary fame, and to find the name of the town in almost every newspaper that gives any space to scientific matters.

This sudden elevation to general prominence was due to no merit on the part of the village, but because astronomers decided from careful computations that the Village of Fryeburg would be directly in the center of zone of darkness during the total eclipse of the sun.

Fryeburg was selected by the greater number of scientific observers because its topographical location was such that the possibilities of clear weather were greater than any place nearer the mountains, as all the records of weather for fifty years indicated the best average in the area considered.

Accordingly expeditions were started from the Lick Observatory, University of California, the University of Michigan and Georgetown University, D. C., and the intricate and valuable apparatus was sent to Fryeburg early in August, sites were selected, and work begun installing the camps for observation.

The site selected for the principal observations was the athletic field of the Academy, because of its clear horizon, its convenience, and the opportunity to use the Academy building for laboratory work. The apparatus was assembled there, and concrete bases for the large structures were made. The University of Michigan force erected a camera forty feet long, with a lens five and one-half inches in diameter, which would fill a plate fourteen by seventeen inches, on which the diameter of the image of the sun would be about four and one-half inches. This camera had been used in India, Labrador, Flint Island in the Pacific Ocean, in Burmah, Sumatra, and California, recording eclipses. It was in charge of Dr. H. D. Curtis, the head of the astronomical department of the University, as also two spectroscopes and an interferometer, for testing the corona for the presence of certain substances, of which knowledge was desired. A camera five feet long was also in use for color photography.

While these preparations were made on the Academy grounds, in another part of the village, Rev. Dr. Paul A. McNally, S.J., director of the Georgetown Observatory, was preparing his special apparatus for a motion picture of the shadow-bands which cross the landscape, just before the last thin crescent of the solar disk disappears. Another camera was in use in making a picture of the eclipse from the first to the last contact.

At Indian Acres, Dr. Oliver J. Lee, of Northwestern University, erected a mast 100 feet high for taking the temperature at different altitudes during the moments of the eclipse. This was done by recording thermometers set at intervals of twenty-five feet. Airplanes for a similar purpose were used at greater altitudes.

The day of the great experiment dawned bright and fair, and was a typical summer day, until about 1 P. M., when fleecy clouds began to come over the mountains, but the clouds happily broke, and allowed intermittent views of the eclipse. It was a spotty sky, but the astronomers worked unremittingly, catching every sight possible. At times the eclipse was seen perfectly, showing that the judgment of the astronomers was justified in selecting Fryeburg for their observations. The development of the negatives revealed some perfect photographs, which were highly satisfactory, for at neighboring points of observation, there were no results.

From the first the local Kiwanis Club worked steadily in preparation to assist the astronomical expeditions. An attractive circular descriptive of the place and the great undertaking was widely circulated, and preparations were made to give the expected throngs of spectators every courtesy. A committee of introduction and assistance to the visitors composed of Robert D. Eastman, Asa O. Pike, 2nd, Alvin D. Merrill, worked zealously to make the day enjoyable and educational for the visitors. Clarence E. Mulford was of great assistance to the astronomers, acting as time-keeper, calling the minutes and seconds during the entire period of the eclipse, which required strict watching of the clock, and gave him no opportunity to see the happenings in the period of darkness. In fact none of the operating astronomers actually saw the phenomenon, their work requiring strict attention to their duties.

Between 4,000 and 5,000 persons were estimated to be in Fryeburg for the day. They accepted the necessary conditions imposed by roping off and guarding the limits of the observation points, to prevent disturbance of the astronomers in any way. Any undue tremor of the ground, any noise of auto horns, and diversion of attention of the observers would have proved disastrous to the results of the photography, so sensitive to outside influences were the delicate instruments in use.

The force of astronomers were: University of Michigan: Dr. H. D. Curtis, Francis C. McMath, Robert McMath, Judge Henry S. Hulbert, Dr. R. M. Petrie, Dr. D. B. McLaughlin, R. B. Curtis.

University of California: Dr. J. H. Moore, Dr. W. H. Wright, Dr. D. H. Menzel, Dr. C. D. Shane, J. F. Chappell, Ben Osen.

Georgetown University: Rev. Dr. Paul McNally, S.J., Rev. Thomas D. Barry, S.J., Rev. Dr. Stein, director of the Vatican Observatory, Rev. Dr. Kolkmeyer, S.J., Rev. William J. Crawford, of Boston College, Rev. E. E. Swift, of Boston College High School, Rev. Daniel O'Connell, S.J., of Riverview Observatory, Sydney, Australia, Rev. T. H. Quigley, S.J., of Lyola College, Baltimore, Rev. Walter Miller, S.J., Dr. S. A. Korff, of Mount Wilson Observatory, Rev. Thomas J. Smith, Weston College, Weston, Mass.

Others present conducting independent observations were: Dr. Oliver J. Lee of Northwestern University, Capt. Barnett Harris, of the U. S. Signal Reserves.

XIX

PEOPLE IN PROFESSIONAL LIFE

> Other verses will sing of fair Fryeburg's great sons
> Other voices will praise them as mine may not do,
> Tell o'er their achievements, recount their bright deeds;
> Though much they may tell, far more would be true.
> —*Ebenezer Knowlton.*

Fryeburg has been fortunate in its professional men and women. The presence of the Academy has influenced the character of the town, so that a member of any profession seemed guaranteed recognition and appreciation on account of his profession.

Lawyers have won their first spurs in Fryeburg; physicians have found, in spite of the health-giving atmosphere, opportunity to help and cure; writers have found in people and environment suggestions for their pens; poets have never lacked inspiration among the beauties of nature; artists hesitate between the many attractive scenes as to which should be given preference on their canvasses; and any who seek inspiration, have always found in Fryeburg something worthy of their best efforts.

Judah Dana won distinction as a lawyer, being the first to open an office in what is now Oxford County. He filled many positions of honor and trust through his profession, and became Associate Justice of the Court of Common Pleas. He was a delegate to the convention that in 1819 framed the Constitution of the State of Maine. In 1836 he was elected to the Executive Council. He was appointed by the Governor to fill an unexpired term in the United States Senate, and served from December 21, 1836, until March 3, 1837. In that short time he measured swords with Henry Clay in debate. This aroused Clay's ire, and he referred to Senator Dana unpleasantly, twitting him of being "A six-weeks' senator." To this charge, Dana replied, administering a scathing rebuke to Clay.

THE OXFORD HOUSE

THE DANA HOUSE

Dana came naturally by his determination and courage, as his mother, Hannah Pope Putnam, was a daughter of Gen. Israel Putnam, the noted Revolutionary officer.

It was in Judge Dana's office that Daniel Webster, second preceptor of the Academy, read law, while he was in Fryeburg. Dana built the large colonial house in the village at the corner of Main and River Streets about 1816. Senator Dana died in Fryeburg, December 27, 1845.

His only son, John W. Dana, was Governor of Maine from 1847 to 1850. He was appointed minister to Bolivia by President Franklin Pierce. After his term of office had expired, he remained in South America, investing largely in sheep ranches, which attracted a number of Fryeburg young men.

Another lawyer, who had association with Judge Dana, was Jacob McGaw, who spent four years in this town, when he and Judge Dana were often opposing counsel. An anecdote is told of these two men, who after a sharp contest in court, in a neighboring town, happened to room together that night. The maid who showed them the room, expressed considerable surprise and anxiety that those two fighters in court should have been assigned to the same room. Judge Dana set her mind at rest, by telling her that opposing lawyers were like the two parts of a pair of shears; they could not cut one another, but only what came between them. Mr. McGaw continued in practice until 1805, when he removed to Bangor, where he had a large practice.

Another lawyer was Col. Samuel A. Bradley, a graduate of Dartmouth, who came from Concord, N. H., in 1803, and lived with his brother, Robert Bradley, a prosperous farmer and influential citizen. He was an honorable practitioner, and it is believed that he never accepted a case which he considered unjust.

Stephen Chase was an able lawyer. He completed the large colonial house, begun by Parson Whiting, now occupied by Major Clayton W. Pike. His son, Henry, a brilliant lawyer, was Senator in the Legislature, in 1846-47 and was president of that body.

Enoch Lincoln before becoming prominent in politics, was in practice about 1812. He had time to take an interest in military affairs, becoming Adjutant of the Brigade, the headquarters of which were in Fryeburg.

John Stuart Barrows, a native of Hebron and son of William Barrows, a Revolutionary soldier who founded Hebron Academy, came to Fryeburg in 1810 and established a partnership with Col. Samuel A. Bradley. He was considered a careful adviser and an upright attorney. He died while in the prime of life. His son, George B. Barrows, read law with him, but did not practice.

Edward L. Osgood, son of Samuel Osgood, was in practice for a number of years and was active in politics. He died in 1864. His son, James Ripley Osgood, became a noted publisher of Boston.

Alexander R. Bradley, son of Robert Bradley, a graduate of Harvard, was in practice in the early 1850-1860s. He was considered one of the best-read lawyers in Maine. His son, Alexander Stuart Bradley, after graduating from Bowdoin and securing his legal education, practiced here a while, but removed to Chicago, where he continued in practice until his death.

Henry Hyde Smith, for a time preceptor of the Academy, after reading law here engaged in practice until 1868, when he removed to Boston, where he took a high place in the profession.

Judge Augustus H. Walker, a graduate of Yale, was in practice in Fryeburg for several years before removing to Bridgton. His nephew, Edward C. Walker, a native of Fryeburg, studied law with him, and later was in partnership with him.

Major David R. Hastings, a native of Bethel, and a graduate of Bowdoin, was in practice in Lovell before he went into the Civil War as Major of the 12th Maine Infantry. He came to Fryeburg and opened an office in 1864. He bought the Stephen Chase house, where he lived for a number of years, and developed a large practice. He later built a fine residence on Elm Street, where he lived until he died, leaving his practice to his son and partner, Edward E. Hastings, a graduate of Bowdoin, and a prominent member of the Oxford Bar. He continued the firm of Hastings & Son, by taking into partnership his son, Hugh W. Hastings, also a graduate of Bowdoin, and a veteran of the World War. He has continued the practice since his father retired.

Seth W. Fife, a native of Chatham, N. H., and a graduate of the Harvard Law School, began practice in 1869, continuing until his death in January, 1915.

In the autumn of 1936, Roy A. Hanson, Esq., opened a law office in Fryeburg Village, and engaged in practice.

Residents of Fryeburg have been accorded high places in the State and National Government. Judah Dana went to the United

States Senate as has been said. Enoch Lincoln sat in the House of Representatives in 1821 and 1826, and James W. Ripley in the sessions of 1827-1828, and again in 1829-1830.

Simon Frye was the first representative of the County to the General Court of Massachusetts, sitting in the House in 1781. Moses Ames was the second representative to the same august body, in 1785. He was elected twice after that, and Simon Frye was elected to the senate in 1797. Rev. William Fessenden entered the political field as representative in 1799, and was twice re-elected in 1801 and 1802.

When the State of Maine was established, James W. Ripley was elected to the Senate, in 1820, 1821 and 1825. His successors in the Senate were: Edward L. Osgood, 1838-1839; John W. Dana, 1843-1844; Stephen H. Chase, 1846-1847, at which time he was President of that body; James Hobbs, Jr., 1849-1850; James Walker, 1851-1852-1853; Timothy Walker, 1855; George B. Barrows, 1863-1864, in the second session President of the Senate; Enoch C. Farrington, 1872-1873; E. Chandler Buzzell, 1925-1926-1927-1928; Earl P. Osgood, 1937-1938.

The members of the State House of Representatives from Fryeburg have been: James W. Ripley, 1815; Samuel A. Bradley, 1816-1817; Nathaniel Charles, 1855; Samuel L. Chandler, 1856; George B. Barrows, 1859-1862; James W. Howe, Jr., 1865; Enoch C. Farrington, 1866-1869; John Locke, 1873; Henry D. Hutchins, 1876; Enoch C. Farrington, 1879; Samuel O. Wiley, 1887; Tobias L. Eastman, 1891-1892; Dean Ballard, 1901-1902; E. Chandler Buzzell, 1911-1912; James W. Eastman, 1921-1922; Earl P. Osgood, 1933-1934. Fryeburg has been included with other towns in the selection of Representative, and so the turn comes infrequently.

Other positions of honor and trust held by Fryeburg men are: Governor's Councilor: Enoch C. Farrington, 1877-1878. Albion P. Gordon, 1899, 1901. Mr. Gordon also held the position of Inspector of Prisons and Jails, 1902-1903.

With the exception of a few years at the beginning of the settlement Fryeburg has not lacked physicians of the best skill. The first to come, was Dr. Joseph Emery, a young man, called to treat Samuel Walker, who had cut himself badly while working in the woods. Dr. Emery was so pleased with the prospects, that he decided to remain, and in 1768 built a house on the Drift Road.

Dr. Josiah Chase came from Canterbury to Fryeburg, in 1764. He married a daughter of Colonel Frye. He had been a surgeon with Gen. Peleg Wadsworth on the Penobscot expedition. He came to the town at the solicitation of Colonel Frye, and continued practice until his death in 1796, by drowning, when his horse fell into the river near the "Black Cat" brook one dark night as he was coming from Conway.

Dr. Joseph Benton, a graduate of Yale, and a skillful physician, came in 1795. He had a large practice, but did not remain long. He was succeeded by Dr. Stephen Porter in 1797, but he died of typhus fever the next year. His body lies in the old cemetery in the village.

Dr. Oliver Griswold, came from Lebanon, N. H., in 1798. He occupied the house built by Capt. Vere Royce, which is still standing on River Street. He continued in practice until his death in 1833. Mrs. Griswold was a daughter of Rev. William Fessenden.

About this time Dr. Locke was in practice at Center Fryeburg.

Dr. Eliphalet Lyman, from Connecticut, a graduate of Yale, came about 1800 and remained several years. He built a large colonial house where now is the Congregational Church. Colonel Edward L. Osgood bought and moved it to the corner of Main and Oxford Streets where it is now known as "Ye Olde Inn."

Dr. Moses Chandler came in 1797, and settled at the Center where he practiced. He died in 1822.

Dr. Reuel Barrows, a native of Hebron, settled in the Village in 1817, continuing with a large practice, until he died in 1857. About the same time, Dr. Ira Towle, a native of Newfield, was in practice. He and Dr. Barrows were among the leading physicians of the County. When he died in 1873 his place was taken by his son, Dr. William C. Towle, who had a large practice. He had been surgeon in a Maine regiment in the Civil War. He died October 1, 1900.

Dr. John Chandler, a native of Boscawen, N. H., and a graduate of Dartmouth in the same class as Daniel Webster, was in practice for a number of years at North Fryeburg. Dr. Noah O. Parker also held a long practice at North Fryeburg, and died there.

Dr. Israel B. Bradley was numbered among the physicians of the Village, but his extensive business associations limited his practice to consultation.

Dr. D. Lowell Lamson came to the Village from Conway Center in 1857, and continued as an active practitioner for many years.

He was a leading citizen in good works, and was a very ingenious man, and a clever inventor.

Dr. Charles Hill came from Bridgton in 1879 and practiced until his death in 1884.

Dr. George H. Shedd, a native of Norway, came from Bartlett, N. H., in 1883. He had an extensive practice. His brother, Dr. John Z. Shedd, assisted him the latter part of his stay. They removed to North Conway where they organized the Memorial Hospital, in which many Fryeburg people have had treatment.

During the same years, Dr. J. L. Bennett was in practice at North Fryeburg, as was Dr. Mitchell, his successor; both of whom removed to Bridgton. Dr. Irving Mabry succeeded to the North Fryeburg field, where he remained for thirty years and more, until he died May 3, 1929.

Dr. Herman L. Bartlett, a native of Stoneham, practiced for a few years before removing to Norway, where he died.

Dr. George Allen, after a practice in Conway, came to Fryeburg for a few years before he removed to Lovell.

Dr. F. H. Jordan from 1902 for some years had a successful practice in the Village, until he removed to South Portland.

Dr. A. C. Ferguson assisted Dr. W. C. Towle during the last years of his life, and succeeded to his practice. He left for practice in New York.

Dr. L. W. Atkinson was in practice from 1901 for a number of years before removing to California.

At this same time Dr. H. L. Craft, who later went to Lovell, and Dr. W. H. Baker, who went from this town to Buxton, practiced at North Fryeburg. Following Dr. Baker, North Fryeburg was without a local physician for a few years, and the situation became so crucial that Town action was taken to pay a physician a certain sum, to insure his residence.

Dr. Arthur J. Lougee, a native of Rochester, N. H., and a graduate of Dartmouth, developed an extensive practice during more than twenty years until he died, Dec. 21, 1933.

Dr. W. B. Twaddle, of Bethel, coming in 1909, practiced several years.

He was succeeded by Dr. Earle P. Gregory, who had a large practice from 1920. He built a colonial house on Main Street. He died suddenly Nov. 20, 1937.

Dr. R. M. Boothby was in practice from 1935, specializing in the practice of Osteopathy.

Dr. Leon Cohen, came from New York and built a house on the Drift Road, in the Village, and was a successful physician from 1930.

Dr. W. A. Monkhouse came to the North Fryeburg field in 1934, and carried on practice for several years.

Fryeburg and its various attractions have been the theme of song and story, from the time of Lovewell's Fight to the present day. The fight on the shore of the pond attracted the bards of the period and the events were embalmed not only in household tales but in ballads, also.

One of the first efforts of this character was "The Ballad of Lovewell's Fight," by an unknown author, the first line of which is:

" 'Twas Paugus led the Peq'kt tribe,"

This poem is kept alive in historic papers, as also the "Song of Lovewell's Fight," the first line of which is:

"Of worthy Captain Lovewell I now propose to sing."

The Centennial of this fight stimulated the poets to action, and Thomas Cogswell Upham produced two, and Henry Wadsworth Longfellow an ode which is given on page 26.

Other persons skilled in poesy have apostrophized Fryeburg and its beauties, among them Rev. Samuel Souther, who loved Fryeburg with a powerful affection and delivered a poem, "Memory," of marked quality, at the Semi-Centennial of Fryeburg Academy, Aug. 17, 1842.

Rev. Henry Bernard Carpenter produced a classic. This brilliant Irish clergyman lived in the Village about 1875.

A daughter of Fryeburg, Mrs. Caroline Dana Howe was always lavish in her tributes to the place. William P. Palmer, a summer resident, laid his offering on the altar of the place. John S. Colby, born in West Fryeburg, of an old family, will be remembered for his graceful ode beginning:

> Dear Fryeburg, fair art thou,
> Time writes upon thy brow
> No furrows deep.

George Strout, son of a Methodist minister in Fryeburg, wrote a dignified and appreciative poem, entitled, "Change," in praise of the scenery of the town.

The list might be enlarged by the names of many lesser lights, who do not claim to be poets but have offered their tributes to the beautiful town.

In rehearsing the list of poets we can not overlook Kate Putnam Osgood, daughter of Col. and Mrs. Edward L. Osgood, who lived at the corner of Main and Oxford Streets, and received the suggestion of scenery from the lane on the opposite side of the street that leads to the farms and pastures on the intervale.

"Private" Joseph W. Fifer, ex-Governor of Illinois, who as a Union soldier in the Civil War knew the real pathos of "Driving Home the Cows," said of the poem:

> There are poems of the heart and poems of the head, and that beautiful wartime poem "Driving Home the Cows" was a poem that went to the heart—and to their hearts our boys took it. Some of them memorized it. I have recited it at many a reunion and campfire. Soldiers from the farm loved it because it was a perfect picture of home—the lanes, the footpath, the clover field, and the apple orchard, the herd coming from pasture, the wheeling bats, the frog pond, the farm gate, and the buttercups amidst the meadow grass. Why, there isn't anything but agriculture in it! It is pure pastoral . . .
>
> The poem struck a chord of yearning in the heart of every farm-born soldier in an army so largely recruited from the farm as ours was.
>
> "Driving Home the Cows" first appeared in the March number of *Harper's*, 1865, but the list of authors didn't come out till the following June. Then it was too late, for meanwhile thousands upon thousands of soldiers at the front had read the poem in newspapers that had immediately reprinted it from *Harper's*—and from one another—and of course without the name. So the name didn't catch up with the poem.
>
> Therefore a mystery grew up and you would hear people say—I said so myself—"Think of the modesty of that man who wrote this beautiful poem and won't give up his name in spite of all the eagerness to know it!" Finally some of the guessers said that they had found out about a place in Iowa that fitted in with all the poet's story and description—the old man, the three sons, the natural features, and so on. But still they didn't find the author's name.
>
> I found out years afterward, the poet was not "that modest man" but a woman. She was Kate Putnam Osgood, born in the little town of Fryeburg down in the southeast corner of Maine, where her folks lived for half-a-century, and she was twenty-three years old when she wrote "Driving Home the Cows."

Rev. Amos Jones Cook, long time Preceptor of Fryeburg Academy, wrote frequently for the press, and compiled in 1813, the

"Students' Companion," a book of selected articles, suitable for reading or declamation, which was a dignified and creditable work for the time.

William Dean Howells, while resting in the Village, found the beginning for one of his novels, "A Modern Instance," in a description of the place in winter.

Elizabeth Shepley Sergeant, a grand-daughter of Fryeburg, found in her vacations here the theme for a delightful novel, "Short as Any Dream," in which she introduced people of the past.

Among the authors who have chosen Fryeburg for a home is Clarence E. Mulford, who though born in Illinois, was so satisfied with the New England country, and Fryeburg in particular, that he bought a residence on Main Street. Mr. Mulford is well known to the American reading public as the author of the stories about his favorite hero, "Hopalong Cassidy." Mr. Mulford is also a skillful mechanic and has specialized in making models of the various forms of transportation which have become historic in this country. He also has made a detailed scale model, fully equipped, of the U. S. S. "Constitution," which stands high among the many models of that ship. He is also a lover and thorough student of the rifle and is an accomplished marksman. In order to engage in his favorite pastime he built a rifle-range of several distances, and has interested his acquaintances in the perfection of the historic art of marksmanship with the American weapon.

Margaret Vere Farrington, (Mrs. W. F. Livingston), who lived in the village and attended the Academy, is among the authors who have added to the fame of Fryeburg. She wrote the story "Fra Lippo Lippi," and her "Tales of King Arthur" is a book that pleases youth.

Anna Barrows, nationally known as a pioneer of the Home Economics movement and for years on the staff of Teachers College, Columbia University, New York, wrote several books on her specialty. She lives in her birthplace in the Village.

Miss Edith A. Sawyer, of New York, found the Village so attractive that she bought one of the old residences. She has won a reputation for her works dealing with Japanese life and literature, "The Fortunes of Umi" being highly praised by Japanese readers. She is known also as a writer of short stories.

It is not surprising that a locality so favored by Nature should prove attractive to the artist, and from the time of the development of landscape painting as an American art, there have been many who have reproduced on canvas the scenery of the town. Among the early artists who spent some time in Fryeburg, were John Kensett and John Casilear, New York men who later were noted for their landscape work. They were brought to Fryeburg in the 1840s by Benjamin Champney, a Boston artist, who later became a summer resident of North Conway, N. H.

Other artists from near and far have painted the scenery of Fryeburg, but none has been so faithful to their beauty in summer or winter as Benjamin T. Newman, a native of Bath, Maine, who was so charmed with the possibilities of Fryeburg scenery, that he became a resident. As a faithful draughtsman and a skillful colorist, his paintings have the charm of the actual scenery. He has made use of a trailer-studio in winter, and thus equipped has made pictures unavailable to the artist in the open. Mr. Newman is also skilled in portraiture.

Douglas Volk, an artist of national reputation, who for many years had a studio in Lovell, and for forty years lived summers in Maine, chose Fryeburg for his residence during his declining years. Here he painted his favorite study, Abraham Lincoln, of whom he had a vivid recollection. His father, Leonard Volk, the noted sculptor who made the death-mask of Lincoln, was well-known to the President, and was often at the White House. Douglas, as a child, sat on Mr. Lincoln's knee while he was sitting for the sculptor. That incident seemed to throw a charm over the life of the child, and when he became a man and an artist he made studies of the face of Mr. Lincoln, and his portraits of the man, which now hang in many notable galleries and public buildings throughout the country, are considered excellent likenesses, and the best character pictures of the martyred President.

During his active years Mr. Volk painted the portraits of many famous persons, among them King Albert of Belgium, by whom he was made an officer of the Order of King Leopold II. He also went to England on commission of the United States Government to paint a portrait of Lloyd George. An example of his ability in portraiture is the picture of his wife, which he gave to the Woman's Library Club.

One of the early painters who has immortalized Fryeburg scenes in his pictures was Eastman Johnson, who was born in the neighboring town of Lovell, but lived in his youth in Fryeburg, in the locality known as "Fish Street," where he obtained impressions of country life that afterward he reproduced in his paintings.

Miss Hattie A. Pike is a Fryeburg artist. A daughter of Mr. and Mrs. Asa Osgood Pike of the "Oxford House," she attended Fryeburg Academy, after which she devoted herself to voice-culture and to music teaching. She also studied under competent teachers and prepared herself to teach Art. She always spends her summer vacations in her home town, where she built a studio on the site of her former home, destroyed in the conflagration of August, 1906. Here she displayed her work in summer exhibitions, and as the patron of young artists, showed their work in public exhibitions.

Among the artists who have exhibited in Miss Pike's studio may be mentioned: Mrs. Rachel Weston Alden, a Fryeburg girl, whose child-studies are fascinating; Miss Florence Whitehead of Boston, a landscape artist who has exhibited also in Boston; Miss Anne Cary Bradley of Fryeburg, who has exhibited elsewhere and whose ability as an artist has received merited and wide appreciation; the late William B. Post, a resident of Fryeburg, where he found wide opportunity for the exercise of his carefully discriminating taste in photography, his subjects being remarkable for their grace and beauty, unique selection of lighting and their appropriate finish, which made all his work veritable works of art.

Appreciation of the beauties of nature, and the artistic presentation of them have not been confined alone to the literary or painter's reproduction. Many flower gardens have been a matter of pride to the owners, among those noted in the past are the gardens of Mrs. I. B. Bradley, Mrs. John Locke, Mrs. W. B. Bradley, Mrs. W. B. Fessenden, Mrs. G. S. Barrows, Mrs. E. G. Fife, Mrs. John Ward, all of which in their season were beautiful and objects of interest to the passer-by. The gardens of Hon. A. A. Perry at his residence and on River Street, were luxuriant in blossoms and variety. The most extensive flower farm and a popular market is that carried on by Mr. James Hobbs, on Main Street, where a wealth of flowers during the season are a source of attraction.

XX

NOTABLE TOWNSFOLK

It is a noble faculty of our nature which enables us to connect our thoughts, our sympathies and our happiness, with what is distant, in place or time; and, looking before and after, to hold communion at once with our ancestors and our posterity. Human and mortal although we are, we are nevertheless not mere insulated beings, without relation to the past or the future.

—*Daniel Webster.*

To catalogue properly the famous men and women who have ever lived in Fryeburg, would require a special definition of the word, "famous", for "Fame is but a slow decay", and people who never went beyond the boundaries of the town, were in their own ways as famous as some whose names were on the lips of thousands. This story is told of "Uncle Johnny" Smith, the noted stage driver and innkeeper, when a visitor sitting in conversation with him asked, "Where shall I find the first men of this place?" Uncle Johnny, in his simple but effective way pointed to the burying ground in sight of the house, and said, "Over there".

So if the names of the famous persons of Fryeburg were to be mentioned, it should include those present now, and many who have completed their work.

Such men as General Frye, the father of the town; Rev. William Fessenden, first minister of the Congregational Church; Preceptor of the Academy, Amos J. Cook, already mentioned, should be included in the list of Fryeburg heroes, but there are other persons entitled to mention for the parts they played in the Town and the Nation.

Colonel Joshua Bailey Osgood, who lived in the Osgood place on Main Street, on the slope of Pine Hill, combined the energy of the old forester and scholarly attainments, being a graduate of Harvard. He came from Haverhill, Mass., and married Elizabeth, the daughter of Capt. Harry Y. Brown. While on his way to visit his dying father at Haverhill, he was taken sick and died, May 30,

1791. On his sick-bed he enjoined upon Captain Brown the establishment of the Academy at Fryeburg, and this led to the founding of Fryeburg Academy.

Fryeburg has had many skillful medical practitioners, who made a local reputation worthy of more extended note, but it is doubtful if there ever was among them so unique a character as Dr. Alexander Ramsay, a physician and surgeon, who in 1805, came to this country from Scotland where he was a member of the family of Dalhousie; rumor has it he was a member of the nobility, resigning his title because of deformity. He came to this valley, bringing his library and anatomical collection, and after looking over the country selected Fryeburg, partly on account of the Academy, as a suitable place to establish a medical school. He presented his plan to the trustees of the Academy but the scheme did not seem feasible to them, and so the Doctor conducted a school on a more modest plan, giving lectures in his room in Robert Bradley's house. He also gave lectures at Parsonsfield and at Conway, and in Montreal, Canada.

Dr. Ramsay did not undertake to practice his profession, but he was often in consultation with local physicians. He was ahead of his time as an anatomist, and he strengthened his position by his published work on "The Heart, Brain and Cranium." He had an extensive museum of anatomical specimens, and when lacking the proper part, would roll up his sleeve and demonstrate on his muscular arm, or on his head, which was unusually large. He remained in Fryeburg until 1810 going back to England occasionally, but returned and established himself in Fryeburg again in 1817. He did not remain long, but travelled, going as far south as Charleston, lecturing and making a reputation among men of his profession.

Dr. Ramsay was noted for his irascible temper, which he could not, or did not attempt to control. His reputation outweighed his personal peculiarities, and he was considered the most talented physician anatomist ever in Maine. He was interested in the work of Sunday Schools, and gave Bibles to his youthful acquaintances with deep conviction in the value of the book. He died in Parsonsfield while he was lecturing in that place.

A useful citizen was Deacon Simon Frye, a nephew of General Frye, and a member of the Church from the time it was organized. He cleared land and built a house at the east end of the Menotomy road. He brought his family to Fryeburg in 1767. He was active in town affairs, acting as proprietors' clerk for a few years, and after the town was incorporated served as moderator of the town meetings and also as a selectman for some years. After the Town was established he was the representative to the General Court of Massachusetts for five or six years in succession. He was senator from the County of York for two terms, having run against Parson Fessenden at the first elections. After Oxford County was formed he was first judge of Court of Common Pleas.

Simon Frye's name is found frequently in the records of the doings of the people of Fryeburg, as he was among the foremost in all good efforts. He was one of the first trustees of the Academy, when it was incorporated. He served his fellows in the town for thirty years, and died in 1822.

During the first ten years of the settlement, three brothers, John, Abner and Samuel, sons of John Charles of Brimfield, Mass., came to the township and established homes. They cleared farms, and became useful citizens. They raised large families, and were the progenitors of the number of families of Charles, in this and adjoining towns. Their descendants married with the Wileys, Walkers, Stevens, Evans and other pioneer families, and descendants of this family of Charles are to be found widely scattered through New England.

Caleb Swan, Jr., son of Caleb, the first settler, followed his father's example as a soldier and enlisted in the Revolutionary Army, and in Nov., 1778, was at Camp Hartford. During his service he wrote letters, but was unable to visit his home. Some of his letters were pathetic in his expressions of affection and his great desire to see his family. In one written April 22, 1780, while in camp at West Point on the Hudson, he asks them to send him a pair or two of stockings, if it would not embarrass the family too much to spare them. He said he had tried to get them from Boston, but could not buy them there for less than $90.00 a pair, and he could not get them in his vicinity, for any price. On April 19, 1781, he was still at West Point, and still was unable to get home; he sent his letter and word by Mr. Frye to his family. He then had been four years in the service, without visiting his home. After the war he was in the Paymaster's Department, and was serving in that capacity with the Western Army some time in President Washington's Administration.

Enoch Lincoln, who gave to Fryeburg the reputation of having inspired a future Governor with the theme for the first poem written and published in Maine, was "to the manner born", as the father, Hon. Levi Lincoln was Lieut. Governor of Massachusetts; his brother, Levi, Jr., and finally, Enoch, a wearer of the gubernatorial toga. He was born in Worcester, Mass., December 28, 1788. He entered the Sophomore class of Harvard, and later received the degree of Master of Arts from Bowdoin. He studied law with his brother Levi, and was admitted to the Bar in 1811. After practicing his profession in Salem and his native town, he came to Fryeburg in 1812. During his years there he served in the militia, sent a challenge to a duel to a man in the village, and otherwise distinguished himself. He became engaged to Mary Chapman Page, daughter of David Page and sister of Captain John Page, who was wounded fatally at Palo Alto. History tells nothing of the romance; Mary, herself, did not tell why the two drifted apart, but for some reason they never completed the romance. Lincoln went to Congress in 1818 and spent the next eight years at Washington, where he was a popular man in society. The next three years he was governor of his home state, and died in office in 1829. He never married.

It must not be forgotten that Fryeburg enters largely into his fame, for it was the charm of the scenery, and the historic associations that inspired him to the composition of "The Village", a little volume that is highly valued by possessors today. None of the poets who gave American poetry its place in the literature of the world had yet reached the age of production.

"The Village" is a descriptive and didactic poem of more than two thousand lines, in heroic measure, common in England at that time. It suggests Pope in the formation of the lines and the expressions of thought. The author's study of the ancient classics is evident in the imagery and style of the poem. It opens with an apostrophe to Fryeburg's woodland and intervale scenes:

> "Range after range, sublimely piled on high,
> Yon lofty mountains prop the incumbent sky.
> Such countless tops ascend, so vast the heap,
> As if, when gushed the deluge from the deep,
> The rushing torrents wrecked the guilty world,
> And all the rocky fragments thither whirled.

> Around their tops the gathering vapours driven,
> In cloudy flight conceal the face of Heaven.
> I see them meet, divide, collect and spread,
> And last convolve around the mountain's head;
> While here and there the sun-beams glimmering through,
> Their borders paint with each prismatic hue;
> Then gathering thick, in one black cloud they lower
> And pour impetuous down the liberal shower.
> Frequent and bright the forked lightning's flash,
> And loud and deep the heavy thunders crash;
> By rushing winds the sturdy woods uptorn,
> From crag to crag by roaring streams are borne;
> Rebellowing echo swells the hills around,
> And every summit trembles at the sound."

The poem is divided into a number of subjects, which the author treats in this same style. His reference to the Saco River is especially forcible:

> "Shallow and deep, by turns, and swift and slow
> There I behold the winding Saco flow.
> In early spring, when showers increase its tides,
> And melting snows pour down the mountains sides,
> I've seen it raging, boisterous, and deep,
> O'erflow its banks and through the upland sweep.
> The farmer's hopes, the lumberer's hard earned thrift,
> Logs, bridges, booms and boats were all adrift;
> Trees, fences, fields, whate'er oppos'd its course,
> Were torn and scatter'd by the o'erwhelming force.
> Loos'd from the fold to crop the tender feed,
> The hungry flock were grazing on the mead.
> Their saving Ararat, a trifling mound,
> Secured them from the deluge spreading round,
> 'Till, taught no more to let the stragglers roam,
> The careless shepherd bore them to their home.
> Then, from the spouting clouds no longer fed,
> Our little Nile return'd within its bed."

This poem, covering 81 pages, was published in Portland, by Edward Little & Co., in 1816. The volume was further expanded by an Appendix, in three parts filling 87 pages, in which the author discusses slavery, lawyers and law courts and the peculiar forms of religious persecutions, with condemnation of popery and the inquisition. The intention of the author, mentioned in his preface, "has been the production of useful information to his countrymen, and the success of that object will be an ample remuneration for his labour and researches."

One of the earliest settlers of Pequawket, whose name is immortalized by the mountain that bestrides the state line between Chatham, N. H., and Gilead, Me., was Captain Vere Royce, who was born in 1733, a member of a noble family of Ireland, and being a younger son and ineligible to the peerage, went into the army, with the commission of ensign. He came to America with Gen. Braddock's army, in 1755, and was in the Indian War, in the attack on the French Fort DuQuesne in the Philadelphia wilderness. While Royce was an engineer in the army he commanded an infantry company in the Battle of the Monongahela. He was acquainted with Colonel George Washington, who was attached to Braddock's staff, and this anecdote is told of them:

After Gen. Braddock was killed, Colonel Washington was riding along the front, trying to bring some order out of the chaotic condition into which the loss of their general had thrown the army, and he came upon Capt. Royce's company, still engaged. The captain was directing the fire of his men, when Washington came up.

"Why haven't you retreated, Captain Royce?" asked Washington.

"I have had no orders to retreat, sir. Steady men, Load, Aim, Fire!" said the Captain.

"But this will not do, Captain Royce, you are exposed here to a severe fire. I order you to retreat, sir!"

"Right about face; forward march, and double-quick!" came the prompt command, and the company made a precipitate retreat from the field, that was already too hot.

Captain Royce participated in the second attack on Louisburg, where he met Major Joseph Frye. This acquaintance was destined to mean much for both men. Royce was at Quebec in 1759, where he met John Farrington, who had been captured by the Indians, another acquaintance that time was to bring into closer relationship after he resigned from the army in 1761, when he became a resident of America; influenced perhaps by his association with Miss Mary Pickard, a Portsmouth young woman, whom he married and took with him into the Pequawket wilderness, where he went with Colonel Frye to help survey the grant. In 1769 he was granted a tract of land of 2,000 acres on the banks of the Saco river, which became Bartlett, N. H.

In 1785 he was living in Fryeburg, in what is now East Conway, in a house built by Nathaniel Smith, one of the first settlers. The house is still standing not far from "Union Hall", on the opposite side. That year the great freshet brought the water around the house, and in the night, Mrs. Royce being disturbed by the sound of the flood awoke and waked her husband. He listened, and then said, "Lie down Mrs. Royce, nothing will harm thee." Mrs. Royce was not so easily satisfied, and putting her foot ankle-deep into the water which had come into the cottage, she immediately informed her husband of the situation by letting out a yell that, it was said, was heard at Colonel Webster's, which was below the Woodward farm. The Captain decided then to act promptly, and made known the situation so that soon people in boats took them and others along the street to more comfortable locations.

Some time later, he and his son-in-law, for John Farrington whom he first met at Quebec, had married his daughter, built a house on the North Fryeburg road, below the Center. It was later known as the "Charles Gordon house". Captain Royce lived there until he died in 1810. Captain Royce was an accurate surveyor and was employed for years by the state of New Hampshire in surveying the new lands. He corrected some of the surveys of the township of Fryeburg, and allotted the third and fourth Divisions.

There is a tradition that, owing to his habits of accurate surveying, "he ate, drank and slept according to the rules of arithmetic," and if any accident happened, he excused it, "because he had missed a figure".

Among prominent citizens was Asa Osgood Pike, whose early life was closely associated with East Fryeburg, where he was born, Nov. 25, 1822, the son of Job K. and Mary (Buck) Pike. He was a grandson of James Osgood, the first tavern keeper. Mr. Pike lived as a farmer and general business man for some years, and built the brick house at the corner of the Bridgton Road and the Toll Bridge-Denmark Road. He occupied this as a dwelling, store, post office and tavern. Here he laid the foundation for an ample competence, which, by hard work and superior business capacity he early secured. He was an extensive dealer in lumber, his good judgment and ability to see a good trade being an important factor in his success.

In 1874 he moved to the Village, and acquired the ownership of the Oxford House.

Mr. Pike was a broad-minded man, awake to all the movements of the town, state and nation. His education put him in touch with the thought of the times, and he was foremost in good works. He was honored by his townsmen, being given high positions of trust, and at the time of his death, April 21, 1888, he was holding the office of Assessor of the Village Corporation, Director of the White Mountain Telephone Company, a member of the State Board of Agriculture, President of the Fryeburg Horse Railroad Company, President of the West Oxford Agricultural Society.

His son, Cassius Warren Pike, by nature modest and unassuming, took up the work his father laid down. He helped whatever he laid his hand to, and at his death left an empty place in the town.

Asa Osgood Pike left his name to a grandson and a great grandson, both of whom are giving their best to their town.

John Smith is recalled with thoughts of the old days of stage coaches. His White Mountain coach used to be seen, on a summer morning, in front of the Elm Tavern on Federal Street, Portland. It had seats on top, covered with an awning, and was called a "double-decker". Smith's coach was conspicuous among those picking up their passengers before starting on their various routes. After carrying on the line for many years, Mr. Smith retired to Fryeburg, and became landlord of the Oxford House, which under his management was noted for its neatness. Later he kept a private and select boarding house opposite. He was a man highly esteemed in the community, and he retained his physical and mental faculties almost to the last of his ninety-five years.

One who gained high eminence in his chosen profession as a publisher was James Ripley Osgood, son of Hon. Edward L. Osgood. Ripley Osgood left Fryeburg in 1860 for a position in Boston, where he advanced in his profession until he was known as a publisher of some of the best works of American and English authors. He was at first associated with the honorable firm of Ticknor & Co., which became Ticknor & Osgood, and finally his own name stood where now the succeeding house of Houghton, Mifflin Co., stands among the leaders of New England.

Osgood left Boston for a better outlook in his profession in New York. He was for a time the advance agent and manager of Charles Dickens in his tour of the United States. Later Osgood went to England to be the London representative of Harper Brothers, a position he held from 1886 until his death in 1892.

He made a place for himself among the publishers of London, where he organized the firm of James R. Osgood, McIlvane & Co., and at the same time won favor for the American house which he represented.

Perhaps the best testimonal was the inscription on the stone that marks his grave in Kensal Green Cemetery, in London, which is:
"To James R. Osgood; a Cherished Companion and
Loyal Friend. Born at Fryeburg, Maine, U.S.A.,
22 February, 1836. Died in London, 18 May, 1892.
This memorial is erected by the many who respected
and loved him."

A man of eccentric genius, but of great business talents, who lived in Fryeburg at times during his long life, was Albert Colby. Born in the town, of the best blood of the early families, he grew up with an ability to acquire both learning and property. His chosen vocation was that of dealer in books, and he had book stores in several New England cities, but he always claimed Fryeburg as his home, clinging to the ancestral farm because several generations of the family are buried there. He stated this fact in many advertisements of his business:

And when my life shall close, There may I decompose, When I've turned up my toes, And the tip of my nose To the roots of the rose, Or whatever grows On the earth where the bones of the Colbys repose: Then good bye friends and foes, With earth's joys and woes, For how this world goes; When it rains or it snows, The summer sun glows, Or the winter wind blows, Saith the Book, He that's dead in his grave never knows.

Mr. Colby's advertising methods were original. He claimed to have sold more good books than any other man in New England. For many years he had a store in Boston, where the Transcript building now stands. Afterward he hired the ground, and built the Archway book store, under the old Marlboro Hotel. He specialized in Bibles and religious books of any denomination, saying in his advertisements:

Can any one tell much about Hell, or is it a sell to make us act well? That little book called "The Roads to Heaven and Hell", telling you all about it, for 10 cents, is a very funny little book; and Old Man Colby's History of the Bible has been commended by good men of all denominations.

He had five sons, two of whom died, but the other three were prosperous men. One was in the book business with his father. As he said in an advertising circular,

But there are still left the "Old Man Colby" and the three "young men Colby", who are "Old Man Colby's" sons, and the "young men Colby" will be "old men Colby" when "Old Man Colby" is gone.

Mr. Colby claimed to have made "Two Great Discoveries": how to make the best cider-vinegar from apples in ten days' time, and how to raise from three hundred to five hundred bushels of grain from a single acre of ground in sixty days' time. The latter discovery was made from planting seeds found in the crop of a wild duck coming from the Arctic regions. He planted this seed and his neighbors also tested it, and found it prolific, and a remarkable rejuvenator for live stock. This "Duck-wheat" was tested in the neighborhood in West Fryeburg, in 1890, and produced twelve hundred and ninety-five sound kernels on a single stalk.

Once at Town meeting Mr. Colby was the spokesman for the citizens of West Fryeburg, desiring a bridge to be built at Swan's Falls as being more convenient and direct to the Village. He advocated the measure in his vigorous manner, and in closing said, "Now let us consider this in the way Jesus Christ would have done—" when he was interruped by witty William Gordon, who cried out, "Mr. Moderator, Mr. Moderator; If Jesus Christ was here, he would not need a bridge. He could walk on the water!" This was received by a shout, in which even the advocates of the bridge could not help joining. The question was put to a vote, and was decided against the proponents of the bridge.

Mr. Colby foretold his death to a day. He was in the Village when he knew his condition was precarious, and said to a man, "I want you to come over Wednesday, and lay me out." The invitation was answered pleasantly, but on that day his active mind and body went to its eternal rest. An honest man who loved Fryeburg, and was proud of his ancestry.

Among citizens of the Village for a number of years in the early 1870s, was Captain John Thomas Bishop, a veteran of the Civil War, and later one of the charter members of the First Post of the Grand Army of the Republic organized at Decatur, Ill. Capt. Bishop was in the Pay Department of the Portland & Ogdensburg Railroad, which took him away from home the greater part of each day, so he was not particularly active in local affairs. He was a quiet and modest man, who made no display of his part in organizing the great War-Veteran association.

Thomas Chase Shirley was a quietly influential citizen who, after years of business experience in Boston, returned to the Village, where he spent the remainder of his life.

He was especially helpful in times of distress in any family. He was always ready to "watch" at the bedside of the sick; to assist in the last offices to the dead; to attend and take charge of the funeral exercises, and accompany the dead to their last resting place. At the same time, he was always ready to make fun, and to help others enjoy the pleasures of social gatherings.

One of the sons of Fryeburg, who never forgot the town of his birth, and was never forgotten by his many friends through several generations there, was Seth Chase Gordon, who was born in 1831, and died at Portland at the age of 90. After he finished his education at the Academy, he taught school in Evansville, Ind. Then he returned to his native town and began the study of medicine with Dr. Ira Towle. He attended the medical schools at Dartmouth and Bowdoin Colleges, graduating from the latter in 1855. He began active practice in Gorham, Me., where he continued until he entered the 13th Regiment Maine Volunteers, Col. Neal Dow's command, in December 1861, as assistant surgeon. He served through the war as surgeon in this and the 1st Louisiana Infantry, being mustered out July 12, 1865.

Dr. Gordon began practice after the war in Portland, Me., where he continued until his death, June 22, 1921. Beside his local practice, in which he excelled as a surgeon, he was appointed in 1874, to the staff of the Maine General Hospital, remaining until he retired from medical practice. He was a consulting surgeon at the Maine Eye and Ear Infirmary for a number of years, and was lecturer at the Portland School of Medical Instruction.

Dr. Gordon was affiliated with all the leading medical and surgical organizations of the country. He served as President of the Maine Medical Association and was Vice-President of the American Medical Association. In 1905 he received the degree of LL.D. from Dartmouth College. He was Commander of the Maine Commandery of the Loyal Legion, a member of Bosworth Post, G.A.R. He was a director of the Portland & Ogdensburg R. R., and was its surgeon many years. A life-long Democrat, he was candidate for Congress from the First District of Maine in 1902.

Dr. Gordon was a trustee of Fryeburg Academy, and was President of the Board. He gave a building, known as "Gordon Hall" to the institution. He made his summer home in the Judah Dana house, on Maine and River streets, in the Village. He never married, his sister, Mrs. Hannah McKenney being his home maker for many years. His two brothers are noticed next.

A man who made himself widely useful and helpful to the community in which he lived, was William Gordon. He was born October 10, 1834, son of Stephen and Lydia Chase Gordon, and always lived in Fryeburg. His early manhood was spent in West Fryeburg, where he carried on a small farm to advantage, and engaged, as many farmers did, in lumbering during the winter. He developed an ability to judge timber lots with considerable accuracy as to their lumber contents and was alert to buy lots in different parts of the town, and in adjoining towns. In his early life he acquired the facility of auctioning goods, and his facile tongue and ready wit made him desired on such occasions through the surrounding country. It was a poor year in which he did not attend at least a dozen auctions.

Mr. Gordon's especial vocation at certain seasons, was surveying lumber and timber trees. He was constantly in demand in the latter part of a winter to survey the cut of logs just as it was put into the river to be floated to the mills, and regardless of cold and storms, he worked faithfully, until the burden of years became too heavy for him to bear the labors with comfort. He varied his employments by securing farmers' contracts to raise corn for packing, and during the season of packing he was in control of the yard, and also kept accounts and settled with employees and farmers.

William Gordon was popular among his townsmen, and his strict honesty made him desirable as a town officer, filling the position of Selectman frequently. His good business judgment was of value in appraising property and adjusting claims under dispute. He was accurate in assessing taxes, and he gave much time to that important part of the work. He was conscientious in his public office, devoting much time to the duties. He was a good neighbor, and always at the service of any man who needed his help.

Mr. Gordon was a keen observer of events around him. He kept a record of weather conditions, temperature, rain and snow fall, and noted these facts in his diary. He enjoyed the beauties of nature; and a beautiful sunset, the snow covered trees and other changes of nature excited his interest and appreciative comment. It is doubtful if many busy men would have given the attention to the beauties of surrounding nature, as did he.

He added to his experience by a term as Postmaster at the Village. There he gave general satisfaction, and resigned his duties to his successor of the opposite political party, without the slightest feelings of hostility, and stood ready to substitute for his successor frequently. During the later years of his life he gave much attention to the history of his town and its inhabitants.

William Gordon was a twin, his brother, Samuel C. Gordon living in the adjoining town of South Chatham, where William eventually found his helpmate, Julia Anderson. The two brothers were close in their relations. In later years they both removed to the Village, where they enjoyed a comfortable living the rest of their lives.

One of the most enterprising men of the town was Francis A. Wiley, who, after a varied experience, returned to his native town in 1872, and went into business in a small way. In Chapter XVI reference is made to his business which increased rapidly, and required a large store-house near the railroad station. In 1883 he shipped to the city markets 54 carloads of potatoes, 153 cases of eggs, and a number of tons of butter, and this beside his large market in the town and surrounding points.

Mr. Wiley was a man with whom the people liked to deal, and he possessed their confidence. At one time he was somewhat embarrassed, and one of his creditors to whom he owed one hundred dollars said, "Mr. Wiley, if you will pay me fifty dollars, I will receipt your account in full." Mr. Wiley replied, "No, I will pay you fifty dollars now, and fifty more if you will give me a little more time." Any settlement of his debts for less than a hundred cents on a dollar did not meet his approval.

Mr. Wiley was born in North Fryeburg, Nov. 12, 1837. When the Civil War began, he enlisted in Co. K, 50th Mass. Vols., and served through the war.

He was a public-spirited citizen, generous and helpful. He was a member of Pythagorean Lodge, A. F. & A. M. and of the Grand Army of the Republic.

William Kelly, familiarly known among his many friends as "Billy Kelly", was a citizen who was of service to the public, carrying on a good Livery Stable for many years, until his failing health compelled his relinquishing his business. He was born in Philadelphia; his father was killed in the Mexican War, and as a child of three years he was brought to Fryeburg, and put in the care of his uncle, William Kelly, who adopted him. He took charge of his uncle's livery stable, which he made a matter of personal pride, and his horses and vehicles were well cared for and reliable. He was a thrifty man, and his farm was well kept, as were the buildings which he inherited. Always courteous, he made friends, and when he departed this life, was much missed. He was the last of the family in town.

Albion P. Gordon, who lived at the Toll Bridge, was one of the best known citizens of the town. He was a skillful surveyor, and was considered one of the best in Oxford County. He conducted a small farm, but his land surveying business required most of his attention. His genial manner won him a host of friends wherever he was. He was appreciated by his fellow citizens, and was elected to the State Senate, where his good business judgment proved of value to the State. He served a term as County Commissioner, his knowledge as a surveyor and engineer being of value in the work. He was so well esteemed in policial circles that he was made Governor's Councilor, and later was appointed one of the State Prison Inspectors. He was a prominent Free Mason and a member of the Odd Fellows of the town.

In the early 1880's Gerry Morgan came to Fryeburg to reside. He was a native of New Hampshire, a veteran " '49-er", and a former member of the New Hampshire Legislature, where among other valuable services he was the father of the bill that gave free text books to the schools of the State, making New Hampshire the first to take such a progressive step. He was engaged in the manufacture of shoe pegs at Bartlett, where he owned a large plant, and had an extensive export trade. He was attracted to this town because of the Academy, where all his five children attended school.

Mr. Morgan's only son, William Gerry Morgan, graduated from the Academy and four years later from Dartmouth College. He chose the profession of physician and later established a practice in Washington, D. C., where he won distinction. Beside his practice, he was Professor of Diseases of the Digestive Tract in the Medical School of Georgetown University, becoming Dean of the School of Medicine, after a service of twenty-five years. He was president of the American Gastroenterological Association, of the Clinico-Pathological Society of America, as well as of the Medical Society of the District of Columbia, and president of the American Medical Association, to which he was elected in 1932. In that position he assisted at the dedication of the Los Angeles County General Hospital, the world's largest single-unit center of mercy and healing.

Dr. Morgan was given the degree of Doctor of Science, by his Alma Mater, on which occasion the President of the College spoke as follows:

> William Gerry Morgan, President of the American Medical Association, physician, and authority upon diseases of the digestive tract, the prestige of whose knowledge and skill extends far beyond national boundaries. Respected as a teacher and painstaking as an editor of professional works, your reputation as a specialist has not been gained at expense of outside contacts or through a narrowness of vision which ignored the world outside your field. Building in later achievement upon the broad base of your earlier experience in general practice as a country doctor, wherein intelligence, judgment and capacity for quick decision are indispensable, you have retained those qualities in cosmopolitan environment while international repute has become yours. Of you it has been said on high authority, that you are generous in friendship, and that you move among your associates with the helpful attitude of the typical bedside doctor. These are qualities which the College delights to honor in one of her sons and I confer upon you the honorary degree of Doctor of Science.

A man who proved himself a useful citizen, though not fully appreciated for his good qualities, was James I. Lovis. He was born in East Fryeburg, but spent the most of his life in the Village, where he was a handy man in many ways. He was invaluable to the Water Company, in the laying and repair of the pipes; he took charge of the town clock for many years, and for eighteen years was janitor of the Graded School building. As a mark of respect during his funeral the public schools of the village were closed. He was a man of marked personality, and somewhat deformed, but he was entitled to the respect of the community, which could say of him, "Faithful in everything he did".

One of the noted characters among the early settlers of Fryeburg was Limbo, an African slave. Simeon A. Evans, M.D., a native of Fryeburg, later a resident of Conway, N.H., compiler of "The Descendants of David Evans" tells these facts about him.

> Any account of the Pequawket settlement would be incomplete without the story of Limbo the slave, who, even in this remote northern locality, was a factor in American civilization. According to his own account, Limbo was kidnapped, on the coast of Guinea, while he was out feeding silk worms. Of his early life there are no records. We first know of him as a slave of William McLellan of Gorham, in the District

of Maine, State of Massachusetts. Before the settlement of the Seven Lots, he, with others, used to drive cattle up to the great Pigwacket meadows and winter them there. He and two white men, Nathaniel Merrill and John Stevens passed the winter of 1762-3 there, and thus formed an acquaintance with the first settlers from Penacook. He was quite an old man when the come-outers and new lights, whose creed was universal freedom and universal liberty for every man to do as he pleased, were flourishing in Gorham. Limbo was fond of going to their meetings, and they finally persuaded him to exchange the comforts of life with slavery for the hardships and privations of a new settlement in the wilderness with freedom, whereupon he ran away to Pigwacket. He must have been the first passenger and Pigwacket the earliest terminus of the "Underground Railway." As Fryeburg is less than forty miles from Gorham, the inference is plain either that slave property did not bear a high value or that facilities for taking runaways were scanty; for it is stated that his former owners never heard of him afterward. In some unexplained way the title to this movable piece of property was later vested in Moses Ames, one of the original and immortal 'Seven'. Tradition says that the new master, Ames, treated Limbo unkindly, and that Col. Samuel Osgood compassionately bought him, the consideration being a yoke of oxen. Mr. Osgood subsequently sold him to his son, Lieut. James Osgood, "for five shillings lawful money". Mr. James R. Osgood, the well-known publisher, discovered, among his grandfather's papers, the bill of sale of Limbo, dated October 4, 1790. Mr. Osgood has heliotyped this interesting document. This last sale was a mere form to hand him down to another generation, and thus keep the title in the family. In his later years Limbo was kindly cared for by "Aunt Nabby" Osgood, the kind-hearted hostess of the Oxford House. He died December 12, 1828, and rests in an honored grave. His humble tomb-stone may still be seen in the old cemetery at Fryeburg Village. The tablet was not erected until several years after his death, which may account for the error in its date, proved by other records:

LIMBO.
A Native of Africa,
Lies Here.
He was while living an honest man,
the noblest work of God.
Died Nov., 1829,
aged 90.

Limbo was not supposed to be quite fully witted, but he maintained himself as a good worker. He could not read or write, but he had a way of counting the sheep and knew at once whether all were present or any missing. He had a favorite chair, which Aunt Nabby kept for him by the fireplace, and when the children, to tease him, used to run and get into it, Limbo would break into a terrible rage.

Another incident is recalled by H. W. Ripley, as follows: "He was a very faithful servant, but like many others in those days, as well as at the present time, he liked his allowance of toddy, and sometimes would go down to Jake Evans' store to reinforce himself. Jake loved fun. Limbo loved rum, and was terribly profane at times. Jake had taught him how to articulate when pretty well 'keyed up', Jake would ask him what his name was; his answer would be, 'God! My name's Limbo, Mingo, Pingo—by jingo,' and his voice could have been heard a full mile."

Limbo was not the only negro slave in town. Abel Cary was a slave owned by Ezekiel Walker, and came with his family from Concord, in 1764 or 1765. He was restless and discontented, and finally ran away from Mr. Walker, and spent fourteen days wandering on Moat Mountain. He lived chiefly upon berries, but at last, tired and weary of the life of a wanderer with such a slender mode of existence, he came out of the forest to Colonel McMillan's home in Conway. There he asked for something to eat, and Colonel McMillan's daughter offered him a bowl of blueberries and milk. Abel had a very fiery and passionate temper, and was given to sudden bursts of rage. He seized the bowl from the girl's hands and dashed it on the floor, refusing to eat the lunch offered him, saying, "No more berries for me". He had enough of such food while wandering, and declared that they were too near his color.

Fryeburg had the honor of furnishing, in 1917-1918, the National President of the Ladies of the G. A. R., Mrs. Wallace R. Tarbox, who had been an earnest worker in that body for some time. Mrs. Tarbox was a native of Belfast, Me. Her father was killed in the battle of Gettysburg, when she was an infant, and she was born imbued with love for the country, its defenders and the flag. Mrs. Tarbox was a member of the organization from its beginning. She had served as State and National Instructor in Patriotic Work, and became so well-known that she was chosen to fill every office in the State body, serving two years as State President. At the National Convention in Boston, in 1917, she was elected National President, having during the ten years previous, filled every office in the national body.

In the discharge of the duties of her office, Mrs. Tarbox crossed the United States from sea to sea, and was a popular speaker at patriotic gatherings. Her administration was highly commended by the officers of the Grand Army of the Republic, for the sympathetic work done in connection with their organization. Hon. Orlando A. Somers, of Indiana, Commander in chief of the G. A. R., at the time of Mrs. Tarbox's administration of the "Ladies", said of her and her work: "Mrs. Tarbox of Maine, is a lady of fine accomplishments, capable in direction and gifted in speech. I know her organization has been elevated and strengthened in every respect by her wise leadership and admonitions. Mrs. Tarbox's grand work has won for her a national reputation."

A man who rendered valuable service to Fryeburg, was Hon. Albion A. Perry, mayor of Somerville, Mass., in 1905-06-07. A lawyer by profession, he was largely interested in banking and business affairs. He came to Fryeburg as a summer visitor, but became so much attached to the place that he made himself an adopted son, and showed a deeper affection and interest than many who were born to citizenship.

Mr. Perry took an active interest in everything that meant betterment of the standard of living in the place. He often took the place of some clergyman in conducting the service, in some neighborhood. He was interested in patriotic matters, and was in frequent demand as a speaker. He showed such a lively interest in town affairs that he was added to the Board of Trustees of Fryeburg Academy, where he found opportunity to increase the efficiency of the school, by prizes for excellence in various ways.

Quotation has been made from the tribute, "Fryeburg", of which the Rev. Henry Bernard Carpenter was the author. He was a resident of the village in 1875-1877, before he was called to the pastorate of the Bridgton Congregational Church, and later to a wider field in Boston. While in Fryeburg, he boarded with "Uncle Johnny" Smith and Miss Molly Brewster. He won his way into the hearts of the people by his charming manners and his graceful Irish wit. He was in demand throughout the surrounding country as a lecturer. His lectures, always given extemporaneously, were on literary topics, and showed a wide knowledge of English men of letters. He contributed freely to the pleasure and interest of the local Reading Circle, of which he was a frequent attendant, and he showed interest in the students of the Academy. He was the author of a serio-comic poem, "The Oatmeal Crusaders", written in commemoration of a walking trip through the White Mountains by a number of young people from Fryeburg. Aside from the amusing local and personal references, it is a gem of its kind, and the published copies are exceedingly rare. In later years he produced a long poem, "Liber Amoris", which was highly commended by Alfred Tennyson.

No list of the names of persons to whom Fryeburg is indebted for a part played as a resident would be complete without that of one of her grandsons, whom the world delighted to honor, Robert Edwin Peary, discoverer of the North Pole. Robert Peary came naturally to Fryeburg, as his mother was a member of the Wiley family. He had been in the town, on frequent visits to his kindred in North Fryeburg, and had explored the surrounding country before he came in 1877, on graduation from Bowdoin College. Mrs. Peary and her son occupied a modest house on Elm Street in the Village, and lived quietly, making friends and doing their part as members of society. Robert took an active interest in affairs of the village and town. Being a well equipped surveyor, he surveyed land in the vicinity, and his habit of taking great care in his work was demonstrated in the accuracy of his surveys. He made a survey of the Village and mapped it. That map is still in existence, and copies are owned by a few fortunate persons. An accomplished taxidermist, he did a lucrative business in mounting birds of the vicinity, and some of his work is still preserved in homes in Fryeburg. He enjoyed society and was active in the affairs of the church society, and whatever he did was done with much skill. He planned and conducted a pageant of historical characters, which attracted much interest. An excellent horseman, he enjoyed touring the town in the saddle.

He devoted some time to establishing a meridian line on an open lot in the village, and spent many clear nights, in the cold of winter, in observing the North Star. Whether he then began to draw that inspiration that led him to the Pole, no one knows, but he left the result of his work marked by two posts, which are used to correct compasses. A memorial stone with a bronze tablet thereon stands near these stones; and a memorial in the form of a director to the mountains, stands on Jockey Cap.

It was while he lived in Fryeburg, that he passed successfully an examination for a draughtsman in the Coast Survey office at Washington, D. C., and decided to accept the position, leaving Fryeburg in the spring of 1879.

Among the citizens of Fryeburg who rose from humble circumstances, until he was numbered among the steamship magnates of New England, was Calvin Austin. The descendant of one of the early families of the town, the son of a farmer, he came to the village to be a student in Fryeburg Academy. During his school life he lived in the family of Thomas C. Shirley where he enjoyed advantages that were of service to him in later life. Through Mr. Shirley's acquaintance he obtained a position in the office of a steamship line, which ran between Boston and Maine ports. He steadily won his way upward by strict attention to his duties, through various clerkships, until he became Manager of the Eastern Steamship Co., and later President of the corporation. He also was President of the Metropolitan Steamship Co., the Clyde Steamship Co., of Maine; Director of the Mallory Steamship Co., Hudson River Navigation Co., First National Bank of Boston, Boston Insurance Co., Old Colony Insurance Co., Massachusetts Bonding & Insurance Co., Renfrew Manufacturing Co.

During his long and busy life he kept in touch with his native home, where his mother remained for many years. He was a trustee of Fryeburg Academy and a generous patron of the institution. His residence was in Boston and he later had a summer home in Dunstable, Mass.

In preparing the history of such a town as Fryeburg, the names of individuals are frequently mentioned in the accounts of past events. These people did their parts in developing and improving the town they had chosen for their homes. Many were born here; others have found Fryeburg a place well adapted to their desires for a home. Even after the lapse of years their names are still remembered, and it is unnecessary to go into details regarding them. Those who were included among the early settlers have been mentioned in the proper place, and others have been referred to as occasion required. Without further attempt at characterization, among the names of those who have helped to make the town what it is today are these:

Abram Andrews, Caleb and John Atwood, Eckley Ballard, Wilson Barker and son, Frank, George B. Barrows, John A. Batchelder, Capt. George H. Bradbury, Col. Samuel A. Bradley, Robert Bradley, Alexander R. Bradley and sons, Alexander Stuart, Frank Y., Lieut. Richard, U.S.V., Dr. George, U.S.N., William B., Daniel W., John J., Philbrick Bradley, David Bradley, E. W. Burbank, Andrew Buzzell, Hon. E. C.

Buzzell, D. D. Carlton, Dennis M. Cole, Charles Chandler, Moses Chandler, Joseph Chandler, Asa Charles, Justus Charles, Stephen Chase, Enoch S. Chase, H. W. Cousins, Thomas Day, Wm. Durgin, John L. Eastman, T. L. Eastman, C. C. Eastman, T. C. Eastman, John Ela, Fred T. Ela, Capt. Wm. Evans, Wm. Evans, A. H. Evans, "Deacon" John Evans and son, Clinton B., Foxwell C. Evans and son, Samuel O., Gen. E. C. Farrington, M.V.M., Maj. Seth Farrington, U.S.V., Eben Fessenden and son, Eben, J. B. Fellows, H. B. Flint, C. E. Fox, F. N. Frye, Caleb Frye, Isaac Frye and son, Amos C., B. M. Glines, S. C. Gordon, M.D., Samuel Gordon, F. E. Haley, S. Hapgood, S. Hardy, John Hastings, C. E. Harris, D.M.D., Robert Harriman, Caleb Harriman and son, J. C., H. Harnden, Solomon Heald, Henry D. E. Hutchins, H. K. Hobbs, Michael Keefe and sons, David Leavitt and son, George, Alonzo F. Lewis, Charles, Frank, John Locke and son, William, F. L. Mark, Rev. J. K. Mason, D.D., E. F. McIntire, Oliver McIntire and son, Nelson O., T. O. McIntire, J. McMillan, F. C. Merrill and son, Alvin D., Calvin Merrill, Rev. Samuel Osgood, J. L. Osgood, Hon. Earl P. Osgood, J. E. Osgood, James Osgood, Albion Page, Russell Page, S. A. Page, F. H. Peterson, John J. Pike, A. O. Pike, 2nd., Rev. P. Richmond, J. J. Rogers, David Sawyer and son, Barnet, Edward Shirley and son, Franklin, Thomas C. Shirley, M. M. Smart, Abial F. Smith, C. F. Smith, Samuel Souther and sons, Rev. Samuel, Thomas, John W. and sons, John C., William, Thomas, Wm. H. Tarbox and son, James W., W. R. Tarbox, Charles Tibbetts and son, C. H. Tibbetts, Berlin F. Tinker, Hon. W. W. Towle, C. A. Walker, M.D., Col. James Walker, Henry Walker and sons, George H., Fred A., Wm. G. Walker, Timothy C. Ward, Amos C. Ward and son, Stephen C., John Ward, Isaiah Warren and son, Otis, and sons, George and Hon. Charles C., Edson Warriner, John W. Webster, Foxwell C. Webster, Dana Webster, John Weston and sons, Edward, George, E. Payson Weston and son, J. Henry, Eben Weeks and son, Seth.

All the influential people of Fryeburg were by no means confined to the male sex. There have always been women of sterling character, and influence, who have had an effect on matters in the town. Among them may be mentioned:

"Aunt Nabby" Osgood (Mrs. Samuel), Sophronia Hurd (Mrs. Carlton), Rosilla N. Page (Mrs. Albion), Mary W. Souther (Mrs. Samuel), Susan Ballard (Mrs. George), Caroline G. McMillan (Mrs. James), Mary A. Evans (Mrs. John), Caroline F. Walker (Mrs. Henry), Sarah J. Bradley (Mrs. I. B.), Abby T. Warriner (Mrs. Chauncey), Georgiana S. Barrows (Mrs. G. B.), Mary O'B. Hastings (Mrs. D. R.), Abby G. Weston (Mrs. John), Annah Glines (Mrs. B. M.), Ruth Atwood, Jane F. Coolidge (Mrs. H. A.), Hattie Gordon (Mrs. A. P.), Huldah Evans (Mrs. A. H.), Mary S. Howe, Laura H. Carlton (Mrs. D. D.), Sarah T. Walker (Mrs. C. H.), Helen S. Locke (Mrs. John), Lydia H. Locke

(Mrs. Frank), Frances H. Weston (Mrs. E. P.), Abby N. Page, Sarah S. Evans, Eliza G. Fife (Mrs. S. W.), Georgia D. Bradley (Mrs. David), Emily F. Stone (Mrs. B. N.), Elizabeth C. Charles (Mrs. Orlando), Sarah K. Ladd (Mrs. C. T.), Mary Warren, Mary W. Lord (Mrs. Charles), Alice O. Hastings, Hattie A. Pike, Harriet L. Abbott, Anna Barrows, Mary W. Post (Mrs. W. B.), Lucia M. Lougee (Mrs. A. J.), Hattie G. Warren (Mrs. George), Laura G. Weeks (Mrs. Seth), Mary L. Gordon.

These are some of the persons whose reputation has gone outside the boundaries of Fryeburg. They did well, but perhaps, no better than many persons who did much in a quiet way, and never were heard of beyond a short distance from their homes. A large list could be enrolled of those rural knights and ladies, who were known for high character, good works and practical Christianity, though today their names may be found graven only on white marble slabs, under the whispering pines, that "clothe the wold and meet the sky."

XXI

CASUALTIES

History, which is, indeed, little more than the register of the crimes, follies, and misfortunes of mankind.
—*Edward Gibbon.*

Because of its favorable location, Fryeburg has been comparatively free from diseases and distempers. Purity of air and water and generally comfortable ways of living have kept the people well. Competent physicians have treated the sick and ailing, so that they have been free from contagious diseases, and deaths have been more from natural causes. The early inhabitants in May, 1800, suffered from what was called, "putrid sore throat," among the children, and there were several deaths. In May, 1815, Dr. Moses Chandler wrote to his nephew:

Very sickly in Lovell and Chatham, and somewhat in Fryeburg. I am almost dead with fatigue. I have had 103 cases—lost four. I charged in the month of April, between 200 and 300 dollars. I am going to see Sally Russell at Gen. Steele's. No expense: care of the widowed and fatherless.

The first case of small pox occurred in 1800. In the winter of 1871 and 1872 a case occurred, brought from Canada, but few cases developed in the Village and surroundings. The physicians were active, and general vaccination and care to avoid contact brought an end to the scare. One death resulted, and burial was at night, when there was less danger of contagion. Since then there has been no trouble from that disease.

Disturbances caused by winter conditions, though serious and troublesome, have rarely resulted in fatalities, except through complications. Influenza, which ran so violently through the country during the World War years, caused considerable sickness, but it yielded to treatment.

Serious accidents have been few, and confined chiefly to those liable to occur among working men. Deaths due to accidents have happened, but from causes understood and generally not preventable. Fryeburg, therefore, has been remarkably free from fatalities. A few serious accidents, drownings, and one murder, in 1861, are in the records. The last was committed by an illiterate farmhand because the victim disapproved of his attentions to her daughter. The man's illiteracy was one of the contributing causes of his arrest, since he made the same error in spelling that was found in a "farewell message", when told to write the message as dictated. Reports of the case can be found in court records.

Perhaps the first fire at the Seven Lots was Moses Ames' house. Mrs. Ames was doing her week's washing, and put some chips on the fire, which caused a quick blaze, and set the roof on fire. Capt. William Evans and another man saw the fire from Mr. Osgood's and ran to it. All they were able to save was the kettle of clothes in the fireplace. The Ames house stood near where afterwards Mr. Ames built the Robert Bradley house, about opposite the Congregational Vestry.

While no country place is immune from fires, especially where the majority of houses are built of wood, Fryeburg was remarkably free from disastrous fires during the early years. Occasional fires broke out in houses where the chimney was old and defective. This condition is responsible for most of the fires in the country, and the losses of old buildings in different parts of the town are due to such poorly built chimneys.

Forest fires have been too common around the Village. In 1816 a fire swept through the woods but the damage done was not recorded. Mr. Amos J. Cook in some of his writings stated that the next year the blueberries were unusually plentiful. That has been the only redeeming feature after fires on the plain.

In May, 1880 a fire started by a locomotive near the railroad crossing of the Porter Road swept the plains from that spot to the swamp between Foxwell C. Evans' place and Highland Park. It crossed four travelled highways, and a number of wood roads. It swept a lot on which were several hundred cords of hard pine wood cut the winter before, all of which was destroyed. The home of Mr. Evans was threatened but was saved. The burned area never recovered fully after this devastation. Since then several fires have run over much of the same area and the plains that once were heavily covered with fine pine trees, today have a sparse and scattered growth of hard pine and scrub oaks.

In the winter of 1878-1879, the little building which was the Village Post Office was burned from a defective chimney. This was the first fire in many years. A few years later, the stable and ell of the Dana house, occupied by Capt. George H. Bradbury, were burned, but the house was saved. The next fire of any magnitude was that of the Oxford House, in February, 1887, which opened the way for the new "Oxford." Mention has been made of many of the other fire losses.

In the great conflagration of August 31, 1906, fourteen buildings of importance in the village were destroyed.

The fire started in a most mysterious way in the attic of the "Oxford", about 10.30 in the forenoon. There were seventy-five guests at the hotel, but most were away from their rooms, and nearly all of them lost clothing and jewelry. The employees, of whom there were twenty-five, lost their belongings and many lost the money they had earned during the previous weeks.

Every effort was made in the hotel to stop the fire, but an unusually low pressure on the water rendered the hose in the house useless. The Village Fire Department responded to the alarm, and laid two lines of hose, but the hydrant streams could not do effective service on the roof and the interior of the fourth story, because of the lack of pressure, which under normal conditions would have been ample.

When the fire broke through the roof of the Oxford, a steady south-westerly wind took up the cloud of embers and carried them directly into the thickly settled part of the village. The fire burned the small storehouse behind the hotel, and was soon communicated to Mrs. M. B. Barker's millinery store, and then to the stable and dwelling house of the Pike family. The next house, that of Mrs. Susan Abbott, was dynamited in hope of stopping the flames, but the debris was soon a menace to the next two fine houses of T. L. Eastman and Mrs. Eben Weeks, which were soon in flames. The next house, that of Mr. H. G. Freeman, and his printing office was dynamited, but the fire was too close to Seth W. Fife's house and Mrs. Fife's millinery store, and that went quickly. A little space between that and the next house, E. P. Weston's, made no difference in the rush of the fire, as the stable nearer the Fife house was quickly on fire, and spread to the large handsome house.

Before the fire had spread far, a telegram to Portland brought on a special train Engine 4, a hose carriage, and company of thirty men, under the command of Chief Eldridge, and they went to attach the apparatus to the hydrants. Here an unfortunate condition rendered the engine useless, as the screw threads of the hydrants were different from the hose couplings of the engine. The engine was drawn out of immediate danger, and the firemen set to work assisting the citizens in clearing houses.

The house next in danger, that of Miss Abby N. Page was quickly cleared of furnishings, and a bucket brigade with water in pails from the sink room of the house kept the roof and side of the house so well wet, that no sparks blazed on the buildings. The whole house and outbuildings were saved, and here the fire was stayed on Main Street.

Brands had twice flamed on the roof and steeple of the Church across the street from Miss Page's, but they were seen in time and extinguished. Buildings on the opposite side of Main Street, from the track of the fire caught from brands, but they too were saved.

The fire worked curiously, although the over-spreading branches of the elms may have had some effect in keeping safe a number of buildings on Portland Street, but, from a burning brand, which blew in the window of the barn, fire was communicated to the home of Andrew H. Evans from which all the family were absent for the day. That set fire to the little house, the home of Nathaniel Walker, which was next, to the southward, of which it made short work. On the opposite side of the street brands fell on the roofs of the vacant Fryeburg House, setting it on fire, and next on the handsome residence of Miss Minnie A. Bradley, and destroyed that with much of its valuable contents. The next buildings, the home of Mr. William Durgin, with its large barn, were wiped out.

Meanwhile the brands were carried by the wind for a mile, scattering in the nearby woods and grass fields. The mill property of the Misses Walker caught fire, but men succeeded in stopping it there.

The Portland firemen withdrew, finding their efforts with the apparatus useless, but their help as workers had been invaluable.

When the sun set, it was on a scene of distress and ruin. Heaps of embers were burning, and coal in cellars continued to glow for several weeks. The stricken families hardly knew which way to turn; their property was in heaps, and was in danger of being looted by those who had been attracted to the fire, from even remote distances. But to the credit of the people of Fryeburg, all the homeless found a place for the night, and the next day were able to find houses where they managed to begin life anew.

In spite of all the excitement, but one person was injured, Mr. Alonzo F. Lewis, who, in protecting his own property, fell from the ladder and broke his hip. He was taken to a Portland hospital, and from the injury and the shock of the conflagration, died the next morning. Thus was removed one of the persons Fryeburg could ill afford to lose, as Mr. Lewis was a talented and public-spirited citizen.

That night, the water power increased. For some unaccountable reason, the pressure had been lessened during the day, and the person in charge was out of town until evening. If normal conditions had existed, the story undoubtedly would have been different.

The financial loss was estimated at nearly $100,000, nearly one-eighth the town's entire valuation. Aside from the loss of valuable real estate, personal property, and embarrassment to business, all of which could not be replaced, the great loss to the village, and a loss irreparable, was the destruction of the great elm trees along the streets, which embowered the residences. It was a terrible blow to the beauty of the village. It is impossible to know how many trees were killed. Though strenuous efforts were made by experts scarcely a tree was saved. Since the time when all were cut down, new trees have been set out, some of different species, quick-growing, to fill the gaps.

The loss of the hotel, which was built at a cost of $40,000 was a blow to the summer travel from which the village has never fully recovered. The site is occupied by two attractive residences; other sites where were large buildings are now occupied by small ornamental cottages. A garage occupies the site where stood the two twin houses, built by the Spring Brothers. The conflagration was a set-back to Fryeburg in many ways.

Since that time the water supply has been increased, and a modern fire apparatus has been installed, and is handled by a prompt fire department, maintained by the Village Corporation.

XXII

MISCELLANY

I am but a gatherer and disposer of other men's stuff.
—*Sir Henry Wotton.*

There stands in the principal square of the streets of Fryeburg Village, a monument, bearing a bronze tablet with this inscription:

> In Memory of
> John Stevens
> An Early Settler of this Town
> Who spent the Winter here in
> 1762-1763;
> Erected by his Great-grandson,
> Henry Pierce,
> of
> San Francisco, California,
> 1902.

It is a grateful tribute to a man, who with two others had nerve enough to winter in charge of a number of cattle, on one of the great meadows of the town. Besides Stevens, the other two were Nathaniel Merrill and Limbo, the colored slave man of a Gorham family. These three antedated the earliest settlers in living for a season in Pequawket, and Mr. Pierce, though a native of Standish, was so proud of his ancestor, that he caused this memorial of white Hallowell granite, designed as a fountain for man and beast, to be set at the junction of Main and Portland Streets, the union of two of the earliest colonial roads. Since it was erected the use of the bowls for watering animals has passed, with the universal use of the automobiles, but the monument stands in all its dignity.

The "Gun House", of the Fryeburg Artillery Company, stood at one time on the lot of the "Alumni House".

It is impossible to tell when this Gun House was built, but it was in the days when the Militia of the State consisted of all able men between the ages of eighteen and forty-five, and also the organized and uniformed companies. There were eight Divisions in the State, and there were more major and brigadier generals, than there are Colonels in Kentucky. The ordnance consisted of Revolutionary War cannon, allotted to the artillery companies in pairs, making a section, according to present establishment. The gun house was large enough to accommodate these two guns and the limbers, caissions, and the equipment for the care and handling of the cannon.

The Fryeburg Artillery Company served a short time during the latter years of the War of 1812, but it continued as an active organization for some time after that, until the enthusiasm waned.

An industry peculiar to a forested area was "Masting", or cutting pines and such large timber trees as were suitable for masts of vessels. Prior to the Revolutionary War all trees in the forests of New England which were suitable for masts for ships of the Royal Navy were marked with "the Broad Arrow" as soon as found. To cut one for private purposes was a crime. The use of such trees was continued after the colonies became free, the growing commerce and the American Navy making a brisk market for them. These trees measured from three to four feet at the butt, and were from fifty to one-hundred feet tall. Masting was a special avocation of experienced lumbermen, and a "Mast Master" held an honored place in a community. It was an art to fell such trees so that they would not break and when felled would be in position for hauling out of the woods. This was accomplished by the use of a large number of yokes of oxen.

At the Town Meeting in March, 1777, the voters elected several "Hogreeves", and this has continued the custom with but few intermissions ever since. The office is by no means an onerous one today, though in the early times, when swine were allowed to run at large, picking up their living where they could, to protect the residents from incursions into the fields and private grounds was within the jurisdiction of the Hogreeve, as also to settle damages that might result. The first vote of the town was to let swine run at large. The Hogreeves were an inheritance from old rural England, but today the office has depreciated to the point that those eligible are the men who have been married during the year since the last town meeting. They always accept the office with good grace, and are duly sworn to the strict performance of the duties, to the great merriment of their towns folks.

In 1794 an interest in the western territories began to develop, and some emigrated to Ohio. Timothy Walker and his family left Fryeburg in a two-horse covered wagon, in which they lived on their three-months journey. They were carrying out the spirit of the popular song of that time: "It is found that we will go, and settle on the banks of the pleasant O-hi-o."

It is appropriate to mention the bells that have sounded for various purposes over the Pequawket valley. The first which woke the silence of the locality, was that in the tower of the second Academy building, and it brought to the woods and fields a new sound to be re-echoed back from the hills around the village, as well as to summon the schoolboy, "creeping like a snail unwillingly to school". It sounded until the building was burned in May, 1851, when it fell in the ruins and was melted by the intense heat. All that is left of the bell is the iron tongue, which was uninjured.

This bell did double duty, for since the Second Parish Meeting House near by did not have a bell, it served on Sundays to call the parishioners together.

An interesting little story is remembered of the influence of that bell in the life of at least one boy who heard it.

One morning in the early years of the last century, a father and son were driving cattle to Fryeburg, on the old stage road over Oak Hill.

The clear ringing sound of the bell came through the still air, and echoed among the surrounding hills. "You never heard a bell ring before, did you?" said the father. "That bell is on the Academy, over there."

The association of bell and Academy was somewhat confusing to the lad, and as they walked along, he asked his father what the Academy was, and what the bell looked like to make such a sound. His father told him about the school, and promised the lad that if he sold his cattle well, he might go to school at the Academy and hear the bell every day. Evidently the cattle brought a satisfactory price, for many years later a Fryeburg man was in Vermont, and had occasion to stay at the home of the leading man of the town, who told him this story. He was the boy who was interested to learn about the bell when he first heard its tones; had profited by the opportunity to go to school at Fryeburg Academy, and thus had become a useful and prosperous man, all because he happened to hear the bell ringing that morning so many years before.

The second bell raised in Fryeburg was in the steeple of the Congregational Meeting House built in 1850. It was a large bell, weighing 1254 pounds, and was hung in the belfry in 1851, when it was received as a gift of Abiel Chandler. There was plenty of novelty about such a bell; because it was for a time the only bell in town, after the Academy bell was destroyed, so for many years its solemn tones sounded over the village, until in recent years a crack developed that ruined it till such a time as it may be recast.

This bell arrived in Fryeburg January 29, 1851, and was stored in the stable of Samuel Souther's "Temperance House", on Portland Street, and its advent was reported by its own voice for it was rung that day; and everybody had to have a chance, so it was kept ringing all the next day.

Saturday, February 1, the thermometer registered 27 degrees below zero, but in spite of the chill in the air, the bell was hoisted to the belfry and put in position, and the next day being Sunday, the people had the satisfaction of being called to services, as a diarist noted the fact, "by our own bell."

The next bell was in the steeple of the Methodist Church, where it sounded the call to the people of that demonination, until one night before the Fourth of July, some over-enthusiastic young patriots pounded it with a hammer until it was cracked, which ended its usefulness.

The bell on the Congregational Vestry, was the gift of Hamilton Willis, of Boston, and bears upon it this inscription: " 'Peace on Earth and Good Will among Men', Fryeburg Ladies' Sewing Circle, Christmas, 1870". It was necessary to construct a proper belfry, as none had ever been planned before. The bell was placed in position in the Spring of 1871.

Following the erection of the Swedenborgian Church in 1879, a large, sweet-toned bell was procured, which was placed in position and used on all proper occasions.

From the time when Fryeburg became one of a chain of towns along the Saco river between the White Mountains and the sea coast, until the advent of the railroad in 1872, transportation of persons, baggage and mails was by the public conveyances, the "Concord" stage coaches. In the middle years, and down to the advent of the railroad, John Smith was the most picturesque of the stage drivers. He conducted a line between Conway and Portland, making a trip each day. It was no small task to keep the run of the places of call, and the errands to be done, but he did his work well.

The advent or departure of the stage coach, was an event of more than passing moment. Four lively horses, and the bright colored coach made a handsome picture now almost obsolete. Such a scene was continued for a number of years in Fryeburg by the Lovell Stage, a four-horse Concord coach, running daily between Lovell and Fryeburg. Many remember the genial Dean Wiley, who for many years owned the line, and carried thousands of persons during his career.

As long as towns remain at a distance from the railroads, so long will they be dependent on vehicular transportation. The business of the neighboring town of Lovell, which perpetuates in a shortened form the name of Captain John Lovewell, must be helped by the use of transportation by automobile. But the memory and the picture of the great truck teams that hauled freight between the two towns, to and from the railroad, will be kept in mind.

These teams hauled by four large horses at a slow pace, loaded with shook for hogsheads, and produce for the markets, the driver sitting under his umbrella with little to do but guide his team as it ambled along, were a picturesque sight, that is now a thing of the past. They are as obsolete as the "Lumber Boxes", which came from Vermont years ago.

Like all places where people make their homes, Fryeburg has had its peculiar names for certain localities; names which grew out of natural conditions, as did the name "Pequawket," which means "Here is a crooked place;" others originated in some fancied resemblance to a place familiar to the settlers, who found comfort in seeing something that appeared natural.

There is every reason for the lower section of North Fryeburg having been dubbed "Mud City", the name being a gift of the river. The area in that locality was not much above the river's level even at low water, and when the freshets came and flooded farms and even the houses, the land was left in a sodden condition. The highways and byways were muddy, and the jocular name of "Mud City", while unpleasant to the inhabitants, described the situation with stern accuracy.

"Fish Street", a section of the highway from the Center to North Fryeburg won its name from the fact that the old channel of the river as it looped around made in one place a great eddy, which even today is of unusual depth. The water became the haunt of many fish of different kinds, peculiar to the river; it was a favorite fishing ground and amply supplied the neighboring inhabitants. They caught and ate many fish, and the fact that one might find fish on the dinner table in half the homes gave to the locality the name "Fish Street".

There is a conspicuous hill, to be seen from almost any point in the valley, called "Mount Tom". The name was given to it by some of the early settlers who were familiar with the hill of that name in the Connecticut valley in Massachusetts. From a certain aspect, it was said to resemble that eminence. In the same way, the road along the northwestern slope of Mount Tom, because it suggested a place in the town of Arlington, Mass., was given by Rev. William Fessenden, the same Indian name, "Menotomy", which it still bears.

To some of the citizens whose associations go back into the past, the cross-roads in East Fryeburg, became known as "Pike's Peak", a natural name, because there a little hill, known as "Little Pleasant Mountain", northward of the main range, stands out quite distinctly; and as the locality was the home of Elder John Pike, a Baptist clergyman who had a numerous family, some of whom settled in the vicinity, the name became attached to the place.

Between East Fryeburg and Toll Bridge was "Frog Alley", a sparsely settled section along a single road, near Great Kezar Pond. Further on is "Hemlock Bridge", and the bridge over the old river still bears that name although today there are few if any hemlock trees in the vicinity.

"Toll Bridge", speaks for itself. It was built above the ferry, on the old river, by private subscription, and a toll was exacted from all passers, to remunerate the builders. The covered bridge has given place to a concrete structure, and the beauty of the river is made more appreciable.

Because many people played the violin, the road from Fish Street to the "Harbor" was known as "Fiddle Row".

Were one to follow the channel of the old river, a pleasant little hamlet would be found, which bears the restful name, "The Harbor". The line of homes is principally on the easterly side of the stream that pours its lazy current, from draining Kezar Lake in Lovell, and Charles and Kimball ponds in Fryeburg. Huge trees line the banks, and it is a charming spot. A substantial bridge crosses the river, connecting the "Harbor", with "Fish Street". How the locality obtained its name is a matter of some discussion, but it is a safe "harbor", for any one today. From "Fiddle Row" to the Lovell road at Toll Bridge, is "Federal Road".

A locality, often referred to as the "Haley Neighborhood", because of the families that lived there at one time, is along the road that leads from the main highway to New Hampshire, to Brownfield, where it meets the road to Porter. (This road in part, winds through a wild and romantic country, beyond Bald Peak, where a ravine comes close to the highway.) In the local vernacular of the village, this section is known as, "Nebraska". The title is explained in this wise: Jason Whitman Towle, son of Dr. Ira Towle, who brought up a splendid family, at one time in his early life, went to the state of Nebraska. On his return he had occasion to visit the Haley Neighborhood, and remarked that it reminded him of what he saw of Nebraska. He said that he should call the locality "Nebraska", and the nickname stuck.

Some places have been known by one name for many years, and are still so called, but no one now knows why. "Choat's Brook", for instance, is an unexplained name.

In the Village it was the custom in the early part of the nineteenth century to refer to "French Corner", which was the corner of Main and River Streets. It was so called because in the neighborhood were a number of "Jacobins".

The junction of Main and Portland Streets was always "The Corner".

While not now in Fryeburg, the long street on the New Hampshire side of the river was called "Fag End". Whether it was the "fag-end" of Fryeburg, when the State Line was run, or whether it was to the Conway people the "fag-end" of that town, because it was separated by the range of Green Hill and the Saco river from the rest of the town, no one knows. Some claimed it was not "Fag End", but "Fair Gain", from Maine to New Hampshire.

During the earlier years of the Village houses and stores were occasionally moved from the site on which they were built, to a different location. This was due to the changes caused by new building to replace the earlier, and buildings were moved to occupy sites left vacant by fires. While many buildings changed position, but one must suffice as a peculiar case.

The front of the farm house for many years occupied by John Atwood, on Main Street in the village, originally was the front of a dwelling built by Philip Page, that stood nearly opposite Portland Street, and was burned in the great fire of August 1906. It was moved from that site to a location on the opposite side of the street, near the rear of the lot where is now the blacksmith shop. It remained there for some time, until it was moved again to the present site. It was then referred to as "The Old Brig", from having cruised around to a final anchorage.

Moving a building was in a way a simple process, but it required considerable careful management and preparation. The building was prepared by removing the underpinning, and inserting long logs called "shoes," which were pointed at the ends. These shoes were fastened to the building by a method of cross-timbers, secured to the sides of the house, in turn fastened by strong pegs to the shoes. The building was let down to the ground, which was made free of all obstructions, and was ready for moving.

The motive power was oxen, of which there were plenty on the farms in and near the village. The number was according to the size of the building, and the distance and difficulties of the streets. These yokes of oxen were fastened to each shoe by long strings of chains. The number of oxen on each chain depended on whether the building required turning to the street, in which case the longer string was fastened to the shoe on the side which was to be turned. Once on the street, the strings of oxen were equalized and the building advanced as rapidly as the number of oxen used could walk away with it. The location on the new site often required turning the building, which demanded skill on the part of the moving-master.

One of the most efficient moving-masters of more recent years was Eli Johnson, and he performed the difficult task of moving the Weston homestead from the original site, near the Bridge, to the final location on Smith Street. This required hauling it up the hill and down, making two changes of direction, before it was finally located, all of which was successfully performed.

With the growth of the cities, and before the western supply of beef was in the market, there was a steady demand for beef-cattle at the abattoirs of the large cities. Among the men who made a specialty of furnishing cattle to these markets were John Weston and Benjamin M. Glines of the Village, who for many years combed the Saco valley for select stock. They went into New Hampshire and Canada buying cattle and taking them to Brighton, Mass. It is recalled that on one trip which lasted well into November (the autumn being the usual time for this commerce) these two men brought down through Pinkham Notch, through the White Mountains, five hundred head of cattle and twenty horses, through between four and five feet of snow, from an unexpected early blizzard. They got through all right, but it was a hard trip.

Sometimes they sold all or nearly all of their drove before they reached Brighton; they bought and sold all along the road. The distance covered each day depended on trading, weather conditions, and other matters incident to the drive. Sometimes only ten miles were made in a day. Thirty miles was a long, hard day's travel, but it was accomplished at times, especially when they had some particular town in view as a stopping place. To feed and water such a herd of animals properly was a proposition not to be overlooked. They also were obliged to find a field sufficient to corral them in for the night. The cattle required easy day's trips, as it was most desirable to bring them to market in as good condition as possible. Their market value for sales on the road was dependent on their condition, so the enterprise of cattle-driving to market was no small art, if it was to be properly lucrative. Since the steady supply of heavy beef from the western ranches has become possible, the country cattle-drives have become things of the past, and the reduction of the number of cattle on the farms fit for beef has made such great droves almost impossible. There are yet large stocks kept by thrifty farmers, as an adjunct to their crop raising, but the days when the droves were a spectacular sight on the roads are gone. "Baby Beef" has not yet been raised in the town.

The great change in agriculture in Fryeburg has been brought about by the development of the sweet corn packing industry. The first effort in this line was made in 1879 when J. P. Baxter of Portland established a factory in the Village, near the railroad station. This provided a new market for a farm product hitherto limited to kitchen gardens. The business thrived, and the factory was enlarged and improved. Another factory was opened by the same firm at North Fryeburg. Later Burnham and Morrill located a factory at the Center.

One of the most important matters requiring annual attention was the condition of the highways. From the early times for many years the work was under charge of district commissioners, called "Highway Surveyors". These men were informed of the appropriation allowed for each district, and called upon the citizens either to pay in money, against their tax assessment, or to pay in work. As workers were necessary, the latter form of payment was welcome, and it was common to see the men in the neighborhood laboring on the repair of roads. As the labor was hard but not insistent, working on the road was coloquially referred to as "Leaning out" the tax, the connection being the handle of a hoe.

This method of conducting the work was later dispensed with, and Town Commissioners were chosen, who took charge of all the work on the highways and employed workers at fixed wages, and drew on the Town Treasurer for other necessary expenses.

The care of the roads in winter was often a heavy task. It was customary to employ the labor of men and ox-teams in breaking out the roads, but in 1888-1889, a more modern method was substituted, the use of large rollers, between five and six feet in diameter, made in two drums of heavy plank, which rolled down the snow, making a road ten feet or more wide. The rollers were hauled by four or six horses, and did good service. In 1902 the town owned seven of these great rollers, held in different parts of the town, which were immediately set to work after a heavy fall of snow.

In 1929 snow plows were substituted for the rollers, on account of the increase of automobiles, which required a solid road. The use of "snow fences" was introduced, which were slender slats fastened on wires, and could be rolled up when not required. Set up with stakes in winter, in locations where the snow was likely to drift badly, they reduced the drifting, making the work of plows much lighter.

The number of Poll Taxes in the town has varied from year to year. Probably the largest number assessed was in 1886, when the enrollment was 475. This number dropped in 1895 to 442; then it steadily gained, until 1935, when it dropped from the preceding year, 455 to 432. Since then it gained to 461 in 1937.

Bench-marks are set in different parts of the township, by the Coast and Geodetic Survey, which show the elevation above the sea level at that point. The elevation of Fryeburg Village is 429 feet; Fryeburg Center, 438; North Fryeburg, at the Chapel, 388; at the Harbor, 381; Walker Farm on the Bridgton Road, 478; East Fryeburg, 487. The average level of the intervales through the town is 380 feet. Frye Hill, the home of the General is 520 feet.
The level of Lovewell's Pond is 358 feet, of Pleasant Pond, 362; the difference is explained by the presence of the rapids where once was a bridge on the Denmark Road, at the "Island".

At one time, there was a plan broached at the Village, to dig a canal from the river, which in that vicinity had an altitude of 380 feet, across the plains, and into Lovewell's Pond, the difference of 22 feet being considered worth the undertaking, for the water power it would generate. Fortunately for all concerned, the plan never developed beyond consideration.

While Fryeburg was not different from other early settled towns through New England, it is interesting to study the way that old families spread their blood throughout the country. Families in the old days were large; and in the limited circumstances of acquaintance it is not surprising that they married among their neighbors, and intermarriage became common. For an illustration of this infiltration of family blood, David Evans, one of the "Seven Lots' Men," may be taken as typical.
David Evans came to "Pigwacket" in 1763, with his younger brother John. They settled at the Seven Lots, David obtaining Grant No. 7, which included the area occupied by the Atwood, Virgin, Robson, Fessenden, Tinker, Evans, Creighton families, during the years of 1860 to 1937. David Evans married Catherine

Walker of Penacook, August 27, 1764, and from that marriage were five children. These five had numerous progeny, and from this family came connections with the following families throughout the United States east of the Mississippi river: Andrews, Abbott, Adams, Buzzell, Brown, Bradley, Blake, Carter, Caswell, Chase, Colby, Cotter, Cutler, Coombs, Devin, Durgin, Dunham, Drown, Eastman, Evans, Fifield, Flint, Farrington, Furness, Gamage, Gerrish, Hamlin, Hanson, Harriman, Hatch, Horr, Hutchinson, Johnston, Knight, Lovejoy, Laird, March, McCollom, Monroe, Newman, Perkins, Proctor, Randall, Richardson, Raymond, Roberts, Swan, Spring, Storr, Taylor, Thoms, Thomson, Trussell, Tucker, Walker, Wallingford, Waterhouse, Webster, Weston, Whitten, Williams, Willis, Woodman, Woodward.

That other families have sprung from these is most probable, and the long stream of blood descent flows on, till the Evans strain can be traced as far as one wishes.

As there is not space in a historical sketch of Fryeburg, to give the families and their nearest descendants, this one reference must be typical of the way in which Fryeburg families have run over the country, and contributed their sterling qualities to other communities.

To show how wide-spread such a family as that of David Evans can be, it is but necessary to note the different places where descendants of his have been located. In Maine, their residences have been: Brownfield, Westbrook, Belfast, Bangor, Foxcroft, Lisbon. In a wider circle are these places in fifteen states: Concord, Conway, N. H.; Haverhill, Springfield, Leicester, Boston, Mass.; Marysville, San Francisco, Sacramento, Little River, Calif.; New York, Brooklyn, N. Y.; Philadelphia, Penn.; Chicago, Waukegan, LaClede, Newman, Sparta, DuQuoin, Ill.; Columbus, Ohio; Kenosha, Anthony, Eau Claire, Wis.; Omaha, Neb.; St. Louis, Mo.; Kinsley, Kan.; Stillwater, Minn.; Sykeston, N. D.; Freehold, N. J.; Leesburg, Fla.; and this is but a fraction of the United States covered by the descendants from one little town in the foot-hills of the White Mountains.

Samuel E. Spring, of Portland, Me., a scion of David Evans, became interested in the possibilities of raising sheep and cattle on ranches in the vicinity of Buenos Ayres, South America. He went there and made large investments. The possibilities attracted Hon. John W. Dana of Fryeburg, a former Governor of the state, who with his son, in 1860, went to South America, and joined Mr. Spring. Mr. Dana died there when a cholera epidemic swept the locality. With him went George Weston, also of Fryeburg, who died there. On his death-bed he married a daughter of Mr. Spring.

Samuel Evans was another who ventured to try the life of a rancher, and while in his lone hut on his ranch, he was attacked one night, robbed and left for dead with a terrible break in his skull. The old blood asserted itself, and he recovered, but his mind was somewhat unbalanced after the assault. He came back to Fryeburg, and lived for a number of years.

Jonathan Stickney, of Brownfield found the South American prospects attractive, and he too, made his home in that country, returning to Brownfield on occasional visits. He died on his way hither from London. James Edward Osgood, a young man, went to the ranches of the Danas, and remained some time, but returned to continue the life of a farmer on the ancestral acres. Thus the influence of Fryeburg was felt in so far-away place as the pampas of Buenos Ayres.

XXIII

LITTLE STORIES

> Oh, Maine, Thy shield is bright and strong,
>   Dirigo!
> Thy patriot spirit's never wrong,
>   Dirigo!
> Behold behind a mighty throng,
> Eager to follow thee along,
> And chant thy dauntless slogan-song
>   Dirigo, oh Dirigo!
>
> —*Anonymous.*

Captain William Evans, a descendant of John Evans of the Seven Lots, was the first male child born in Fryeburg, April 11, 1765. He served in the Revolutionary War, and was a prominent citizen until he died, March 8, 1855.

One of the earliest annoyances of the settlers was from the wolves which infested the forests. According to Captain Evans these beasts could be heard at night howling in the woods which covered the plains about the Seven Lots, from Stark's Hill to Jockey Cap, and he told of an instance when they killed nineteen sheep back of where now stands the stable of Ye Olde Inn, and back of the old burying ground. He said that on one occasion Mrs. Samuel Osgood drove off the wolves from the sheep, being armed only with her broom. The women of those days were not afraid of the terrors that roved by night.

Mrs. Jane Walker, daughter of Hugh Stirling, lived with the widow of James McMillan at the Moosehorn, where he had moved the old blacksmith shop of Timothy Frisbie, which stood where now stands the Fryeburg Tavern. One night when the two women were alone, as they sat in the kitchen, they heard a most unearthly howling, as if all the fiends of the forest were abroad. On looking out they saw a wolf near the barnyard where were their two cows. He could be seen plainly. Presently, in answer to his howls, more wolves came, until there were eleven of the vicious beasts watching the barnyard. They made no attempt to attack it, and finally they left. Fearing that perhaps the wolves might come back and attack the house, the women covered the windows with shawls and blankets, that no ray of light might cause the wolves to think there were human being within. They also turned out their little dog, in the hope that his barking might frighten the animals, but the dog immediately crawled back into the house, through the "cat-hole" in the door. Fortunately no second visit of the wolves was made.

Fryeburg people in the early days did not hesitate to undertake long journeys on horseback. A number of the women who came from other towns seventy-five or a hundred miles distant rode horses over the long journey through the woods. In the latter part of 1793-1794 Samuel Osgood and his sister Mehitable rode on horseback from Fryeburg to Concord, N. H., a distance of seventy-seven miles, in two days. In the summer of 1805 Miss Mary Osgood, Miss Mary Sherburne, with Henry Y. B. Osgood and James W. Ripley rode on horses through the Crawford Notch, to Hanover, N. H., to attend the graduation of Samuel Osgood at Dartmouth College. One day they rode forty-two miles. Osgood and Miss Sherburne were afterward married, and he was pastor of a church in Springfield, Mass., for many years.

General John, Samuel and Major William Stark, all sons of Archibald Stark, of Dunbarton, N. H., held commissions in the British Colonial Service during the Seven Years War. William served at Louisburg and at Quebec. General John was noted as in command of the New Hampshire contingent at the rail fence at Bunker Hill, and as the hero of the battle at Bennington, Vt., in the Revolution. All three brothers received grants of land at Pequawket from Colonel Frye, in recognition of comradeship in arms. No one of them settled on his right, but John and Samuel gave theirs to their sister, Isabel Stark Stirling, who with her husband Hugh Stirling, settled on them.

Joshua Gammage, a veteran of the Revolutionary War who was at the affair at Lexington and was a drummer at Bunker Hill, came to Fryeburg soon after he left the army. He was the first tailor in the town. In June, 1845, in company with Mr. Stephen Gordon (father of several sons who have been a credit to the family and to Fryeburg) and Colonel Webster, Mr. Gammage went to Boston to the dedication of Bunker Hill Monument. He was then about ninety years old, and the journey overtaxed his failing strength. He was prostrated on his return to his home, and died a few days later.

Deacon Richard Eastman, who lived for a time at the north part of the town, was a very useful man in the community in the absence of a clergyman. Until they had a minister he was accustomed to lead the religious services on the Sabbath, attend funerals, and perform other duties of a regular clergyman. He died in Lovell, Dec. 29, 1807, aged 95.

Parson Fessenden had a parish that developed some determined, even beligerent persons. Toward the latter part of his pastorate he divided the time with Elder Zebediah Richardson, preaching half of the time at the Seven Lots, the other half at the Center Meeting House.
One Sunday, Mr. Barker, one of the upholders of the established denomination, shut one door of the Meeting House, and stood in the other doorway, to keep out the Baptists.
Uncle Nathaniel Frye came to enter the doorway where Barker stood. Barker pushed him back.
"What does the damned fool mean!" exclaimed Uncle Nathaniel, and attempting to go in again, Barker pushed him back a second time.
That angered Mr. Frye, and he determined on more forcible action. He took up a stake, and said to the door-keeping Barker, "Step out of that door, or I'll split you down!"
Mr. Barker seeing that he would be driven to defend himself, with prospect of being defeated, stepped back from the door-way, and allowed Mr. Frye to enter.
They took their denominationalism seriously in those days, and were ready and willing to fight to defend it.

There were smart women in Fryeburg in the early days, when the pioneers were obliged to work for everything they had. Mrs. Carter, who was a Fifield, on one occasion after dinner spun the yarn, washed and scoured it; and after her children were in bed knit a pair of breeches, bound and finished them, so that her brother could wear them the next morning.

Mary Stirling, daughter of Hugh, was nursing Mrs. Carter, when one of her children was born. She took her pay in flax. She carried the flax home, walking on snowshoes to "Goshen". She combed and dressed the flax, spun it on a linen wheel, wove the web of cloth, then whitened it, and when completed her father took it on horseback to Kennebunk, and exchanged it for family necessaries.

Another instance of the work of women, was when Mrs. Webster and daughter Jane, spun shoe-thread from flax, till they had sufficient quantity for Edward Weston, who carried the mail to Portland, to take in his saddle bags and exchange for spices and tea before Thanksgiving, 1815. This was in the last year of the War of 1812, when the country was helping itself by patronizing home industry. All sewing thread was home spun.

The same Mary Stirling, who then lived in what is now East Conway, and her sister Martha, got up and washed, getting through at noon, so as to go to a quilting at their sister's at Sodom. At dinner their mother said, "Girls, the sheep must be sheared before you go." They had nothing but common shears, and it was nearly night when they finished. Mary was for giving up going to the quilting, but Martha said, "We shall have a good time. Let's go."

It was sunset when they crossed the river at Wilson's. They danced all night, but lay down a short time, and got up in the morning in season to walk the four miles home, and milk the cows.

After she was married to John Webster, Mary would take a baby, or perhaps two, and go into the field after doing the morning work; pull flax until 11 o'clock; come home, pick up wood, cook dinner for the family, and go again to the flax field until she would pull a bushel's sowing.

One winter day the Dinsmores came, five or six of them to spend the day; the next day at Colonel Walker's keeping pretty late hours. The next morning, after they had gone, while cleaning up, who should drive up but four Starks, three of them with their wives. Of course the turkey had to be killed, and at night, among other amusements, they danced. At 2 o'clock, they made field-beds, for the men in one room, and for the women in the other; the family slept in the attic. That was a story told to the grandchildren, and it shows how energetic the women were, for work or amusement, in the early days.

A young man who became a credit to Fryeburg Academy was Abiel Chandler, who was born in Concord, N. H., Feb. 26, 1777. John Bradley was so impressed with the industry which the lad showed in his work there, that he gave him a farm of forty acres in Stow, Maine. When about twenty-one years old, he took the farm and at the same time showed a great desire for an education. He overheard the conversation of two men who were graduates of Dartmouth College, and being impressed by the different manner of their speech from that of the local people with whom he associated, he expressed a wish to be able to speak as they did. Accordingly he went to Fryeburg Academy in the winters, and so well did he spend his time, that he was able to graduate from Harvard in 1806. He amassed a fortune in business in Boston, and gave to Dartmouth the Chandler Scientific School.

In Fryeburg and Lovell are large ponds, both bearing the name of "Kezar". These ponds were named for George Kezar, who came from Canterbury, N. H., about 1788, and settled in Parsonsfield, where he had previously hunted. He had roved the country around the Kezar ponds, also, hunting, and knew the territory between Fryeburg and the Ossipee River. His name was given to the village and the falls, now known as "Kezar Falls", which are between Parsonsfield and South Hiram.

Daniel Webster, in his recollections of Fryeburg, referred to a ride to Conway. That destination seemed to be favored among the young people of the village as a place where they could get a good supper, for a letter written in December, 1855, mentions the fact that "twelve couples were to ride to Shattagee the next evening". Chatauque, to give the proper spelling, was a place of attraction, as the Adams Hotel set a good table, and on this occasion it kept up its reputation, for the bill of fare as reported, included "turkeys, ham and tongue, with all the necessary sauces and tarts, and eight kinds of cake, together with an elegant dessert of raisins, nuts, peppermints, etc. At eleven we set sail, arriving at home at one o'clock."

This story shows to what heights the freshets of the Saco sent the waters. Joseph Knight was living with Squire Joseph Chandler at the time of the great freshet, October 6, 1785. The barn stood on a knoll near the old channel of the river, opposite the house. The cattle gathered on another knoll where is the burying ground, standing there until the water was up to their sides, then they went with the current, which was setting toward Kezar Pond. One ox came ashore at Toll Bridge. Mr. Knight had but one cow. She disappeared in the flood. After the water had subsided, he found her hanging by her horns from the crotch of a tree, so high that he could just reach her tail. The live stock were not the only sufferers, as Squire Chandler's house was submerged to the chamber windows, and the family were forced to find other quarters.

The Walker family, one branch of which has occupied "The Island" farm since 1778, has a clear line of descent from Deacon Samuel Walker, who came to this country from England. His grandson, who lived in Saugus, Mass., and was an Indian fighter, had a son, Captain Samuel of Wilmington, whose wife was Hannah Fowle, of Woburn. Their son Timothy inherited the farm from his father. He married Eunice Brewster, of Duxbury, a direct descendent from Elder Brewster, who came with other Pilgrims in the "Mayflower" in 1620, and was the pastor of the Plymouth colony. The family claimed that his name was not William, but "Truelove", and a son of Timothy Walker was named Truelove, for the Elder. Colonel James Walker, son of Timothy, occupied the Island farm during his life. His son was named for the Rev. Carlton Hurd, and was prominent in the town.

Recruiting for the war of 1812 was carried on in the store of Capt. Seth Spring, now occupied by E. L. Skillings.

Mr. Moses Chandler told how his mother, a daughter of Paul Langdon, was so accustomed to riding horseback, that she rode from the base to the summit of Mount Kearsarge at the age of sixty-five, a distance of two miles over ledges, through ravines and the forest. She said on reaching the summit that she could have easily carried a child in her arms on the trip. Mr. Chandler with two others built the house that will be remembered by the old citizens as crowning the summit of Kearsarge, until the great wind of November, 1883, swept it away, and it was several years later that the present smaller house was built.

For a number of years attention was directed to the settlement of the town according to the first division of land into lots. This kept the settlement practically on the inside of the Great Bend of the Saco. The section to the eastward, south of Kezar Pond, was not settled until the early part of the Nineteenth Century. The first man to occupy land here was Elder John Pike, a Baptist minister. Others who came in included Humphrey Chadbourne, Phendeas Hurd, Elbridge Harnden, William Hapgood, Job Pike, Deacon Sanborn, Major Smith. The area where they settled was good upland with some intervale and meadow lands. These settlers improved their time and their claims, until that section became one of the best neighborhoods in the town. The people paid attention to their farms and were thrifty, as the lands in that neighborhood show.

An incident occurred "once upon a time" which might have been a fatality, instead of the accident that it was, when two boys, McNeal and Buck were squabbling on the "Shelf" of Jockey Cap. The Shelf is a little projection on the southerly side, forming the "visor" of the "Cap", some distance above the tops of the pines on that side of the cliff. No one knew exactly how it happened or who was at fault, but Buck fell off. Instead of being crushed to death, as his horror-stricken companion imagined, he fell into the saving branches of a pine tree, which bending under his weight dropped him a less distance to the ground, where he was picked up, bruised and thoroughly frightened, but uninjured.

The clear, cold temperature of Fryeburg has gone on record. There were times when a careful register was kept for the Government. In 1848 Dr. Reuel Barrows reported under date of January 11 that the cold was more severe then than ever known before, that morning the mercury having reached from 36 to 39 below zero, and that when mercury was exposed in a dish it froze to a consistency of putty and could be turned over and cut like lead. In 1855, it was reported to the Portland papers, that the morning of February 7, a mercurial thermometer reached 38½ degrees below zero on Main Street, and that the mercury congealed when exposed to the air in a dish. The highest summer mark on record was 104 degrees in the shade, on July 3, 1868. An average of 99 degrees was reached frequently in mid-summer.

Governor John W. Dana, of Fryeburg, had the distinction of vetoing in 1847 the first Prohibition bill to reach the executive chamber. He took this stand because he claimed that the statute could not be enforced, and that it would increase, rather than lessen drunkenness.

By a singular coincidence, three families of Fryeburg lived as neighbors on the same side of the road from Fryeburg Center through "Fish Street" to North Fryeburg. Speaking the names in order, as one passed along from the Center, the advice was: "Pray, Day and Knight."

Governor John A. Andrew used to tell an amusing story of his experience with Aunt Molly Brewster, whom he encountered when he visited the Oxford House. Aunt Molly was the hostess of that famous tavern, and she "ran" the house. At that time window screens were not in use. Governor Andrew opened a window in the parlor; a moment later Aunt Molly entered the room and closed the window. Governor Andrew a second time opened the window, and a second time Aunt Molly closed it. The third time the window was opened by the Governor Aunt Molly entered the room with wrath in her eye, and remarked with considerable asperity, "Look here, you may run the State of Massachusetts, but you can't run the Oxford House", and she closed the window the third time, with a bang that firmly emphasized her determination to "run" the Oxford House herself. The circumstance gave Governor Andrew a story that he told years afterward.

In the dooryard of the Isaiah Warren House on Portland Street, is an elm that is noted and known all over the country. It is called, "The Doughnut Tree", because a large branch has grown in such a way as to make a complete circle near the ground, and then has kept on, growing up to a proportionate height to the other limbs. It is perhaps the most-photographed elm tree in Maine, and it has held in its curve children of several generations, adding to the picturesqueness.

In 1867 Usher W. Cutts, a recent graduate of Bowdoin came to the principalship of Fryeburg Academy, a position which he held for two years. One of his strong holds on the youth of the place was the fact that he introduced them to the game of baseball, which gained a national popularity during and following the Civil War. The "Pequawket Baseball Club" was organized, and was continued for a number of years with great success, winning many games from the neighboring nines, and giving the citizens of the town a nine to be proud of.

One of the apostles of the national temperance cause was Rev. Wilbur F. Crafts, who was born in the Village during the residence of his father, the minister of the local Methodist Episcopal church, in the house on upper Main Street, lately occupied by Joseph H. Johnson and his wife. Mr. Crafts only occasionally visited his birthplace, but his wife was a teacher in the Chautauqua Assembly, in 1884.

The late Mary L. Gordon left a fund of ten thousand dollars, which she named the "Seth C. Gordon Fund," its income to be used for the surgical and medical treatment of children in the town whose parents are unable to provide such care.

The first woman in Oxford County appointed to serve on a Jury, at the Superior Court of the County, was Miss Harriet L. Abbott, who was a valued town official in many capacities, as Town Clerk and on the School Board, with manifold duties connected with both positions.

Fryeburg furnished few men to the naval service. The most conspicuous instance was that of Charles Tappan Chase, who was born in 1827. He had a varied career. He went to California in the great exodus of 1849, where he became interested in politics, and served in the state legislature three years. Afterwards he went to South America, where he was the engineer in charge of building a railroad in Bolivia. He returned to the United States in 1858, and soon after entered the U. S. Navy. He was under Admiral Farragut at the capture of New Orleans, April 29, 1862. He was on the steamship Mississippi when she was burned at Port Hudson, to prevent her falling into the hands of the Confederates. He and his crew escaped to the river bank where they were rescued by the boats of the fleet. Later he was in command of a cruiser in the Gulf of Mexico, suppressing the blockade runners. While engaged in this duty, he went ashore near the mouth of the Rio Grande and was captured and taken to Brownsville. He expected to be shot as a spy, but because he was captured on Mexican soil the captors decided it would save complications if he were released, which was done. At the end of the war he transferred to the Revenue Marine, with the rank of Lieutenant. He received promotion to a captaincy later. He was stationed during his Revenue service at Key West, Baltimore, New York, Philadelphia, Portland and Eastport. His last service was at Portland, in command of the Revenue cutter "Dallas."

George Perley Bradley, son of A. R. Bradley, was a Fryeburg man who served with honor in the U. S. Navy, as a medical officer. He studied medicine in Fryeburg, and entered the Navy as an assistant surgeon. He passed through the successive stages of rank in his department, becoming a surgeon, in which capacity he served until his retirement. His cruises brought him to different parts of the world, where he had opportunity to study and observe, and he rendered important service by his reports and by his translations of medical works from foreign languages.

For a long time the population of Fryeburg was homogeneous. Intermarriage between the early families helped to perpetuate the strains of New England blood among a widening circle. The influx of residents during the last century has been slow, while the outgo has spread Fryeburg family associations throughout the country. The lack of class manufacturing in the town has prevented a movable people, and has kept old homes in the families for a long period of years.

That Fryeburg has welcomed to its residence people of other lands, as readily as those in the earlier days from other places in New England, has always been a characteristic.

Some time about the 1840s there came to the Village, James J. Rogers, a native of England, who conducted a furniture shop. He lived on Main Street opposite Pine Hill. Another Englishman was Robert Tonge, a tailor by trade, and an agent for an oven which took the place of the time-honored brick oven. He lived for a time in the house which he built close to Main Street, on the old Town Line; later he lived on Dana Street. Mrs. Tonge was a noted beauty.

Still another from the old country, was George Davidson, a Scotchman by birth, who had been a soldier in a Highland Regiment. He was a tailor, and his sign bore the legend, "Davidson, from London". He served the town as a selectman, at one time.

In later years people whose ancestry was from the Emerald Isle came to the town to make good citizens, among them William Devine. The railroad brought Michael Keefe, who was in charge of the Fryeburg section until it was consolidated with the Conway section. He was a good citizen, who left a good name, and a family who keep up his record.

When Asa O. Pike assumed the conduct of the Oxford House in 1876, he removed the sun dial from the site where it had stood since the early 1860s beside the building used as a store by John Locke. It was placed in front of the Oxford House, between the sidewalk and the highway. There it has stood ever since, during the destruction by fire of the Oxford House and of its successor the Oxford.

The sundial, which is of iron, stands about a foot and a half high above the cubical stone base, about three feet square and high. On this granite base is engraven, "Level in Latitude 42". A part of one of the sections of the iron work has been broken off, but it does not interfere to any appreciable extent with the time keeping qualities of the dial.

Comparing the solar time with that of Daylight Saving, the sundial is about one-half hour slower, if the edge of the shadow nearest the gnomon is taken as the index of the time.

This dial, which marks the changing hours on sunny days, is an object of great interest to visitors who may pass it, though it is such an old story to the people of the town that it is practically unnoticed. It is an interesting relic of the age when people lived slower and were willing to let the world go by without trying to regulate it too much, or to run everything by a time schedule.

An event of more than passing moment was the observance of the first hundred years of Fryeburg Academy, which took place August 16-17, 1892, at the Academy and at the Chautauqua Assembly grounds, as no room in the village would have accommodated the gathering. The social reunion was held Tuesday, August 18 in Academy Hall, and brought together former students from all over New England, New York, New Jersey, Illinois, Kansas and other Western states. The more formal exercises were held the next day at the Assembly Auditorium, at which the program included an historical address by Hon. George B. Barrows; Singing of the Ode, written by Mrs. Caroline Dana Howe; Oration by President William DeW. Hyde of Bowdoin College, in which he showed "The Place of the Academy in the Educational System"; Poem by John Stark Colby of Concord, N. H.

The banquet in the Dining Hall followed, and at the after-dinner exercises reminiscent remarks were made by Rev. Daniel Furber, D.D., Hon. A. P. Stone, Hon. Nelson Dingley, S. C. Gordon, M.D., S. H. Weeks, M.D., Hon. A. A. Strout, Rev. B. P. Snow, Henry H. Smith, Esq., C. A. Page, A.M., Hon. J. M. Bradbury, Prof. W. A. Robinson, Isaac Walker. Letters were read from absent friends, and poems were read from Prof. E. Knowlton, a former Principal, of San Francisco, and Miss Ellen Hamlin Butler, of Hallowell, a former teacher. The occasion was one of fragrant memories, and the renewal of old acquaintances.

On page 250 there is mention of the destruction by fire of Moses Ames' house. The many references to Mr. Ames show his position as one of the Seven Lots men and as representative from the Town to the General Court of Massachusetts. By singular good fortune, after this book was nearly through the press, the authentic picture of the original Ames house was obtained and is reproduced for frontispiece.

In a story of his life that Dr. Simeon A. Evans wrote for his children, he included this picture, drawn by Samuel A. Bradley, which had been pronounced "a perfect representation" by those familiar with the house. The picture adds interest to diary entries given earlier; young Mr. Timothy Walker on Aug. 17, 1765, "Breakfasted at Mr. Ames"; and on June 5, 1775, Parson Fessenden "Drank coffee at Mr. Ames." So here we see the place of their entertainment rise Phoenix-like from its ashes.

John Greenleaf Whittier spent the summer months of 1880, at the Village, in the T. C. Ward house, with the family of his niece, Mrs. Samuel T. Pickard, of Portland. Mr. Whittier was a frequent visitor at the homes of those with whom he became acquainted, though his natural shyness caused him to avoid anything that seemed like hero-worship. He frequently walked the streets, his tall, spare form being a conspicuous figure, especially in those directions that would give him an extended view of the mountains and hills around the village. On being asked to write his autograph in the album of a friend, Mr. Whittier accompanied it with these lines appreciative of the mountain view which he enjoyed contemplating:

> O Mountains of the North, unveil
>   Your brows, and lay your cloudy mantles by!
> And once more, ere the eyes that seek ye fail,
>   Uplift against the blue walls of the sky
> Your mighty shapes, and let the sunshine weave
>   Its golden network in your belting woods;
>   Smile down in rainbows from your falling floods,
> And on your kingly brows at morn and eve
> Set crowns of fire! So shall my soul receive,
>   Haply, the secret of your calm and strength;
> Your unforgotten beauty interfuse
> My common life; Your glorious shapes and hues
>   And sun-clothed splendors at my bidding come,
> Loom vast through dreams, and stretch in billowy length
>   From the sea-level of my lowland home.

SOURCES OF INFORMATION

History of Concord, N. H., by N. Bouton.
History of Haverhill, Mass.
History of Manchester, N. H.
History of Porter, Me., by Thomas Moulton.
History of the White Mountains, by Benj. G. Willey.
Lovewell's Fight, Francis Kidder.
Lovewell's Fight, Thomas Symmes.
The Abnakis, by Rev. Eugene Vetromile.
Maine Historical Society Publications.
Rev. Paul Coffin's "Trip to Pigwacket."
Rev. Timothy Walker, Concord, N. H., Journal.
Rev. T. Smith, Portland, Me., Journal.
The Descendants of David Evans, by S. A. Evans, M.D., Conway, N. H.
Fryeburg Town Records.
Fryeburg Town Officers' Reports.
Historical Notes collected by George B. Barrows and Mrs. Barrows.
Historical Notes collected by Rev. Samuel Souther, Worcester, Mass.
Historical Notes collected by James R. Osgood, Fryeburg.
Diaries of William Gordon, Fryeburg.
Rev. Samuel Souther's Address at Fryeburg Centennial.
Records of Congregational Church, Fryeburg.
Records of Fryeburg Academy.
Records of Societies and Organizations.
Statutes of the State of Maine.
Maine Registers.
New England Directory.
Registry of Deeds, Western District Oxford County.
The Farmer's Monthly Visitor.
Files of the Oxford Democrat.
Files of the Lewiston Journal.
Files of the Oxford County Advertiser.
Files of the Oxford County Record.
Files of the Christian Mirror, Portland, Me.
Files of the Portland Transcript.
Historical Collections of John F. Pratt, Chelsea, Mass.

History of Indian Wars, Samuel Penhallow.
History of Bethel, Me., by N. T. True.
Narrative of Lieut. Nathaniel Segar.
Diary of Darby Field.
A Century of Conflict, by Francis Parkman.
Writings of Rev. Amos J. Cook.
Letters of Enoch Lincoln.
"The Village", by Enoch Lincoln.
"Our Forbears", by Rebecca Perley Read.
"Mothers of Maine", by Helen Coffin Beedy.
Hoyt's History of Indian Wars.
The Journal of Major Robert Rogers.
The Granite Monthly, Vol. 8.
The New England Magazine.
Journals of Rev's. Smith and Deane.
History of the Town of Paris.

INDEX

Abnaki Indians	1
Academy,	
47, 92, 99, 121, 122, 123-132, 213, 228, 229, 238, 244, 246, 256, 271, 275	
Buildings	126, 128, 130
Centennial	277
Grant	124
Semi-centennial	127, 222
Acadian Peasants	34
Act of Incorporation	103
Alarm List	109
American Legion	166, 177, 212
Amherst College	128, 129
Aqueduct Corporation	181
Around River	142
Artillery Company	159, 255
Artists	225-226
Authors	223-224
Baldface	145
Baldpeak	146
Baldwin	191, 193
Baptist Society	85, 89
Bartlett	58, 90, 191, 232
Bates College	129
Batteaux	41, 51
Battle at the Pond	13
Bear Pond	55, 74, 83, 136, 138, 139
Beaver Dam	161
"Bees"	67
Bells	256-257
Bethel (Sudbury, Canada)	8
Bench Mark	147, 264
Birch Hill	75, 83, 91, 140, 147, 189
Blacksmiths	67, 174
Bog Pond	83, 136, 139, 148
Book Club	206
Boston	115
Bounds of Frye's Grant	31
Bowdoin College	26, 127, 218, 230, 275

284   FRYEBURG

Bradley Park 54, 147, 165, 194
Brass Band 203-204
Bridges 141
Bridgton 145, 161, 191, 193, 233
Bridgton Road 53, 141
British King 114
Brooks 150, 186
Brownfield 33, 49, 120, 123, 147, 156, 169, 189, 190, 193
Bunker Hill Monument 269
Burying Ground 55, 73, 74
By-ways 75

C. C. C. 145
"Calm Content" 44
Canal 135-139, 143
Candles 65
Carter Hill 147
Casco Bank and Trust Co. 184
Cattle Drives 262
Cemeteries 188-189
Centennial of Academy 277, 278
  of Town 199
Center Fryeburg 55, 189, 264
Chandler Scientific School 271
Charles River 141
  Pond 141, 148
Chase House 53
Chatham, N. H. 191, 218
Chautauqua Union, Maine 179, 208-209, 275
Chautauque 271
Cheese Factory 176
Choats Brook 152, 260
Chocorua 144
Christian Science Association 92
Church of the New Jerusalem (Swedenborgian) 91
Concord Coaches 196, 258
  Double-decker 234
Congregational Church Building 91
Constitution, Convention for Ratification of 112
Conway, N. H.,
        33, 58, 82, 90, 95, 96, 123, 156, 191, 197, 220, 228, 243, 260, 271
  East 118, 232, 270
  North 221, 225
Corn Packing 263
Cornish (Francesborough) 191
Court Hall 176
Courts of Common Pleas 111
Culler of Shingles 62, 107

Dartmouth College	126, 127, 217, 220, 221, 268, 271
Death Hole	150
Denmark	120, 145, 161, 189, 190
Detaching Men	109
Division of Land—	
First	71
Second	72, 73
Re-laying	76
Third-Sixth	76, 233
Doublehead	145
Doughnut Tree	274
Drift Roads	75, 170
"Driving Home the Cows"	223
East Fryeburg	141, 147, 189, 241, 264
Eastern Artillery	161
Eastern Star	212
Eastman, Mount	145
Store	152
and Bradley's Grant	33
Eaton	191
Eclipse in 1932	213-215
Evans Notch	145
"Fag End"	260
Falmouth	37, 41, 77, 78, 113
Federal Road	260
Ferries	140
Ferry Boats	49, 56
Fessenden Hill	147
"Fiddle Row"	260
Fight Brook	149
Fire Department	182, 251
Fire of Aug. 31, 1906	251
"Fish Street"	55, 141, 189, 226, 259, 274
Flax	66, 111, 270
Foods of Pioneers	65
Footstoves	69
Fords	140
Foundry	174
Freedom	191
Free Will Baptist Society	91
"French Corner"	260
French and Indian Wars	153
Charts	2
Voyagers	2
"Frog Alley"	259
Frye Hill	55, 58

Fryeburg Addition 33
Frye's Grant 28
Furniture, Early 64

G. A. R., Bosworth Post 237
   Grover Post 164
   Ladies of 243
General Court of Massachusetts,
       30, 43, 75, 76, 101, 113, 115, 123, 130, 136, 138, 154, 181
   Remonstrance to 155
Geological Conditions 134-135
Gilead 145
Glacial Action 134
Gordon Hall 238
Gorham 193, 242
"Goshen" 270
Granges 191, 204, 205
Green Mountain 56, 144
Grist Mill 54, 141, 150, 186
Gun House 254

Haley Neighborhood 260
Hans Gram Musical Society 203
"Harbor" 55, 75, 141, 189, 260, 264
Harvard College 34, 51, 97, 118, 218, 227, 230
Hearse 183
Hemp 111
Highway Surveyors 263
Highways 75
Hiram 189, 190, 193
History of Fryeburg 210-212
Hogreeves 255
Horse Railroad 179-180
House Construction 61-63
Hoyt's History of Indian Wars 35
Hurricane Mountain 144
Hutchins Farm, Spring on 151

Illiterates 122
Implements 66
I. O. G. T. 202
I. O. O. F. 212
"Indian Acres" 55, 214
Indian Hole 5
Indians 6, 9, 10, 153
Instructions to Representatives 110, 112
"Island" 56, 264, 272

Index

Jackson 191
"Jockey Cap" 10, 135, 146, 147, 149, 187, 245, 273

Kearsarge 144, 272
   Village 144
Kennebunk 270
Kezar Falls 271
   Lakes 28, 135, 260
   Pond 135, 147, 150, 271, 272, 273
   River 150
Kimball Brook 140
   Pond 148
Kiwanis Club 213, 214
Knights of Pythias 212

Lawyers 216-218
"Leather Lane" 172
Locke's Mill 150
Log Houses 60
Long Hill 146
Loom 64
Lord's Supper, Celebration of 97
Lottery 73
Louisburg, Siege of 35, 232, 268
Lovell 33, 145, 189, 190, 226, 258, 260
   Stage 258
Lovewell's Brook 53, 75
   Fight 14-23
      Ballads on 222
      Centennial of 24
   Pond 51, 54, 56, 80, 135, 142, 148, 149
Lug Pole 62
Lumber Boxes 58, 258

Maine Chautauqua Assembly 149
   Eye and Ear Infirmary 238
   General Hospital 238
   Power Company 195
Martha's Grove Camp Ground 151, 208
Masting 255
Mast Master 255
Meeting House 67, 69, 73, 74, 83, 84, 86
   South 69, 84, 88
Memorial Hospital 221
"Menotomy" 56, 140, 189, 259
Methodist Episcopal Church 90, 179, 275

Mill Brook	53
Irons	41
Lot	54
Milliken Regiment	167
Minister's Right	55
Moat Mountain	144
Moosehorn	179, 208, 267
Brook	74, 149, 152
Moose Rock	54, 142
Mount Bradley	147
Tom	135, 140, 145, 259
Mountains	144, 145
Moving Buildings	261
"Mud City"	258
Museum, Academy	126
Music in Fryeburg	203
Musters	161
Naples	193
"Nebraska"	260
North Bridgton Brass Band	199
North Chatham	134, 187
North Fryeburg	75, 91, 140, 141, 150, 189, 221, 258, 264
North Star	184
Northern N. E. S. S. Assembly	179
Notch	58
"Numbering the People"	108
Nurse, State Field	119
Oak Hill	146, 148, 188
"Oatmeal Crusaders"	244
Odd Fellows	212
Hall	84
Olde Inn	177, 267
Old River	55
Organ, First	204
Ossipee Trail	193
Oven, Brick	62, 63
Dutch	62
Oxen	68, 261
Oxford	53, 177, 251
Bank	183
House	5, 53, 54, 172, 174, 176, 226, 233, 234, 242, 251, 274, 277
Page Hill	74, 147
Paper Money	111
Parish, First	89
Second	89
Third	89

Index

Parsonsfield 228, 271
Paugus Day 24
Pearlash 111
Peas 111
Pequawket Baseball Club 275
    Hills 146
    Indians 2
    Spelling 4
    Trail 186, 193
    Village 5
Petitions:
    Frye's for a Grant 30
    For Authorization to Sell Spirituous Liquors 43
    Proprietors for Organization 71
    Frye's for Exchange of Land 75
    Re Road to Falmouth 76-79
    Proprietors for Incorporation 101
    For Reduction of Taxes 113
    Re Mistake in Valuation 115
    For Incorporation of Fryeburg Academy 123
    For Amendment of the Act Incorporating the Proprietors of the
    Canal 136
Phillipstown (Sanford) 49, 50, 77
Physicians 219-222
"Pike's Peak" 259
Pillion 68
Pine Grove Cemetery 45, 100, 188
    Hill 141, 147, 187, 194, 199, 276
"Pitch" Lot 31, 83, 84
Pleasant Mountain 28, 133, 145
    Pond 148
Poets 222-223
Poll Taxes 264
Ponds 148-149, 260
Porter 189, 190
Portland and Ogdensburg R. R. 178, 197, 238
Post, Fryeburg 186
Postmasters 195-198
Potash 111, 172
Pot-hooks 62
Price-fixing 105
Prohibition Bill, First 274
Proprietors, Account with Frye 40
    Locating 56
    Petition for Incorporation 101
Pythagorean Lodge, A. F. A. Masons 171, 212, 239
Pythian Sisters 212

Quiltings 67

Raisings 67
Rattlesnake Hills 144
Reading Circle 206
    Chautauqua 207
Rebekahs 212
Recruiting for War of 1812 272
"Red Men" 213
Registry of Deeds 177, 183, 193, 209-210
Reporter, Fryeburg 186
Revolution, War of 154
Revolver Horse-rake 66
Roads 37, 74
Rogers' Rangers 153
Roosevelt Trail 193
Royce 145
Russell's Echo 184

Sabatis Mountain 145
Sable Mountain 145
Saco 113
    Pond 17
    River 3, 5, 28, 29, 32, 41, 56, 71, 78, 115, 133-143, 181, 231, 258, 273
Sawmills 150, 175, 186
School, Appropriation for 108
    First 118
School Districts 119
School Houses, Location of 108, 119
Sesquicentennial of Town 200
Seth C. Gordon Fund 275
"Seven Lots" 53, 54, 58, 59, 74, 86, 264, 269
Singing Schools 68, 203
Skating Rink 173
Ski Coasts 187
Slaves 44, 241, 243
Smart's Hill 147, 189
Society of Colonial Wars 22, 23
"Sodom" 50, 81, 270
Sources of Information 280
Speckle Mountain 145
Spinning Wheels 64
Standish 193
Stark's Hill 57, 146, 147, 149, 151, 187, 267
Steep Falls 193
Stickney's Tavern 161
Stirling Literary Club 206

Index

Stoneham	145, 189
Stow	33, 120, 134, 145, 150, 189, 271
Streets of Village	192
Sundial	277
Swan's Falls	53, 74, 139, 140, 141, 142, 195, 236

Tannery	174
Tavern, Fryeburg	177, 267
Telegraph Office	179
Temperance	201-202
House	177, 210, 257
Temperature Records	273
Thread	270
Tin Kitchen	64
"Toll Bridge"	55, 141, 189, 259
Tories	114
Town Clock	191
Town Commissioners	263
Farm	121
Line	32
Meeting, First	104
Date set for	108
Officers, First	105
Train Band Soldiers	109
Training Field	55, 73, 75
Trammels	62
Transportation	68
Trees, Indigenous	29, 30

Unitarian Society	90
U. S. Trust Co.	183
Universalist Chapel	91
Society	88, 89

Valuation of Estates, First	108
"Village, The"	230-231
Village Corporation	182, 195, 253

Walker Genealogy	272
Wars, Fryeburg in	153
Water Company	56, 180
Waterford	189
Webster Association	199
West Fryeburg	75, 186, 189, 236
West Oxford Agricultural Society	74, 179, 204
Grounds	193

West Point 229
Westbrook 193
Weston's Bridge 140, 141, 142
Wheat 111
    Duck 236
"Whirlpool" 171
White-Lot Brook 56, 180
Williamson's History of Maine 6
Winter Sports Committee 187
Wolves 267-268
    Bounty on 107
    Destruction by 156
W. C. T. U. 202
Woman's Library Club 201, 205-206
Woodward Farm 56, 233
Wool 66

Yale College 127, 218, 220

NAMES

Abbott, Aaron, 39, 51, 70, 79, 102
  Asa, 159
  Augustus, 196
  Ernest H., 93, 209
  George H., 177
  Harriet L., 168, 205, 211, 248, 275
  Isaac, 39, 51, 55, 79, 83, 84, 89, 105, 106, 136, 157, 158
  Isaac, Jr., 9, 44
  Lyman, 209
  Micah, 159
  Moses, 159
  Philip E., 166
  Silas, 159
  Simeon, 9
  Stephen, 136, 160
  Susan, 251
  Thomas, 152
  William Henry, 177, 190, 196
Achenbach, Solomon T., 93
Adams, Emerson L., 23, 129
  Fred Emerson, 209
  John, 51
  Wendell H., 129
Albert, King of Belgium, 225
Alden, Rachel Weston, 226
Alexander, Lafayette, 162
Allard, Thomas J., 207
Allen, George, 221
  Peter, 102
Ambrose, Edwin F., 128
Ames, Moses, 9, 50, 53, 70, 79, 83, 87, 95, 102, 105, 106, 109, 110, 112, 124, 157, 195, 219, 242, 250, 278
  Nathan, 79, 105
Amherst, General, 153

Andrew, John A., 132, 199, 274
  Mary Pierce, 132
Andrews, Abby, 210
  Abraham, 142
  Abram, 246
  Charles, 162
  George C., 120
  Henry, 162
  James, 162
  John, 164
  Langdon F., 166
Appleton, E. W., 183
Atkinson family, 51
  L. W., 221
Atwood, Caleb, 164, 246
  James, 160
  John, 246, 261
  Ruth, 247
Austin, Abiel, 17, 19, 21
(Also spelled Astin and Austen)
  Calvin, 246
  George, 162
  Hezekiah, 40, 56, 70, 73, 79, 83, 102, 105
  Maria P., 131
  Peter, 9, 79, 105
Ayer, Ebenezer, 17, 19, 21

Bachelder, John, 197, 246
Badger, Daniel, 196
Bailey, Edwin, 162
Baker, W. H., 221
Ballard, Abby, 210, 211
  Aimee, 168
  Dean A., 206, 210, 219
  Eckley, 164, 206, 210, 246
  Edward, 164
  George, 187, 206

BALLARD—Con.
    Jackson H., 166
    Susan F., 206, 247
    Uriah, 159, 187
Barbour, Amadel, 162
Barker, Albion G., 166
    Benjamin, 56, 70
    Charles F., 164
    Frank, 246
    John P., 162
    Mary B., 172, 251
    Walter D., 166
    Webster, 162
    Willard, 162
    Wilson, 246
Barron, Elias, 17, 19
    Oliver, 9
Barrows, Anna, 206, 209, 224, 248
    Charles D., 128
    Ellen A., 131
    George B., 132, 190, 199, 211, 217, 219, 246, 278
    Georgiana S., 205, 226, 247
    John Stuart, (1) 161, 217
        (2) 23
    Reuel, 188, 190, 201, 220, 273
    William, (1) 217
        (2) 125
    William G., 132
Barry, Thomas D., 215
Bartlett, Edith S., 206
    Herman L., 221
Bashford, J. W., 209
Bates, Arlo, 129
Battery, Henry, 162
Baxter, James Phinney, 22
Bean, Fred W., 166
Beckley, Peter, 162
Bell, Erving, 167
    Merton L., 166
Bemis, Amos, 159
    Thaddeus, 89
Bennett, J. L., 221
Benton, Joseph, 220
Berry, Harmon V., 197, 198
Bigelow, Timothy, 138
Bishop, John Thomas, 236

Blaine, James G., 209
Blanchard, Charles R., 164
Bodwell, Governor, 209
Boody, Alvin, 127
    S. E., 131
Booth, George, 167
    George F., 207
    Harold G., 93
Boothby, Mr., 47
    Horatio, 176
    R. M., 222
Bosworth, Wilfred H., 166
    Mary, 206
Bouton, Nathaniel, 22
Brackett, Elmer, 172, 175
    Uranus O., 177
Bradbury, George H., 246, 251
    J. M., 278
Braddock, General, 232
Bradford family, 51
Bradley, Abraham, 9, 55, 70, 79, 95, 102, 105, 124
    Alexander R., 148, 218, 246
        Stuart, 217, 246
    Anne Cary, 211, 226
    Daniel W., 246
    David, (1) 159
        (2) 246
    Frank Y., 246
    George P., 132, 246, 276
    Georgia D., 194, 248
    I. B., 177, 188, 194, 211, 220
    Jeremiah, 159
    John, (1) 271
        (2) 170, 210
    John Jay, 148, 246
    Mary F., 205
    Minnie A., 252
    Philbrick, 246
    Richard, 162, 246
    Robert, 5, 137, 148, 170, 217, 228, 246, 250
    Samuel, 39, 102
    Samuel A., 24, 25, 127, 203, 217, 219, 246
    Sarah Johnston, 194, 226, 247
    Timothy, 79
    Mrs. W. B., 226

Bragdon, Charles H.,	162	Frances L.,	131
William,	162	Hubbard,	56
Bray, Oliver,	203	Mrs.,	269
Brewster, Eunice,	272	Samuel F.,	160
Molly,	244, 274	Cary, Abel,	243
Ralph O.,	200	Casilear, John F.,	225

Bragdon, Charles H., 162
  William, 162
Bray, Oliver, 203
Brewster, Eunice, 272
  Molly, 244, 274
  Ralph O., 200
  William, 272
Briggs, Captain, 48
Brooks, George, 160
Brown, Amos, 127, 188
  Earle, 165
  Harry Young, 32, 43, 49, 52, 95, 96, 124, 147, 227
  Jonas, 160
  Loren, 52, 53
Bryant, Gridley J. F., 128
  Walter, 6, 146
Buck, Asa, 52
Bucknell, John, 54, 79, 102, 105
(Becknell)
  John, Jr., 102
Burbank, Ezekiel W.,
    165, 171, 175, 246
  H. H., 170
Burgin, Isaac, 159
Burke, John, 162
Burnham, H. H., 176, 192
Buswell, Henry C., 170, 188
Butler, Ellen Hamlin, 278
Butters, Levi, 162
Buzzell, Andrew, 246
  E. C., 83, 194, 219, 246
  Francis, 84
  John, 146
  Mary E., 131
Byron, Parker D., 166

Card, And. Pierce, 47
Carlt, Edward, 56
Carlton, D. D., 247
  Laura H., 247
  Theodore, 73
Carpenter, Henry Bernard,
    222, 244
Carruthers, John B., 93
Carter, Donald W., 166, 168
  Ezra, 56, 70, 71, 73, 79, 102, 105, 106, 186

Frances L., 131
Hubbard, 56
  Mrs., 269
  Samuel F., 160
Cary, Abel, 243
Casilear, John F., 225
Chadbourn, Humphrey A.,
    162, 273
Chamberlain, Eliza, 131
  John, 17, 19, 22, 25
Champney, Benjamin, 225
Chandler, Abial, 70
  Abiel, 132, 271
  Charles, 175, 198, 247
  Daniel, 55, 89
  Horace, 162
  Isaac, 159
  James E., 164
  Jeremiah, 159
  John, 70, 73, 102, 159
  John, Jr., 70
  John, Dr., 221
  Joseph, (1)
    55, 85, 88, 89, 136-137, 272
    (2) 198, 211, 247
  Moses,
    55, 89, 160, 220, 247, 249, 272
  Nathan, 159
  Peter, 79
  Samuel L., 219
  Stephen, 162
  Thomas P., 166
Chapman, John E., 166
Chappell, J. F., 215
Charles, Abner,
    9, 55, 79, 89, 102, 229
  Asa,
    53, 188, 196, 199, 201, 210, 247
  Bliss, 55, 89
  Cora, 205
  Elizabeth C., 248
  Frances, 210
  Frank C., 162
  Isaac, 55, 89, 159
  James, 89, 159
  John,
    56, 70, 79, 83, 85, 89, 102, 159

CHARLES—Con.
  John, Jr., 89, 105, 159
  Joseph, 55, 89
  Justus, 175, 198, 247
  Lyman R., 197
  Moses, 95
  Moses L., 162
  Nathaniel, 219
  Norman, 173
  Osborn, 187
  Samuel, 9, 56, 85, 89, 102
  Sewall, 128, 162
  Simeon, 55, 89, 159
  Solomon, 89, 229
  Stephen, 162
  Thomas W., 120
  Timothy, 160
  Walter A., 162
Chase, Charles Tappan, 275-276
  Enoch S., 160, 162, 247
  Hall, 159
  Harry, 167
  John S., 170
  Josiah, 47, 220
  Seth S., 159
  Stephen, 188, 203, 217, 218, 247
  Stephen Henry, 132, 217, 219
Cheney, True P., 167
Child, Isabella, 131
Church, Hannah T., 131
Clark, R. C., 120, 129
Clay, Henry, 216
Clement, Charles L., 120
  Daniel, 196, 210
Clements, James, 53, 70
  Timothy, 41
Clough, Orville, 162
  Steven F., 162
Coe, Joseph F., 164
Coffin, Paul, 51, 82, 125, 146
  Peter, 157, 159
Cohen, Leon, 52, 222
Colby, Albert, 235-236
  Ephraim, 70
  Jacob, 102
  John S., 222, 278
  Joseph, 159
  Robert, 56, 160

  Simon, 118
Cole, Abner A., 162
  Dennis M., 247
  James B., 162
Collins, B. R. T., 166
Connor, Richard, 162
Converse, E. S., 129
Cook, Amos J., 5, 14, 126, 127, 203, 223, 227, 250
  George W., 164
  Mehitable J., 131
  Thomas D., 162
Coolidge, Jane F., 247
Coombs, David, 160
Copeland, David, 90
Cousins, H. W., 247
Craft, H. L., 221
Crafts, W. F., 275
  Mrs., 209
Crawford family, 51
  William J., 215
Cressey, A. Tyler, 172
Crocker, Samuel R., 162
Cross, Daniel M., 79
Cummins, William, 16
Curtis, Cyrus H. K., 129
  H. D., 215
  R. B., 215
Cushman, Bezaleel, 125
Cutler, Edward, 102
Cutter, Ammi, 128, 190
Cutts, Colonel, 108
  Usher W., 123, 275

Dana, John W., 132, 217, 219, 265, 274
  Judah, (1) 25, 90, 196, 216-217, 218
  (2) 127
Dascomb, Alfred B., 128
Davidson, George, 277
Davies, Thomas, 24
Davis, Captain, 47
  Eleazer, 16, 19, 20
  Josiah, 16, 18
  Robert N., 167
Day, David, 102
  Ebenezer, 55, 73, 79, 89, 102, 105

DAY—Con.
F. W., 164
Jabez, 55, 89
Moses, 52, 70, 79, 102, 105
Orland, 164
Thomas, 55, 89, 160, 247
Devine, William W., 162, 277
Dingley, Nelson, 278
Dinsmore, John E., 129
  Stephen, 47
Dole, Anita, 206
  Louis A., 92
Dolloff, John, 47
Dresser, Benjamin, 40
  Frank R., 184
  Job, 160
  Jonathan,
    7, 55, 79, 102, 158, 159, 170
  Levi, 158, 159
  Nehemiah C., 159
  Simeon, 158, 159
  Stephen, 102
Drew, Jonathan, 52
Dunlap, Elizabeth, 131
Dunn, A. T., 209
Dunnack, Henry E., 200
Dunning, A. E., 209
Durgin, William, 247, 252
Dutch, Samuel, 159
Dyer, Henry L., 167

Eastman, Adelia S., 205
  Andrew J., 162
  C. C., 247
  James W.,
    166, 167, 168, 173, 194, 219
  Jeremiah, 55, 89
  Job, 102
  John L., 164, 196, 247
  Obadiah, 70
  Philip,
    24, 25, 48, 70, 73, 160, 161, 172
  Ralph, 165
  Richard,
    55, 70, 102, 105, 106, 140, 269
  Robert, 162
  Robert D., 173, 214
  Seth W., 164

T. C., 247
Tobias L.,
  165, 173, 196, 219, 247, 251
Eaton, James, 162
  William,
    55, 70, 102, 158, 159, 160
Ekstrom, Frank C., 167
Ela, David W., 163
  Fred T., 247
  John, 247
  Lyman E., 167
Emerson, Alice M., 131
  Jacob, 160
  Ralph Waldo, 90
Emery, Joseph,
  52, 95, 102, 170, 177, 219
Evans, Andrew H., 164, 247, 252
  Clinton B., 132, 247
  David, 50, 70, 79, 102, 105, 106,
    153, 158, 241, 264-265
  David, Jr., 124
  Enoch, 199
  Foxwell C., 247, 250
  Huldah, 247
  Jacob, 160, 171, 243
  John, (1) 11, 50, 53, 54, 70, 79,
    81, 102, 105, 113, 124, 145,
    153, 158, 160
    (2) 172, 173, 188, 247
  Jonathan, 160, 188
  Mary A., 247
  Moses, 132
  Prentice H., 132
  Samuel, 74
  Samuel O., 247, 266
  Sarah S., 248
  Simeon A., 132, 163, 241, 278
  S. Wilson, 132
  William, (1)
    74, 124, 158, 159, 267
    (2) 247

Farnham, Abiel, 160, 161
  Mary F., 131, 209
Farrah, Jacob, 16, 18
  Joseph, 16, 19
Farrar, Caroline E., 132

Farrington, Daniel, 39, 51, 70, 73, 74, 102, 105, 109, 154, 158
  Ebenezer, 157, 158
  Enoch C., 171, 207, 219, 247
  Henry G., 198
  Jacob, 89, 160
  John, 9, 51, 70, 79, 102, 105, 232, 233
  Jonathan, 160
  Josephus, 174
  Margaret Vere, 224
  Philip, 160
  Putnam, 39, 89
  S. A., 163
  Samuel, 160
  Seth C., 163, 247
  "Singer Sam," 203
  Stephen, 8, 56, 70, 73, 79, 83, 94, 102, 105, 106, 109, 113, 158, 160
  Stephen, Jr., 89
  Stephen, (2) 164
  Thomas, 160
Farris, Nancy B., 131
Farwell, Josiah, 16, 18, 19, 20
Felch, Alpheus, 132
Fellows, Jerome B., 186, 247
  John C., 163
Fenton, James J., 183
Ferguson, A. C., 120, 221
Fessenden, Ebenezer, (1) 55, 160, 161
  Ebenezer, Jr., 136
  Ebenezer, (2) 247
  Enoch, 24, 25
  Huldah P., 131
  Jonathan, 160
  Joseph, 132
  Samuel, 125, 132
  Samuel C., 132
  Sarah Clement, 96, 100
  Thomas, 132
  W. B., 226
  William, 7, 55, 82, 86, 87, 88, 94-100, 104, 107, 109, 124, 125, 126, 170, 219, 220, 227, 229, 259, 269

  Capt. William, 160, 161
  William Pitt, 46
Field, Darby, 5
Fife, E. G., 171, 195, 226, 248, 251
  Seth W., 175, 180, 218, 251
Fifer, Joseph W., 223
Fifield, Benjamin, 160
  John, 158, 159
  Jonathan F., 160, 190
  Mary Swan, 202
  William R., 163
Files, Elsie, 131
Fiske, John W., 129
Fitzgerald, Betty, 50
Flint, H. B., 247
  Henry S., 167
Forest, Arthur S., 167
Foster, Mrs., 47, 48
Fox, Blanche, 206
  C. E., 53, 186, 247
  Ephraim, 160
  Gustavus V., 144
  John, 165
Frazier, Thomas, 163
Freeman, H. G., 185, 251
  Samuel, 103
  William, 47
Frisbie, Timothy, 267
Frost, Hazen O., 164
  William, 118
Frye, Amos C., 196, 247
  Caleb, (1) 74
  (2) 164, 247
  Charles W., 164
  Dolly, 118
  Eben'r, 73
  Frederic, 160
  Fred N., 74, 247
  Isaac, 38, 160, 161, 176, 190
  Jane W., 196
  Jonathan, (Frie), 16, 17, 18, 19, 20
  Joseph, 28-46, 51, 52, 55, 58, 59, 70, 71, 73, 74, 75, 76, 79, 80, 81, 82, 83, 94, 101, 102, 103, 104, 108, 113, 116, 121, 135, 136, 147, 154, 157, 158, 159,

NAMES 299

FRYE—Con.
  170, 199, 220, 227, 232, 268
  Joseph, Jr., 46-48, 55, 70, 79,
    115, 157, 158, 159
    (2)   163
  Mary E.,   196
  Nathaniel,
    37, 55, 85, 132, 158, 159, 269
  Richard,   38
  Samuel, (1)   38
    (2)   163
  Simon, 51, 56, 70, 79, 97-98, 102,
    105, 106, 109, 113, 124, 125,
    136, 140, 154, 158, 219, 228-229
  William,   160
  William H.,   163
  William P.,   46
Fullam, Jacob,   16, 18
Fuller, Alvin T.,   200
Furber, Daniel,   278
Furlong, Atherton,   207

Gage, M. E.,   171
Gammage, John,   160
  Joshua,   158, 175, 268
  Joshua, Jr.,   159
  Nelson,   172
Gee and Son,   177
George, Lloyd,   225
Gerry, John C.,   171
Gibson, Abel,   160
  Abel A.,   169
  Harvey D.,   129, 132
  Paris,   132
Giles, Charles P.,   197
  Frank F.,   197
  Loring R.,   197
Gilman, William,   163
Gilson, Joseph,   17, 19
Glines, Alice B.,   206
  Annah,   247
  B. M.,   247, 262
Goldthwait, Olive,   210
Goodwin, General,   46
Googins, John,   40
Gordon, Albion P.,   219, 240

Charles,   37
Hattie,   247
Henry,   79
Henry, Jr.,   159
Hugh,   9, 85, 118
John,   9, 55, 89, 159
Joseph,   159
Lydia Chase,   237
Mary L.,   205, 248, 275
Samuel C.,   207, 239, 247
Seth C.,   132, 207, 237, 247, 278
Stephen,   237, 269
Susan,   205
William,
  186, 196, 207, 211, 236, 238
William H.,   163
Grant, General,   168
  R. D.,   209
Gray, Angevine,   163
  Daniel V.,   164
  John C.,   164
  Melville,   163
Greenlaw, John J.,   197
  Richard L.,   163
Gregory, Earle P.,   221
Griswold, Oliver,   53, 220
  Mrs.,   100, 220
Guptill, Isaiah,   163
  Stephen H.,   163

Hale, Edward Everett,   209
  Truman E.,   167
Haley, Emma T.,   198
  F. E.,   247
Hall, Alonzo W.,   167
  Barbara B.,   131
  Gilson A.,   163
Hamilton, E. C.,   92
Hanscom, Elmira,   131
Hanson, Roy A.,   218
Hapgood, Sherman,   197, 247
  William,   160, 273
Harbard, Mr.,   41
Hardy, Jonathan,   160
  Nathaniel R.,   164
  Stephen G.,   160, 247
Harmon, R. C.,   171

Harnden, Elbridge,	273
H.,	247
Judith F.,	198
Samuel H.,	163
Harper, Daniel,	158
Harriman, Caleb,	247
John C.,	170, 247
Robert,	247
Sampson P.,	187
Harris, Barnett,	215
Charles E.,	195, 247
George,	163
Harvey, John,	163
Harwood, John,	16, 18
William,	159
Haseltine or Hazeltine,	
Barnes,	9, 56, 140
Ebenezer,	160
James,	70
Haskell, John,	127
Hassell, Benjamin,	22
Hastings, Alice O.,	
	194, 205, 211, 248
David R.,	168, 190, 211, 218
Edward E.,	177, 218
Hugh W.,	167, 168, 200, 218
John,	247
Mary,	168
Mary O'B.,	247
Hasty, Ella F.,	131
Hatch, Carl S.,	120
John,	160
Samuel,	159
William H.,	197
William H., Jr.,	197
Head, Asa,	160
Heald, Solomon,	247
William S.,	163
Heath, Charles W.,	163
John W.,	160
Joseph,	163
Hill, Amos,	159
Charles,	221
Daniel,	159
Frank A.,	174
John L.,	163
Ralph W.,	167
Roy W.,	167

Hitchings, S. K.,	151
Hobbs, Enoch W. B.,	163
H. K.,	247
James,	176, 226
James, Jr.,	219
Lewis C.,	163
Seymour C.,	210
Hodsdon, Herbert D.,	173
Lucy C.,	168
Holden, Samuel C.,	163
Holt, Eunice J.,	196
James G.,	163
Thomas K.,	163
William,	163
Howard, Alfred E.,	167
William,	51
Howe, Caroline Dana,	222, 278
Christopher,	46
Eben,	171
James W.,	163
James W., Jr.,	219
Mary S.,	171, 247
Seneca,	160
Simeon C.,	163
Howells, William Dean,	224
Hubbard, John P.,	190
Hulbert, Henry S.,	215
Hull, John C.,	129, 200
Huntress, Hannah M.,	131
Samuel D.,	159
Hurd, Carlton,	
	24, 89, 91, 161, 188, 201
Herbert A. D.,	167, 200
Phendeas,	273
Sophronia,	247
Hurlin, Arthur M.,	167
Hutchins, Frank F.,	164
Harry L.,	167
H. D. E.,	247
Henry D.,	89, 175
Ichabod,	159
James,	175
James E.,	198
Jonathan,	39, 102
Jonathan, Jr.,	9
John,	160
John W.,	196

HUTCHINS—Con.
　Lillian C., 168
　Nathaniel, 56, 154, 157, 158, 159
　Richard K., 167
Hutchinson, John W., 207
Hyde, William DeW., 209, 278

Ilsley, John, 201
　Louise H., 196
　Samuel, 163, 183, 196
Indians, Names of, 9
Ingalls, Daniel, 95
　Rufus, 132
　Samuel, 56, 70, 79, 81
Irish, Stephen, 159
　William H., 177

Jack, Ira T., 164
Jackson, Harvey L., 167
Jacobs, Mrs. Hale, 207
James, George P., 167
Jefts, John, 17, 18
Jenkins, Willard M., 163
Jenner, James T., 163
Jenness, A. R., 175, 180, 212
Jewett, Ernest O., 176
　Hannah B., 131
　Nathaniel G., 159
　Norman R., 167
Johnson, Andrew, 159
　Daniel, 163
　Eastman, 176, 225
　Eli, 262
　George 162
　Ichabod, 16, 18
　James, 160
　Joseph H., 162, 275
　Joseph J., 165
　Josiah, 16, 19
　M. P., 177
　Noah, 16, 19
　Philip C., 176
　William H., 162
Johnston, William, 188, 201
Jones, Josiah, 16, 19, 20
Jordan, F. H., 120, 221
　Minnie Howe, 203

Tristram, 103, 104
　William Gerald, 196

Keefe, Michael, 247, 277
Kelly, "Billy," 174, 239
　William, 174, 193
Kenerson, Percival H., 167
Kenison, Andrew, Jr., 162
Kennedy, John, 162
Kensett, John F., 225
Kerr, John W., 167
Kezar, George, 271
Kidder, Benjamin, 16
　Francis, 188
　Frederick, 15
Kies, Solomon, 16, 19
Kilgore, Benjamin, 79
　James, 157, 159
　Joseph, 79
　Trueworthy, 157, 159
Kimball, Clarence, 37
　H. W., 209
　John L., 190
　Miss, 202
　Obed, 161
　Richard, 9, 79, 105, 106, 109, 157
Kinsman, Colonel, 46
Kittridge, Jonathan, 16, 18
Kneeland, O. A., 177
　Victor L., 167
Knight, Caleb, 55, 89
　Eliphalet, 160
　John, 89, 160
　Joseph,
　　7, 8, 51, 55, 89, 158, 159, 272
　Moses, 55, 89
　Mr., 176
　Noyes, 160
　Oliver, 55, 89
　Stephen,
　　52, 79, 83, 102, 157, 159
Knowlton, Ebenezer, 128, 278
Knox, Frank E., 167
　Wendell H., 167
Kolkmeyer, Rev. Dr., 215
Korff, S. A., 215
LaCasce, Elroy O., 129

LaCome,	35	Longfellow, H. W.,	25, 26
Ladd, Charles T.,	174	Lord, Augustus F.,	162
Sarah F.,	172, 192, 248	Charles E.,	164
Lakin—also Larkin,		Enoch B.,	164
Isaac,	17, 19	George H.,	164
Lamson, D. L.,		Henry M.,	167
179, 180, 191, 194, 204, 220		Herbert P.,	167
Langdon, Paul,		Isaac W.,	164
99, 112, 113, 115, 117, 124, 125		Mary W.,	206, 248
Samuel,	125	Loudoun, Gen. Lord John,	34
Lassells, Israel,	160	Lougee, Arthur J.,	221
Lawless, Patrick,	162	Lucia M.,	120, 194, 205, 248
Leadbeater, John M.,	167	Richard J.,	134
Mary,	211	Lovejoy, Abial,	96
Leavitt, David,	247	Lovewell, John,	
George,	247	9, 14-18, 25, 54, 258	
Lee, Oliver J.,	214, 215	Lovis, Charles H.,	162
Lewis, Alonzo F.,		James I.,	192, 241
172, 207, 211, 247, 253		Lyman, Eliphalet,	91, 220
Harris A. P.,	162	Lynd, Benjamin,	42, 71
Hazen,	162		
Ivory, J.,	164	McArthur, R. S.,	209
Jesse,	160	McCarty, Michael,	162
Nelson,	162	McCay, Mr. and Mrs.,	176
William,	162	McElroy, Harry D.,	166
Libby, Belle,	209	McGaffey, Joseph,	127
Limbo,	241-243, 254	McGaw, Jacob,	217
Lincoln, Abraham,	225	McGuire, James,	162
Enoch, 24, 25, 125, 160, 217, 219,		John,	162
230, 231		McIntire, Asa S.,	162
Levi,	230	Ebenezer,	160
Levi, Jr.,	230	Edward,	164, 187
Lindsay, George D.,	209	E. F.,	247
Lingfield, Edward,	16, 19	Joshua C.,	162
Little, David,	125	Laura E.,	131
Livermore, Mary A.,	209	N. O.,	120, 247
Livingston, Stephen T.,	93	Oliver G.,	162
William F.,	92, 209	Oscar,	247
Locke, Charles,	247	Samuel F.,	162
Dr.,	220	T. S.,	247
Frank,	187, 247	McKay, Frank,	162
Helen S.,	247	McKeen, B. Walker, 120, 191, 194	
John,	172, 173, 247	McKenny, Hannah,	237
Lydia H.,	247	Mr.,	196
Sara M.,	131	McLaughlin, D. B.,	215
S. B.,	150, 187	McLellan, Charles S.,	166
Long, Augustus,	162	McMath, Francis C.,	215
		Robert,	215

NAMES

McMillan, Andrew, 70, 71
  Caroline G., 247
  Carolyn, 143
  James, (1) 50
    (2) 178, 210, 247
  John, 39, 46, 79, 95, 96, 160
McNally, Paul A., 214, 215
McNeal, Daniel, 188
  Harrison, 192
McNeil, William W., 164
Mabry, Irving, 221
Mann, William G., 93
Mansfield, Charles, 164
  Hollis, 175
  Mary, 205
  Willard L., 177
Marden, John, 160
Mark, Frank L., 173, 177, 247
Marriner, George T., 165
Mason, Javan K., 92, 247
  John, 160
  Oliff, 166
Mattson, Mrs. Charles R.,
    193-194, 206
Melvin, David, 16, 19
  Eleazar, 16, 19
Menzel, D. H., 215
Merrill, Alvin D., 184, 214, 247
  F. C., 247
  James H., 127
  John, 124
  John C., 164, 247
  Margaret, 131
  Marion, 131
  Moody, 175
  Nathaniel, 39, 49, 50, 53, 70, 79, 95, 96, 102, 105, 106, 113, 124, 154, 158, 242, 254
  Rev. Mr., 82
  Susan Walker, 200, 206
Miller, Henry H., 190
  John Bolt, 56, 84, 102
  Robert, 41
  Walter, 215
Mitchell, Dr., 221
  Joseph, 162
Monkhouse, W. A., 222
Moore, J. H., 215

Morgan, Gerry, 53, 240
  William G., 240-241
Morin, Joseph, 162
Morrell, Helen, 131
Morton, Harrison G., 163, 164
  Sidney G., 162
  William B., 162
Muckley, Simon, 162
Mulford, C. E., 53, 214, 224
Munger, Lillian, 209
Murphy, Francis, 202
  James, 162
Murray, James, 84

Nash, 58
  J. Waldo, 165
Nason, Mrs., 95
Newman, Arthur Dow, 164
  Benjamin T., 169, 194, 225
  Carrie G., 205
  George B., 166
Nichols, George W., 162
  James L., 162
Norton, Harry G., 162
Noyes, Joseph, 76
Nute, Philip C., 166
Nutter, Charles, 197
  Martha, 208
Nutting, Wallace, 92

O'Brien Bros., 175
  Daniel W., 197
O'Connell, Daniel, 215
  Michael, 162
Ober, F. A., 209
Odlin, John W., 203, 204
Oliver, S. T., 174
Osen, Ben, 215
Osgood, Annie R., 210
  "Aunt Nabby," 242, 247, 267
  Carrol M., 166
  Charles, 164
  Charles H., 164
  Earl P., 219, 247
  Edward L.,
    90, 190, 196, 218, 219, 220, 234
  Edward Sherburn, 207

OSGOOD—Con.
  Elbridge G., 174
  Elizabeth, 227
  Hannah C., 205
  Henry B., 127, 132
  Henry Y. B., 268
  Henry D., 166
  Isaac, 160
  James, 38, 47, 52, 54, 70, 86, 124, 125, 145, 154, 158, 247
  James, Jr., 124, 160
  James Edwin, 247
  James R., 132, 210, 218, 234, 242
  John, 124
  John L., 211, 247
  Joshua B., 160, 227
  Joshua, Mrs., 90
  Kate Putnam, 132, 223
  Mary, 268
  Mehitable, 268
  Samuel, (1) 50, 53, 54, 70, 79, 83, 102, 104, 108, 145, 154, 158, 176, 218, 242
    (2) 132, 247, 268
  Sarah, 191
  Timothy, 203
Ostrander, Mrs. J. S., 209
Otis, James, 31

Paddelford, Paul, 141
Page, Abby N., 172, 207, 247, 252
  Albion, 55, 188, 192, 247
  Blanche S., 177
  Caleb, 132
  Caleb A., 128, 278
  David, 49, 53, 55, 70, 79, 96, 124, 125, 154, 158, 230
  George, 171
  Horatio Nelson, 132
  Jeremiah, 41, 42
  John, 132, 160, 168, 230
  Julia A., 207
  Mary Chapman, 230
  Philip, 172, 261
  Robert, 87
  Rosilla N., 247
  Russell, 172, 188, 247
  Seth A., 171, 247
Palmer, Albert S., 162
  Alice Freeman, 209
  G. H., 209
  William P., 222
Paris, Albion K., 132
Parker, Francis R., 162
  James, 9, 56, 102, 105
  Moses, 46
  Noah O., 220
Parkman, Francis, 22
Patten, Benjamin, 158
Paugus, 9, 14, 20, 22, 25
Peabody, Henry C., 132
  John Q., 92
  Oliver, 70, 71, 73
Peach, Robert E., 185
Peary, Robert E., 53, 143, 206, 245
Pease, Ernest A., 166
  John M., 128
Perkins, Sidney F., 192
Perkins and Pendexter, 174
Perry, Albion A., 194, 226, 244
  Virginia, 168
Peterson, F. H., 247
Petrie, R. M., 215
Pettee, David, 158, 159
Pettingill, Joseph, 79, 157, 159
Philbrook, Harry I., 166
Phillips, John, 138
  John Jr., 126
Pickard, Joseph C., 127
  Mary, 232
  Samuel T., 278
Pickering, Ebenezer, 162
Pike, Asa Osgood, (1) 176, 197, 226, 233-234, 277
  (2) 176, 214, 234, 247
  (3) 176, 234
  Cassius W., 204, 234
  Clayton W., 53, 132, 167, 211, 217
  Hattie A., 194, 209, 211, 226, 248
  Job K., 233, 273
  John, 259, 273

PIKE—Con.		Amos,	30, 127, 201
John J.,	164, 247	Caleb,	160
Martha A.,	131	George,	164
Mary Buck,	233	G. H.,	163
Thomas S.,	164	Joshua,	160
Pingree, William,	177	Luther,	160
Pinkham, Ivory O.,	166	Thomas,	16, 19
Piper, Ruth,	131	Timothy,	16, 19
Pitman, Merle W.,	166	William B.,	164
Pitts, Edgar T.,	93	Zebediah,	85, 86, 88, 269
Plummer, Frank S.,	177	Richmond, P.,	247
Poor, Enoch,	45	Ricker, George H.,	129
Henry Varnum,	10	George H., Mrs.,	202
Lozien,	163	Hattie G.,	131
Mehitable,	34	Ridlon, Ernest,	167
Porter, Nathaniel,		Preston R.,	167
	82, 88, 124, 125, 127	Riedel, Wesley U.,	93
Rufus,	132	Riley, John,	162
Stephen,	220	Ripley, Edward,	203
William R.,	127	General,	25
Post, Mary W.,	248	H. W.,	243
S. L., Jr.,	178	James W.,	
W. B.,	177, 226		132, 160, 196, 219, 268
Potter, Harold E.,	167	Robins, Cleveland O.,	167
John B.,	167	Robbins, Jonathan,	16, 18
Powers, Charles H.,	164	Roberts, Clifton E.,	167
Daniel,	162	George H.,	167
Fred W.,	120	Robinson, Mary,	46
Jacob,	55	Walter A.,	
Pratt, Harold B.,	167		23, 128, 207, 209, 278
Putnam, Colonel,	158	Rogers, James J.,	173, 247, 276
		Robert,	153
Quigley, T. H.,	215	William L.,	167
Quimby, Joseph,	142	Rose, John,	162
Martha,	188	Ross, Albion H.,	92
Quinan, John,	162	Rounds, Leonard P.,	163
Quint, Monroe,	162	Royce, Vere,	
			53, 55, 154, 158, 220, 232, 233
Ramsay, Alexander,	228	Russell, Abraham,	102
Randall, Harry H.,	171	Benjamin,	79, 102, 105, 106, 107
Nathaniel,	171	Elijah,	184
Rasle, Sebastian,	1, 2, 3, 13, 14	John,	70, 73
Rawson, Grindall,	42, 43, 82	Joseph,	197
Reed, Rebecca Perley,	152	William,	55, 97, 136, 160
Rice, Wilfred G.,	92		
Richards, Sewall N.,	164	Sampson, Lowell B.,	164
Richardson, Albert F.,	129	Sanborn, Abel F.,	207
Albion,	162	Frank B.,	207

SANBORN—Con.
  Job L., 163
  John S., 9
  Lorenzo B., 167
  Ruth, 206
Sargent, John E., 167, 196
Saunders Bros., 186
Savard, Albert J., 167
Sawtelle, Fred W., 165
Sawyer, 58
  Arthur R., 167
  Barnet, 247
  David, 247
  Edith A., 224
Seavey, Benjamin G., 163
  Phineas, 187
Sergeant, Elizabeth Shepley, 224
Severance, George F., 167
Sewall, David B., 92
  Helen, 131
  Jane, 202
Shane, C. D., 215
Shaw, Frank W., 166
Shedd, George H., 221
  John Z., 221
Sherburne, Mary, 268
  Thomas R., 167
Shirley, A. and J., 14
  Edmund, 186
  Edward, 56, 150, 158, 175, 247
  Franklin, 55, 172, 175, 247
  Jonathan, 160
  Leon A., 167
  Lizzie C., 203
  Ralph W., 166
  Ruben W., 164
  T. C., 180, 236-237, 246, 247
  William, 160
Shirley & Cousins, 171, 186
Shirley & Lewis, 185
Simmons, Augustine, 128
Simpson, Bertha H., 206
  Charles, 187
Skillings, E. L., 170, 272
Small, L. W., 207
  Reuben H., 163
Smart, Marcus M., 163, 247
  William T., 163

Smith, Abial F., 163, 247
  Asa, 160
  Benjamin, 163
  Charles F., 175, 247
  Daniel, Jr., 163
  Henry Hyde, 128, 218, 278
  James F., 163
  J. Edwin, 167
  John, 176, 177, 182, 227, 234, 244
  Jonathan, 158
  Mr., 47
  Nathaniel, 50, 79, 232
  Owen P., 166
  Thomas J., 215
Snow, Benjamin P., 128, 278
  Charles A., 120
  Ivory F., 163
  Ray A., 167
Solari, Joseph, 174
Somers, Orlando A., 244
Souther, John C., 247
  John W., 177, 188, 247
  Mary W., 247
  Samuel, (1) 177, 210, 247
    (2) 8, 132, 164, 199, 210, 222, 247
  Thomas, (1) 127, 132, 190
    (2) 247
  Williams, 247
Sowdon, A. J. C., 22
Spalding, George B., 93
Spiller, Isaac, 163
Spring, Betty, 52, 80
  Fred W., 197
  Hannah M., 131
  Isaac, 190
  Jedediah, 50, 52, 79, 80
  Lewis, 170
  Samuel E., 265
  Seth, 170, 272
  Wm. G., 173
Stacy, Jordan, 160
  Mark, 70, 71
  Oliver, 160
Stanley, John L., 163
  Oramel, 167
  Samuel C., 163
Stanyan, John, 41

NAMES

Staples, Helen M., 131
Stark, Archibald, 268
  John, 57, 70, 71, 268
  Samuel, 46, 268
  William,
    57, 58, 70, 71, 146, 154, 268
Steele, William, 47, 56, 84
Stein, Rev. Dr., 215
Stearns, J. F., 165
Sterns, John S., 160
Stevens or Stephens,
  Benjamin, 41
  Charles E., 164
  Ebenezer, 55, 85, 89
  John, 49, 56, 70, 79, 108, 140, 159, 242, 254
  John, Jr., 9, 85
  John P., 163
  Jonathan, 55, 89
  Joseph, 160
  Lloyd, 187
  Mrs. L. M. N., 209
  Samuel, 55, 85, 89
  Seth, 164
  William, 159
Stickney, Mrs. E. A. G., 202
  Jonathan, 266
  Samuel, 189, 190
  William, 132
Stiles, John, 163
Stirling, Hugh, 56, 79, 267, 268
  Isabel, 57, 58, 268
  John, Jr., 160
  Martha, 270
  Mary, 270
Stone, A. P., 278
  Baman N., 92, 120
  Clarence N., 211
  Emily F., 248
  Katherine F., 131
  Ralph, 167
Strout, A. A., 278
  George, 222
  & Higgins, 172
Sutcliffe, James, 180
Swain, John, 89
Swan, Caleb, 34, 51, 69, 70, 73, 74, 79, 118, 142

  Caleb, Jr., 159, 229
  Francis D., 194
  James, 73, 79, 102
  Joseph, 160
  Joseph Greeley, 9, 79
  Joseph G., 190
  Naamah, 51
  Olive J., 207
  Samuel, 142
Swift, E. E., 215
Symmes, Thomas, 14, 21, 23

Tarbox, James W., 247
  Wallace R., 173, 247
  Wallace R., Mrs., 243-244
  W. H., 177, 247
Tenney, Abbie Powers, 202
Thomas, Alfred E., 163
  Charlotte J., 207
  George A., 207
Thoms, Frank, 177
  Mrs., 177
Thompson, George W., 163
  Ralph W., 167
  Rev. Mr., 82
  William, 159
Thurston, Fred R., 167
  John P., 125
Tibbetts, Charles, 53, 247
  Charles H., 171, 197, 247
  Fannie, 53
  John W., 163
  Samuel, 159
Tinker, Berlin F., 247
Tonge, Robert, 192, 276
Towle, Howard E., 167
  Ira, 193, 210, 220, 237, 260
  Jason W., 164, 207, 260
  John W., 164
  William C., 163, 165, 199, 220
  William Warren, 23, 247
True, N. T., 3, 11, 199
  Otis, 176
Twaddle, W. B., 221
Tynge, Colonel, 9, 20

Usher, Robert, 16, 18, 19

Volk, Douglas, 225
　Leonard, 225
Von Steuben, Baron, 158
Vose, Edwin F., 151

Wade, M. Augusta, 131
Wadsworth, Peleg, 189, 220
Waldo, John, 40
Walker, Alden B., 163, 176, 177
　Augustus H., 218
　Benjamin, 160
　Carlton, 272
　Caroline F., 247
　Charles, 55, 89
　Clement A., 132, 247
　Dexter, 163
　Edward C., 218
　Ezekiel, 43, 52, 55, 70, 71, 75, 79, 81, 83, 95, 102, 105, 106, 124, 243
　Fred A., 247
　Gardiner, 171
　George H., 247
　Henry, 247
　Isaac, (1) 8, 56, 102, 105, 107, 109, 157
　　(2) 164
　James, (1) 46
　　(2) 56, 190, 211, 219, 247, 272
　Jane, 267
　Jesse, 9
　John, 8, 55, 79, 89, 105, 154, 157, 158
　John, Jr., 89, 159
　John B., 163
　John S., 163
　Joseph, 52, 79, 95, 102
　Joseph C., 163
　Judith, 131
　Lewis A., 167
　Lewis M., 165
　Marshall, 197
　Nathaniel, (1) 9, 55, 89
　　(2) 173, 252
　Peter, 136, 172
　Samuel, 9, 79, 83, 84, 96, 102, 105
　Samuel, Jr., 79
　Sarah T., 247
　Supply, 52
　Susan M., 131
　Timothy, Rev., (1) 80, 82
　　(2) 81
　　(3) 49, 53, 70, 73, 79, 102, 157, 159
　Truelove, 272
　Wiley, 163
　William G., 247
Wallis, John S., 127
Walton, Anastasia, 131
Ward, Amos C., 247
　Artemus, 132
　John, 164, 247
　Mrs., 226
　Jonathan, 160
　Stephen C., 247
　Timothy C., 171, 212, 247
　William Fessenden, 203
Warren, Benjamin O., 167, 168
　C. C., 120, 247
　E., 204
　Florence, 131
　George O., 171, 247
　Hattie G., 152, 248
　Isaiah, 150, 152, 160, 161, 170, 174, 175, 188, 247, 274
　Mary, 248
　Nathaniel, 159
　Orin, 22
　Otis, 175, 247
Warriner, Abby T., 247
　Edson, 247
Washington, George, 37, 232
Waterhouse, C. W., Jr., 164
Webb, Burt C., 197
Webster, Dana, 247
　Daniel, 126, 176, 209, 271
　David, 56, 187, 188
　Isaac, 70
　James E., 163
　Jane, 270
　John, 47, 52, 56, 70, 79, 113, 150, 154, 158, 159, 186, 233, 269
　John W., 247

NAMES 309

WEBSTER—Con.	
Jonathan,	164
Ralph,	167
Weeks, Eben,	172, 175, 247
Ernest E.,	129
James M.,	164
Laura G.,	152, 248
Seth,	247
S. H.,	278
Welch, Edwin K.,	129
Wellington, Isaac M.,	128
Mrs.,	191
Wentworth, Governor,	58
Herbert H.,	167
Marion,	205
Mrs.,	131
Weston, Abby G.,	247
Daniel,	125
Edward, (1)	196, 270
(2)	247
Edward Payson,	170, 247, 251
Frances H.,	206, 247
George,	247
John,	33, 207, 247, 262
John Henry,	247
Rachel,	194
Susanna,	206
White, Wallace H.,	46
Whitehead, Florence,	226
Whittemore, J. T.,	171
Whiting, Francis,	88, 217
Oliver, Jr.,	159
Samuel,	16, 17, 19
Whittaker, N. T.,	209
Whittier, John G.,	278
Wiggin, Benjamin,	55, 89
Lot,	201
Wild, Edwin W.,	93
Wilde, John,	128
Wilder, Captain,	47
Wiley, America,	159
Benjamin,	9, 85, 89, 159
Caleb,	165
Dean,	164
Dexter,	55
Francis A.,	173, 239
Herbert L.,	167
James,	55, 89
Job,	159
John,	89, 159
John H.,	164
Joseph,	163, 164
Mason,	89, 157, 159
Samuel, (1)	159
(2)	164
Samuel O.,	219
Simeon C.,	197
Stephen J.,	163
Sullivan J.,	163
William,	51, 79, 84, 102
William H.,	164
Willard, Charles G.,	129
Mr.,	41
Sara Locke,	131
Willey, Francis,	172
Ralph,	165
Willis, Hamilton,	257
Mr.,	25
Wilson, Edwin P.,	93
Frederic A.,	128
John,	73
Wiswell, William H.,	163
Witham, Bertram L.,	167
Morris,	47, 56
Woodbury, Enoch W.,	190
Ernest R.,	129
Victor A.,	167
Woodman, Benjamin,	159
Woods, Daniel,	17, 18
Thomas,	17, 18
Woodsides,	171
Woodward, Bradley B.,	181, 207
Harriet F.,	206
Mary,	206
Wormwood, R. Fult,	185
Wright, W. H.,	215
Wyman, Merrill,	182
Seth,	16-21, 25
Young, Charles S.,	92

www.ingramcontent.com/pod-product-compliance
Lightning Source LLC
Chambersburg PA
CBHW070935230426
43666CB00011B/2448